SECOND EDITION

RESEARCH
METHODS

ARE YOU
EQUIPPED?

Kendall Hunt
publishing company

Jennifer Bonds-Raacke
Fort Hays State University

John Raacke
Fort Hays State University

Cover image © 2014 Shutterstock, Inc.

Kendall Hunt
publishing company

www.kendallhunt.com
Send all inquiries to:
4050 Westmark Drive
Dubuque, IA 52004-1840

DEDICATION

Our work is dedicated to our daughters,

Callie and Brooke,

and to the memory of Eugene C. Bonds.

BRIEF CONTENTS

Part 1: Introduction to Research

    Chapter 1: Psychology as a Science 3

    Chapter 2: Goals and Methods of Psychology 17

    Chapter 3: Ethics 33

Part 2: Nonexperimental Research Methods and Variables

    Chapter 4: Nonexperimental Research Methods 59

    Chapter 5: Variables, Reliability, and Validity 81

Part 3: Experimental Research Methods

    Chapter 6: Hypothesis Testing 101

    Chapter 7: Selection of Variables, Operational Definitions, and Measurement Issues 123

    Chapter 8: Selection and Assignment of Participants 145

    Chapter 9: Controls and Threats to Internal Validity 161

Part 4: Types of Designs

    Chapter 10: Between Subjects Designs 181

    Chapter 11: Within Subjects Designs 195

    Chapter 12: Factorial Designs 211

    Chapter 13: Single Case Designs 229

Part 5: Hypothesis Testing Continued and Interpreting Results

    Chapter 14: Hypothesis Testing Revisited and Interpreting Results 245

    Chapter 15: APA Style: Sixth Edition 263

Appendix: Sample APA-Style Manuscript 285

References 305

Glossary 311

Index 317

CONTENTS

Preface xv

Part 1: Introduction to Research

 Chapter 1: Psychology as a Science 3
  Are You Equipped? 3
  Research Methods and You 4
   Sources of Information 4
   Importance of Being an Educated Consumer 5
   Disconnect between Media and Psychological Research 7
   Recommendations 7
   Section Summary. 8
  Science versus Pseudoscience 8
   Pseudoscience 9
   Science. 10
   Section Summary. 11
  What You Can Expect .12
   "You Try It!" and "Are You Equipped?" Exercises 13
  Are You Equipped Now? 13
  Chapter Summary 14
  APA Learning Goals Linkage 15

 Chapter 2: Goals and Methods of Psychology 17
  Are You Equipped? 17
  Introduction 18
  Goals of Psychological Research 19
   You Try It!. 20
   Section Summary. 25
  Use of the Scientific Method: Steps and Importance. 25
   You Try It!. 27
   Section Summary. 28
  The Research Process .28
   Section Summary. 30
  Are You Equipped Now? 30
  Chapter Summary 30
  APA Learning Goals Linkage 31

Chapter 3: Ethics 33

Are You Equipped? 33

Consumers of Research 34

Institutional Review Board 35

You Try It!. 36

Section Summary. 37

APA's Ethics Code 38

You Try It!. 43

You Try It!. 45

Section Summary. 47

Are You Equipped Now? 52

Chapter Summary 54

APA Learning Goals Linkage 55

Part 2: **Nonexperimental Research Methods and Variables**

Chapter 4: Nonexperimental Research Methods 59

Are You Equipped? 59

Differentiating among Methods 60

Introduction to Correlational Methods 61

You Try It!. 62

Section Summary. 64

Nonexperimental Methods. 65

You Try It!. 67

You Try It!. 69

You Try It!. 73

Section Summary. 74

Factors to Consider with Nonexperimental Designs 75

Converging Research Methods 75

Are You Equipped Now? 76

Chapter Summary 77

APA Learning Goals Linkage 78

Chapter 5: Variables, Reliability, and Validity 81

Are You Equipped? 81

An Introduction 82

Variables: Independent and Dependent 82

You Try It!. 83

Subject Variables 84

You Try It!. 85

Treatment Condition 86

You Try It!. 87

Section Summary. 89

Reliability and Validity. 89
    Reliability. 89
    Validity 91
    Internal, External, and Construct Validity 91
    Section Summary. 93
Are You Equipped Now?. 94
Chapter Summary 95
APA Learning Goals Linkage 97

Part 3: Experimental Research Methods

Chapter 6: Hypothesis Testing 101
Are You Equipped? 101
Formulating a Research Question 102
    Getting Your Research Idea. 104
    Conducting Searches. 107
    Starting a Search 108
    Section Summary. 110
Generating Hypotheses 110
    You Try It!. 113
Testing the Hypothesis 116
    Section Summary. 116
Are You Equipped Now?. 117
Chapter Summary 118
APA Learning Goals Linkage 119

Chapter 7: Selection of Variables, Operational Definitions, and Measurement Issues. 123
Are You Equipped? 123
Selecting the Levels of the Independent Variable 124
    You Try It!. 127
    Section Summary. 128
Measuring the Dependent Variable and Number of Dependent Variables 129
    You Try It!. 130
    You Try It!. 132
    Section Summary. 132
Operational Definitions 133
    Section Summary. 134
Types of Scales 134
    You Try It!. 136
    Section Summary. 138
Are You Equipped Now?. 138
Chapter Summary 140
APA Learning Goals Linkage 142

Chapter 8: Selection and Assignment of Participants 145

Are You Equipped? 145

Populations versus Sample 147

Probability Sampling Procedures 147

    You Try It!. 150

    Section Summary. 151

Nonprobability Sampling Procedures 151

    You Try It!. 152

    Section Summary. 153

Random Assignment to Conditions 153

    You Try It!. 154

    Section Summary. 155

Determining Sample Size 155

Power 155

    Section Summary. 156

Are You Equipped Now? 156

Chapter Summary 157

APA Learning Goals Linkage 158

Chapter 9: Controls and Threats to Internal Validity 161

Are You Equipped? 161

Control 162

    Answer 163

    Section Summary. 165

Threats to Internal Validity 165

    You Try It!. 166

    You Try It!. 167

Minimizing Threats 172

    Section Summary. 172

Are You Equipped Now? 173

Chapter Summary 176

APA Learning Goals Linkage 177

Part IV: Types of Designs

Chapter 10: Between Subjects Designs 181

Are You Equipped? 181

Introduction to Between Subjects Designs 182

    You Try It!. 184

A Classic Research Example 184

    You Try It!. 185

    Contemporary Research Examples 185

    Section Summary. 187

Factors to Consider 187
    You Try It! 190
    Section Summary. 190
Ways to Minimize Disadvantages 191
Are You Equipped Now? 191
Chapter Summary 192
APA Learning Goals Linkage 193

Chapter 11: Within Subjects Designs 195
Are You Equipped? 195
Introduction to Within Subjects Designs 196
    Examples from Chapter 7. 196
    You Try It! 197
    A Classic Research Example 198
    You Try It! 199
    Contemporary Research Examples 199
    You Try It! 200
    Section Summary. 201
Factors to Consider 201
    Ways to Minimize Disadvantages. 203
    You Try It! 204
    Section Summary. 206
Matched Subjects Designs 206
Are You Equipped Now? 207
Chapter Summary 208
APA Learning Goals Linkage 209

Chapter 12: Factorial Designs 211
Are You Equipped? 211
Introduction to Factorial Designs 212
    Between Subjects Factorial Designs 213
    You Try It! 214
    Within Subjects Factorial Designs 216
    You Try It! 217
    Mixed Subjects Factorial Designs 218
    You Try It! 219
    Section Summary. 220
Results of Factorial Designs. 221
    Main Effects 221
    Interactions. 223
    Section Summary. 224
Are You Equipped Now? 224
Chapter Summary 225
APA Learning Goals Linkage 226

Chapter 13: Single Case Designs 229

    Are You Equipped? 229

    An Introduction to Single Case Designs 230

        You Try It!. 231

        Section Summary. 232

    Why Use Single Case Designs? 232

        You Try It!. 233

        Section Summary. 235

    Conducting Single Case Designs 235

        AB Designs (Pretest–Posttest) 235

        ABA Designs (Reversal Designs) 235

        Multiple Baselines 237

        You Try It!. 238

        Section Summary. 239

    Limitations of Single Case Designs 239

    Are You Equipped Now?. 240

    Chapter Summary 240

    APA Learning Goals Linkage 241

Part 5: Hypothesis Testing Continued and Interpreting Results

    Chapter 14: Hypothesis Testing Revisited and Interpreting Results. 245

    Are You Equipped? 245

    Examining the Results: Rejecting the Null or Failing to Reject the Null Hypothesis . 246

        The Cheerleader Effect Revisited 246

        You Try It!. 248

        Type I and Type II Errors 249

        The Role of Replication. 250

        Section Summary. 251

    Introduction to Interpreting Statistical Results. 251

        Drawing Conclusions from Descriptive Statistics. 252

        Conclusions from Inferential Statistics 254

        You Try It!. 256

        Statistical Significance versus Practical Significance. 257

        Section Summary. 258

    Are You Equipped Now?. 258

    Chapter Summary 260

    APA Learning Goals Linkage 261

Chapter 15: APA Style: Sixth Edition 263

    Are You Equipped? 263

    An Introduction to APA-Style Writing 264

        The Title Page 265

        Abstract. 265

        Introduction 266

        Method 267

        Results 268

        Discussion 268

        Tables and Figures 269

        You Try It!. 269

        Section Summary. 269

    References. 270

        Within-Text Citations 271

        Reference List 274

        Typical Sources. 275

        You Try It!. 278

        Section Summary. 279

    Are You Equipped Now?. 279

    Chapter Summary 281

    APA Learning Goals Linkage 283

Appendix: Sample APA-Style Manuscript 285

References 305

Glossary 311

Index 317

PREFACE

We are all consumers—each one of us, every day. Consider your role as a consumer in today's world. When you start your day by taking a shower and eating breakfast before classes, you consume energy in the form of heated water and nutrients. When you listen to the radio in your car on the way to work, you consume fossil fuel and information in the form of news reports, talk radio debate, or music. And when you decide which college to attend and pay your tuition bill, you consume an educational experience. As consumers, we make very personal choices about what, where, and how we experience most things in our daily lives. Similarly, psychologists are consumers of research. Psychologists use the principles of research methods to study topics of interest to the field and society. For example, through the application of research methodology, psychologists have conducted studies which have helped us better understand allocation of resources while driving and talking on a cell phone, the role of subliminal advertising and buying behaviors, and potential benefits to children from viewing series such as *Baby Einstein*. As you can see, psychological research plays a vital role in our ability to make educated decisions about our lives. Students who are equipped with skills to understand research methodology and interpret research findings carry this knowledge with them always. Thus, the central goal of our text is to provide you with an understanding of research methods with a focus on helping you become a more educated consumer of research.

Toward that goal, this textbook offers several pedagogical tools to reinforce research methodology and its relevance in psychology and the world around us. For the new edition, these tools have been updated to further enhance the learning experience.

- **Are You Equipped? Boxes**   Featured at the beginning and end of each chapter, these boxes present examples from everyday life or from classic psychological research. You are introduced to new topics and asked to critically evaluate each to demonstrate mastery of previously covered concepts. Examples include "Does the input of the *American Idol* judges influence how viewers vote?" and "How much can you trust the feedback about your professors posted online?"

- **You Try It! Exercises**   You get hands-on practice in testing various research methodologies and conducting research. For example, you will obtain practice at differentiating between positive and negative correlations, identifying variables used in a research design, and generating hypotheses. These exercises will help prepare you to conduct your own research.

- **Student-Centered Writing Style and Organization**   Each chapter is written with a goal of optimizing your experience for greater understanding and class success. A direct, concise, and engaging writing style supported by relevant examples works to help you tackle concepts more easily. In addition, key terms are bolded within the narrative, with full definitions provided on page in the running glossary. A chapter summary highlights key points for you to aid in the review and study process.

- **APA Learning Outcomes**   To better provide you a way to assess your knowledge of the concepts discussed, each chapter opens with a list of relevant learning outcomes as outlined by the American Psychological Association (APA) and ends with an overview of examples from the chapter showing how those outcomes were covered. For nonpsychology majors, this feature both provides another way to gauge understanding of the chapter material and provides a guideline for review. For psychology majors, this feature allows you to track which APA outcomes you have mastered as you work through the course. In addition, the outcomes and review use APA language to correspond to courses employing these outcomes across the discipline. This edition uses the latest APA Guidelines for Undergraduate Psychology which are as follows:

- **Goal 1. Knowledge Base in Psychology**

  You will demonstrate fundamental knowledge and comprehension of the major concepts, theoretical perspectives, historical trends, and empirical findings to discuss how psychological principles apply to behavioral problems.

- **Goal 2. Scientific Inquiry and Critical Thinking**

  You will demonstrate scientific reasoning and problem solving, including effective research methods.

- **Goal 3. Ethical and Social Responsibility in a Diverse World**

  You will apply ethical standards to evaluate psychological science and practice and you will develop ethically and socially responsible behaviors for professional and personal settings in a landscape that involves increasing diversity.

- **Goal 4. Communication**

  You will demonstrate competence in writing and in oral and interpersonal communication skills.

- **Goal 5. Professional Development**

  You will apply psychological content and skills to career goals and develop meaningful professional direction for life after graduation.

We hope that you find these pedagogical techniques useful and that you actually enjoy reading your textbook. Research methods relate not only to the field of psychology but also to many facets of everyday life. It is our hope that through the variety of examples used in the textbook, you will see the importance of the material for you. If you ever have any ideas or suggestions, please let us know. We would love to hear from you!

SUPPLEMENTS FOR THE INSTRUCTOR

The following supplements are available to qualified instructors who have adopted this textbook.

- **Instructor's Resource Manual**   Written by the authors of this book, the *Instructor's Resource Manual* includes learning objectives, key terms and concepts, self-contained lecture suggestions and class activities for each chapter with handouts, supplemental reading suggestions, and an annotated list of additional multimedia resources.

  This Instructor Supplement includes the following:
  - **Chapter-at-a-glance** tables to summarize all of the resources available to the instructor for each chapter
  - **Learning Objectives** for each chapter
  - **Chapter Summaries** to provide a quick overview of each chapter
  - **Lecture Outlines**, which provide a detailed overview of each chapter to help instructors plan their lectures
  - **Lecture Launchers and/or Discussion Topics**, which are ideas to introduce topics or get students involved in discussing issues
  - **Key Terms**
  - **Website Resources**
  - **Bibliography**

- **PowerPoint® Lecture Slides**   The lecture slides have been authored by the textbook's authors Jennifer Bonds-Raacke and John Raacke, and feature prominent figures and tables from the text.

SUPPLEMENTS FOR THE STUDENT

- **eBook** This eBook version of the textbook offers students an online subscription to *Research Methods: Are You Equipped?* At 20% savings. With the eBook, students can search the text, make notes online, print our reading assignments that incorporate lecture notes, and bookmark important passages.

Introduction to Research

Part 1

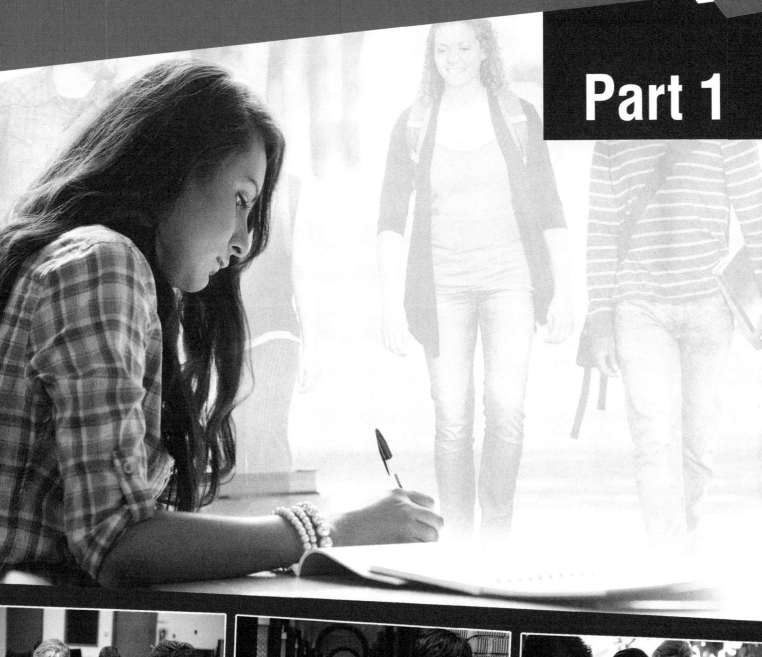

CHAPTER 1

Psychology as a Science

CHAPTER OUTLINE

Are You Equipped?

Research Methods and You

Science versus Pseudoscience

What You Can Expect

Are You Equipped Now?

Chapter Summary

APA Learning Goals Linkage

ARE YOU EQUIPPED?

Are you familiar with Penn and Teller? These entertainers are magicians and comedians. They have a show in Las Vegas and a television show called *Penn & Teller: Bullshit!* The show focuses on debunking myths people commonly believe to be true. One episode focuses on the power of suggestion. Penn and Teller send actors into a local mall and the actors pretend to be professionals in the medical community. These "professionals" attempt to convince shoppers of the benefits of magnet therapy. Shoppers experiencing pain are asked to wear fictitious products such as magno-mitts (oven mitts with magnets) and a magno-hat (construction-like helmet with attached magnets) and report if their pain is reduced while using the product. To ensure the magnets could not have caused any pain relief, they were demagnetized in advance without the shoppers' knowledge. Other shoppers allowed the professionals to place snails on their face for a mucous massage! Thus, Penn and Teller were able to show that the power of suggestion can influence some people. You can view part of this episode at http://www.youtube.com/watch?v=MzjoKhBklYg.

You might want to know what would possess Penn and Teller to try and trick shoppers. The reason is they want to demonstrate a valuable life lesson: Do not confuse pseudoscience with science. As you will learn in this chapter, there are some fields masquerading as real science. However, when empirically and systematically tested, a pseudoscience will not measure up to its claims. Furthermore, Penn and Teller's demonstration illustrates the point we should not blindly obey or believe authority figures. Pseudoscience relies on the so-called experts and authority figures to convince people of the message. Sometimes, people with limited knowledge of the field of psychology will assume it is a pseudoscience. Yet, psychology is a true science. In the following chapters, we will discuss how psychology uses the scientific method to arrive at conclusions. It is understandable that some shoppers in the mall believed in the claims made by the fake medical doctors and equipment. However, by the end of this chapter, you should be skeptical of anyone making such claims.

As you go through this chapter, we also want you to keep in mind how the material relates to the American Psychological Association (APA) goals for psychology majors. Specifically, this chapter will address the following goals:

- **Goal 1. Knowledge Base in Psychology**

  You will demonstrate fundamental knowledge and comprehension of the major concepts, theoretical perspectives, historical trends, and empirical findings to discuss how psychological principles apply to behavioral problems.

- **Goal 2. Scientific Inquiry and Critical Thinking**

  You will demonstrate scientific reasoning and problem solving, including effective research methods.

- **Goal 5. Professional Development**

  You will apply psychological content and skills to career goals and develop meaningful professional direction for life after graduation.

We will relook at these goals again at the end of the chapter.

RESEARCH METHODS AND YOU

Psychologists use a variety of research methods to investigate topics of interest. This textbook will equip you to use these methods to conduct your own research. In addition, the information contained in this textbook will prepare you to be an educated consumer of research. This means you will be able to read, understand, and draw conclusions based on the published work of other social scientists. This is important because when you graduate from your college or university you will no longer have professors to teach you about current developments within the field of psychology. It will become your responsibility to remain up-to-date and knowledgeable. Therefore, no matter whether you are interested in becoming a clinical psychologist, an industrial/organizational psychologist, or any other kind of professional, you will need to stay current within your area.

SOURCES OF INFORMATION

APA: American Psychological Association.

APS: Association for Psychological Science.

One way to know about recent developments is through scholarly resources. You can attend national conferences held by psychological organizations such as the APA and the Association for Psychological Science (APS). This is an opportunity to hear about new theories, trends, and practices from colleagues across the country. Both APA and APS allow students taking psychology courses to join their organizations as student affiliates. The cost is under $40 per year and benefits include reduced conference rates, magazines, journals, and newsletters to name a few. If you are interested in learning more about the organizations or joining, visit the respective websites at the following addresses: www.apa.org and www.psychologicalscience.org.

Another way to learn of new developments in psychology is to read published research findings. Although some journals are broad in scope and publish articles spanning all areas of psychology, others are specific to subareas of psychology. You can subscribe to journals as an individual or, if you are affiliated with a university, you can access the journals through the library. In addition, as we mentioned above, membership in psychological organizations provides access to some journals.

You can also conduct your own research. Many psychologists have a research line or research agenda whereby they add to the existing body of knowledge within their area of expertise. By being actively engaged in research, psychologists remain current and have the latest information on a topic. At this point, the idea of conducting your own research might sound like a daunting task. But, by the end of this textbook, you will have the basic skills and foundations needed to investigate areas of psychology that are of interest to you. We think it is important for you to know that conducting research is not restricted to individuals with PhDs. The field of psychology has a strong tradition of involving undergraduate students in research. There are organizations (e.g., Psi Chi) and conferences (e.g., Great Plains Students' Psychology Convention) devoted to promoting and supporting student research. Be sure to ask your professor about what opportunities are available in your location.

A final source of information about developments within the field is media outlets. Journalists and editors are particularly interested in social science research findings, and it is not uncommon to see or read about psychological research in particular. However, as you will see in this chapter, media outlets do not always do such a great job of accurately conveying findings from social science research. In addition, entertainment media regularly contribute to popular myths about psychology through inaccurate portrayals. Therefore, it is important you have a healthy skepticism when you are a consumer of research information from the media.

IMPORTANCE OF BEING AN EDUCATED CONSUMER

Many times we obtain information about psychological topics from the media. We may purposively seek out information on psychological topics by conducting searches on the Web or we may form ideas about psychological topics through media we consume for entertainment purposes. Yet, the information we obtain is not always accurate. Lilienfeld, Lynn, Ruscio, and Beyerstein (2010) recently published a book examining myths in popular psychology. Take a look at some of the chapter titles below:

- "Most People Use Only 10% of Their Brain Power"
- "Extrasensory Perception Is a Well-Established Scientific Phenomenon"
- "Subliminal Messages Can Persuade People to Purchase Products"
- "Playing Mozart's Music to Infants Boosts Their Intelligence"
- "Most People Experience a Midlife Crisis in Their 40s or Early 50s"
- "Intelligence Tests Are Biased Against Certain Groups of People"

- "The Defining Feature of Dyslexia Is Reversing Letters"
- "Researchers Have Demonstrated That Dreams Possess Symbolic Meaning"
- "Opposites Attract: We Are Romantically Attracted to People Who Differ from Us"
- "People's Responses to Inkblots Tell Us a Great Deal about Their Personalities"
- "People with Schizophrenia Have Multiple Personalities"
- "Most Mentally Ill People Are Violent"

We can't help but think of how media portrayals have helped to reinforce these popular myths. For example, *Ghost Busters* (1984) was about "parapsychology" professors and included scenes with the professors testing extrasensory perception of participants. This could have contributed to the myth stating that extrasensory perception is a well-established phenomenon. In *Father of the Bride Part II* (1995), George Banks (played by Steve Martin) goes through a midlife crisis as his wife and daughter are pregnant at the same time. It is possible that such a depiction gives the impression that a midlife crisis is typical or expected. Even the movie *Me, Myself, and Irene* (2000) confuses multiple personalities with schizophrenia.

Of course, there are other popular myths other than those described by Lilienfeld et al. (2010). For example, countless portrayals in movies and television communicate to viewers married people have little to no sex. However, this depiction is not accurate either! Dr. Bella De Paulo explains to readers such misconceptions on her website in a post titled, "Getting Married and (Not) Getting Sex." Survey research indicates married and cohabiting individuals report more frequent sexual activity than single people. You can read more at http://belladepaulo.com/2014/01/14 /getting-married-and-not-getting-sex/

Certainly, media sources are not entirely to blame for the existence of these myths. Nevertheless, media channels do contribute to the popularization of the myths through inaccurate depictions. The examples we just presented were depictions from entertainment media. However, media outlets can also misinterpret research findings. For example, Larson (2003) notes in the 2000 general election, 47% of the news stories did not accurately report the margin of error and Bushman and Anderson (2001) also note while the scientific community is reaching a consensus on the negative effects of exposure to violent media, news reports paint a different picture saying there is only a weak link between media violence and aggression. More recently, Yavchitz et al. (2012) found misrepresentation of randomized controlled trials in press releases and news coverage could bias consumers' understanding of research findings. Specifically, this misrepresentation of controlled trials could lead to consumers overestimating the value of an experimental treatment.

DISCONNECT BETWEEN MEDIA AND PSYCHOLOGICAL RESEARCH

Although there is not one reason in particular why a disconnect exists between media and psychological research findings, scholars have proposed a few possible explanations. For example, Harris (2009) points out journalists and psychologists use very different languages. Psychologists are very careful not to imply cause and effect from correlational results and prefer to stay away from sweeping generalizations. Yet, this approach does not always make for interesting reading. Psychologists do not receive any formal training in how to bridge this gap, and thus the two groups have difficulty communicating on a topic. Harris also mentions when journalists present both sides of an issue, they may be lending credit to positions not supported in the scientific community. Journalists may feel that presenting both sides of an issue is balanced reporting. But, balanced reporting, in cases where one side is supported by extensive research findings and the other side is conjecture, is not always accurate reporting. For example, researchers have examined how balanced reporting impacted public perceptions on the autism vaccine controversy (Clarke, 2008; Dixon & Clarke, 2013). Even introductory textbooks on mass communication provide examples of how balanced reports can lead to inaccurate coverage (Vivian, 2011) or fail to accurately convey the complexity of a situation (Campbell, Martin, & Fabos, 2014).

RECOMMENDATIONS

Throughout this textbook, we provide you with specific information to help you interpret research findings presented in the media. The specific information will be related to the content covered in the chapter and examples from the media will be provided. At this point, we would like to share with you some general guidelines you should consider. You will be able to understand more about each guideline later in the semester, but it is a good idea to begin thinking about each of them now.

GENERAL GUIDELINES FOR INTERPRETING RESEARCH IN THE MEDIA

1. **Locate original sources:** To begin, it is always a good idea to locate the original source of the story. Typically, the researchers' names and affiliations are provided. With a simple Internet search, you can find the scholarly reference. Then, you can use your university library to locate the reference. Although this sounds time consuming, we have found you can locate original sources pretty quickly. Moreover, having the original source will give you access to all of the research findings and you can draw your own conclusions.

2. **Look for correlational findings:** Many times psychological research examines how factors in life are related to one another. Later in this textbook, we will discuss how this type of research, known as correlational research, does much to advance our knowledge on psychological issues. However, correlational research does not establish cause and effect. It is not uncommon for media sources to imply correlational research findings do more than establish a link between variables of interest. Having the original sources (as mentioned in the previous point) will allow you to know what conclusions can be drawn.

3. **Watch for balanced reporting, misinterpretation of numbers, and generalizations:** We hope after reading this textbook you will have developed a keen eye for issues to be aware of when consuming research. For example, balanced reporting can be a less preferred approach because it can give the impression that the psychological community is divided on an issue when the reality is very different. Similarly, interpreting numbers requires an understanding of statistics and it is not unheard of for media reports to inaccurately explain results or margins of error. Finally, you should watch for sweeping generalizations. Psychological research is conducted in such a way that findings can be applied to specific groups of people. If research findings are presented in a manner implying that *all* people think or behave in a certain way, this is probably not accurate.

Now that we have discussed how research methods relate to you in terms of your career in psychology and in terms of being an educated consumer of research findings in everyday life, we want to talk about psychology as a science. To do so, we will begin by differentiating between science and pseudoscience.

SECTION SUMMARY

- There are many sources from which someone can obtain information in the field of psychology. Information can be obtained (p. 4)
  - from conferences conducted by organizations such as APA and APS;
  - by reading journal articles, books, or book chapters on the field of psychology;
  - by conducting your own research on a topic within psychology; and
  - through the media (p. 5).
- However, there are some caveats when obtaining information through the media (p. 6).
  - Media outlets do not always present information accurately.
  - This can occur because of the disconnect in the use of language by psychologists and media outlets.
  - Also, the media typically presents both sides of an issue in a way lending credibility to nonscientific viewpoints.
- In order to be confident in information reported in the media, make sure to
  - locate the original sources (p. 7).
  - look for correlational findings (p. 7).
  - watch for balanced reporting, misinterpretation of numbers, and generalizations (p. 7).

SCIENCE VERSUS PSEUDOSCIENCE

Have you ever read your horoscope? If so, you are not alone. Newspapers around the world print a daily horoscope for anyone who wishes to have a foreshadowing of the coming day. Reportedly, a horoscope uses the placement of the Sun on the day of a person's birth in conjunction with celestial events to make predictions about the daily dealings for that individual. Horoscopes were developed by those who study astrology. Astrology, the study of the position of celestial bodies and their influence over human behavior, has been studied and followed for thousands of years. By utilizing the placement of celestial bodies in relation to the Earth, astrologers claim to explain past behavior and use it to predict future events.

We started off with this example to help explain the difference between a science and a pseudoscience. Astrology, including its aspects such as horoscopes, is classified as a pseudoscience. A pseudoscience is any theory, method, or belief appearing to be based in science but in reality is not. Even though the description of astrology provided above sounded very scientific, it is not a science. This is because when subjected to scientific evaluation, astrology fails to produce any substantial results. Let us explore the differences between a science and pseudoscience further.

PSEUDOSCIENCE

As mentioned earlier, a **pseudoscience** is any theory, method, or belief appearing to be based in science but is not. The word itself means "false science." A pseudoscience gives the appearance of being a science without the technical rigor or empirical evidence to back it up. Rather a pseudoscience benefits from gathering information via (a) intuition, (b) tenacity, or (c) authority to maintain its scientific appearance. The key is that a pseudoscience acquires its knowledge in ways not lending themselves to open criticisms or challenges. Let us take a look at the three ways a pseudoscience typically operates.

When evaluating arguments, we rely on our **intuition** every day. Intuition can be defined as understanding through the use of common sense based on observation. This means a person uses common sense in forming a judgment about the believability of an observed event. When using intuition, a person assumes if something sounds plausible and looks to be plausible, then it must be true. For example, on the surface, some people would believe the following statements to be true:

- Cholesterol is bad.
- Criminal profilers can be found in most law enforcement agencies.
- The number-one killer of women is breast cancer.
- Criminal activity is on the rise nationally.

However, are these examples true? The answer is no. Although it seems plausible cholesterol is bad for you, there are types of cholesterol which are good for you and aid in neuronal development. In addition, despite the rise in popularity of criminal profiling shows on television, there are only a couple of hundred profilers in the United States (Holmes & Holmes, 2009). Likewise, there

Pseudoscience: Any theory, method, or belief appearing to be based in science but is not.

Intuition: Understanding through the use of common sense based on observation.

has been much publicity about breast cancer and its effects on women; however, the number-one killer of women is heart disease. Heart disease leads to about 10 times as many deaths as compared to breast cancer. Lastly, while much of the US population believes crime is on the rise, the truth is far less dire. Criminal activity in the United States has stayed relatively stable or declined slightly over the past 30 years (Barkan & Bryjak, 2011). Hence, relying solely on your intuition will not always lead to the truth.

Tenacity is defined as the persistence to maintain over time. For a pseudo science, tenacity is seen in the persistent ability of a belief, theory, or method to last over a significant amount of time. In particular, tenacity occurs when something is repeated over and over again to the point where people believe it to be true because (a) of the sheer number of times they have heard it or (b) they have heard it for a long amount of time. However, just because a belief, method, or theory has stayed around without anyone providing counterinformation does not make it a valid or true argument. In other words, just repeatedly saying something is true does not make it true. For instance, it is a commonly held belief among college students that those who are single engage in and enjoy more sexual activity compared to people who are married. This belief has been portrayed in movies and on television shows for years. Each year college students come to campus believing this to be a scientific fact. However, General Psychology students learn the opposite is the case. Research has shown that those who are married or cohabiting not only engage in greater amounts of sexual activity but also report higher levels of satisfaction with their sexual lives (think back to the work by Dr. Bella De Paulo we mentioned earlier in this chapter). Yet, because of the tenacity of this belief about single people, students next year will no doubt come to campus thinking this to be a proven fact.

Lastly, a pseudoscience benefits from **authority**. A pseudoscience gains traction when there is an authoritative figure who conveys the message. This figure can be real but is often imagined. People who are believers of pseudoscience will use terms such as "they said" or "they have shown" without actually being able to identify who "they" are. You probably have seen television commercials where an actor or a real person is promoting a product. Often, this is a doctor who is supporting a new drug or weight loss remedy, or the fifth dentist who approves a certain brand of toothpaste. Typically, these advertisers will use terms such as "the experts" or "those researchers" to provide authority to back up the claims in the advertisement. People believe these claims by making the mental jump that the expert must be the person talking on the television or someone at the product's home company. After all, the advertising company would never insinuate a falsehood just to sell a product; they have "experts." Within a pseudoscience, this lack of clarity in authority is purposeful. It is this anonymity in the authoritative figure that allows the pseudoscience to go unchallenged. Specifically, a pseudoscience chooses an attitude of blind obedience to authority without challenging any of the beliefs held. This is unlike a science which continually challenges the held beliefs of authority. The problem with relying on intuition, tenacity, or authority to form opinions is that it is done without any reliance on critical objectivity or logical reasoning. Thus, a pseudoscience is called a false science. Let's take a look at what makes a science a science and distinguishes a science from a pseudoscience.

SCIENCE

Science is defined as the accumulation of knowledge via systematic observation or experimentation using the scientific method. The scientific method is a step-by-step process by which hypotheses are tested and retested. We will discuss

Tenacity: The persistence to maintain.

Authority: The appearance of expertise in a field of study.

Science: The accumulation of knowledge via systematic observation or experimentation using the scientific method.

the scientific method further in Chapter 2. Right now, we focus on how a science distinguishes itself from a pseudoscience. The biggest differences between a science and a pseudoscience are how information is obtained and the extent to which science is challenged. Unlike a pseudoscience, a science relies on three stable ideals to acquire and distribute knowledge.

First, science is **empirical**, meaning knowledge is gained via observations, experience, or experimentation. However, we have already shown mere observation and experience is not enough. Therefore, the use of the word "empirical" in science means knowledge is obtained via objective and systematic collection of data. After data collection, scientists draw conclusions and make inferences about the topic of study. This is in direct contrast to a pseudoscience, which uses subjective evaluations.

Empirical: Acquisition of knowledge via objective and systematic collection of data.

Second, science is **self-correcting**. Unlike a pseudoscience which avoids challenges to its claims, science encourages challenges. In fact, researchers provide other researchers with the information needed to conduct the work again. This process allows information to be verified. This provides science with a system by which claims can be verified as being true or false. In other words, science allows for a system of checks and balances to ensure any information put forth is accurate. Again, this claim cannot be made by pseudoscience.

Self-Correcting: A system of challenges by which scientific claims can be verified.

Finally, science applies measures of **control**. In scientific research, control is determined by either (a) direct manipulation of a desired variable or (b) management or removal of unwanted factors influencing observations or experiments. Thus, control allows science to determine which factors are important in research and which are not. Control also allows science to make direct comparisons and in many cases demonstrate cause and effect. Without the use of scientific control, researchers will be unable to determine which factors influence which behaviors. For example, psychics (who would come under the category of pseudoscience) most often fail to demonstrate special powers when tested by researchers in controlled environments. Specifically, when a psychic is placed in a situation where a researcher removes the ability of reading body language or facial expression, the psychics' abilities are greatly diminished. The management or removal of unwanted factorsallows the researcher to demonstrate the psychic's mental abilities as false.

Control: Direct manipulation of a desired variable or the management or removal of unwanted factors influencing observations or experiments.

In this section, we have investigated the differences between science and pseudoscience. In the next chapter, we will begin to explore the idea that psychology falls under science. In particular, we will be discussing the use of the scientific method to illustrate how findings of psychologists are scientific.

SECTION SUMMARY

- A distinction must be made between pseudoscience and science (p. 8).
- Pseudoscience is any theory, method, or belief appearing to be based in science but is not (p. 8).
  - Pseudoscience is aided by three principles: intuition, tenacity, and authority.
  - Intuition is the understanding through the use of common sense based on observation (p. 9).
  - Tenacity is the persistence to maintain (p. 10).
  - Authority is the appearance of expertise in a field of study (p. 10).

- Science is the accumulation of knowledge via systematic observation or experimentation using the scientific method (p. 10).
  - Science is empirical. Empiricism is the acquisition of knowledge via objective and systematic collection of data (p. 11).
  - Science is self-correcting. Specifically, science allows for a system of challenges by which scientific claims can be verified (p. 11).
  - Science exerts measures of control. Control is the direct manipulation of a desired variable or the management or removal of unwanted factors influencing observations or experiments (p. 11).

WHAT YOU CAN EXPECT

Just as at the beginning of a semester you wonder what your professors will be like, you might want to know what you can expect from us as the authors of your textbook. To begin, Experimental Psychology (research methods) is one of our favorite courses to teach. This is because most students come to the class with a preconceived notion that they will not like the material. This gives us the unique opportunity to show students how the material can be exciting and relate to the real world. Second, our approach in this textbook is to communicate the material to you as if you were one of our own students. To help you succeed in the course, we have incorporated many student-friendly features in this textbook, which are presented in the list below.

Relevant and Interesting Examples.   We provide you with many examples to help you understand key concepts. We use examples relating to your life and examples that are well known within the field of psychology. We also offer examples appealing to students with a broad range of backgrounds and interests. This includes traditional and nontraditional students, as well as those pertaining to the many different areas of interest in psychology. We hope by giving such examples you will find it easier to remember and apply the information.

Section and Chapter Summaries.   We provide you with summaries at the end of each section within a chapter and at the end of each chapter. The summaries draw your attention to important concepts and terms. Included in the summaries are page numbers, allowing you to easily locate concepts and terms within the chapter. The summaries are also a great way to check your comprehension of the material presented.

Easy-to-Understand Definitions.   When introducing new terms, we avoid using technical or jargon-filled language. Rather, we explain the concept in easy-to-understand language. After you are comfortable with the new information, we illustrate how the term is used within the field. You will find new terms and concepts are presented in bold font within the paragraphs and new terms are also defined in the margins. This will help you to easily spot new information as you are reading the textbook.

Conversational, Engaging Tone.   Our tone in the textbook is very friendly and approachable. This is reflective of our teaching styles. Our goal is that you will want to read the textbook! We also believe it is important to talk to you about the material rather than at you in a lecture style.

Opportunities for Practice.   Finally, you will find this textbook is packed full of opportunities for you to practice. We find students appreciate the opportunity to practice what they have learned and this helps to prepare you for quizzes and exams. We would like to call your attention to two types of practice opportunities: "You Try It!" and "Are You Equipped?"

"You Try It!" and "Are You Equipped?" Exercises.   Two ways we give you the opportunity to practice the material is through "You Try It!" and "Are You Equipped?" exercises. The "You Try It!" exercises are found throughout the chapters after a new topic is presented. It is not uncommon to have more than one such exercise in a given chapter (except for this chapter). Typically, we walk you through an example and then give you the chance to try it on your own. After you try the material for yourself, we talk about the answers. "Are You Equipped" exercises are found at the beginning and at the end of chapters. These exercises at the beginning of the chapters are designed to introduce you to a new topic. For example, the "Are You Equipped" at the beginning of this chapter introduced us to the topic of pseudoscience. You are not expected to know the answers. It is a fun way to get you thinking about the upcoming topics in the chapter. The "Are You Equipped Now" exercises at the end of the chapters are designed to ensure you understand the material before moving onto the next chapter. This is an opportunity for you to test your knowledge of the material before you take an exam. We provide you with the answers to these exercises so you can see how you are doing. To get you familiar with the "Are You Equipped Now?" exercises, take a look at the one below.

ARE YOU EQUIPPED NOW?

On December 15, 2010, The Federal Trade Commission issued a press release titled, "Dannon Agrees to Drop Exaggerated Health Claims for Activia Yogurt and DanActive Dairy Drink: FTC Charges that Evidence Supporting Benefits of Probiotics Falls Short." The press release states Dannon will stop claiming: (a) Activia relieves irregularity and (b) DanActive can help individuals avoid the cold or flu. In short, scientific evidence to support these specific claims was lacking. The FTC stated that consumers need accurate information and companies should not exaggerate the scientific support for products. The press release provides specific examples of wording and graphics in the ads, which could have given consumers inaccurate information. We find the issue discussed in this release interesting, as it relates to the idea of being an educated consumer of media, in particular advertising.

As we mentioned at the beginning of this chapter, it is wise to be hesitant at believing everything you hear and read through media. In fact, some of the guidelines we discussed in this chapter would have been helpful to consumers when deciding whether to purchase the yogurt to help improve digestion. What are two of the guidelines and how might these guidelines have helped?

This textbook has five main parts. Part I of the textbook contains the first three chapters. In the next two chapters, you will read about goals and methods of psychology and ethics. These chapters taken together provide a foundation for the remainder of the course. As we proceed through the material, information will become more challenging. However, our approach of presenting the material in a way you can understand and relate to will remain the same.

CHAPTER SUMMARY

- There are many sources from which someone can obtain information in the field of psychology. Information can be obtained (p. 4)
    - from conferences conducted by organizations such as APA and APS;
    - by reading journal articles, books, or book chapters on the field of psychology;
    - by conducting your own research on a topic within psychology; and
    - through the media.
- However, there are some caveats when obtaining information through the media (p. 6).
    - Media outlets do not always present information accurately.
        - This can occur because of the disconnect in the use of language by psychologists and media outlets.
        - Also, the media typically presents both sides of an issue in a way that lends credibility to nonscientific viewpoints.
- In order to be confident in information reported in the media, make sure to
    - locate the original sources (p. 7).
    - look for correlational findings (p. 7).
    - watch for balanced reporting, misinterpretation of numbers, and generalizations (p. 7).
- A distinction must be made between pseudoscience and science (p. 8).
- Pseudoscience is any theory, method, or belief appearing to be based in science but is not (p. 8).
    - Pseudoscience is aided by three principles: intuition, tenacity, and authority.
    - Intuition is the understanding through the use of common sense based on observation (p. 9).

- Tenacity is the persistence to maintain (p. 10).
  - Authority is the appearance of expertise in a field of study (p. 10).
- Science is the accumulation of knowledge via systematic observation or experimentation using the scientific method (p. 10).
  - Science is empirical. Empiricism is the acquisition of knowledge via objective and systematic collection of data (p. 11).
  - Science is self-correcting. Specifically, science allows for a system of challenges by which scientific claims can be verified (p. 11).
  - Science exerts measures of control. Control is the direct manipulation of a desired variable or the management or removal of unwanted factors influencing observations or experiments (p. 11).

APA LEARNING GOALS LINKAGE

- **Goal 1. Knowledge Base in Psychology**

  You will demonstrate fundamental knowledge and comprehension of the major concepts, theoretical perspectives, historical trends, and empirical findings to discuss how psychological principles apply to behavioral problems.

  Sections Covered: Are You Equipped? Importance of Being an Educated Consumer, Disconnect between Media and Psychological Research, Recommendations, Science versus Pseudoscience, Are You Equipped Now?

  Explanation of the Goal: It is important to understand the nature of psychology as a discipline. To begin, psychology is a science. Therefore, we have examined the characteristics of psychology making it a science. This included the use of (a) empirical data, (b) a system to challenge scientific claims, and (c) controls in observations and experiments. We have also focused on the interpretation and use of psychological research findings. As we have seen, interpreting psychological claims correctly has important personal and societal ramifications.

  It is also important you are able to explain how psychological principles can be used in society. Therefore, we have given many examples in this chapter where concepts, theories, and research findings can be applied to your everyday life. This includes applying psychology principles to everyday activities like buying yogurt and being aware of how psychological research findings are often misunderstood by the public, such as the belief that a midlife crisis is typical and expected.

- **Goal 2. Scientific Inquiry and Critical Thinking**

  You will demonstrate scientific reasoning and problem solving, including effective research methods.

  Sections Covered: Are You Equipped? Importance of Being an Educated Consumer, Disconnect between Media and Psychological Research, Recommendations, Science versus Pseudoscience, Are You Equipped Now?

Explanation of the Goal: Many of the sections in this chapter involved Goal 2. This is because scientific reasoning and problem solving are commonly used by psychologists in daily activities. Thus, we have introduced you to topics and situations where you would use critical and creative thinking, in addition to skeptical inquiry. The popular myths of psychology and blind obedience to authority by those in pseudoscience are two examples. As we have illustrated with these examples, it is by using critical thinking skills that we can recognize common fallacies in thinking and avoid being swayed by appeals to authority. Critical thinking also involves approaching topics with a skeptical inquiry. One way skepticism can be demonstrated is by following the recommendations outlined when interpreting research in the media.

- **Goal 5. Professional Development**

You will apply psychological content and skills to career goals and develop meaningful professional direction for life after graduation.

Sections Covered: Sources of Information, Recommendations

Explanation of the Goal: While completing your major, it is important to learn how your knowledge and skills in psychology will be used after graduation. At the beginning of this chapter, we devoted time to explaining how you will obtain information on the recent developments within the field later in your career. We also encouraged you to join APA and APS as student affiliates and to become involved in undergraduate research. Becoming familiar with these national psychological organizations will provide you with information on the academic experiences needed to achieve your career goals.

In the recommendations section, we have provided general guidelines that you can use when interpreting research findings presented in the media. Following these guidelines will help you to apply psychological principles to promote personal development. In addition, you are engaging in metacognition. This will enable you to evaluate the quality of your own thinking.

CHAPTER 2

Goals and Methods of Psychology

CHAPTER OUTLINE

Are You Equipped?

Introduction

Goals of Psychological Research

Use of the Scientific Method: Steps and Importance

The Research Process

Are You Equipped Now?

Chapter Summary

APA Learning Goals Linkage

ARE YOU EQUIPPED?

Have you ever sat in a movie theater and wondered why snack foods are always advertised before the start of the movie? Or, furthermore, does anyone actually go out and buy the snack foods because of the advertisements? The advertisement of snack foods before a movie starts can be traced back to an early research study. In the mid-1950s, research came out claiming if a movie theater used subliminal advertising, snack sales could be increased. Specifically, an owner, and in this case also the researcher, of a movie theater decided to flash a subliminal message during the screening of a show. The owner flashed "Eat Popcorn" and "Drink Coca-Cola" at an exposure rate of 1/3,000 per second on the screen during the presentation of a movie. The messages flashed on the screen were far below a person's threshold for conscious experience (i.e., subliminal). The owner conducted this experiment over a 6-week period and his results indicated a 50% increase in Coca-Cola sales and an 18% increase in popcorn sales (McConnell, Cutler, & McNeil, 1958).

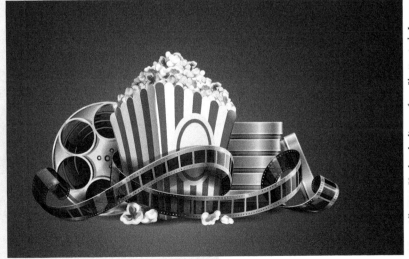

This experiment was hailed as a breakthrough in advertising. So popular were these results that the researcher of this experiment opened his own subliminal advertising firm and charged clients for his new technique. This one event also sparked a plethora of research on the topic of subliminal messages. In fact, subliminal messages and subliminal advertising became part of the global culture after the reporting of these findings. The interesting part of this story was that a few years later, the results were discredited and consequently the researcher admitted to falsifying his results. You might wonder how it came to pass that the results were called into question.

The answer is a result of a simple method psychologists adopted years before: the scientific method. The scientific method provides a framework from which psychologists are able to systematically study behavior and mental processes. As we will discuss, part of the scientific method involves the reporting of research methodologies and findings. In this case, when the research on subliminal advertising was first publicized, other researchers could not reproduce the claimed results, even when using the exact methodology as the theater owner. It was through this process of reporting (commonly referred to as dissemination) and replication that the researcher was shown to be fabricating his results. In this chapter, we will discuss the steps of the scientific method, as well as the goals of psychological research, hypothesis generation, and theory development. By the way, you might find this related video on Buzz Feed to be of interest. This example of subliminal advertising is one of the myths discussed: http://www.buzzfeed.com/video/mdeicke1/7-myths-about-the-brain-that-you-probably-believe

As you go through this chapter, we also want you to keep in mind how the material relates to the APA goals for psychology majors. Specifically, this chapter will address the following goals:

- **Goal 1. Knowledge Base in Psychology**

  You will demonstrate fundamental knowledge and comprehension of the major concepts, theoretical perspectives, historical trends, and empirical findings to discuss how psychological principles apply to behavioral problems.

- **Goal 2. Scientific Inquiry and Critical Thinking**

  You will demonstrate scientific reasoning and problem solving, including effective research methods.

- **Goal 3: Ethical and Social Responsibility in a Diverse World**

  You will apply ethical standards to evaluate psychological science and practice and you will develop ethically and socially responsible behaviors for professional and personal settings in a landscape that involves increasing diversity.

INTRODUCTION

This chapter will introduce you to the goals of psychological research and the method psychologists use to achieve these goals, which are known as the scientific method. The scientific method is used by many disciplines and allows psychologists, in particular, to investigate areas of interest regarding human thought and behavior. Finally, this chapter will begin to show you how to utilize those student-friendly features we discussed in Chapter 1. Let's get started!

GOALS OF PSYCHOLOGICAL RESEARCH

Psychologists carry out research with four goals in mind (Figure 2.1). These four goals build upon one another, creating a pyramid for researchers. The four goals are to (a) describe, (b) explain, (c) predict, and (d) influence behavior and mental processes.

The underlying goal laying the groundwork for all research is to **describe** an event or process. This need to describe events is inherent in our nature as curious human beings. For instance, we overheard our students discussing how sometimes after an individual passes away his or her Facebook account is still active and friends of the individual will post on their wall. When we heard about this behavior, we wondered, "What is going on here?" This is exactly what a researcher does too. A researcher sees a behavior or process and wants to describe it. For example, a researcher hearing about people posting messages on the wall of someone who has passed away would wonder, "What is this?" As the researcher attempts to describe the behavior, he or she is using the first goal of psychological research. In fact, researchers have studied messages directed to the deceased on Facebook memorial group walls and published findings describing the behavior. For example, wall posts to the deceased are a unique form of communicating. This is because research found the messages are typically written as if the deceased could read them (DeGroot, 2012). As can be seen, this is a description of the event.

Describe: The first goal is to describe behavior or mental processes.

Once a description of a behavior or process has been adequately provided, researchers move onto explain the behavior or process. Now, the question changes from "What is going on?" to "Why is this happening?" The process moves from describing the behavior or event to attempting to explain why this behavior or pr ocess is occurring. Let's go back to the Facebook example. Previously, we described what types of messages were written on Facebook memorial group walls. The next goal is to explain why people engage in this form of communication. You might predict people write these types of messages to help them deal with the loss or feel connected to others. In fact, research has found these posts helped people to make sense of the loss and helped people to feel connected to the deceased (DeGroot, 2012). For the purpose of Goal 2, the key is that the research goal has moved beyond documentation to generating explanations for the behavior.

Explain: The second goal is to explain behavior or mental processes.

Predict: The third goal is to predict behavior or mental processes.

The third goal of psychological research is to **predict** the occurrence of a behavior or process. Knowing what the event is and also why it happens allows researchers to begin to predict where it will, or will not, occur. The question for this goal is: "Where will this behavior or event be exhibited?" Researchers working on this goal will look to predict events in specific situations. Therefore, a researcher who knows what messages directed to the deceased on Facebook are (describe) and knows

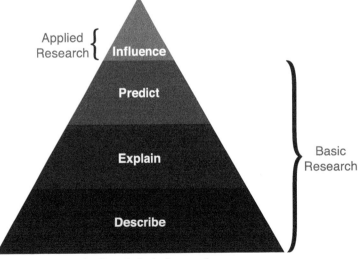

Fig 2.1   Four goals of psychological research

why people make these post (explain) will now try to predict the occurrence of the posts. For example, if a researcher knows that messages to the deceased on Facebook are a unique form of communication (describe) used by those who need to make sense of the loss or feel connected to the deceased (explain), the researcher might predict these messages will be more common after a sudden death (versus a death that an individual has time to prepare for). To confirm the prediction, he or she might investigate how common it is for people to post messages to the deceased when the death was expected or unexpected.

Up until this point, the goals of psychological research have fallen into a category known as **basic research**. Basic research is conducted to further the collective knowledge about a topic within a field of study. In the cases discussed, the field is psychology but basic research can be conducted in any field. With the last goal of psychological research, we move into a category known as **applied research**. Applied research occurs when research is conducted to solve a practical problem within a field of study.

The last goal of psychological research is to **influence** the studied behavior or process. The question for this goal becomes, "How can I enhance or reduce the exhibited behavior or process?" When a researcher attempts to influence a behavior or process, he or she is essentially looking to solve a problem (applied research). A researcher would look to take from all previous research and try to enhance or reduce the behavior or process. For example, if a researcher was investigating messages to the deceased on Facebook with this goal in mind, they might try to reduce the number of messages. One way this might occur is by working with a local school district that had a student pass away unexpectedly. The school district could provide information on support services, hotlines and where to turn for help on the Facebook page. This might provide students with resources they did not know about.

Basic Research: Research conducted to further the collective knowledge about a topic within a field of study.

Applied Research: Research conducted to solve a practical problem within a field of study.

Influence: The fourth goal is to influence behavior or mental processes.

© JaysonPhotography, 2014. Used under license from Shutterstock, Inc.

YOU TRY IT!

In Chapter 1, we mentioned two ways in which we wanted to help you practice the material covered. One of the ways was through exercises called "You Try It!" Here is our first one. Don't worry if you struggle at first; you will get the feel for how to work through these exercises the more you do them.

Questions

We have just gone over the four goals of psychological research and presented them with a running example about messages on Facebook. We would like you to try and apply each of these goals to a topic area in psychology. In this exercise, we will use the topic area of depression. Think about how researchers would investigate the topic of depression using the four goals of psychology, and answer the questions below.

1. For the first goal, what would be the research question? Explain what the researcher would hope to accomplish in terms of information gained on the topic of depression.

2. For the second goal, what would be the research question? Explain what the researcher would hope to accomplish in terms of information gained on the topic of depression.

3. For the third goal, what would be the research question? Explain what the researcher would hope to accomplish in terms of information gained on the topic of depression.

4. For the fourth goal, what would be the research question? Explain what the researcher would hope to accomplish in terms of information gained on the topic of depression.

ANSWERS

Psychologists have been interested in clinical topics such as depression for many years. The information we know about depression has come via research using each of these four goals:

1. A researcher using the first goal would focus on the question, "What is depression?" The researcher would attempt to describe depression. This would include a definition and the ways to identify depression (i.e., symptoms). In psychology, this has been done by researchers and can be found in the *Diagnostic and Statistical Manual of Mental Disorder (DSM-V)*. Most college libraries have a copy of this manual and you might find it interesting to read about various disorders as they are described. This is the most recent edition of the manual released in May 2013 and you can learn more about the updates to the edition at http://www .dsm5.org/Pages/Default.aspx

2. Researchers using the second goal would focus on the question, "Why do people get depressed?" Here, researchers would attempt to identify those situations that lead to depression, such as environmental/social situations (e.g., being homesick, being lonely), biological factors (e.g., a chemical imbalance in the brain), or other plausible explanations.

3. When looking at the third goal, researchers ask the question, "Where or when will people get depressed?" A researcher might predict that freshman college students are susceptible to depression because they have left home for the first time and may feel isolated. Understanding specific situations in which depression occurs will help researchers with the fourth goal.

4. Researchers who engage in the last goal of influence ask the question, "How can I reduce depression?" In this area, therapies and drug treatments have been developed to alleviate or reduce the symptoms of depression. Again, you might find the manual to be useful as it provides information on common treatments for each disorder described.

As you were completing the "You Try It exercises", your answers might have been similar to ours or a little different. As long as your answers addressed the correct question for each goal (e.g., what is going on? why is this happening? where will it happen? and how can I influence it?), you are on the right track. Be sure to ask your professor if you have any concerns. As can be seen, the goals of research determine the direction your studies will take.

Now that we have practiced applying the goals of psychological research, let's return to the issue of basic and applied research. Although the distinction between the two types of research appears clear in the definitions provided earlier, distinguishing between the two can sometimes be problematic. In part, this is due to the fact that some research studies are both basic and applied in nature. Listed below are abstracts from recent issues of the journal *Psychological Science* (a professional journal published by APS) and the *Journal of Psychological Inquiry* (an undergraduate journal published by the Great Plains Behavioral Research Association). We would suggest for you to read each abstract. As you are reading the abstract, do not get overwhelmed with the details of the study. Rather, look for information that helps you determine if the nature of the study was basic (i.e., furthering collective knowledge on a topic), applied (i.e., solving practical problems), or both. After reading each abstract, we will discuss the appropriate categorization.

- Hogan, J., & Sobel, K. V. (2014). Conceptual and perceptual features in guided visual search. *Journal of Psychological Inquiry, 19*, 5–11.

  Visual search experiments have long concluded perceptual features such as color and shape can guide visual search to efficiently locate a target object. Krueger (1984) argued manipulating conceptual features (i.e., '6' is a number and 'G' is a letter) entails manipulating perceptual features ('6' and 'G' have different shapes) so there is no way to disentangle the influence of conceptual and perceptual features on visual search. Nevertheless, Lupyan (2008) carefully controlled for shape while manipulating letter categories, and showed conceptual features such as one letter's identity can be used to guide search. We expanded on this by looking at numbers. Our results were largely consistent with Lupyan's, but also revealed a surprise: participants were faster to find targets based on numerical magnitude than numerical parity (even vs. odd). This could be due to the way numbers were arranged on the number line or to the fact judgments of numerical magnitude were more familiar than judgments of numerical parity. Future experiments are described to explore the role of the mental number line and familiarity in visual search for conceptual features.

Category: Based on the information available in this abstract, you could argue that this research is basic in nature. This is because the goal of the research is to further our understanding of processes involved with visual searches. In particular, the article focuses on how conceptual and perceptual features impact visual searches for numbers.

- Olsson, M. J., Lundström, J. N., Kimball, B. A., Gordon, A. R., Karshikoff, B., Hosseini, N., Sorjonen, K., Höglund, C. O., Solares, C., Soop, A., Axelsson, J., & Lekander, M. (in press). The scent of disease: Human body odor contains an early chemosensory cue of sickness. *Psychological Science*, available online at: http://pss.sagepub.com/content/early/2014/01/21/0956797613515681

Observational studies have suggested that with time, some diseases result in a characteristic odor emanating from different sources on the body of a sick individual. Evolutionarily, however, it would be more advantageous if the innate immune response were detectable by healthy individuals as a first line of defense against infection by various pathogens, to optimize avoidance of contagion. We activated the innate immune system in healthy individuals by injecting them with endotoxin (lipopolysaccharide). Within just a few hours, endotoxin-exposed individuals had a more aversive body odor relative to when they were exposed to a placebo. Moreover, this effect was statistically mediated by the individuals' level of immune activation. This chemosensory detection of the early innate immune response in humans represents the first experimental evidence that disease smells and supports the notion of a "behavioral immune response" that protects healthy individuals from sick ones by altering patterns of interpersonal contact.

Category: This abstract would be categorized as basic research. The authors investigated how diseases have particular smells and how individuals exposed to a toxin have more aversive body odors than when not exposed to a toxin. In doing so, the manuscript meets the goals of basic research by furthering our knowledge on the innate immune system.

○ Vohs, K., Sengupta, J., & Dahl, D. W. (in press). The price had better be right: Women's reactions to sexual stimuli vary with market factors. *Psychological Science, 25*, 1–7. doi: 10.1177/0956797613502732

Two experiments tested when and why women's typically negative, spontaneous reactions to sexual imagery would soften. Sexual economics theory predicts that women want sex to be seen as rare and special. We reasoned that this outlook would translate to women tolerating sexual images more when those images are linked to high worth as opposed to low worth. We manipulated whether an ad promoted an expensive or a cheap product using a sexually charged or a neutral scene. As predicted, women found sexual imagery distasteful when it was used to promote a cheap product, but this reaction to sexual imagery was mitigated if the product promoted was expensive. This pattern was not observed among men. Furthermore, we predicted and found that sexual ads promoting cheap products heightened feelings of being upset and angry among women. These findings suggest that women's reactions to sexual images can reveal deep-seated preferences about how sex should be used and understood.

Category: This abstract might have been difficult to place into a category. That is because it is both basic and applied in nature. On the one hand, the research is basic in nature as it advances our understanding of women's reactions to sexual imagery. On the other hand, it also addresses a practical problem. Specifically, what should advertisers know about using sexual imagery when promoting cheap and expensive products to men and women? Thus, it is also applied in nature.

○ Hendrickson, B., & Ferraro, F. (2013). Assessing the clinical value of cannabis-based treatments on fibromyalgia pain. *Journal of Psychological Inquiry, 18 (2)*, 6–14.

This paper investigates the effectiveness of treating pain attributed to Fibromyalgia Syndrome (FMS) with cannabis-based medicine. Fibromyalgia is a debilitating condition characterized by widespread pain and related symptoms that affects 2–4% of populations worldwide (Fitzcharles & Yunus, 2012). A comprehensive explanation for the underlying causes is still developing and current pharmacology provides little symptom relief. Unlike typical manifestations of pain, fibromyalgia is not a response to pathology or physical injury, but rooted in the functioning of pain signals within the nervous system (Schmidt-Wilcke & Clauw, 2010). When case studies began reporting fibromyalgia-related symptom relief from using preparations of the Cannabis sativa *plant, clinical trials were performed to investigate their validity (Lynch & Campbell, 2011). This review examines these clinical trials, along with the current understanding of fibromyalgia, the history of cannabis use and its chemicals' effects on the endocannabinoid system, and how this recently discovered system relates to fibromyalgia. Drawing on the promising results of this review, the values and drawbacks of cannabis and its emerging pharmaceutical counterparts can be more accurately considered when treating fibromyalgia and other pain conditions.*

Category: This research addresses a current problem in society. The problem is how best to treat pain for individuals suffering from Fibromyalgia Syndrome (FMS). This is an example of applied research as it illustrates how cannabis-based medicine can be effective in treating FMS.

○ Zarkadi, T., Wade, K. A., & Stewart, N. (2009). Creating fair lineups for suspects with distinctive features. *Psychological Science, 20*, 1448–1453.

In their descriptions, eyewitnesses often refer to a culprit's distinctive facial features. However, in a police lineup, selecting the only member with the described distinctive feature is unfair to the suspect and provides the police with little further information. For fair and informative lineups, the distinctive feature should be either replicated across foils or concealed on the target. In the present experiments, replication produced more correct identifications in target-present lineups—without increasing the incorrect identification of foils in target-absent lineups—than did concealment. This pattern, and only this pattern, is predicted by the hybrid-similarity model of recognition.

Category: In this final abstract, we see another example of applied research. In this article, researchers are trying to understand the influence of lineups on eyewitnesses' abilities to identify suspects with distinctive features. By providing police officers with information on how to improve lineups, this research is solving a practical problem in our society.

We shared these examples with you to illustrate how current research can be conducted to further collective knowledge, solve practical problems, or, in some cases, accomplish both goals. This is the first time in the textbook we have presented you with excerpts from published manuscripts. If you have little previous experience with reading published manuscripts in the field, this may have been challenging for you. However, we will practice this skill throughout the chapters so your comfort level in reading journal articles will increase.

SECTION SUMMARY

- There are four goals psychologists have when conducting research.
  - The first goal is to *describe* behavior or mental processes. The question researchers ask is, "What is this?" (p. 19).
  - The second goal is to *explain* behavior or mental processes. The question researchers ask is, "What is going on?" (p. 19).
  - The third goal is to *predict* behavior or mental processes. The question researchers ask is, "Where will this take place?" (p. 19).
  - The fourth goal is to *influence* behavior or mental processes. The question researchers ask is, "How can I impact this?" (p. 20).
- The first three goals fall under *basic research*. Basic research is conducted to further the collective knowledge about a topic within a field of study (p. 20).
- The last goal falls under *applied research*. Applied research is conducted to solve a practical problem within a field of study (p. 20).

USE OF THE SCIENTIFIC METHOD: STEPS AND IMPORTANCE

In order to accomplish the goals of psychological research, psychologists have borrowed the scientific method from other fields. The scientific method provides a framework for the systematic study of behavior and mental processes. There are six steps in the scientific method psychologists use when conducting research. The steps are (a) problem identification, (b) hypothesis formation, (c) collection of data, (d) analysis of data, (e) conclusion, and (f) reporting of findings (Figure 2.2).

The first step in the scientific method is known as problem identification. Sometimes, this is known as question identification. No matter what the title, this step involves identifying a topic to research, as well as doing an initial review of the literature to determine what previous research has been conducted on the topic. We will discuss further how to identify a topic of interest and conduct a literature review later on in Chapter 6. The second step in the scientific method is to formulate a hypothesis. A popular definition of a hypothesis is an educated guess. However, for the purposes of conducting research, that definition is not sufficient. A more useful definition is that a **hypothesis** is a statement about the relationship between variables. When going through the scientific method, a researcher must develop a hypothesis. Typically, the hypothesis is derived from the first step after which a thorough review of information regarding the topic of interest has been completed. The hypothesis is also used to guide the next step in the scientific method, designing a study or experiment.

Hypothesis: A statement about the relationship between variables.

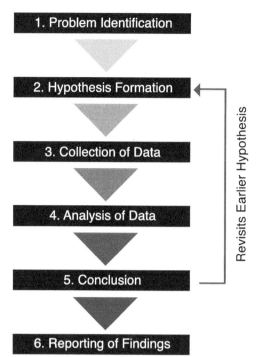

1. Problem Identification

2. Hypothesis Formation

3. Collection of Data

4. Analysis of Data

5. Conclusion

6. Reporting of Findings

Revisits Earlier Hypothesis

Fig 2.2 Steps of the Scientific Method

The third step is to collect data on your topic to test your hypothesis. To do this, researchers typically design an experiment or develop a study in which the variables of interest can be tested. One of the purposes of this textbook is to explain the types of research designs that can be used. The fourth step is to take the data collected and conduct data analysis. Data analysis involves the use of statistics. The results the statistical analyses yield are used to guide the fifth step, conclusion. The fifth step is very important in the research process. This is the step where a researcher revisits the hypothesis. At this point, the researcher, using the results from the analysis of the data, will make a judgment about the hypothesis. Based on the results of the study, a researcher will then decide to either support or reject the earlier hypothesis. Interestingly, it is at this step that many researchers will reevaluate the hypothesis and research design. This reevaluation can lead the researcher to make changes to the study. If a change does occur, the steps in the scientific method are carried out again starting with Step 2. In essence, the fifth step allows for a feedback loop in the scientific method, giving researchers the opportunity to correct any problems discovered along the way.

Replication: A research experiment or study that is reproduced using the exact methodology and procedure.

The final step, although crucial, is often overlooked. This step is reporting your findings. To conduct the research is not enough. As a researcher, you must make sure the information you have learned from your experiment or study is disseminated. Keeping the information to yourself only hinders the advancement of the field. The manner in which you disseminate your research is also important. In particular, research must be shared in such a way that the experiment or study can be replicated. **Replication** occurs when a research experiment or study is reproduced using the exact methodology and procedure. Thus, when reporting findings, the procedure and methodology need to be clearly communicated, with no ambiguity. Failure to do so could result in conflicting information on a topic. However, if a study is communicated accurately and the researchers replicating the study find similar results, the original researchers can have greater confidence in the accuracy of the results. It should be noted that, for the most part, research studies that find new results are typically published, whereas studies failing to add to the body of knowledge are not. (As a side note, whether this practice of only publishing new results is the best approach is a topic of much discussion in the field.) Researchers prefer to publish their findings in what is known as peer-reviewed sources. This means that other scholars have reviewed the content of the manuscript and judged it to be worthy of publication and free from error.

To further illustrate these steps applied to psychological research, let's look at an example. Recently, there has been a push for young females to receive the human papillomavirus (HPV) vaccine. This vaccine can prevent some types of cervical cancer and genital warts. This topic has received a lot of attention from the media, health-care providers, and parents alike regarding the risk of contracting HPV, which can lead to cervical cancer in females. Cox, Cox, Sturm, and Zimet (2010) decided this was a worthy topic to research. In other words, they identified a problem (Step 1). After researching the topic further, Cox et al. developed several hypotheses (Step 2). For the purpose of this example, we will focus on their first hypothesis. This hypothesis stated the graphic representation of risk statistics regarding HPV and cervical cancer in young women would increase mothers' intention to have their daughters vaccinated.

In order to test their hypothesis, Cox et al. (2010) developed an experiment in which they presented information on the risks of developing cervical cancer as a result of contracting HPV with and without graphical statistics to mothers of female children (Step 3). Upon the completion of the study, the researchers analyzed their results using several different statistical techniques (Step 4). Interestingly, the researchers found mothers who viewed the graphical message had significantly higher levels of intention to have their daughters vaccinated than those who did not view a graphical message. From these results, the researchers concluded a graphical message used by health-care providers could lead to higher levels of HPV vaccination (Step 5). The last step is to report the findings (Step 6). This occurred given that we are sharing with you the published findings. In the future, another researcher will more than likely replicate this study to verify that the results obtained by Cox et al. are accurate.

When followed, the scientific method allows a researcher to systematically study a topic. It is this approach psychologists follow when conducting research. Although this approach was borrowed over a 100 years ago, it still has an impact on science. The remainder of this textbook will provide you with the necessary tools to engage in the first three steps of the scientific method in psychology.

YOU TRY IT!

QUESTIONS

Using the information about the scientific method we have just discussed, answer the following questions about the research processes in the field of psychology:

1. A researcher is interested in determining if the racial makeup of an audience influences perceptions of humor. The researcher has conducted a review of previous research and has developed the hypothesis that the audience racial makeup will influence perceptions of humor. Using the scientific method, what is the next step that needs to be taken by the researcher?

2. A group of undergraduate students are investigating whether the skills acquired when playing a real-world game are helpful when a simulated version of it is played as a video game. The students have hypothesized that taking a class in dance will improve a person's skill and confidence level when playing *Just Dance* on the *X-Box One*. The undergraduate researchers have designed a study and collected their data. However, they are now unsure of what to do. What is the next step that these undergraduates must take in the scientific method?

1. Once a researcher has decided on a topic, reviewed the relevant work on that topic, and developed a hypothesis, the researcher is ready to pursue the third step of the scientific method. In particular, this is the point where the researcher must develop a research design (i.e., an experiment or a study) and collect data to test the hypothesis.

2. In this example, the researchers have gone through the first three steps in the scientific method. This puts the researchers halfway through the steps in the scientific method. The next steps would be to analyze the data, draw conclusions, and report the findings.

SECTION SUMMARY

- There are six steps in the scientific method psychologists use when conducting research (p. 25).
  - The steps are (a) problem identification, (b) hypothesis formation, collection of data, (d) analysis of data, (e) conclusion, and (f) reporting of findings.
    - The step of problem identification involves identifying a topic of study and conducting an initial review of the work already done on the topic (p. 25).
    - The step of hypothesis formation involves the development of a hypothesis. A hypothesis is a statement about the relationship between variables (p. 25).
    - The third step involves data collection. Data collection occurs through the design of an experiment or development of a study in which the variables of interest can be tested (p. 25).
    - The fourth step of data analysis involves using statistics to analyze the data collected in the third step (p. 26).
    - The fifth step involves drawing conclusions about the data that were collected and analyzed. It is in this step that many will revisit their original hypothesis to make any changes that are necessary (p. 26).
    - The last step involves the dissemination of the findings. This allows others to confirm or disprove the findings of the study (p. 26).

THE RESEARCH PROCESS

Before concluding this chapter, we have two more things we would like to discuss. Earlier, we mentioned the term "hypothesis" when explaining the scientific method. We defined a hypothesis as a statement about the relationship between two or more variables. However, the tricky part of a hypothesis is developing one. A hypothesis has to be worded in such a way that it can be tested.

For example, a researcher would never have a hypothesis such as, "Religious groups are moral." This hypothesis is not testable. In this case, the question is of morality and how that is defined is determined by the individual. However, a researcher could have a hypothesis such as, "Members of religious groups consider themselves to be moral." Now, the question is not whether religious groups are moral. Rather, the question is whether those in religious groups believe they are moral. This can be tested. We will discuss hypothesis generation in detail in Chapter 6.

The other concept we want to mention before closing the chapter is that of a **theory**. A theory is an overarching principle explaining separate research findings in an area. After researchers have produced consistent findings on a topic, psychologists need to propose a theory accounting for those findings. Specifically, a theory uses a set of interrelated concepts to explain a large body of findings on a topic which will then be used to make future predictions about the topic.

Theory: An overarching principle that explains separate research findings in an area.

© scyther5, 2014. Used under license from Shutterstock, Inc.

For example, in the area of media research, researchers have consistently shown that (a) people who watch a lot of TV think that the world is more crime-ridden than it really is and (b) the more TV you watch, the more your political views reflect the mainstream. A theory known as the "cultivation theory" was proposed to account for these separate findings (Gerbner & Gross, 1976). Cultivation theory states after repeated exposure to media, one's worldviews are shaped and changed. This would account for each of the aforementioned separate findings about media exposure and can be tested with future research.

Another example comes from the area of human aggression. Researchers have consistently shown that (a) a large proportion of violent acts are performed by young males toward other young males and (b) that young males are much more likely to engage in violent acts when they are born into poverty. A theory known as "sexual selection theory," originally developed by Darwin (1871), has been proposed as an explanation for the patterns of aggression previously described (Wilson & Daly, 1985). Briefly, sexual selection theory suggests that young males will compete with other young males for the attention of young females, and that this competition may escalate—perhaps violently—when the stakes are highest (e.g., when resources are scarce, as is the case in many impoverished areas). This theory would account for each of the aforementioned separate findings about human aggression and can be tested with future research.

As researchers, we look not only to create theories but also to disprove them. Attempts to disprove theories typically yield two outcomes, both of which are positive for researchers. First, if a theory is disproven, then the scientific community will discard it and work to create a new and improved theory that will benefit all researchers. Second, when researchers attempt to disprove a theory and fail, they are strengthening the likelihood that the theory is good. This is beneficial in that when a theory stands up to scrutiny, the validity of the theory becomes stronger.

SECTION SUMMARY

- A hypothesis must be worded in such a way that it can be tested. Hypotheses are not worded using ambiguous language (p. 28).
- A theory is an overarching principle that explains separate research findings in an area (p. 29).
- A theory is more difficult to develop than a hypothesis (p. 29).

ARE YOU EQUIPPED NOW?

To end this chapter, let's look at one more example of research on the topic of Facebook messages to individuals who are deceased. Pennington (2013) examined what types of behaviors participants reported engaging in, for example, looking at pictures and writing messages, and why participants did these things. Results indicated participants found this to be helpful and a form of a coping mechanism.

QUESTIONS

1. Can you identify the psychological goal(s) that the researcher was investigating in the study?
2. What step is the researcher currently taking in the scientific method? And, what steps in the scientific method should come next?

ANSWERS

1. For this particular study, there are two goals that are being addressed. The first is the goal of *describe*. Specifically, the researcher is describing the types of behaviors people reported on Facebook pages for friends who are deceased. Second, the goal of *explain* is being addressed. Once the researcher described the behavior, she sought to explain it. Specifically, the researcher was able to show why individuals maintain contact with deceased friends through social networking sites.
2. The researcher is currently on the last step of the scientific method. She conducted all the other steps including problem identification, hypothesis formation, collection of data, analysis of data, and conclusion. The researcher has reported her findings. Now, other researchers can replicate the experiment to see if similar results are achieved.

CHAPTER SUMMARY

- There are four goals psychologists have when conducting research (p. 19–20).
  - The first goal is to *describe* behavior or mental processes. The question researchers ask is, "What is this?" (p. 19).
  - The second goal is to *explain* behavior or mental processes. The question researchers ask is, "What is going on?" (p. 19).

- The third goal is to *predict* behavior or mental processes. The question researchers ask is, "Where will this take place?" (p. 19).
- The fourth goal is to *influence* behavior or mental processes. The question researchers ask is, "How can I impact this?" (p. 20).

- The first three goals fall under *basic research*. Basic research is conducted to further the collective knowledge about a topic within a field of study (p. 20).

- The last goal falls under *applied research*. Applied research is conducted to solve a practical problem within a field of study (p. 20).

- There are six steps in the scientific method psychologists use when conducting research. These steps are (a) problem identification, (b) hypothesis formation, (c) collection of data, (d) analysis of data, (e) conclusion, and (f) reporting of findings.
  - The first step of problem identification involves identifying a topic of study and conducting an initial review of the work already done on the topic (p. 25).
  - The second step of hypothesis formation involves the development of a hypothesis. A *hypothesis* is a statement about the relationship between variables (p. 25).
  - The third step involves data collection. Data collection occurs through the design of an experiment or development of a study in which the variables of interest can be tested (p. 25).
  - The fourth step of data analysis involves using statistics to analyze the data collected in the previous step (p. 26).
  - The fifth step involves drawing conclusions about the data that were collected and analyzed. It is in this step that many will revisit their original hypothesis to make any changes that are necessary (p. 26).
  - The final step involves the dissemination of the findings. This allows others to confirm or disprove the findings of the study (p. 26).

- A hypothesis must be worded in such a way that it can be tested. Hypotheses are not worded using ambiguous language (p. 28).

- A theory is an overarching principle that explains separate research findings in an area (p. 29).

- A theory is more difficult to develop than a hypothesis (p. 29).

APA LEARNING GOALS LINKAGE

- **Goal 1. Knowledge Base of Psychology**

  You will demonstrate fundamental knowledge and comprehension of the major concepts, theoretical perspectives, historical trends, and empirical findings to discuss how psychological principles apply to behavioral problems.

  Sections Covered: Goals of Psychological Research, Use of the Scientific Method, The Research Process.

Explanation of the Goal: In this chapter, we have identified and explained the primary goals of psychology, which are to describe, explain, predict, and influence behavior and mental processes. We have also discussed major concepts in the field such as basic research, applied research, and theory. Finally, we continued our discussion from Chapter 1 regarding why psychology is a science through learning the steps of the scientific method.

- **Goal 2. Scientific Inquiry and Critical Thinking**

You will demonstrate scientific reasoning and problem solving, including effective research methods.

Sections Covered: Goals of Psychological Research, The Research Process.

Explanation of the Goal: It is important to be able to describe how various research methods address different types of questions. We began to develop this skill through examining how the goals of the research influence the type of research question formed. While learning the steps of the scientific method, we introduced the idea of replication. As psychologists, we must be cautious in predicting behavior from a single study. However, as findings are replicated, we can become more confident in our predictions.

- **Goal 3: Ethical and Social Responsibility in a Diverse World**

You will apply ethical standards to evaluate psychological science and practice and you will develop ethically and socially responsible behaviors for professional and personal settings in a landscape that involves increasing diversity.

Sections Covered: Goals of Psychological Research, Use of the Scientific Method.

Explanation of the Goal: We expanded our critical thinking skills by learning to apply the scientific approach to solve problems related to behavior and mental processes. You also completed numerous exercises requiring you to think critically. These included forming research questions for each goal in psychological research, identifying basic and applied research, and determining what step is needed next to complete the scientific method.

Sections Covered: Are You Equipped, Goals of Psychological Research, Use of the Scientific Method, Are You Equipped Now?

Explanation of the Goal: We have applied topics from psychology to numerous personal and social issues in this chapter including subliminal advertising and creating fair police lineups.

CHAPTER 3

Ethics

CHAPTER OUTLINE

Are You Equipped?

Consumers of Research

APA's Ethics Code

Are You Equipped Now?

Chapter Summary

APA Learning Goals Linkage

ARE YOU EQUIPPED?

Back in the 1950s, researchers wanted to better understand how members of a jury reached a verdict. In particular, the researchers wanted to know if the behavior of the attorneys influenced how jury members thought about the case. The researchers needed to be able to listen to a jury deliberate but without the members of the jury knowing their conversations were being heard. This was an important aspect to control because jury members might change what they were saying if they knew other individuals were listening.

© bikeriderlondon, 2014. Used under license from Shutterstock, Inc.

The researchers set about conducting the study by obtaining permission from the judge and both attorneys to record the deliberations. However, the jury members were not informed that the discussions were being recorded. After the trial had ended, information regarding the research became known to the public through presentation of the research at a professional conference. The news that the researchers had recorded conversations without obtaining permission (consent) from the jury members caused many people to become upset. Although the researchers had good intentions, people were concerned that this event might influence the integrity of the system in future cases.

More specifically, future jury members might be reserved and less willing to speak their minds, knowing that their conversation might be on tape. Shortly thereafter, a law was passed by U.S. Congress preventing jury deliberations from being recorded. If you would like to know more about this study, known as the Wichita Jury Study, please refer to Amdur and Bankert (2011) and the website of the Drug Institute (www.drugstudy.md/resource3.html).

This study helped shape the way we conduct research today. The researchers were interested in a very valid research question and the results had the potential toadvance our knowledge within the field. However, does this potential knowledge give researchers the right to not inform individuals of their participation in an experiment? In this chapter, we will discuss ethical questions just like this one. Although there are now federal guidelines to help protect research participants, psychologists and social scientists still face situations where the answer is not always clear. For example, is it acceptable to use deception if there is no other feasible way to conduct a study? By the end of this chapter, we want you to be informed of your rights as a participant in research and as a consumer of research. In addition, we want you to know how to conduct experiments that meet ethical guidelines. Let's begin!

As you go through this chapter, we also want you to keep in mind how the material relates to the APA goals for psychology majors. Specifically, this chapter will address the following goals:

- **Goal 1. Knowledge Base in Psychology**

  You will demonstrate fundamental knowledge and comprehension of the major concepts, theoretical perspectives, historical trends, and empirical findings to discuss how psychological principles apply to behavioral problems.

- **Goal 2. Scientific Inquiry and Critical Thinking**

  You will demonstrate scientific reasoning and problem solving, including effective research methods.

- **Goal 3. Ethical and Social Responsibility in a Diverse World**

  You will apply ethical standards to evaluate psychological science and practice and you will develop ethically and socially responsible behaviors for professional and personal settings in a landscape that involves increasing diversity.

CONSUMERS OF RESEARCH

When our oldest daughter was in first grade, we went to her elementary school for a parent–teacher conference. In addition to discussing our daughter's progress, we were given a survey to complete. Our daughter's teacher did a great job of conveying to us that a teacher at another school in our school district was currently working on his or her master's degree and the survey was part of the work. Our daughter's teacher also emphasized that completing the survey was voluntary. We nodded our heads to indicate we understood and took the survey home. That evening we sat down to complete the survey. Having gone through the process of conducting research for our degrees, we wanted to be as helpful as possible. The survey was on the topic of students wearing uniforms and the resulting behavior in the school. The questionnaire required us to share our current feelings about the elementary school and how uniforms might help improve behavior. This placed us in a difficult situation. We had candid opinions to share. However, the way the surveys were to be returned was not anonymous. In fact, the surveys were to be returned in our daughter's homeroom folder so our responses could be easily identified. Furthermore, the survey was not accompanied by a consent form. This meant that we had no way of knowing how the confidentiality of our responses would be maintained. We have both served on Institutional Review Boards (IRBs), which we will discuss in this chapter, so we found it strange that a survey requiring us to divulge such opinions would not have guidelines to protect our rights. Although we completed the survey, Jenn placed a note on the back indicating that a consent form or debriefing statement explaining how the responses would be shared with the school administrators and how our responses would be protected should have been included.

You might think that we overreacted to this situation. However, research participants should not fear their responses can be identified or used against them by a governing body. As a consumer of research, you should be aware of the federal guidelines protecting you. In this chapter, we will tell you about these federal guidelines and also guidelines developed especially for psychologists by the APA.

INSTITUTIONAL REVIEW BOARD

An IRB is a committee that reviews proposals of intended research and evaluates if the research is ethical and if the rights of the participants are being protected. Although colleges and universities have IRBs which review all research conducted on campus, IRBs are not confined to only the academic world. They can also be found in hospitals, government agencies, and private corporations. IRBs are a relatively new entity and have been developed, in part, because of past research that could be considered unethical. The Wichita Jury Study from the beginning of this chapter was one research study that led the government to intervene in how research is conducted. However, the Wichita Jury Study was not the only study which prompted the formation of IRBs. Amdur and Bankert (2011) provide a listing of other questionable research playing a role. Some examples include the research conducted by Nazi leaders in concentration camps, the administration of a drug called thalidomide to pregnant women without informing the women the drug was in an experimental testing stage, and injecting hepatitis into mentally impaired children who were residents of a state school.

You probably noticed the previous examples of questionable research are not just from the social sciences. Rather, the examples are from many areas of inquiry. This chain of events prompted the government in 1974 to pass the National Research Act, which established the IRB system and formed a commission to protect participants of research. This commission developed a report known as the Belmont Report in the late 1970s, which outlined three principles to be used by the IRB: respect, beneficence, and justice (Amdur & Bankert, 2011).

According to the Belmont Report, the first principle of **respect** for persons emphasizes protecting the autonomy of people and those with diminished autonomy. Simply, the first principle ensures research is conducted in such a way that people have the right to determine their own destiny (i.e., have the right of choice in participation). However, some populations do not have the ability to act autonomously and are, therefore, offered special protection by the IRB. If you plan to conduct

Respect: Protect the autonomy of research participants as well as those with diminished autonomy.

research with minors (under the age of 18), prisoners, the mentally impaired, or pregnant women, you can expect the IRB to require you to describe how you will protect the rights of your participants. Using these populations might also involve additional steps in the research process. For example, several of our colleagues have investigated gender roles and career development in preschool children from a local church day care. Even before data collection, the researchers had to secure permission from the child-care advisory board of the church, teachers, and parents.

Beneficence: Research is conducted with the well-being of the participant in mind.

The second principle outlined in the Belmont Report is **beneficence**. This principle focuses on investigators conducting research with the well-being of the research participants in mind. Although this seems straightforward, this principle argues that research should be conducted in a manner which maximizes any benefits while minimizing all risks. When conducting research, following the golden rule of do unto others as you would have them do unto you will help a researcher meet this principle (Amdur & Bankert, 2011).

Justice: Any risks or benefits of the study are distributed among the population equally.

The last principle in the Belmont Report is **justice**. This principle is the hardest of the three to understand. In short, the principle of justice was in response to those studies which exploited vulnerable segments of the population. Therefore, the principle of justice states that when conducting research an investigator ensures to distribute any risks or benefits among the population equally, thereby avoiding the likelihood of exploiting certain segments of the population.

These three principles are used by committee members to evaluate the research being proposed in terms of informed consent, assessment of risk/benefit, and selection of participants. If you plan to conduct research at your college or university, you will be required to go through the IRB. This means you will outline your research and present it to the IRB committee. Once submitted, the committee will evaluate your proposed research on the principles above and will place your proposed research into one of the three categories: Exempt, Expedited, or Full Board. Each category represents a level of review by the IRB and is based on the complexity of your proposed study as a function of the three guiding principles. Most universities have a standard form you will need to use. If your university does not provide a standard format for you, ask the faculty member you are working with to provide you a sample from his or her previous research. Once you have practiced completing the forms, it is a rather simple task.

YOU TRY IT!

For the following, we would like for you to reference the Wichita Jury Study from the beginning. Specifically, using the information from that study, answer the questions below.

QUESTIONS
1. Think about the Wichita Jury Study. In your opinion, what were some of the potential benefits to society from conducting the study?
2. In addition to the one mentioned, what were some of the risks to participants who were involved with the study?
3. Do you think that the benefits to society outweighed the individual risks to participants?

1. For this "You Try It!" section there are really no right or wrong answers. We just wanted you to get practice thinking about research projects in terms the IRB uses. One benefit to the Wichita Study would be to see how a lawyer can influence jury members and thus the verdict on a case. Understanding how juries make decisions (and the role the lawyer plays in that decision) is very important information.

2. We had already mentioned this study might prevent future jury members from speaking freely. However, there could have been potential risks for individuals in the study as well. It is possible the individuals could have been identified by their voices and confronted by others regarding the content of the deliberations. In a worst case scenario, a convicted criminal might try and seek revenge on jury members or their families. A researcher must consider all foreseeable risks and describe these to the IRB.

3. This is a tough question. It is not easy to decide if the benefits gained from a study are greater than the possible risks to participants. However, this is the job of the members of the IRB. The Belmont Report acknowledges this difficult situation and stresses that a study should be designed to minimize such risks. Researchers can aid the IRB committee by explicitly stating how risks are minimized and the importance of the findings to the scientific community.

Now that we have given you some background information on the establishment of today's IRB system, we would like to switch gears and discuss the topic of ethics and research with respect to the standards provided by the APA. If you have questions right now about informed consent, assessment of risk/benefit, and selection of participants, they will be answered in the next section.

SECTION SUMMARY

- The IRB is a committee which reviews proposals of intended research to determine if the research is ethical and that the rights of the participants are being protected (pp. 35–36).
- IRBs can be found on university campuses, hospitals, and in many corporations where research on human participants is conducted (p. 35).
- IRBs are a result of government intervention in 1974 by promulgating the National Research Act (p. 35).
  - This Act set up a commission which developed the Belmont Report, which outlined three guiding principles for human participant research: respect, beneficence, and justice (pp. 35–36).
    - The principle of respect protects the autonomy of participants as well as those with diminished autonomy.

- The principle of beneficence ensures research is conducted with the well-being of the participant in mind.
- The principle of justice ensures any risks or benefits of the research are distributed among the population equally.
- The three levels of IRB review are exempt, expedited, and full board (p. 36).

APA'S ETHICS CODE

The APA developed an ethics code (most recently revised in 2010) to guide psychologists in their professional work. For our purposes, we will focus on the ethical standard related to research and publication. The ethical standard related to research is 8.0 and it contains 15 guidelines. As we discuss each of these guidelines, please see the accompanying table for a summary.

- **8.01 Institutional Approval.** The first guideline for psychologists conducting research is that they secure permission from the institution (usually a college or university) before conducting their research. This institutional approval is typically given after going through the IRB process we just described. It is very important psychologists obtain permission from their university before conducting any research and not after the fact. It should also be noted that APA expects psychologists to conduct the research as outlined in the proposal to the university. If, for some reason, the research procedure needs to be modified during the experiment, the psychologist needs to contact the university and go through the proper steps to have the modified procedure approved.

- **8.02 Informed Consent.** Before participating in a research study, participants are given an informed consent (commonly referred to as a consent form). APA requires the consent form address specific topics.
    - To begin, your consent form should tell participants information about the research being conducted. It should also give the participants an estimate of how long it will take them to participate and a brief overview of what they will be required to do.
    - The consent form should clearly inform participants that they do not have to participate in the study. This means participation in the research is voluntary. Participants should also be told they may stop, withdraw, from the study at any point. This includes withdrawing participation even after the study has started.

- If there are consequences to not participating or withdrawing from the study, these should be explained to the participant.
- Any potential risks of participating (if there are any) and research benefits should be stated.
- It should be made clear to participants if their responses are anonymous or confidential. Often, researchers and participants confuse these two concepts. When a study is **anonymous**, the researcher has ensured no identifying information is gathered and participants cannot be identified once the study is concluded. If a study is **confidential**, the participants can be identified by information that is gathered. However, this information is kept in a manner that participant responses are not shared with others and the participants cannot be identified. Finally, if there are limits to the confidentiality, the limits should be addressed.
- When incentives are offered for participation such as a monetary compensation, the incentives should be explained.
- Finally, the consent form should close with information on how participants can contact the researcher(s) if they have questions.

Anonymous: Research that is conducted which ensures no identifying information is gathered and participants cannot be identified by information that is gathered.

Confidential: Research that is conducted in which participants can be identified by information that is gathered but data is restricted to those conducting the research.

A former student, Josh, was conducting his Master's thesis on decision making when it comes to moral dilemmas. He used the consent form below when collecting data at our institution. You will notice, Josh's consent form addresses the specific topics required by APA. In addition, his consent form is written in a simple language that college freshmen will most likely understand.

CONSENT TO PARTICIPATE IN RESEARCH

Department of Psychology Fort Hays State University

Personal Beliefs: How People Interpret Ambiguous Situations

Researcher: xxxxx@fhsu.edu   xxx-xxx-xxxx

Project Advisor: xxxxx@fhsu.edu   xxx-xxx-xxxx

You are being asked to participate in a research study. It is your choice whether or not to participate. Your decision whether or not to participate will have no effect on benefits of the research, the quality of your care, or academic standing to which you are otherwise entitled. Please ask questions if there is anything you do not understand.

What is the purpose of this study?

The purpose of the study is to explore how participants interpret and make decisions about scenarios involving difficult moral dilemmas. You will be asked to think about your personal values and beliefs when making your decisions.

What does this study involve?

The study involves filling out five surveys. If you decide to participate and sign this form, you will be given the questionnaires with adequate instructions. Instructions for each questionnaire are explained at the beginning of each. The surveys are not experimental in nature. The only experimental aspect of this study is the gathering of information for analysis. If you have any questions, feel free to ask the researcher. General instructions for completing the surveys and handing them in after completion will be read aloud prior to distribution. If you decide to participate in this study, you will be asked to sign this consent form after you have had all your questions answered and understand what will happen to you. The length of time of your participation in this study is approximately thirty minutes. Approximately 250 participants will take part in this study.

Are there any benefits from participating in this study?

Your participation will help us learn more about how people interpret scenarios that involve difficult moral dilemmas. It is important to learn about how people's values relate to how they make decisions. In participating in this study, you are helping this cause.

Will you be paid or receive anything to participate in this study?

Yes, there may be course credit or extra credit points for participation as outlined in the course syllabus.

Courtesy of Janett M. Naylor

What about the costs of this study?

There are no costs for participating in this study other than the time you will spend completing the surveys.

What are the risks involved with being enrolled in this study?

It is unlikely that participation in this project will result in any harm than it is expected in our everyday life. However, sometimes thinking about these subjects cause people to be upset. Therefore, there is a slight psychological risk. You do not have to respond to any question that you feel uncomfortable responding to, and you may stop participating at any time. If you feel distressed or become upset by participating, you may seek help at the Kelly Center on campus, which provides support services for students. They are located on the bottom floor of Picken Hall and their number is xxx-xxx-xxxx.

As with every study, there is a risk with confidentiality. However, every step will be taken to ensure the confidentiality of your data. Once you place the surveys in the manila envelope, they will be kept secure and eventually entered electronically into computer. This data will be de-identified and remain securely in a password-protected folder. Also, the only people who know you participated in this study are myself, thesis chair and any professors who you receive extra credit from for participation.

How will your privacy be protected?

Data is collected only for research purposes. Your data will be identified by ID number designated by the researcher, not by your name, and will be stored separately in a locked file cabinet. The data will be entered electronically into password-protected computer files and will remain de-identified. All personal identifying information such as compensation forms or reminder emails will be deleted immediately after you have been reminded or compensated. Access to all data will be limited to my thesis advisor and myself. All of the data will be destroyed after five years by shredding files or deleting computer files. The information collected for this study will be used only for the purposes of conducting this study. What we find from this study may be presented at meetings or published in papers but your name will not ever be used in these presentations or papers.

Other important items you should know:
- Withdrawal from the study: You may choose to stop your participation in this study at any time. Your decision to stop your participation will have no effect on your academic standing or possible compensation.
- Funding: There is no outside funding for this research project.

Whom should you call with questions about this study?

Questions about this study may be directed to the researcher in charge of this study: at xxxxx@scatcat.fhsu.edu or xxx-xxx-xxxx. You may also contact at xxxxx@fhsu.edu If you have questions, concerns, or suggestions about human research at FHSU, you may call the Office of Scholarship and Sponsored Projects at FHSU (xxx) xxx-xxxx during normal business hours.

CONSENT

I have read the above information about the current study and have been given an opportunity to ask questions. By signing this I agree to participate in this study and I have been given a copy of this signed consent document for my own records. I understand that I can change my mind and withdraw my consent at any time. By signing this consent form I understand that I am not giving up any legal rights. I am 18 years or older.

_____   _____

Participant's Signature and Date   Print Name

Guideline 8.02 of the ethics code also provides guidelines for research that involves an experimental and control group. This section is primarily written for research involving drug or therapeutic treatments and therefore is not usually needed by undergraduates conducting research.

- **8.03 Informed Consent for Recording Voices and Images in Research.** This guideline explains to psychologists that participants' permission to be recorded must be obtained prior to data collection. The only exceptions to this guideline are if the recordings take place in a naturalistic observation or psychologists are using deception and permission will be obtained at the conclusion of the study.

- **8.04 Client/Patient, Student, and Subordinate Research Participants.** Sometimes, it occurs that a client, student, or research assistant is recruited to participate in a research study. If this situation occurs, it is the psychologist's responsibility to protect the participant from negative consequences should the participant decide not to participate or terminate participation once the study has started. Also, psychologists must offer alternative activities to research participation, if it is required for a class or offered as extra credit in a class. When this happens, the alternative activity must be similar in length and duration to the research participation. Ensuring similarity between the alternative activity and the research participation avoids the chances the alternative activity is seen as a punishment for not participating in research.

Tiffany is a new faculty member at a state college. She has designed a research study and is ready to collect data. Furthermore, she would like to provide students who are enrolled in her class the opportunity to participate in the study for extra credit. Based on what you know thus far about APA's ethical guidelines for research, answer the following questions:

1. What should Tiffany do before she collects any data?
2. What information can you tell Tiffany about allowing her students to participate in the study for extra credit?

ANSWERS

1. Before Tiffany begins the data collection process, it is important that she check to see if her state college requires institutional approval. If it does (and it more than likely will), Tiffany will need to complete the IRB process.

2. You could tell Tiffany the APA ethics code does permit her to allow students in her classes to participate for extra credit. However, because the potential participants are enrolled in her class, Tiffany will need to protect the students from negative consequences if they decide not to participate or to withdraw. In addition, Tiffany must provide students in her class an alternative to the research study should they decide not to participate.

- **8.05 Dispensing with Informed Consent for Research.** There are some situations in which APA does not require informed consent. Please note that even if APA does not require informed consent in specific situations, an institution still may, and thus you will need to follow your institution's guidelines. See the table containing the ethical standards to learn more about specific situations when informed consent can be dispensed with.

- **8.06 Offering Inducements for Research Participation.** It is not uncommon for psychologists to offer inducements for research participation. The most common inducement is financial. But, it is important that the inducement or financial compensation is equivalent to the amount of effort put forth by the participant. For example, if researchers offer an excessive amount of cash to participate in a study, the participants might feel coerced to participate and this situation should be avoided. This ethical guideline also provides information on how to use psychological services as inducement. Because undergraduates typically do not do so in their studies, we will not go into more detail on this caveat.

- **8.07 Deception in Research.** Deception in research can occur in two ways, either as active deception or as passive deception. Active deception is deception by commission. In particular, this is deception that occurs when a researcher deliberately misleads the participant. This can happen when a researcher gives participants false information or when a researcher embeds a confederate into a study. A **confederate** is a participant in the study but is also part of the research team. Confederates' participation is meant to influence other participants who are not members of the research team. In the famous study on conformity conducted by Asch (1951), he used confederates

Confederates: A participant in a study but is also part of the research team. The participation of confederates is meant to influence other participants.

alongside participants to influence behavior. Specifically, Asch had confederates respond incorrectly to questions to see if "real" participants would conform to the incorrect answers, which they indeed did. Here, Asch actively deceived the participants to gain results for his study.

The other type of deception is passive deception. Passive deception is deception by omission. This type of deception occurs when a researcher withholds information about the nature of a study from the participants. For example, sometimes psychologists are prevented from explaining fully the purpose of their research design at the onset of a study. Doing so might change the way participants respond in the study. This occurs many times when researchers attempt to study concepts where participants are less likely to disclose their true behavior (e.g., cheating instances).

The topic of deception is continually debated to this day. Specifically, researchers and others have debated whether deception is helpful or harmful in research. APA states psychologists may use deception in research if it is needed to study a particular topic and if its use is justified by the knowledge gained. When deception is used, participants should be told about the deception as soon as possible and it should be clearly explained why this method was used and the anticipated benefits should be clearly explained. Participants are given the opportunity to withdraw their data if they want. Although deception is permitted in special cases, APA has made it clear that psychologists are not allowed to deceive participants with regard to physical or emotional pain.

- **8.08 Debriefing.** We will never forget the first time Jenn told an undergraduate assistant that he or she needed to "debrief" the participants, and the assistant thought she meant to take their underwear off. Fortunately, the assistant asked for clarification before following instructions! In general, you want to provide participants with information about the study immediately after the data are collected. If the results are not yet available, you can provide participants with the contact information of the researcher so the participants can learn of the findings when they are prepared. Sometimes, it is necessary to withhold a debriefing until all participants have completed the study. If this situation occurs, psychologists must be sure to reduce the risk of harm to the participants if debriefing is delayed. It is also important if psychologists know that a participant has been harmed during the study (either physically or emotionally) that they immediately try to minimize the harm.

- **8.09 Humane Care and Use of Animals in Research.** Psychologists who conduct research with animals have additional government policies to be aware of than those we discussed for humans earlier in this chapter. The purpose of this section is not to provide a detailed account of policies with animals. However, you should be aware that in addition to the APA guidelines, animal researchers also must follow local, state, and federal guidelines. If you are interested in learning more about research with animals, you can visit the website for the Institutional Animal Care and Use Committee (IACUC): www.unmc.edu/iacuc.

The APA requires psychologists first meet all government laws and standards with animal research. Furthermore, APA states psychologists trained in research methods and with experience working with lab animals are responsible for caring for the animals and training assistants to care for the animals. In addition, animal pain should be minimized and procedures involving pain to animals are only used when other methods are not feasible. If pain is to occur, the result should greatly advance scientific knowledge and the study should be conducted with the use of anesthesia and post-surgery care. If an animal's life needs to be terminated, psychologists are required to again minimize pain and follow current government policies.

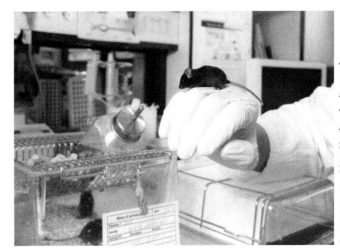

© anyaivanova, 2014. Used under license from Shutterstock, Inc.

Research using animals has been controversial for many years. People can fall into one of two categories when discussing animals in research. The first group is that of the animal rights activists. These individuals assert animals are no different from humans and should be given the same rights. Typically, these individuals do not support animal research in any form. The second group is that of the animal welfare activists. The animal welfare activists believe animal research is necessary but should be conducted in the most humane manner possible. It is more common that researchers who work with animals subscribe to the animal welfare activist point of view.

YOU TRY IT!

A former student once conducted a study to examine the relationship between ethnicity, faculty mentorship, and cocurricular activities. The student was interested in determining if students of different ethnicities were equally likely to have a faculty mentor and be involved in campus activities. The debriefing statement that the student used is given below. What is missing from the debriefing statement?

> Thank you for participating in this experiment. The purpose of this experiment was to see whether a difference existed among ethnicities when it comes to commitment to ethnicity, faculty mentorship, and cocurricular activities. Specifically, we were interested in how students among various ethnicities experienced on-campus activities, and if they had a faculty advisor.
>
> If any questions or concerns arise about the experiment you participated in, please feel free to contact me Student A at XXX-XXX-XXXX or Dr. Smith at XXX-XXX-XXXX. Once again thank you for participating.

ANSWER

In this case, the student failed to include information about the results of the study. Specifically, after explaining to participants the purpose of her study, she should have given participants the opportunity to learn of the results. This is important because some participants may be interested in the topics covered in a research study and appreciate the chance to hear the findings. By simply including the following, she would have been in line with APA ethical standards.

> If you would like to know the results from this experiment, we would be happy to provide you with a copy of them. No names or identifying information would be on the results. Rather, we can provide you only with information as to the differences among ethnicities and their involvement with their campus activities and faculty mentorship. Results are typically ready to share with the public in about 10–12 months' time period. Please let me know if this is something you would like to have.

- **8.10 Reporting Research Results.** The ethical guidelines we have discussed up to this point (8.01–8.09) were provided for psychologists conducting research. The remaining ethical guidelines (8.10–8.15) are provided to guide psychologists during the publication process. To begin, psychologists do not make up data. This is known as fabricating data. In addition, once results have been published, psychologists correct any errors found later through reasonable means.

- **8.11 Plagiarism.** This APA ethical guideline appears straightforward: psychologists should not plagiarize. This means not presenting the work of others as your own work. However, we want to expand on this as many people are unsure of when plagiarism occurs. Therefore, we want to mention the three most common types of plagiarism, as well as give a brief overview of each: blatant, cut-and-paste, and careless.

  The most egregious type of plagiarism is what we are going to call blatant plagiarism which occurs when an individual takes someone else's work and represents it as their own (even when purchased online). The second type of plagiarism is called cut-and-paste plagiarism. Cut-and-paste plagiarism occurs when an individual (a) takes work from someone else's ideas, fails to cite the work properly, and mixes it with their own; (b) takes information (cut-and-paste) from multiple sources and pieces it together with some of their own ideas to complete a paper; or (c) takes work from other sources and, even if properly cited, completes a paper with very little original thought or ideas beyond the borrowed sources. The last type of plagiarism is lazy plagiarism. Careless plagiarism occurs when an individual fails to include a proper citation, and quotes or paraphrases from someone else without giving proper credit for the ideas represented in the final product. Unlike blatant plagiarism, careless plagiarism occurs when much of the product is the individual's own work and only a few instances exist of taking from others' work.

- **8.12 Publication Credit.** It is important that authorship is given to individuals based on their contributions to the study. This means that rank, position, or status does not equal authorship. When faculty members and students work together on projects, authorship should be discussed as soon as possible and reevaluated when needed.

- **8.13 Duplicate Publication of Data.** Typically, psychologists publish data only one time. However, sometimes data can be republished or cross-published. This process is acceptable as long as it is clearly documented. For example, a colleague was invited to submit an expert commentary to an edited book and was later asked by the same publishers to cross-publish the commentary in one of their journals. This colleague denotes on her resume (known as a *vitae*) that the journal publication is a cross-publication from the edited book.

In addition, psychologists can publish data a second time if they have reanalyzed the data in a different way or chosen a new perspective to look at their data. For example, while in graduate school the Federal Aviation Administration (FAA) asked John and another student, Rick, to reanalyze previously published data using a technique that John's professor had developed. Rick and John took the original data and reanalyzed it from a new perspective. The results were interesting and different from the original publication. This allowed Rick and John to publish a new paper based on data previously published.

- **8.14 Sharing Research Data for Verification.** When psychologists publish data, they should share the data with other professionals if such a request is made for verification purposes. Psychologists can request published data only for the purpose of reanalysis and are responsible for any cost associated with the process.

- **8.15 Reviewers.** When psychologists complete their research, they typically submit the research for publication. During the publication process, professionals in the field (reviewers) will review the work to ensure it is ready for publication. Those serving as reviewers are expected to respect confidentiality. In addition, reviewers are not to steal the work of others.

We hope that you have seen in this chapter how the IRB process and that APA ethical guidelines work together. It is important to remember that as psychologists we must be aware of and consult APA's ethical guidelines throughout the research process. However, this does not mean we have the right to ignore any additional information or steps required by the IRB. Conversely, if APA requires steps the IRB does not, we still need to follow them. For example, at our previous institution, the IRB does not require a debriefing statement. However, the APA does. In this situation, we are required to go above the basic requirements of the IRB and also prepare a debriefing statement. If a situation arises where the IRB and APA's ethical guidelines are in conflict (what we described above is not a conflict), you should make known your commitment to the ethics code but in the end obey state and federal laws. Both the IRB process and the APA ethical guidelines are designed with you in mind. Your rights as a participant and your rights as a researcher are better protected with these regulations in place.

SECTION SUMMARY

- The APA began developing an ethics code in 1949. The most recent version of the code was published in 2010 (p. 38).
- Within the APA ethics code, there is Section 8.0 for ethics in research. This section contains 15 guidelines for ethical research (pp. 38–47).
    - 8.01 Institutional Approval (p. 38)
    - 8.02 Informed Consent (pp. 38–42)
    - 8.03 Informed Consent for Recording Voices and Images in Research (p. 42)
    - 8.04 Client/Patient, Student, and Subordinate Research Participants (p. 42)
    - 8.05 Dispensing with Informed Consent for Research (p. 43)

- 8.06 Offering Inducements for Research Participation (p. 43)
- 8.07 Deception in Research (pp. 43–44)
- 8.08 Debriefing (p. 44)
- 8.09 Humane Care and Use of Animals in Research (pp. 44–45)
- 8.10 Reporting Research Results (p. 46)
- 8.11 Plagiarism (p. 46)
- 8.12 Publication Credit (p. 46)
- 8.13 Duplicate Publication of Data (pp. 46–47)
- 8.14 Sharing Research Data for Verification (p. 47)
- 8.15 Reviewers (p. 47)

8. RESEARCH AND PUBLICATION

8.1 INSTITUTIONAL APPROVAL

When institutional approval is required, psychologists provide accurate information about their research proposals and obtain approval prior to conducting the research. They conduct the research in accordance with the approved research protocol.

8.2 INFORMED CONSENT TO RESEARCH

a. When obtaining informed consent as required in Standard 3.10, Informed Consent, psychologists inform participants about (1) the purpose of the research, expected duration, and procedures; (2) their right to decline to participate and to withdraw from the research once participation has begun; (3) the foreseeable consequences of declining or withdrawing; (4) reasonably foreseeable factors that may be expected to influence their willingness to participate such as potential risks, discomfort, or adverse effects; (5) any prospective research benefits; (6) limits of confidentiality; (7) incentives for participation; and (8) whom to contact for questions about the research and research participants' rights. They provide opportunity for the prospective participants to ask questions and receive answers. (See also Standards 8.03, Informed Consent for Recording Voices and Images in Research; 8.05, Dispensing With Informed Consent for Research; and 8.07, Deception in Research.)

b. Psychologists conducting intervention research involving the use of experimental treatments clarify to participants at the outset of the research (1) the experimental nature of the treatment; (2) the services that will or will not be available to the control group(s) if appropriate; (3) the means by which assignment to treatment and control groups will be made; (4) available treatment alternatives if an individual does not wish to participate in the research or wishes to withdraw once a study has begun; and (5) compensation for or monetary costs of participating including, if appropriate, whether reimbursement from the participant or a third-party payor will be sought. (See also Standard 8.02a, Informed Consent to Research.)

8.3 INFORMED CONSENT FOR RECORDING VOICES AND IMAGES IN RESEARCH

Psychologists obtain informed consent from research participants prior to recording their voices or images for data collection unless (1) the research consists solely of naturalistic observations in public places, and it is not anticipated that the recording will be used in a manner that could cause personal identification or harm, or (2) the research design includes deception, and consent for the use of the recording is obtained during debriefing. (See also Standard 8.07, Deception in Research.)

8.4 CLIENT/PATIENT, STUDENT, AND SUBORDINATE RESEARCH PARTICIPANTS

a. When psychologists conduct research with clients/patients, students, or subordinates as participants, psychologists take steps to protect the prospective participants from adverse consequences of declining or withdrawing from participation.

b. When research participation is a course requirement or an opportunity for extra credit, the prospective participant is given the choice of equitable alternative activities.

8.5 DISPENSING WITH INFORMED CONSENT FOR RESEARCH

Psychologists may dispense with informed consent only (1) where research would not reasonably be assumed to create distress or harm and involves (a) the study of normal educational practices, curricula, or classroom management methods conducted in educational settings; (b) only anonymous questionnaires, naturalistic observations, or archival research for which disclosure of responses would not place participants at risk of criminal or civil liability or damage their financial standing, employability, or reputation, and confidentiality is protected; or (c) the study of factors related to job or organization effectiveness conducted in organizational settings for which there is no risk to participants' employability, and confidentiality is protected or (2) where otherwise permitted by law or federal or institutional regulations.

8.6 OFFERING INDUCEMENTS FOR RESEARCH PARTICIPATION

a. Psychologists make reasonable efforts to avoid offering excessive or inappropriate financial or other inducements for research participation when such inducements are likely to coerce participation.

b. When offering professional services as an inducement for research participation, psychologists clarify the nature of the services, as well as the risks, obligations, and limitations. (See also Standard 6.05, Barter With Clients/Patients.)

8.7 DECEPTION IN RESEARCH

a. Psychologists do not conduct a study involving deception unless they have determined that the use of deceptive techniques is justified by the study's significant prospective scientific, educational, or applied value and that effective nondeceptive alternative procedures are not feasible.

b. Psychologists do not deceive prospective participants about research that is reasonably expected to cause physical pain or severe emotional distress.

c. Psychologists explain any deception that is an integral feature of the design and conduct of an experiment to participants as early as is feasible, preferably at the conclusion of their participation, but no later than at the conclusion of the data collection, and permit participants to withdraw their data. (See also Standard 8.08, Debriefing.)

8.8 DEBRIEFING

a. Psychologists provide a prompt opportunity for participants to obtain appropriate information about the nature, results, and conclusions of the research, and they take reasonable steps to correct any misconceptions that participants may have of which the psychologists are aware.

b. If scientific or humane values justify delaying or withholding this information, psychologists take reasonable measures to reduce the risk of harm.

c. When psychologists become aware that research procedures have harmed a participant, they take reasonable steps to minimize the harm.

8.9 HUMANE CARE AND USE OF ANIMALS IN RESEARCH

a. Psychologists acquire, care for, use, and dispose of animals in compliance with current federal, state, and local laws and regulations, and with professional standards.

b. Psychologists trained in research methods and experienced in the care of laboratory animals supervise all procedures involving animals and are responsible for ensuring appropriate consideration of their comfort, health, and humane treatment.

c. Psychologists ensure that all individuals under their supervision who are using animals have received instruction in research methods and in the care, maintenance, and handling of the species being used, to the extent appropriate to their role. (See also Standard 2.05, Delegation of Work to Others.)

d. Psychologists make reasonable efforts to minimize the discomfort, infection, illness, and pain of animal subjects.

e. Psychologists use a procedure subjecting animals to pain, stress, or privation only when an alternative procedure is unavailable and the goal is justified by its prospective scientific, educational, or applied value.

f. Psychologists perform surgical procedures under appropriate anesthesia and follow techniques to avoid infection and minimize pain during and after surgery.

g. When it is appropriate that an animal's life be terminated, psychologists proceed rapidly, with an effort to minimize pain and in accordance with accepted procedures.

8.10 REPORTING RESEARCH RESULTS

a. Psychologists do not fabricate data. (See also Standard 5.01a, Avoidance of False or Deceptive Statements.)

b. If psychologists discover significant errors in their published data, they take reasonable steps to correct such errors in a correction, retraction, erratum, or other appropriate publication means.

8.11 PLAGIARISM

Psychologists do not present portions of another's work or data as their own, even if the other work or data source is cited occasionally.

8.12 PUBLICATION CREDIT

a. Psychologists take responsibility and credit, including authorship credit, only for work they have actually performed or to which they have substantially contributed. (See also Standard 8.12b, Publication Credit.)

b. Principal authorship and other publication credits accurately reflect the relative scientific or professional contributions of the individuals involved, regardless of their relative status. Mere possession of an institutional position, such as department chair, does not justify authorship credit. Minor contributions to the research or to the writing for publications are acknowledged appropriately, such as in footnotes or in an introductory statement.

c. Except under exceptional circumstances, a student is listed as principal author on any multiple-authored article that is substantially based on the student's doctoral dissertation. Faculty advisors discuss publication credit with students as early as feasible and throughout the research and publication process as appropriate. (See also Standard 8.12b, Publication Credit.)

8.13 DUPLICATE PUBLICATION OF DATA

Psychologists do not publish, as original data, data that have been previously published. This does not preclude republishing data when they are accompanied by proper acknowledgment.

8.14 SHARING RESEARCH DATA FOR VERIFICATION

a. After research results are published, psychologists do not withhold the data on which their conclusions are based from other competent professionals who seek to verify the substantive claims through reanalysis and who intend to use such data only for that purpose, provided that the confidentiality of the participants can be protected and unless legal rights concerning proprietary data preclude their release. This does not preclude psychologists from requiring that such individuals or groups be responsible for costs associated with the provision of such information.

b. Psychologists who request data from other psychologists to verify the substantive claims through reanalysis may use shared data only for the declared purpose. Requesting psychologists obtain prior written agreement for all other uses of the data.

8.15 REVIEWERS

Psychologists who review material submitted for presentation, publication, grant, or research proposal review respect the confidentiality of and the proprietary rights in such information of those who submitted it.

ARE YOU EQUIPPED NOW?

In 1924, Landis conducted a study with the purpose of determining what facial expressions, if any, are produced for given emotions. When participants arrived to the experiment, burnt cork was used to draw lines on participants' facial muscles and a picture was taken. Next, participants were exposed to a total of 16 conditions, including smelling ammonia, imagining self being exposed to skin diseases as depicted in pictures, examining a set of French pornographic photographs, placing a hand in a pail filled with frogs, and being told to cut off the head of a rat. Pictures were taken as participants were exposed to each of the conditions. Landis then compared the facial expression from the picture taken at the beginning of the experiment with the pictures taken after being exposed to each of the conditions. He compared the pictures by noting the amount of change in the muscles. Examples of the pictures taken can be found in the appendix of the research article. Landis found that while individuals have variations in their emotional responses, there was not a typical expression for any of the conditions examined. However, he did note the differences between how men and women responded. Landis found men were more expressive in the conditions than women. Furthermore, men were more likely to express anger while women were more likely to cry.

As you were reading over this experiment, the last condition of cutting off a rat's head probably got your attention the most. It is hard to believe but participants were instructed to hold the rat with one hand and cut off the head with the other hand. If the participants refused to do so, the researcher cut off the rat's head while the participant watched. We also found it interesting that one of the participants in the experiment was a 13-year-old boy who had been admitted to a hospital for high blood pressure that was likely caused by "emotional instability." The hospital referred the boy to the PsychologyDepartment and Landis included the boy in the experiment, noting that the boy's reactions did not differ significantly from the reactions of the other participants.

In this chapter, we have discussed the IRB process and APA guidelines for ethical research. However, Landis' research was conducted prior to the establishment of these bodies. After reading this chapter on ethics, answer the questions below regarding Landis' work.

QUESTIONS

1. If Landis were to conduct his experiment today, he would need a regular informed consent and an addition that addresses the recording of images. Why would Landis need an informed consent for the recording of images?

2. Psychologists must inform participants if their participation might cause severe emotional distress. Do you believe Landis' participants should have been informed that their participation might cause distress?

3. The IRB committee pays special attention to research involving minors as participants. What additional steps might the IRB require of Landis?

4. With the current regulations for animal care, do you think Landis would be allowed to behead a rat if he were to replicate the experiment?

ANSWERS

1. Landis would need to address the recording of images in his informed consent because pictures of the participants were taken at the beginning of the experiment and during the experiment. Participants would need to further grant their permission for Landis to publish the pictures in the appendix of his research article.

2. We believe participants in this situation should have been forewarned. Participants could have been informed the purpose of the experiment was to elicit emotional responses and thus some stimuli might cause strong reactions such as anger. Landis might have argued that telling participants in advance about the nature of the stimuli might have reduced the initial response to the conditions. However, we would respond by stating that participants have the right to know in advance if they will be exposed to more than minimal risk and make an informed decision about if they would like to participate. Beheading an animal is certainly above the events of a typical day for most people.

3. Today, the IRB would require the boy's parents or legal guardians give their permission and the boy give his assent. The IRB might also require the boy's medical doctor review the experimental procedure and decide if the procedure posed a risk to the boy's physical health.

4. We do not think the current policies would allow Landis to replicate his experiment and behead a rat. APA explicitly states that only those individuals trained in the care of lab animals are allowed to handle the animals and the termination of an animal's life should involve minimal pain. The procedure described in Landis' research does not fit with either requirement. In fact, Landis describes in his article that because the participants had many false starts and were unsure of how to cut off the head, the process was "prolonged." Furthermore, there are other feasible procedures to induce emotions besides beheading animals.

CHAPTER SUMMARY

- The Institutional Review Board (IRB) is a committee which reviews proposals of intended research to determine if the research is ethical and that the rights of the participants are being protected (p. 35–36).

- IRBs can be found on university campuses, hospitals, and in many corporations where research on human participants is conducted (p. 35).

- IRBs are a result of government intervention in 1974 via the National Research Act (p. 35).
    - This Act set up a commission which developed the Belmont Report, which outlined three guiding principles for human participant research: respect, benefits, and justice (pp. 35–36).
        - The principle of respect protects the autonomy of both participants and those with diminished autonomy.
        - The principle of beneficence ensures research is conducted with the well-being of the participant in mind.
        - The principle of justice ensures any risks or benefits of the research are distributed among the population equally.
    - The three levels of IRB review are exempt, expedited, and full board (p. 36).

- The APA began developing an ethics code in 1949. The most recent version of the code was published in 2010 (p. 38).

- Within the APA ethics code, there is Section 8.0 for ethics in research. This section contains 15 guidelines for ethical research (pp. 38–47).
  - 8.01 Institutional Approval (p. 38)
  - 8.02 Informed Consent (pp. 38–42)
    - Anonymous research is to ensure no identifying information is gathered and participants cannot be identified by information that is gathered during the research process (p. 39).
    - Confidential research is conducted in which participants can be identified by information that is gathered but data is restricted to those conducting the research (p. 39).
  - 8.03 Informed Consent for Recording Voices and Images in Research (p. 42)
  - 8.04 Client/Patient, Student, and Subordinate Research Participants (p. 42)
  - 8.05 Dispensing with Informed Consent for Research (p. 43)
  - 8.06 Offering Inducements for Research Participation (p. 43)
  - 8.07 Deception in Research (pp. 43–44)
  - 8.08 Debriefing (p. 44)
  - 8.09 Humane Care and Use of Animals in Research (pp. 44–45)
  - 8.10 Reporting Research Results (p. 46)
  - 8.11 Plagiarism (p. 46)
  - 8.12 Publication Credit (p. 46)
  - 8.13 Duplicate Publication of Data (pp. 46–47)
  - 8.14 Sharing Research Data for Verification. (p. 47)
  - 8.15 Reviewers (p. 47)

APA LEARNING GOALS LINKAGE

- **Goal 1. Knowledge Base in Psychology**
  You will demonstrate fundamental knowledge and comprehension of the major concepts, theoretical perspectives, historical trends, and empirical findings to discuss how psychological principles apply to behavioral problems.

  Sections Covered: Are You Equipped?, Consumers of Research, APA's Ethics Code, Are You Equipped Now?

  Explanation of the Goal: Many historical aspects of the field of psychology were examined in this chapter on ethics. For example, we discussed key studies outside of the field (e.g., Wichita Jury Study) and within the field (e.g., Landis' research) leading to the development of the Belmont Report and today's IRBs. For each study presented, we discussed relevant ethical issues and provided a general understanding of the APA's Code of Ethics. We also took an in-depth look at ethical standard 8.0 and the corresponding 15 guidelines, which relate to conducting research.

- ## Goal 2. Scientific Inquiry and Critical Thinking

  You will demonstrate scientific reasoning and problem solving, including effective research methods.

  Sections Covered: APA's Ethics Code, Are You Equipped Now?

  Explanation of the Goal: As psychologists, we are expected to follow APA's code of ethics in the treatment of human and nonhuman participants when conducting research. This includes designing a study, data collection, data interpretation, and reporting of psychological research. In the APA's ethics code section of the chapter, we examined these issues. For example, we discussed institutional approval, informed consent, debriefing, deception, and the use of animals, to name a few. In the review at the end of the chapter, we assessed how these ethical issues were related to a historical psychological research experiment.

  Sections Covered: Are You Equipped?, Consumers of Research, APA's Ethics Code, Are You Equipped Now?

  Explanation of the Goal: It could be argued there is no single topic in which psychologists use critical thinking more than the topic of ethics. Although the APA provides ethical standards and corresponding guidelines for many topic areas, implementing the standards is not always easy and requires the use of effective critical thinking. To help prepare you for this task, we examined several research scenarios and asked you to solve problems consistent with ethical standards. In completing the scenarios, you engaged in critical thinking. In some scenarios such as evaluating the benefits and risks of the Wichita Jury Study, the answers were not always simple.

- ## Goal 3. Ethical and Social Responsibility in a Diverse World

  You will apply ethical standards to evaluate psychological science and practice and you will develop ethically and socially responsible behaviors for professional and personal settings in a landscape that involves increasing diversity.

  Sections Covered: APA's Ethics Code, Are You Equipped Now?

  Explanation of the Goal: It is important to recognize the necessity for ethical behavior in all aspects of the science and practice of psychology. Our coverage of standard 8.0 was an introduction to engaging in ethical behavior in carrying out the science of psychology through research.

  Sections Covered: Consumers of Research, APA's Ethics Code, Are You Equipped Now?

  Explanation of the Goal: IRBs and the APA's ethics code specifically address how psychologists should engage in research to protect special populations (e.g., minors, pregnant women, and the mentally impaired) and respect animal and human rights as research participants. This is an important task, as privilege and power may affect inequities in research.

Nonexperimental Research Methods and Variables

Part 2

CHAPTER 4

Nonexperimental Research Methods

CHAPTER OUTLINE

Are You Equipped?

Differentiating among Methods

Nonexperimental Methods

Factors to Consider

Converging Research Methods

Are You Equipped Now?

Chapter Summary

APA Learning Goals Linkage

ARE YOU EQUIPPED?

How do you pick what restaurants to eat at when you are traveling? Many people we know visit a website called Yelp (www.yelp.com). At this website, people can literally rate restaurants by providing a review with comments and the website will also filter restaurants by features such as distance from your location, price, and neighborhood, to name a few. You can read the reviews and use the filters to select a restaurant to visit, especially when you are in an unfamiliar city and want to reduce the risk of picking a bad place.

The use of this website (and others which are similar) brings up an interesting question. Specifically, is the price point of an establishment related to customer satisfaction? In other words, does what you pay for a meal impact your satisfaction with the restaurant? How could we answer this question? Take a minute and think about how you could gather information to address this question. What would you do?

There are numerous ways to gather information to find out if price of a restaurant is related to customer satisfaction with the meal. The fact that there is more than one way to gather information

on this topic illustrates that social scientists have a plethora of research methods at their disposal. In this chapter, we are going to focus on nonexperimental research methods. We could use nonexperimental research methods to examine the relationship between price and customer satisfaction in several ways. First, we could use the existing records provided by the websites mentioned above. This would allow us to see if the two variables were related to one another. Using existing records such as those from yelp.com is known as archival research. Another way to see if the two variables were related to one another would be to ask customers. You could have customers complete a questionnaire asking about their opinions as they left different restaurants. This is known as survey research. Archival and survey research are just two examples of nonexperimental research which seeks to examine relationships among variables. We will talk in more detail about these methods and others throughout the chapter. Before we begin, you might want to know that research has been conducted on this topic and a relationship does exist between price and customer satisfaction. For example, Ye, Li, Wang, and Law (2014) found price was related to customer satisfaction when examining reviews of hotels through online reviews.

As you go through this chapter, we also want you to keep in mind how the material relates to the American Psychological Association goals for psychology majors. Specifically, this chapter will address the following goals:

- **Goal 2. Scientific Inquiry and Critical Thinking**

  You will demonstrate scientific reasoning and problem solving, including effective research methods.

- **Goal 3. Ethical and Social Responsibility in a Diverse World**

  You will apply ethical standards to evaluate psychological science and practice and you will develop ethically and socially responsible behaviors
  for professional and personal settings in a landscape that involves increasing diversity.

- **Goal 4. Communication**

  You will demonstrate competence in writing and in oral and interpersonal communication skills.

Qualitative: Research methodologies where researchers seek subjectivity through in-depth collection of information and emerging hypotheses.

Quantitative: Research methodologies that seek objectivity through testable hypotheses and carefully designed studies.

DIFFERENTIATING AMONG METHODS

Psychology is the scientific study of thoughts and behaviors. Therefore, psychologists, and social scientists in general, use a variety of research methods to study what people think and do. There are two main ways to differentiate among types of research. First, you can describe a research method as being either qualitative or quantitative. **Qualitative** research is inductive by nature. Researchers using this methodology seek subjectivity through in-depth collection of information and emerging hypotheses. Researchers gather the data and draw conclusions on the basis of their observations. On the other hand, **quantitative** research is deductive by nature. Researchers using this methodology seek objectivity through testable hypotheses and carefully designed studies. Researchers gather data that can be reported in numbers and statistics. Conclusions are drawn from statistics and generalized to populations of interest. It is interesting that most researchers are trained in either the qualitative or the quantitative approach. Very few researchers routinely use both approaches. However, the two approaches need not be viewed in opposition, as both can shed light on understanding variables of interest. Another way to differentiate among types of research is by describing if the research is experimental or nonexperimental. **Experimental research** involves the manipulation of a variable of interest and assignment of participants to treatment conditions. We will spend more time in later chapters talking about how to design and interpret experimental research. **Nonexperimental research** does not rely on manipulating variables. Rather, it makes observations about how variables are related to one another and describes the findings.

INTRODUCTION TO CORRELATIONAL METHODS

As mentioned above, nonexperimental research does not manipulate variables of interest. However, even without direct manipulation, you can still explore relationships between variables using **correlational research methods**. Correlational research methods are very important to the field. This methodology provides us with information on the initial link between variables of interest. Correlational research methods are also frequently reported in the media. We want to tell you about two correlational studies recently reported in the media examining issues related to weight and obesity. The first study was conducted by Kopycka-Kedzierawski, Auinger, Billings, and Weitzman (2008) at the Eastman Dental Center, which is part of the University of Rochester Medical Center. Kopycka-Kedzierawski eta al. found that for children between the ages of 6 and 18 there was a relationship between weight and tooth decay. Surprisingly, as weight increased, the risk of tooth decay decreased. We will talk a little later on about why these results might have been obtained. For now, we want to focus your attention on how this study shows that two variables (i.e., weight and tooth decay) are related to one another. Our second news story reported that Gazdzinski, Kornak, Weiner, Meyerhoff, and Nat (2008) found that weight was related to biochemical deficiencies. Specifically as weight increased for individuals, researchers found lower-than-normal levels of markers for neuronal health and cell membrane synthesis. We will return to understanding these results in just a minute when we discuss the advantages and disadvantages of this method.

When you have a correlational research method, your results will tell you if the two variables are related. Variables can be either positively or negatively related. Do not be confused by the labels of positive correlation and negative correlation. This does not mean that positive correlations are good and negative correlations are bad. Rather, **positive correlations** have variables that vary in the same direction and **negative correlations** have variables that vary in opposite directions. To make this clear, we want to tell you about some examples of positive and negative correlations. We have also provided you with the figure below to visually represent each type of correlation. Two variables that are positively correlated are years of education and salary. This is a positive correlation because as scores on one variable increase so too do scores on the second variable. Similarly, as scores on one variable decrease so too do scores on the second variable. In this situation, the more number of years of

Experimental: A class of research methodologies that involve manipulation of a variable.

Nonexperimental: A class of research methodologies that involve the study of how variables are related.

Correlational Research Methods: Research methodologies that evaluate the relationship between variables.

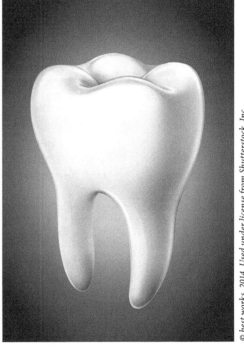

Positive Correlation: Two or more variables vary in the same direction.

Negative Correlation: Two or more variables vary in opposite directions.

education a person has, the higher the salary. Conversely, the fewer number of years of education a person has, the lower the salary. In both instances, the two variables either increased or decreased together, making this a positive correlation. Another example of a positive correlation is time spent studying for a test and performance on the test. In general, the more you study for a test, the higher your grade on the test, and the less you study for a test, the lower your grade on the test. Again, this is a positive correlation because both variables are increasing or decreasing together. Another example of a positive correlation is the amount of food consumed and weight. The more food that you consume, the higher your weight and the less food that you consume, the lower your weight.

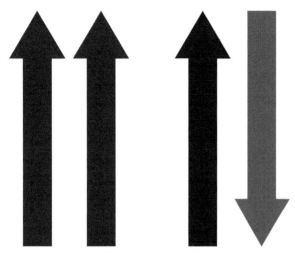

Fig 4.1 Arrows for Positive and Negative Correlation

With negative correlations, the two variables of interest are related to one another as well. However, as one variable increases, the other variable decreases, or as one variable decreases, the other variable increases. An example of a negative correlation is marital satisfaction and likelihood of divorce. As marital satisfaction increases, the likelihood of divorce decreases, and as marital satisfaction decreases, the likelihood of divorce increases. The two examples that we presented earlier from news reports were also examples of negative correlations. Remember that as weight of children increased, the risk for tooth decay decreased. The reverse can also be stated. As the risk of tooth decay increased, the weight of children decreased. Thus, these two variables were related to one another but in opposite directions. Similarly, in the second report, as weight of individuals increased, nor mal levels of brain functioning decreased, or as normal functioning increased, weight of individuals decreased. We find it helpful to draw arrows for each of the variables that we are reading about. If the variable is increasing, we draw an up arrow. If the variable is decreasing, we draw a down arrow (Figure 4.1). We can then look at the arrows to see if they are both pointing in the same direction (positive correlation) or in different directions (negative correlation).

YOU TRY IT!

We want you to get some practice in determining if correlational results are positive or negative. Take a look at the findings below and state whether each of them is a positive or negative correlation.

RESEARCH FINDINGS:

1. As ice-cream sales increase, murder rates increase. The following research findings are from a study published in JPI by Black, Lindberg, Garansi, and Sleigh (2013). The study examined the relationships between perceived sense of fairness as a child and adverse outcomes as an adult.

2. As the sense of unfairness in the childhood home increased, current emotional openness to others decreased.

3. As sense of unfairness increased, individual's pessimistic views of the future increased.

4. As the sense of unfairness in the childhood home increased, individual's self-esteem decreased.

ANSWERS

1. It is hard to believe but this first example is a true one. Research on this topic has found that as ice-cream sales increase, rates of murder also increase. We will talk about what is going on in this situation in a minute. For right now, we want to draw your attention to the fact that this example is a positive correlation because as one variable goes up (ice-cream sales) so too does the second variable (murder rates). It would be visually represented as follows:

2. This is an example of a negative correlation because the two variables are pointing in opposite directions. As one variable increases (sense of unfairness), the other variable decreases (emotional openness to others). Again, you could draw arrows to help determine the type of correlation. For this, the arrows would be as follows:

3. This is also an example of a positive correlation because both variables (sense of unfairness and ratings of pessimistic view of the future) are increasing together. Also, note the reverse statement is true: as sense of unfairness decreases, pessimistic views of the future decrease.

4. Finally, there is a negative relationship between sense of unfairness in the childhood home and self-esteem. As one variable increases (sense of unfairness), the other variable decreases (self-esteem). This brings us to an interesting point to consider. Specifically, how do you interpret these correlational research findings? Should you hold your baby all the time so he or she does not cry? Not necessarily. We will discuss three questions for you to ask yourself when interpreting correlational research findings.

How did you do with these four examples? We should mention that sometimes the direction of a variable is not as clearly stated in the media or in a research article as we did in our examples. However, if you stop and think about the results, you will be able to determine if the scores are increasing or decreasing for the variable.

As with any research method, there are advantages and disadvantages to examining correlations between variables. One major advantage of correlation al research is that it allows us to make predictions. For example, if we know marital satisfaction and likelihood of divorce are negatively correlated, it can help us in counseling couples who are experiencing low marital satisfaction. Many times, examining correlations between variables is a great starting point to researching a topic. Plus, it is a useful method when conducting a true experiment would not be ethical. This brings us to a limitation of the method, determining cause and effect. Using a previous example, should we stop buying ice-cream so that we can reduce the number of murders committed? This even sounds like a strange question to ask. When you have a correlation, you must think about the directionality of the correlation and ask yourself the following questions:

- Is X causing Y?
- Is Y causing X?
- Is there a third variable causing both X and Y to be related?

In the example of ice-cream sales and murder rates, you would ask yourself the following questions:

- Does eating ice-cream (X) cause you to commit murder (Y)?
- Does committing murder (Y) cause you to eat ice-cream (X)?
- Is there a third variable that is causing ice-cream sales (X) and murder rates (Y) to be related?

It really does not make sense that eating ice-cream would cause you to commit murder or that murdering people would cause you to eat ice-cream. However, it does make sense that a third variable (like heat) is related to both. Specifically, as it gets hotter, ice-cream sales increase. Also, as it gets hotter, murder rates increase. Therefore, in this example, it is likely that a third variable was influencing both variables. We cannot emphasize enough on how important it is to not infer cause and effect from correlational research. Remember that this method provides very useful information as to how variables are related, but other factors could be causing the finding.

SECTION SUMMARY

- Qualitative research methodologies seek subjectivity through in-depth collection of information and emerging hypotheses (pp. 60–61).
- Quantitative research methodologies seek objectivity through testable hypotheses and carefully designed studies (pp. 60–61).
- Experimental research is a class of research methodologies that involve direct manipulation of a variable (p. 61).
- Nonexperimental research is a class of research methodologies that do not rely on manipulating variables (p. 61).
- Correlational research methods evaluate the relationship between variables (pp. 61–64).
  - Positive correlations have variables that vary in the same direction. (pp. 61–63)
  - Negative correlations have variables that vary in opposite directions. (pp. 61–63)

NONEXPERIMENTAL METHODS

So far, we have provided you with introductory information that will be helpful as you learn about nonexperimental designs. In this chapter, we will discuss the following nonexperimental designs: ethnography, naturalistic observation, case studies, archival research, content analysis, and survey. It is important to note that all these nonexperimental designs can examine relationships among variables as mentioned previously under correlational methodologies. We will begin with **ethnography**. Typically, ethnographies are associated with the field of anthropology and are used to describe new cultures. The purpose of this method is to describe a culture in detail. In doing so, the researcher records and transcribes events that he or she witnesses and shares these findings with others. Many times, ethnographic questions concern the relationship between culture and behavior, and thus other social scientists are interested in the method. For example, Russell (2011) used ethnographic techniques to learn more about homeless women in Baltimore. One advantage of this methodology is that you can get "rich" or detailed information from an insider's perspective. Disadvantages include the lack of a testable hypothesis, the inability to infer cause and effect, and little ability to generalize the results to other groups (to be discussed further in Chapter 5).

Ethnography: Used to describe a culture in detail by recoding and transcribing events that are witnessed.

Naturalistic Observation: A research methodology where a researcher observes people or animals in their natural setting.

Naturalistic observation is where you observe people or animals in their natural settings. These observations can occur in the field (sometimes, called field studies) or in the laboratory (referred to as laboratory observations). Studying people in their natural setting means many things. One of the most famous naturalistic observations was conducted by Jane Goodall. In the summer of 1960, Goodall went to East Africa to live among the chimpanzee population. There were many aspects about chimpanzees that Goodall wanted to learn such as if chimps used tools. She believed the best way to understand the chimp behavior was to observe them in their natural environment. Goodall's work has led to numerous publications on the life of chimps.

© Vincent St. Thomas, 2014. Used under license from Shutterstock, Inc.

We want to follow up this classic example of naturalistic observation with more everyday examples to illustrate that natural settings are diverse and you are not required to travel to far-off destinations. First, Middlemist, Knowles, and Matter (1976) wanted to know how the presence of another man in the bathroom influenced men's selection of a urinal and urinating behaviors. To do so, the researcher hung out in front of the bathroom mirror. The researcher gathered information on which urinals men used and their urinating behaviors (i.e., length of time to begin urinating and duration of urination). Results indicated that men prefer not to use a urinal next to another man.

© javi_indy, 2014. Used under license from Shutterstock, Inc.

In addition, the closer a man is to another man in terms of urinal distance, the longer it takes for them to begin urinating and the shorter the duration of urination. It would be interesting to see if gender differences occur in this behavior. Another example of a naturalistic observation comes from developmental psychologists who routinely use laboratory observations to study children. Important developmental information has been gained by bringing children into the lab and observing their interactions with their mom and dad. Examples include information on attachment style and stages of development such as object permanence. Finally, we use naturalistic observations in the world of teaching. It is not uncommon for fellow professors to observe one another in the classroom. These observations are used early on in a faculty member's teaching career to provide them with constructive criticism and later on in a career to support decisions regarding promotion and tenure.

The three examples of naturalistic observation that we have shared with you are varied in topic and scope. However, there are some commonalities in these observations. To begin, the researcher had to decide on a topic of behavior to observe and whether his or her presence would be known or hidden to the participants. In Goodall's situation, it was almost unavoidable that the chimps were aware of her presence. Similarly, when a professor has their teaching observed by a colleague, the professor and the students in the class are aware of the observation. In fact, students will quickly recognize a new face in the crowd. However, it was possible for the researcher in the urinal research example to hide his true purpose and pretend to be using the restroom too. Developmental psychologists often hide their presence by videotaping children's interactions with parents and responses to new stimuli from another room. Another commonality in our examples was that the researcher engaged in a systematic observation of specified activities. Sometimes, a coding system is used to describe the observed behaviors and researchers must be trained prior to their observations. Finally, to carry out their observations, researchers will need equipment to note their observations and may use a video camera.

There are many advantages to this methodology. To begin, the behavior being observed is natural and spontaneous. For the most part, participants being observed in naturalistic observations are just doing what they normally do in life. This is an advantage over research procedures that require people to participate in a lab setting or participate in tasks that are unfamiliar to them. It would be very difficult to answer questions about male bathroom behavior in a more realistic way. However, this method also has several disadvantages that you must consider. One main disadvantage is how the observer changes people's behavior by his or her presence. For instance, we can talk about this limitation with the example of teaching observations. Every time a peer has observed our classes, the students act differently. They become shy and well behaved compared to a typical day. This could be due to the fact that the students are trying to behave and make us look good to the observer or we are acting differently and the students are picking up on our changed behavior. Either way, the observation itself changed the natural setting. If a researcher decided to avoid this disadvantage by hiding his or her presence, he or she must consider the participant's right to privacy as well. Another disadvantage is that the researcher has to wait for events to occur. It might have taken a few hours before a man came to use the restroom; and Goodall waited months before seeing chimps use tools. Researchers also need to be careful not to introduce bias in their observations. For example, researchers might be looking for a particular behavior and report "seeing it" when others would not. A well-known example of this has occurred with observation research of chimps using sign language. Some researchers reported seeing animals use sign language, while other researchers reported the animals were not signing. Finally, cause and effect cannot be determined from naturalistic observations.

YOU TRY IT!

We have just covered information on naturalistic observations. If you wanted to examine how children play with one another and how frequently aggressive behaviors occurred, how could you use a naturalistic observation to investigate these topics? Discuss in your answer how you could conduct the study when your presence was known and unknown to the children.

ANSWER

You could investigate how children play with one another and their aggressive acts during play by going to a place where children naturally play together, like a playground. This could be at a community park or at a school. You could hide your presence if you are worried that children will play differently knowing you are watching. For example, you could watch children on a school playground from a classroom window or you could take your own child to the park and be just another parent. On the other hand, you might decide that children knowing you are around will not terribly influence their behavior so you could just sit and watch. In making your observations, you would probably have devised a coding system in advance. This way you would know what was considered violent behavior. If possible, another person could watch with you and make observations, allowing for you to compare observations.

The next nonexperimental research method that we want to discuss is a case study. A **case study** is an in-depth observation of an individual, animal, event, or treatment method. Typically, an intensive observation is done and detailed account is taken because the event is extremely rare and unusual. Case studies in the field are not just limited to Freud's psychiatric applications. There are other classic examples of case studies in the field. These include Phineas Gage and cases of feral children. Phineas Gage provided us with information on the link between personality and parts of the brain. Specifically, in 1848, an explosion sent a tamping iron through Gage's skull. Surprisingly, Gage survived the explosion but his behavior changed greatly due to the damage in the frontal lobes of his brain. Researchers have long been interested in providing a detailed account of what took place and how Gage's behavior changed as a result. Cases of feral children have provided the field with information on the importance of early exposure to language. For example, a child who is referred to as Genie was found around the age of 13. Until she was found, Genie had been kept in isolation and deprived of any exposure to language. This case study was an opportunity to see how language deprivation would influence

Case Study: A research methodology that is an in-depth observation of an individual, animal, event, or treatment method.

Genie's ability to later acquire a language. Genie was able to learn some level of English. However, her fluency was impaired and the actual level of her fluency is debated among experts (Curtiss, 1977).

When telling students about case studies, we always mention the two classics above. In addition to these, we have two more case studies that we heard about during our studies and have not forgotten. The first case study is from the area of human sexuality (Linnau & Mann, 2003). A male patient was admitted to the hospital for severe abdominal pain. When questioned, the patient admitted to swallowing Barbie doll heads (including hair) for sexual gratification. Researchers were interested in understanding how this provided the patient with sexual gratification and how such a behavior develops. A final case study is that of Clive Wearing. Clive Wearing was a brilliant musician. However, due to a case of viral encephalitis, Clive lost the ability to form new memories. This is known as anterograde amnesia. *The Mind*, a series by BBC, documents the events leading up to and after Clive's memory loss. Researchers are particularly interested in the parts of the brain damaged and the result on Clive's memories and behaviors.

The major advantage to case studies is that we can study rare events that would be unethical to study otherwise. It would be extremely unethical to deprive a child of language, make people swallow objects, or damage parts of the brain to see how the event influenced an individual's behavior. Therefore, case studies provide us with unique opportunities to better understand situations that we could not study experimentally. Despite this advantage, there are limitations to this method. First, we do not always know the cause of the behavior. In trying to understand the male patient admitted to the hospital, researchers attempted to reconstruct events from his past to explain his current situation. Yet, this procedure introduces bias because the researchers are selecting what information from his past they think is important. There could be other variables that the patient and the researchers were unaware of that influenced him. Second, these unusual events might not influence everybody in the same manner. For example, Gage was extremely fortunate to have survived the explosion. Not all people would have survived. Furthermore, not all people would have experienced the same resulting behavior. Thus, when using case studies, it is important to keep in mind the limitations of the findings.

Archival Research: A nonexperimental method where the researcher uses existing records and selects portions of the records to examine.

Archival research is a nonexperimental method where you use existing records and select portions of the records to examine. These existing records were collected by other people as a form of public records. Some examples include census information, marriage applications, police arrests, and reports prepared by your university. One of Jenn's first studies as an undergraduate student was an archival study. Jenn was examining sex and age differences in couples applying for marriage. To do so, she obtained the local newspaper's listing of couples applying for marriage licenses in Shelby County, Tennessee, for 1 month. This provided 783 couples. For each listing, the newspaper provided the name and age of the applicants with the male's name listed first. Jenn found that in 63% of the couples the male was older than the female. She discussed these findings in relation to sociobiological theories (Bonds & Nicks, 1999). Jenn has continued to use archival studies in her career. For example, she has used existing records to (a) compare the number of women to men journal editors in psychology, (b) determine the level of engagement in the classroom of Native American students compared to other ethnic groups at an East Coast university, and (c) examine rates of graduation for honors students compared to nonhonors students. Within the field, archival research is used to investigate a variety of topics. For example, Granhag, Ask, Rebelius, Öhman, and Giolla (2013) used descriptions reported to the police by witnesses of a murder to look at accuracy of basic and detailed attributes of offenders and Brenner, et al. (2013) used an archival method to assess rates of brain injury for Veterans seeking psychological help.

YOU TRY IT!

Many universities have a research day at the end of the academic year. This is one day out of the year where students showcase to the university community the products of their scholarly endeavors. Typically, a program is provided for the event which lists the following information: student's name, student's major, title of work, and faculty advisor. The information in the program is collected by the program director. However, you could use the existing data in the program to conduct an archival study. How would you examine rates of student participation across majors using the program?

ANSWER

The program provides the readers with a record of the events that took place. By examining the program, you could compare the number of students across majors to examine rates of participation. You might find that 50% of the student presenters at the research day were from majors in the natural sciences, and fewer numbers were from the arts and humanities. This information could be helpful in numerous ways. First, the people who sponsor the research day might want to consider actively advertising the event to professors and students in the arts and humanities. Second, they may also need to reconsider how work is displayed so that artists can display physical pieces of work and theater/music majors can perform their work.

There are many positive points to using an archival method. For example, you do not have to spend time collecting data yourself. In addition, you might find that more information on the topic was gathered for public records than you would have gathered on your own. Jenn found this to be the case with her archival study on Native Americans at an East Coast university. She used existing records collected by the university and was able to examine variables that she had not originally considered because the information was available. On the other hand, sometimes the records that you need have not been collected or are incomplete. Another disadvantage is that you cannot infer cause and effect. For example, you could not claim that a student's major causes him or her to be more involved with the research day. It could be additional factors (as mentioned above) leading to varying rates of participation across majors.

Content Analysis:
A research methodology where a researcher counts the number of times a particular piece of content occurs.

Survey Research:
A research methodology where one designs a questionnaire to obtain information regarding behaviors, attitudes, or opinions.

Before we move onto survey research, we want to briefly discuss content analysis. **Content analysis** is very similar to archival research in that you are examining existing documents. In this research method, you basically count the number of times a particular content of interest occurs. This is a common method used to examine media. For example, researchers will count the number of characters of different racial, gender, or ethnic groups on television. Researchers using content analysis need to utilize similar definitions of content to obtain the same results. We will talk about this issue of similar definitions in Chapter 7. Typically, content analysis is conducted before an experiment in media research. Here is an example. First, researchers might use a content analysis to examine the frequency of racist portrayals of a minority group in the media. If such portrayals of the minority group do exist, researchers could then conduct an experiment to see if these racist portrayals influenced viewers' attitudes and behaviors toward that minority group. Recently, Burgess, Dill, Stermer, Burgess, and Brown (2011) conducted a content analysis of video game magazines and results indicated that minority women were rarely depicted and minority men were more likely to be depicted as athletes or aggressive.

The last type of nonexperimental research that we will cover in this chapter is survey research. **Survey research** is where you design a questionnaire to obtain information regarding individuals' behaviors, attitudes, or opinions. This questionnaire can be administered in a variety of formats. Maybe the most common format is the written format. Questions are typed and can be administered to participants in person by having them answer on paper or computer, through a mailed survey, and even over the Internet. Another format of administering the questionnaire is via telephone. You can ask people questions verbally in person, which is known as a face-to-face interview, or gather a small group of people together to discuss the questions, which is known as a focus group. Each of these formats has its own advantages and disadvantages. A lengthy discussion of each is out of the scope of this book. However, pros and cons regarding the use of surveys in general will be discussed later in the chapter.

In April 2008, the National Sleep Foundation (NSF) released findings from a survey they conducted. The NSF collected information regarding participants' behavior and sleep patterns. Among the results reported, 36% of respondents fell asleep while driving, 29% reported becoming very tired at work within the last month, and 20% reported having sex less often due to a lack of sleep. Survey research has also examined sleep patterns in children. Specifically, survey research found a link between sleep, television viewing, and weight in children. Taveras et al. (2008) found that children are more likely to be overweight by age three if (a) the child sleeps less than 12 hours per day and (b) the child watches television more than two hours a day. Survey research has even found sleep is related to where you live. Specifically, those individuals living in a disadvantaged neighborhood report lower ratings of sleep quality, which is also related to survey responses of mental and physical health (Hale et al., 2013). Thus, survey research provides us with a wealth of information in terms of what people are doing and thinking on a given topic.

In order to obtain this information from participants, researchers must carefully construct surveys. Survey construction is a skill that takes practice to learn. For those thinking of graduate school, learning how to ask other people questions in a systematic manner will be an extremely valuable skill. Even if you are not planning on attending graduate school, we believe knowledge of survey construction to be of value to you. We have put together a few general suggestions on survey construction. Refer to Table 4.1 as we will talk you through these suggestions with an example.

The first step to survey construction is to determine what information you want to gather from participants. In other words, you want to think about the purpose of your survey. Although this may sound simple, it is an important step. It is easy to get carried away and ask too many questions, which may be off topic from your original purpose.

Table 4.1 Suggestions for survey construction.

Determine the purpose of questionnaire
Determine the type of questions
Ask about one issue per question
Make alternatives clear
Write questions in an unbiased manner
Avoid negative wording
Avoid leading questions
Most importantly, obey the law of parsimony

For our example, the purpose of the questionnaire will be to measure a faculty member's teaching ability.

In the second step, you will want to determine the type of question to ask. This includes deciding whether you will use open-ended questions or closed ended questions. **Open-ended questions** are written to elicit detailed and thoughtful answers from respondents. With open-ended questions, the respondents do not have a set way to answer. For example, you might want to ask students how prepared a faculty member was for class. You could ask, "How prepared was the faculty member for class?" and leave the response section open so students could write in an answer to the question. This would be an open-ended question. On the other hand, you could ask, "How prepared was the faculty member for class?" and have students select from a predetermined list of options (e.g., 1 = never prepared, 2 = somewhat prepared, 3 = always prepared). This would be a **closed ended question**. There are pros and cons to both types of questions. Open-ended questions allow you to gather responses that you might not have thought of, whereas closed ended responses limit you to only the responses provided by the researcher. However, closed ended responses are typically easier to score, whereas open-ended responses take time to quantify. Remember that not all of your questions have to be of the same type. It is possible to have a combination of both.

Open-Ended Questions:
Questions in which a response is elicited and there is not a predetermined list of responses.

Closed Ended Questions:
Questions in which the answers must be selected from a predetermined list of responses.

Third, be sure when you are asking questions that you only ask about one item or factor per question. For example, you would not want to ask about a faculty member's preparedness for class and promptness in returning assignments in the same question.

> To what degree do you agree with this statement?
>
> I find the professor to be prepared for class and prompt at returning graded work.
>
> Not at all   1   2   3   4   5   6   7   Very Much

This is because the student may have different ratings of each. The student might want to rate the faculty member highly on preparedness and poorly on promptness. However, if both factors are asked about in one question, you will not be able to see the difference between the two factors in students' responses.

The fourth suggestion that we have for you when constructing a survey is to make the alternatives clear. Below is an example of a closed ended question with alternatives that are not clear.

> How often did you seek help from the faculty member outside of class? (Check only one alternative.)
> ☐   1–2 times during the semester
> ☐   2–3 times during the semester
> ☐   3–4 times during the semester
> ☐   4 or more times during the semester

The alternatives in this example are very ambiguous. If you had sought help from the faculty member three times during the semester, what option would you check? There are two options (i.e., 2–3 and 3–4) that include the number 3. It is much easier for a participant to answer questions when the alternatives are clearly presented and only one option is possible.

Number five on our list of suggestions is to write questions in an unbiased manner. For example, you would not want to refer to the faculty member as a "he" throughout the survey. This is because the faculty member could be a man or a woman. Sixth, it can also be helpful to avoid negative wording or wording that is complicated. Take a look at the example below.

> The faculty member was not fair in his or her grading procedures.
> Not at all true   1   2   3   4   5   6   7   Very True

To begin, the student completing the survey might not even notice that the word "not" is in the sentence. This could result in the faculty member receiving more negative evaluations on this item. You can help this situation by offsetting the word "not" (see below).

The faculty member was *not* fair in his or her grading procedures.

Not at all true   1   2   3   4   5   6   7   Very True

However, even with measures to draw students' attention to the negative word, some students still might find the question confusing. You do not want to give participants a headache trying to determine if higher scores on the scale are a good or a bad thing. Seventh, you should avoid the use of leading questions. If you want to ask students about how professional a faculty member was in class, it would be unwise to do so in the following manner:

Directions: Sometimes faculty members fail to act in a professional manner. To what extent did the faculty member act in a professional member?

Not at all professional   1   2   3   4   5   6   7   Very professional

Beginning the directions by stating that sometimes faculty members will fail to act professionally will prime students to think about times in which this did occur. You want to be sure that you ask questions in such a way that participants are not primed or led to think of events in a certain way. The eighth, and the most important, step is to obey law of parsimony. In other words, you want to keep the survey as simple as possible to complete. When participants become confused or frustrated, they are more likely to give up or provide responses that are less accurate.

Before moving on to the last "You Try It!" section, we want to mention that survey research is not always nonexperimental in nature. Sometimes, surveys are used to gather data after participants have been exposed to the variable of interest, which the researcher manipulated. However, if no manipulation occurred prior to completing the survey, the survey would be nonexperimental in nature. Jenn et al. (2007) primed participants to recall either a positive or a negative portrayal of a homosexual person in the media. After being either positively primed or negatively primed, participants completed a survey on their attitudes toward gay men and lesbians. This is an example of how a survey can be used in an experimental research design.

YOU TRY IT!

We are going to tell you about a survey that a group of students working for Jenn constructed. Take a look at one question below from their survey. Which of the eight suggestions regarding survey construction did they fail to use?

Please indicate your current religion? (Check only one.)

☐   Catholic   ☐   Baptist

☐   Lutheran   ☐   Presbyterian

☐   Protestant   ☐   Jewish

☐   Methodist   ☐   Other

Probably the biggest suggestion that this group of students failed to use was the fourth suggestion—make the alternatives clear. The alternatives listed are just not clear. For example, Lutheran, Methodist, Baptist, and Presbyterian are all examples of Protestant religions. This made looking at the data very confusing. We were unsure if those who checked Protestant were from a sect different from those listed or from one of the Protestant faiths listed. So it is always important to be sure that the alternatives are clear and that only one alternative is possible. As we mentioned, learning how to write questions is not a skill that comes easy to most people. It takes time and lots of practice. In Chapter 7, we will return to the issue of survey construction and wording questions to obtain specific types of data.

As with the other methods discussed in this chapter, there are advantages and disadvantages to using surveys. Surveys are convenient to use as they are easy to administer and you can obtain responses from numerous participants. Another big advantage is that you can gather information on a variety of issues and with regard to behaviors, attitudes, and opinions. However, surveys can be costly to administer. Copies need to be made and possibly an assistant hired to administer the survey. Depending on the format of the survey (such as with a telephone or a mail survey), there are typically a low number of participants who respond. Also, those participants who do respond could be different from those participants who do not respond. For all surveys, you must consider the fact that participants might lie or that the wording of the question could influence a participant's response. In face-to-face interviews, the characteristics of the researcher (e.g., ethnicity and sex) could influence how people respond to particular questions. Finally, participants may answer questions in such a way as to be viewed positively by the researchers. This is known as social desirability.

SECTION SUMMARY

- Ethnography is used to describe a culture in detail by recoding and transcribing events that are witnessed (p. 65).

- Naturalistic observation occurs when a researcher observes people or animals in their natural setting (p. 65).

- A case study is an in-depth observation of an individual, animal, event, or treatment method (p. 67).

- Archival research occurs when a researcher uses existing records and selects portions of the records to examine (p. 68).

- Content analysis is a research methodology similar to archival research. However, in a content analysis the researcher counts the number of times a particular piece of content occurs (p. 70).

- Survey research involves designing a questionnaire to obtain information regarding behaviors, attitudes, or opinions (pp. 70–74).

FACTORS TO CONSIDER WITH NONEXPERIMENTAL DESIGNS

We have discussed many types of nonexperimental research methods: ethnography, naturalistic observation, case studies, archival research, content analysis, and survey. For each method, we discussed the benefits and limitations. However, as a collective group, nonexperimental designs have a benefit of providing researchers with information that would many times be unethical or practically impossible to obtain otherwise. The primary limitation for these methods is the inability to determine cause and effect. Nevertheless, nonexperimental designs are extremely important to advancing the field.

CONVERGING RESEARCH METHODS

We have introduced and discussed nonexperimental designs thus far as an independent group in research methodologies. We have done this to highlight the uses and benefits of nonexperimental designs, as well as to separate nonexperimental designs from experimental designs. However, many researchers use both types of research methods when conducting a study. This is known as converging research methodologies. Converging research methodologies occur when a researcher uses more than one research methodology to study a single problem. By doing so, the researcher is able to use the strengths of one methodology to make up for the weaknesses of the other and vice versa.

© Constantine Pankin, 2014. Used under license from Shutterstock, Inc.

For example, a researcher studying cheating has decided to use both a survey and an experimental methodology. Specifically, the researcher develops a survey to question participants on their history of cheating in the classroom. The researcher collects data on participants' self-reports of cheating behavior. After collecting data through the survey, the researcher develops an experiment in which the participants have the opportunity to earn money. However, unbeknownst to the participants, the only way they can earn the money is to cheat. The researcher then compares the participant's reported behaviors (through the survey) with their actual behaviors (through the experiment). Interestingly, this was an actual study conducted by Ong and Weiss (2000). By using both methodologies (experimental and nonexperimental), the researchers were better able to understand cheating while avoiding the disadvantages of both survey and experimental research.

College campuses can be diverse in many ways. The U.S. News ranks the most racially diverse campuses in different regions of the country (i.e., North, South, Midwest, etc.) as well as the most economically diverse campuses in these same regions every year. The selected universities view their racial and economic diversity in a positive light, believing that it enriches the college experience. If a university wanted to investigate students' behaviors and opinions regarding how this diversity related to the overall college experience, how could a university do so using the nonexperimental research methods of case study, archival data, naturalistic observation, and survey?

ANSWER

Case Study

In order to conduct a case study, a university could select a student and follow that student during his or her college career. Throughout the study, the university could assess both the student's behaviors and his or her opinions in regard to the diversity on campus and the college experience. The key here is that the study is an in-depth investigation of a single individual.

Archival Data

Most universities have an Office of Institutional Research or Institutional Effectiveness, where large amounts of data are collected and housed. If a researcher wanted to conduct an archival study, this office would be a great place to start.

The researcher could examine data to answer this research question from several years back and begin to develop a clear picture on diversity as it relates to the college experience. Rather than collecting data, this researcher would only have to examine data that were already collected.

Naturalistic Observation

To conduct a naturalistic observation, researchers would want to observe students' behaviors in a diverse environment. Specifically, researchers could sit in a university cafeteria and systematically observe interactions that students have with other students of different racial and economic backgrounds. The researchers could assess who students eat with, how conversations occur, and how the similarities and differences impact students' behaviors.

Survey

The easiest way for a researcher to evaluate the impact of diversity on a student's college experience is to administer a survey. In particular, a researcher could develop a survey to assess students' behaviors and opinions on diversity. Then, the researcher could obtain a sample of students from the larger university population that is representative of the university as a whole (we will discuss sampling procedures in Chapter 8). Finally, the researcher would administer the survey to the students and collect data on the impact that diversity has on their college experience.

CHAPTER SUMMARY

- Research methodologies can be broken down into two types: qualitative and quantitative (pp. 60–61).
    - Qualitative research methodologies seek subjectivity through in-depth collection of information and emerging hypotheses (p. 60).
    - Quantitative research methodologies seek objectivity through testable hypotheses and carefully designed studies (p. 60).
- Often, researchers prefer to distinguish research as either nonexperimental or experimental research methods (pp. 60–61).
    - Experimental research is a class of research methodologies that involve direct manipulation of a variable (p. 61).
    - Nonexperimental research is a class of research methodologies that examine relationships among variables (p. 61).
- Correlational research establishes relationships between variables. Correlations can be either positive or negative (pp. 61–64).
    - Positive correlations have variables that vary in the same direction (pp. 61–63).
    - Negative correlations have variables that vary in opposite directions (pp. 61–63).
- There are six main types of nonexperimental research methods: ethnography, naturalistic observations, case study, archival research, and survey research (pp. 65–74).
    - Ethnography is used to describe a culture in detail by recoding and transcribing events that are witnessed (p. 65).
    - Naturalistic observation occurs when a researcher observes people or animals in their natural setting (p. 65).
    - A case study is an in-depth observation of an individual, animal, event, or treatment method (p. 67).
    - Archival research occurs when a researcher uses existing records and selects portions of the records to examine (p. 68).
    - A similar type of research methodology to archival research is a content analysis. However, in a content analysis the researcher counts the number of times a particular piece of content occurs (p. 70).
- Survey research involves designing a questionnaire to obtain information regarding behaviors, attitudes, or opinions (pp. 70–74).
- When conducting survey research, the construction of the questionnaire is vital to gathering data. To construct a strong questionnaire, there are eight steps you need to follow (p. 71):
    - Determine the purpose of questionnaire.
    - Determine the type of questions.
    - Ask about one issue per question.
    - Make alternatives clear.
    - Write questions in an unbiased manner.
    - Avoid negative wording.
    - Avoid leading questions.
    - Most importantly, obey law of parsimony.

- ## Goal 2. Scientific Inquiry and Critical Thinking

  You will demonstrate scientific reasoning and problem solving, including effective research methods.

  Sections Covered: Differentiating among Methods, Introduction to Correlational Methods, Nonexperimental Methods

  Explanation of the Goal: Throughout this chapter, we have explored basic research methods in psychology such as the difference between qualitative and quantitative research designs. In addition, we have worked on distinguishing the nature of designs that permit causal inference from those that do not. The designs that do not permit causal inferences would include those that fall into the category of nonexperimental methods. Furthermore, we have described how various designs (i.e., correlational research, ethnography, naturalistic observations, survey, content analysis, and so on) address different types of questions and hypotheses, while also articulating the strengths and limitations for each of these methods.

  Sections Covered: You Try It! in Introduction to Correlational Methods, Nonexperimental Methods, You Try It! in Surveys

  Explanation of the Goal: In many places in this chapter, we have worked on critical thinking skills. In order to complete the "You Try It!" section on identifying positive and negative correlations, you had to make linkages between diverse observations such as increases in ice-cream sales and murder rates. In addition, you worked on developing sound arguments based on reasoning while solving the "You Try It!" section using archival methods to understand students' participation in the research day. Finally, we spent time approaching problems effectively and evaluating the quality of a solution in the "You Try It!" section on survey construction.

- ## Goal 3. Ethical and Social Responsibility in a Diverse World

  You will apply ethical standards to evaluate psychological science and practice and you will develop ethically and socially responsible behaviors for professional and personal settings in a landscape that involves increasing diversity.

  Sections Covered: Nonexperimental Methods

  Explanation of the Goal: As psychologists, we want to study behaviors and mental processes. However, often it is not ethical to conduct a true experiment with experimental manipulations. Therefore, this chapter covered alternative methodologies under the topic of nonexperimental designs that allow us to understand behaviors that ethically we cannot manipulate.

• Goal 4. Communication

You will demonstrate competence in writing and in oral and interpersonal communication skills.

Sections Covered: Nonexperimental Methods

Explanation of the Goal: In Chapter 4, we have discussed the importance of communicating effectively. This is especially true during survey construction. Specifically, we have shown that by articulating questions thoughtfully and purposefully when constructing a survey instrument, we can strengthen research results and limit spurious outcomes.

CHAPTER 5

Variables, Reliability, and Validity

CHAPTER OUTLINE

Are You Equipped?

An Introduction

Reliability and Validity

Are You Equipped Now?

Chapter Summary

APA Learning Goals Linkage

ARE YOU EQUIPPED?

Do you ever text while walking? We all do it! However, it is probably not a safe thing to do. Can you think of how we could use basic research elements to determine if texting has a negative impact on our ability to walk? Lopresti-Goodman, Rivera, and Dressel (2012) conducted a study to see if texting impacted speed of walking. Participants were divided into two groups. Half of the participants texted while walking and the other half of participants did not. As you might predict, those participants who texted while walking were found to walk at a slower pace than those participants not texting.

In this example, the two conditions served as the independent variable. An independent variable is a variable you think will produce a change or will influence the results. The researchers used two conditions because they believed texting would influence speed of walking. The speed of walking would be the dependent variable. A dependent variable is the variable observed and measured to see if the independent variable had an influence. In this chapter, we will provide more examples of independent and dependent variables. This will allow you to spot research design elements in everyday life.

As you go through this chapter, we also want you to keep in mind how the material relates to the APA goals for psychology majors. Specifically, this chapter will address the following goals:

- **Goal 1. Knowledge Base in Psychology**

  You will demonstrate fundamental knowledge and comprehension of the major concepts, theoretical perspectives, historical trends, and empirical findings to discuss how psychological principles apply to behavioral problems.

- **Goal 2. Scientific Inquiry and Critical Thinking**

  You will demonstrate scientific reasoning and problem solving, including effective research methods.

- **Goal 3. Ethical and Social Responsibility in a Diverse World**

  You will apply ethical standards to evaluate psychological science and practice and you will develop ethically and socially responsible behaviors for professional and personal settings in a landscape that involves increasing diversity.

AN INTRODUCTION

In order to discuss different types of methodologies in research, we must first start with the basics. In this chapter, we will focus on some of the elementary concepts of research. To begin, the chapter will introduce you to types of variables common in research. This will be followed by an overview of the importance of reliability in research designs. Finally, we will conclude with a discussion on validity and its role in maintaining sound research.

VARIABLES: INDEPENDENT AND DEPENDENT

Variable: An event or characteristic that has at least two possible values.

Independent Variable: The variable in a study that is being manipulated.

Dependent Variable: The variable in a study that is observed or measured.

A **variable** is an event or characteristic with at least two possible values. For example, what would be the variable if we were to ask you, "How stressed are you about taking research methods?" In this example, the condition with an assigned or attached value is your level of stress. Furthermore, the amount of stress you indicate in your answer is the value associated with the variable. There are two variables essential to research. These two variables are the independent variable and the dependent variable.

The **independent variable** is the variable in a study manipulated by the researcher. It is being manipulated because it is the variable the researcher believes will produce a change in his or her study. The other variable of interest is the dependent variable. A **dependent variable** is the variable within a study that is observed or measured. Specifically, the dependent variable is the variable a researcher believes will change or will be influenced in the study. Usually, any change seen within the dependent variable is a result of the independent variable. In other words, any measureable change from the independent variable's influence will be seen in the dependent variable. The way in which a dependent variable is measured is very important to the success of a research study. To help understand these two new terms, we will go through the example below.

A marketing researcher has developed advertisements for television and Facebook to promote a new type of toothpaste. The researcher is looking to conduct a study to determine which advertisement is better at getting people interested in the toothpaste. The research question is, "Does the type of advertisement influence the level of interest in the toothpaste?" In order to test this research question, the researcher has participants watch the television advertisement or view a Facebook advertisement for the toothpaste. After viewing the advertisements on TV or Facebook, the researcher asks the participants how interested they would be in using the toothpaste in the advertisement by responding on a 7-point scale, with 1 indicating "not at all interested" and 7 indicating "very interested."

For this research study, the independent variable is the type of advertisement used (i.e., television or Facebook). Remember, the independent variable is the variable the researcher believes will produce a change. In this case, the researcher wanted to know if a difference would be seen in the types of advertisements (i.e., television or Facebook). The dependent variable is the level of interest in the toothpaste expressed by the participants. Keep in mind, the dependent variable is the measurable variable in a study. Thus, it is the variable where a change can be observed. In this study, the level of interest can be measured for each participant using the 7-point scale. This measurement can be used to see if there was a difference between participants who viewed a television or Facebook advertisement.

YOU TRY IT!

The Mozart effect is a psychological topic that has received much publicity over the past few decades. The Mozart effect is the theorized temporary increase in spatial reasoning abilities following listening to Mozart. The general public is very interested in this idea. In fact, when our oldest daughter was born, the hospital sent us home with a CD of classical music, instructing us to play the music to increase our daughter's intelligence. The scientific community has continuously studied the topic to determine if support for the effect can be found.

Recently, the Mozart effect was again studied by two researchers, Jones and Estell (2007). Part of the study was to assess whether listening to Mozart's music improves spatial reasoning skills in certain high-school populations. In order to determine this, the researchers conducted a simple study. High-school students were divided into two groups of participants. The first group listened to Mozart's music for 7.5 minutes and the second group did not. Following the 7.5 minutes of either listening to music or not, both groups completed a series of spatial problems tasks. Results showed that the group of participants who listened to Mozart's music had higher scores on the spatial problems tasks compared to the group of participants who did not listen to Mozart's music.

QUESTIONS

1. What is the independent variable in this study? Specifically, what was the variable manipulated because it was hypothesized to produce a change?

2. What is the dependent variable in this study? Specifically, what was the variable observed and measured in this study?

3. According to Jones and Estell's (2007) results, was support for the Mozart effect found?

ANSWERS

1. In this study, music was the independent variable. It was manipulated by having participants either listen to Mozart or no music at all. Researchers manipulated the variable of music because they hypothesized it would influence spatial abilities.

2. The dependent variable in this study was spatial reasoning skills. Remember, the dependent variable is the variable measured because it is believed to be impacted by the independent variable. In this particular study, the variable believed to be impacted by the music was a participant's spatial reasoning skills, which were tested by a series of spatial tasks.

3. Yes, based on the results obtained from Jones and Estell's study (2007), the Mozart effect did occur. We mentioned earlier that the Mozart effect is the temporary increase in spatial reasoning following listening to Mozart. Upon listening to Mozart's music and completing the spatial tasks, participants who had listened to the music performed better than those who did not listen to the music. Therefore, in this experiment, the Mozart effect was supported.

SUBJECT VARIABLES

Subject Variable: A characteristic or attribute of a participant that can impact a study.

There is another type of variable we want to discuss that is used in research and has some of the same qualities as the independent variable. This variable is known as a subject variable. A **subject variable** is a characteristic or attribute of a participant that can impact the participant's behavior or thoughts within a study. Subject variables are often traits specific to a participant, such as sex, age, or ethnicity, and these traits can influence the dependent variable.

A subject variable is similar to an independent variable in that it is predicted to influence the dependent variable and cause a change. However, subject variables are not true independent variables. This is because a researcher can manipulate an independent variable and choose how the participant will be exposed to it. Yet, a researcher cannot truly manipulate a subject variable. For example, let's go back to the advertising study at the beginning of this chapter. In that study, the participants had a chance to be exposed to either a television or Facebook advertisement. On the other hand, if the researchers wanted to know the influence of participants' sex on interest in the toothpaste, the researchers could not have exposed participants to the variable of sex. Participants would have arrived to the study with the subject variable as part of their identities. Although you cannot directly manipulate a subject variable like a true independent variable, it is still possible to see if the responses on the dependent variable are influenced.

© Kae Deezign, 2014. Used under license from Shutterstock, Inc.

YOU TRY IT!

QUESTIONS

In the following mini-research studies, can you identify which variable is the independent variable or subject variable and which variable is the dependent variable?

1. A researcher is interested in determining if different exercise programs have an influence on the amount of weight participants lose. Upon arriving to the experiment, the researcher assigns the participants to different exercise programs and measures the amount of weight lost over a 2-month period.

2. You predict people from different religious backgrounds will vary in terms of their racial tolerance. You have participants complete a survey gathering information on their current religion and measure racial tolerance.

3. Your university wants to know if its graduates make more money compared to high-school graduates. So, the university surveys a sample of college graduates and high-school graduates and asks participants to indicate their current salary.

4. A professor wants to know if the amount of time spent studying for a test influences test performance. She has participants study for either 30 minutes or 1 hour before taking the test.

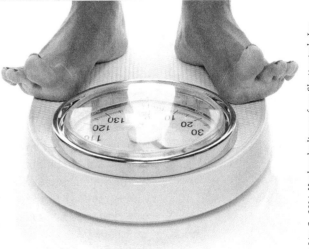

© Lisa S., 2014. Used under license from Shutterstock, Inc.

1. The exercise programs are the independent variable. This is because the researcher manipulates the exercise program given and predicts it will influence weight loss. The dependent variable is the amount of weight lost. This is the dependent variable because it is observed and measured for change.

2. The variable of religion is a subject variable in this study. Religion is like an independent variable in that you can predict it will influence racial tolerance. However, you cannot directly manipulate a participant's religion. The dependent variable is racial tolerance.

3. The variable of level of education is a subject variable in this study. Researchers can examine the influence of a participant's educational level (e.g., whether they graduated from high school or college) but cannot directly manipulate this variable. The dependent variable is job salary. This is the variable the university measured.

4. The independent variable is the amount of time spent studying. This is the independent variable because the researcher can manipulate how the participants are exposed to study time and because study time is predicted to influence test performance. The dependent variable is the scores on the test. This is where the researcher predicts the change can be observed.

TREATMENT CONDITION

Treatment Condition: Levels or number of groups in the independent variable.

Experimental Group: The group that is exposed to the independent variable in a study.

Control Group: The group that is not exposed to the independent variable.

An independent variable will always have at least two conditions. These are referred to as **treatment conditions**. Typically, the treatment conditions are the experimental and the control group. The **experimental group** is the group exposed to the independent variable. In other words, the experimental group is the group of participants given the independent variable and is the group where we would expect to see a measurable change occur. The **control group** is the group of participants not exposed to the independent variable. This group does not receive the independent variable and, therefore, we do not expect to see any measurable change in the participants.

In the study on Mozart discussed above, the experimental group was the group of participants exposed to the independent variable. This was the group that listened to Mozart's music for 7.5 minutes before completing the spatial problems task. The control group was the group of participants who did not listen to any music for 7.5 minutes before completing the spatial problems task. The control group provided a comparison so the researchers could determine if listening to Mozart influenced performance on the spatial problems task. (We will discuss treatment conditions further in Chapter 7 when we discuss levels of the independent variable.) It should be noted that although traditionally a control group is not exposed to the independent variable, there is an exception. If a researcher is comparing a new method to the current (or old) method, then the current (or old) method is serving as the control group. The new method would serve as the experimental group. An example comes from one of our classes. Jenn wanted to know how teaching statistics in her traditional manner compared to a new method where students were to develop skits to explain the material. To see if there was a difference in student learning, she compared exam scores of those students in the traditional section with those students in the new method section. In this case, the traditional manner is serving as the control group. Scores from the new method group, experimental group, are then compared with the traditional group to examine the influence on learning. So, even though we typically refer to the control group as the absence of exposure to the independent variable, in some cases the control group might involve exposure to the standard or typical independent variable.

In addition to the experimental and control groups, there is another group often used as a treatment condition in research. This group is known as the **placebo control group**. The placebo control group is similar to the control group in that participants assigned to this condition are not exposed to the independent variable. However, the placebo control group is different from the control group because the participants are exposed to a placebo. A placebo is an inert substance or object similar to the independent variable but having no direct effect. Essentially, the placebo control group acts as an insurance policy. Sometimes researchers see measurable changes in the experimental group that are not due to the independent variable but due to the participant's belief that a change will occur. Therefore, the placebo control acts as a way for the researcher to determine how much measurable change is due to the independent variable and how much change is due to the participant's belief in a change occurring. For example, if you wanted to know if caffeine influences levels of alertness, you could have three treatment conditions. The first treatment condition, the experiment group, would receive the independent variable in the form of a caffeinated beverage. The second treatment group, the control group, would receive nothing. The third treatment group, the placebo control group, would receive a beverage believed to contain caffeine. However, in reality the beverage would not contain caffeine (such as a caffeine-free beverage). You could then measure participants' levels of alertness in all three groups. Having the placebo control group would allow you to see if alertness levels changed not due to caffeine but due to the participants' belief in the influence of caffeine on behavior.

Placebo Control Group:
The treatment group which is exposed to an inert substance or object that is similar to the independent variable but has no effect.

YOU TRY IT!

There are many advertisements on television for antidepressants. Have you ever wondered how a researcher knows if these drugs will reduce symptoms of depression? Drug companies conduct research studies to determine the effectiveness of medications. Take a look at this scenario. A drug company wants to know if a new antidepressant is effective at reducing the symptoms of depression. The drug company has sampled people who are depressed and placed them into an experimental group and a control group. The participants in the experimental group will receive the new drug and

© Brian A Jackson, 2014. Used under license from Shutterstock, Inc.

the participants in the control group will receive nothing. For 8 weeks, the experimental group will receive daily doses of the new drug and the control group will receive nothing. After 8 weeks, the drug company measures the level of depression in the participants again. The results show that participants in the experimental group are less depressed compared to participants in the control group. Therefore, the drug company concludes that its drug is effective at reducing symptoms of depression.

QUESTIONS

Now that we have introduced the idea of a placebo control group, we want you to (a) describe why having a placebo control group would be of benefit to this design and (b) describe what participants in the placebo control group would do during the experiment.

ANSWERS

(a) When looking at the scenario above, you might wonder if the drug really worked. It could easily be the case that those participants in the experimental group wanted the drug to work and participants' belief alone in the drug reduced the symptoms of depression. Adding a placebo control group to the design ensures observed changes in the symptoms of depression were due to the drug itself (independent variable) and not participants' belief in the drug's effectiveness. (b) Participants in a placebo control group would have gone through the same events as participants in the experimental group, taking a pill every day for 8 weeks. The pill given to the placebo control group would look exactly the same as the pill given to the experimental group, but would be an inert substance (e.g., a sugar pill). In other words, the participants in the placebo control group would have received something that looked like the independent variable but had no direct therapeutic effect. If, after 8 weeks, the participants in the placebo control group showed the same reduced levels of depression as participants in the experimental group, the researchers should question if the drug alone is causing the change. However, if the participants in the placebo control group demonstrated similar levels of depression to participants in the control group after 8 weeks, the researcher would have reason to believe the drug is effective in reducing symptoms of depression. We will return to the topic of placebos and placebo control groups in Chapter 9.

SECTION SUMMARY

- A *variable* is an event or characteristic with at least two attached values (p. 82).
- When conducting a study, there are two important variables to be considered (pp. 82–84):
  - The *independent variable* is the variable in a study manipulated by the researcher (p. 82).
  - The *dependent variable* is the variable within a study observed or measured (pp. 82–83).
  - A *subject variable* is a characteristic or attribute of a participant that can impact the participant's behavior or thought within a study (pp. 84–86).
    - Subject variables are often traits specific to a participant, such as sex, age, or ethnicity (pp. 84–85).
- *Treatment conditions* refer to levels or number of groups in the independent variable (pp. 86-88).
  - The *experimental group* is the group exposed to the independent variable (pp. 86–87).
  - The *control group* is the group not exposed to the independent variable (pp. 86–87).
  - The *placebo control group* is exposed to an inert substance or object similar to the independent variable but having no effect (p. 87).

RELIABILITY AND VALIDITY

In the first part of this chapter, we introduced you to the concept of variables and discussed independent and dependent variables. When you read about independent and dependent variables, it is important to consider two measurement concepts. The first concept is reliability. Reliability deals with the consistency when measuring variables in a research study. The second concept is validity. Validity is concerned with the accuracy of the measurements used to assess different variables. In the remainder of this chapter, we will present you with specific techniques used to establish the reliability and validity of variables. We will begin with reliability.

RELIABILITY

Reliability of a variable is very important when conducting research. **Reliability** is the consistency of your measure to produce similar results on different occasions. Therefore, reliability is primarily concerned with being able to replicate or reproduce the findings. To make sure a measure is consistent in its ability to evaluate a variable, there are several types of reliability assessments.

The most common type of reliability assessment is known as **test–retest reliability**. When using a test–retest assessment, you give your measure to a sample of participants individually (*test*) and then again at a later date (*retest*). Usually, the testing is done a few weeks apart. In order to make sure the measure is reliable, you look at the two scores for each participant. If the measure is reliable, the individual will have comparable scores on the two points in time. For example, if we were to give

Reliability: The consistency of your measure to produce similar results on different occasions.

Test–Retest Reliability: A reliability assessment where your measure is tested on two different occasions for consistency.

an intelligence test to your class at the beginning of the semester and then again midway through the semester, we would expect to see similar scores for each person. We would not expect the scores to be exactly the same, just close. To determine whether the measure is reliable, you compute a correlation coefficient for the scores. A correlation coefficient of 0.80 in a measure is generally seen as very reliable. At this point, you do not need to know how to compute a correlation coefficient. Rather, the goal is to have you prepared to know what to look for when reading about this procedure in research articles. One disadvantage of the test–retest procedure is that it is time consuming.

Another method which does not require the same amount of time to assess reliability is known as the **split-half method**. The split-half method occurs when you administer a measure to a sample of participants. Unlike a test–retest method, where you would wait several weeks before giving the measure again, the split-half method uses only the results from the first collection of data. Specifically, you would split the measure in half. It might sound strange to split a measure into half. However, consider assessing the reliability of a 50-question multiple-choice exam. This could be done by randomly assigning questions from the exam to two groups, dividing the exam between odd and even questions, or by dividing the exam at the midpoint. You then compute scores for each half finding a correlation coefficient between the two halves. One concern is the method in which you split the halves can impact the correlation. Specifically, if you unknowingly have several similar questions in the same half and none in the other half, the correlation will be low. Therefore, many researchers use a modified version of the split-half method known as internal consistency.

Split-Half Reliability: A reliability assessment in which a measure is split into half and the two halves are compared. If the correlation is high, the measure is said to have high reliability.

Internal Consistency: A reliability assessment similar to the split-half method. However, the splitting occurs more than once and an average of the correlations is taken.

Parallel Forms: A reliability assessment in which a measure is divided into half and given to two groups of people. The reliability is high if each measure given is highly correlated.

Interrater Reliability: A reliability assessment used when a research design calls for observations of an event. Two or more observers compare results from their observations. The higher the observer consensus, the higher the reliability.

The **internal consistency** method is the same as the split-half method with one exception. In the internal consistency method, you repeat the split-half procedure multiple times, thus collecting multiple correlation coefficients. Then, you average the multiple correlation coefficients. This method counteracts the impact of having too many similar questions in only one-half of the split. A commonly used statistic for computing internal consistency is Cronbach's alpha.

Another way to assess the reliability of a measure is to use the **parallel-forms method**. In this method of reliability assessment, you divide a measure into two parts. Questions from the original measure are randomly divided among the two parts. You then administer both of the parts to a sample of participants. Following the administration, you compute the correlation coefficient for the two parts. The higher the correlation between the parts, the more reliable the measure is said to be. The benefit of this approach is the brief amount of time it takes to assess reliability. However, one disadvantage is you must generate a large number of questions in order to divide into two parts.

The last assessment of reliability we want to discuss is **interrater or interobserver reliability**. The previous assessments of reliability were focused on how you would construct a measure (such as constructing an exam in a class). However, interrater or interobserver reliability is focused on using a measure consistently in research. Interrater reliability is used when a research design calls for observations of an event. This type of reliability assessment is used to ensure the observations being made are consistent and not biased. For example, if you want to evaluate bullying behavior in children, you could observe 100 instances of bullying and categorize the bullying into one of the four categories. If you were the only researcher making the observations, there is no way to know if you consistently categorized the 100 observations. However, if there is more than one observer, you can become more confident in the ratings. Interobserver reliability uses more than one observer and the observations of the observers are compared to assess the level of agreement. In the bullying example, two or more observers would compare the categorizations of the 100 instances of bullying. If the observers were to agree 92 times out of a 100, the reliability would be 92%, which is quite reliable. However, if the observers only agreed 48 times out of a 100, the reliability would be 48% and the measure is not very reliable. Essentially, you are calculating a correlation coefficient between the degree of similarities in the observations of the observers. To be confident in the reliability of your results, you want to obtain a high degree of similarity.

VALIDITY

As we have mentioned, selecting your variables is an important part to any research design, as is measuring them. In this section, we will talk about the concept of validity. **Validity** is defined as the ability of your measurement to accurately measure what it is supposed to measure. This is different from reliability, which is about being able to replicate scores on future instances. Let's begin with an example.

Validity: The accuracy of a measure to evaluate what it is supposed to measure.

Recently, we had a student decide to pursue his graduate degree in psychology. In order to apply to graduate school, he had to take the Graduate Record Examination (GRE). In this example, the GRE score is the measurable variable. The GRE measures a person's verbal and quantitative skills. Our student took the test and did not do very well. Believing the score was an anomaly, he took the GRE a second time. Unfortunately, the student received a similar score. It was after this second exam we discovered that the student had been taking the wrong test. Specifically, the student had been studying for the GRE-General but had taken the GRE-Psychology (or GRE subject test). The GRE-Psychology exam tests a student's knowledge of the field of psychology. You can use this example to think about validity. The GRE-Psychology is not a valid measure of a person's verbal and quantitative skills. This is because the GRE-Psychology is designed to measure knowledge in the area of psychology. Thus, it makes sense why the student was complaining that the information he studied was not on the test. You can also use this example to compare the concepts of reliability and validity. The GRE-Psychology is a reliable measure. This is because the student received similar scores both times he took the test. (By the way, if you are thinking about graduate school, you will need to take the GRE. You can learn more about the GRE at http://www.ets.org/gre.

INTERNAL, EXTERNAL, AND CONSTRUCT VALIDITY

When measuring a variable, there are several types of validity to consider. The three most common types of validity are internal validity, external validity, and construct validity. Each of these types of validity deals with a different aspect of measurement. However, the commonality in all is that they are concerned with the accuracy of the measures used in a research design. The first type of validity we will discuss is internal validity. Internal validity is an important factor for independent variables. **Internal validity** is confidence in saying the observed change in the dependent variable is due to the independent variable and not due to

Internal Validity: It is confidence in saying the observed change in the dependent variable is due to the independent variable and not due to any outside influences.

any outside influences. This allows you to make a causal inference regarding the influence of the independent variable on the dependent variable. This is important when conducting a study because you want to be able to show the manipulation had an impact.

Rothbaum, Anderson, Hodges, Price, and Smith (2002) examined different types of therapies to relieve fear of flying. Specifically, over a 6-week period, participants were placed into one of the three groups, where each group was exposed to a different type of therapy. After 6 weeks, the researchers measured participants' fear of flying. The interesting part to this study was that the researchers again assessed participants' fear of flying one year after the conclusion of the study. Results showed the levels of fear had remained relatively stable since the end of the study. Therefore, the researchers concluded that the introduction of the independent variable (types of therapy) had caused a measurable change in the dependent variable (fear of flying). We mention this study to bring up the idea that researchers need to remain vigilant as to factors that might threaten the internal validity of their study. For example, do you think the follow-up results (i.e., results after 12 months) would have been different had the events on September 11, 2001, occurred during that time? The answer is probably yes. Had the results been different and the fear level was higher, the researchers would not have been able to conclude that the independent variable had a lasting influence. There are many threats to internal validity that a researcher must be aware of when conducting research. We will discuss many of these threats later in Chapter 9.

External Validity:
The extent to which the obtained results in a study can be generalized to other settings.

The next type of validity we want to discuss is external validity. **External validity**, also known as ecological validity, is the extent to which the obtained results in a study can be generalized to other settings. When considering external validity, you examine if any changes in the dependent variable can be applied to similar events. Specifically, can the results you obtained in the laboratory occur in a real-world setting? Researchers are often confronted with problems due to external validity. This is because a large percentage of research is conducted in a laboratory environment, where the researcher can isolate a single independent variable to determine its influence on a dependent variable. However, since research is done in such controlled environments, it is sometimes difficult to know if the causal inference drawn in the laboratory will apply to the real world.

One way to combat threats to external validity is to design experiments as close to the real world as possible. For example, researchers in the area of cognitive psychology have done much research using microworld simulations and virtual computer games. Researchers continue to think outside of the box and design experiments that are as close to the real world as possible. This allows researchers to extend results obtained in the lab to the real world.

Construct Validity:
The likelihood that the device or scale used to measure a variable actually is related to the topic or theory of interest.

The final type of validity that we will discuss is construct validity which is perhaps the most difficult to understand. **Construct validity** refers to the likelihood that the device or scale used to measure a variable actually is related to the topic or theory of interest. In other words, does the way we measure a variable accurately capture the theoretical construct behind that variable? If we are interested in measuring college student obesity, we could ask the following questions:

Do you overeat?

Not at all   1   2   3   4   5   6   7   All the time

How often do you eat fast food?

Not at all   1   2   3   4   5   6   7   All the time

Do you eat vegetables?

Not at all   1   2   3   4   5   6   7   All the time

On the surface, these questions might appear as though they will measure the variable of obesity. (This is known as face validity, where the device or scale has the superficial look to assess a variable's theoretical construct.) However, what is the likelihood that participants in your study would be truthful in their answers? In addition, just because you eat a lot of food or fast food does not necessarily mean that you are obese. Conversely, eating lots of vegetables does not mean you are skinny. If these were the questions you used to assess college student obesity, you might have low construct validity.

In order to have higher construct validity, you can assess two different components related to construct validity. The first component is **convergent validity**. The logic behind convergent validity is that your measure should converge or be similar to other measures of the same variable. Therefore, to have high construct validity your measure for a variable should show similar results to other valid measures of the same variable. Going back to the example on obesity, your measure should yield results similar to that of a valid measure of obesity. The second component related to construct validity is **divergent** or **discriminant validity**. This is the opposite of convergent validity. Whereas convergent validity argues your measure of a variable should be similar to other valid measures of the same variable, divergent validity argues your measure should be dissimilar to measures of different variables. Looking at the example of obesity again, your results from your measure should look similar to other obesity measures, but should not look similar to say a measure on diabetes. By using these two related components when developing measures of variables, researchers are able to increase construct validity in their study.

Convergent Validity: A type of construct validity that states that your measure should converge or be similar to other measures of the same variable.

Divergent Validity: A type of construct validity that argues that your measure should be dissimilar to measures of different variables.

SECTION SUMMARY

- *Reliability* is the consistency of your measure to produce similar results on different occasions. There are several ways to assess reliability (pp. 89–91):
  - *Test–retest reliability* is a reliability assessment where your measure is tested on two different occasions for consistency (pp. 89–90).
  - *Split-half reliability* is a reliability assessment in which a measure is split in half and the two halves are compared. If the correlation is high, the measure is said to have high reliability (p. 90).
  - *Internal consistency* is a reliability assessment similar to a split-half method. However, the splitting occurs more than once and an average of the correlations is taken (p. 90).

- The *parallel-forms* method is a reliability assessment in which a measure is divided in half and given to two groups of people. The reliability is high if each measure given is highly correlated (p. 90).
- *Interrater reliability* is used when a research design calls for observations of an event. Two or more observers compare results from their observations. The higher the observer consensus, the higher the reliability (pp. 90–91).

- *Validity* is the accuracy of a measure to evaluate what it is supposed to measure. The three most common types of validity are internal, external, and construct validity (pp. 91–93).
  - *Internal validity* provides confidence in saying that the observed change in the dependent variable is due to the independent variable and not due to any outside influences (pp. 91–92).
  - *External validity* is the extent to which the obtained results in a study can be generalized to other settings (p. 92).
  - *Construct validity* refers to the likelihood that the device or scale used to measure a variable actually is related to the topic or theory of interest. Construct validity is composed of two components, convergent validity and divergent validity (pp. 92–93).
    - *Convergent validity* states your measure should converge (or be similar) to other measures of the same variable (p. 93).
    - *Divergent validity* argues your measure should be dissimilar to measures of different variables (p. 93).

ARE YOU EQUIPPED NOW?

Let's revisit the topic of texting from the beginning of the chapter. This time we will pose the question, do you ever text and drive? Again, we have probably all done this before. However, is this safe to do? Research suggests it is not. For the purposes of this exercise, we are going to give you a modified version of an experiment conducted by Owens, McLaughlin, and Sudweeks (2011). Owens et al. wanted to manipulate texting conditions while driving (i.e., driving with no texting, driving while texting on a personal phone, and driving while texting using an in-vehicle texting system) to see if this influenced visual and steering behaviors of drivers. Participants completed these conditions by texting the researcher on a closed course. Results indicated that driving with no texting produced the best results, followed by the in-vehicle system and lastly the personal phone. Thus, texting does reduce performance and is a mental distraction for drivers.

For this experiment, answer the following questions:

1. What is the independent variable?
2. What is the dependent variable?
3. How did the researchers try to increase the ecological validity of the experiment?

ANSWERS

1. The variable the researchers manipulated was the driving condition. Specifically, the researchers verified if the participants were driving without texting or driving while texting on a personal phone or through the use of an in-vehicle testing system. The researchers manipulated this variable because they predicted it would influence driving abilities.

2. The variable the researchers measured was the performance of the drivers on visual and steering behaviors. Thus, performance was the dependent variable. The researchers did find the dependent variable was influenced by the independent variable, with texting negatively impacting driving behaviors.

3. The researchers increased the ecological validity of the experiment by having participants actually drive in a car. This increases the likelihood that the results can be generalized to the real world.

CHAPTER SUMMARY

- A *variable* is an event or characteristic with at least two possible values (p. 82).
- When conducting a study, there are two important variables to be considered (pp. 82–84):
  - The *independent variable* is the variable in a study manipulated by the researcher (p. 82).
  - The *dependent variable* is the variable within a study observed or measured (pp. 82–83).
- A *subject variable* is a characteristic or attribute of a participant that can impact the participant's behavior or thought within a study (pp. 84–86).
  - Subject variables are often traits specific to a participant, such as sex, age, or ethnicity (pp. 86–87).

- *Treatment conditions* refer to the levels or the number of groups in the independent variable (pp. 86–88).
  - The *experimental group* is the group exposed to the independent variable (pp. 86–87).
  - The *control group* is the group not exposed to the independent variable (pp. 86–87).
  - The *placebo control group* is exposed to an inert substance or object similar to the independent variable but having no effect (p. 87).
- *Reliability* is the consistency of your measure to produce similar results on different occasions. There are several ways to assess reliability (pp. 89–91):
  - *Test–retest reliability* is a reliability assessment where your measure is tested on two different occasions for consistency (pp. 89–90).
  - *Split-half reliability* is a reliability assessment in which a measure is split in half and two halves are compared. If the correlation is high, the measure is said to have high reliability (p. 90).
  - *Internal consistency* is a reliability assessment similar to a split-half method. However, the splitting occurs more than once and an average of the correlations is taken (p. 90).
  - The *parallel-forms* method is a reliability assessment in which a measure is divided into half and given to two groups of people. The reliability is high if each measure given is highly correlated (p. 90).
  - *Interrater reliability* is used when a research design calls for observations of an event. Two or more observers compare results from their observations. The higher the observer consensus, the higher the reliability (pp. 90–91).
- *Validity* is the accuracy of a measure to evaluate what it is supposed to measure. The three most common types of validity are internal, external, and construct validity (pp. 91–93).
  - *Internal validity* is confidence in saying the observed change in the dependent variable is due to the independent variable and not due to any outside influences (pp. 91–92).
  - *External validity* is the extent to which the obtained results in a study can be generalized to other settings (p. 92).
  - *Construct validity* refers to the likelihood that the device or scale used to measure a variable actually is related to the topic or theory of interest. Construct validity is composed of two components, convergent validity and divergent validity (pp. 92–93).
    - *Convergent validity* states your measure should converge (or be similar) to other measures of the same variable (p. 93).
    - *Divergent validity* argues your measure should be dissimilar to measures of different variables (p. 93).

- ## Goal 1. Knowledge Base in Psychology

You will demonstrate fundamental knowledge and comprehension of the major concepts, theoretical perspectives, historical trends, and empirical findings to discuss how psychological principles apply to behavioral problems.

Sections Covered: Are You Equipped? An Introduction, Are You Equipped Now?

Explanation of the Goal: The field of psychology uses specific concepts to account for psychological phenomena. This chapter introduced concepts such as independent, dependent, and subject variables. The exercises at the beginning and the end of the chapter helped you practice identifying these variables.

- ## Goal 2. Scientific Inquiry and Critical Thinking

You will demonstrate scientific reasoning and problem solving, including effective research methods.

Sections Covered: An Introduction, Reliability and Validity, Are You Equipped Now?

Explanation of the Goal: This chapter covered two areas in basic research methods. First, we introduced different research methods used by psychologists. The methods included the use of an experimental group, a control group, and a placebo control group. Next, we introduced two important terms in research: validity and reliability. After learning about these terms, you should be able to (a) evaluate the validity of conclusions presented in research reports, (b) select and apply appropriate methods to maximize internal and external validity and reduce plausibility of alternative explanations, and (c) use reliable and valid measures of variables of interest.

- ## Goal 3. Ethical and Social Responsibility in a Diverse World

You will apply ethical standards to evaluate psychological science and practice and you will develop ethically and socially responsible behaviors for professional and personal settings in a landscape that involves increasing diversity.

Sections Covered: Are You Equipped?, An Introduction, Reliability and Validity, Are You Equipped Now?

Sections Covered: An Introduction

Explanation of the Goal: Psychological explanations are complex in nature. Thus, to answer research questions, more sophisticated designs (e.g., the use of a placebo control group) are sometimes needed. In addition, to ensure that explanations are correct, reliability and validity are key.

Experimental Research Methods

Part 3

CHAPTER 6

Hypothesis Testing

CHAPTER OUTLINE

Are You Equipped?

Formulating a Research Question

Generating Hypotheses

Testing the Hypothesis

Are You Equipped Now?

Chapter Summary

APA Learning Goals Linkage

ARE YOU EQUIPPED?

Over the past 10 years, we have had an ongoing discussion about our writing abilities. This stems from the fact that we disagree over who is the better writer. During graduate school, our professors confirmed Jenn was the better writer. However, John's writing skills significantly improved during graduate school and this accomplishment was recognized at his dissertation defense. So, this brings us to today. As we begin to write chapters students traditionally find more problematic, Jenn insists she should do the majority of the writing, while John insists he is equally qualified. In other words, John is arguing there is *no difference* in writing abilities and Jenn is arguing there *is a difference* in writing abilities and that she is a *better* writer than John.

We are telling you about our ongoing discussion to illustrate research and statistical hypotheses. In this chapter, we will present the topics of null and research hypotheses. You will then be able to see how our discussion presented above actually relates to hypothesis testing.

© barang, 2014. Used under license from Shutterstock, Inc.

As you go through this chapter, we also want you to keep in mind how the material relates to the APA goals for psychology majors. Specifically, this chapter will address the following goals:

- **Goal 1. Knowledge Base in Psychology**

  You will demonstrate fundamental knowledge and comprehension of the major concepts, theoretical perspectives, historical trends, and empirical findings to discuss how psychological principles apply to behavioral problems.

- **Goal 2. Scientific Inquiry and Critical Thinking**

  You will demonstrate scientific reasoning and problem solving, including effective research methods.

- **Goal 3. Ethical and Social Responsibility in a Diverse World**

  You will apply ethical standards to evaluate psychological science and practice and you will develop ethically and socially responsible behaviors for professional and personal settings in a landscape that involves increasing diversity.

- **Goal 4. Communication**

  You will demonstrate competence in writing and in oral and interpersonal communication skills.

FORMULATING A RESEARCH QUESTION

To introduce this topic, we would like for you to take a moment and recall a famous psychology experiment. This could be an experiment you learned about in a General Psychology course. Can you describe some of the details of the experiment? Now, what if we asked you tell us what the research question for that experiment was? All of a sudden, this task has taken on a more complex nature. What we have just demonstrated to you is there is a difference between a research topic and a research question.

Research Topic: A broad concept or idea.

A **research topic** consists of an idea that is not very well defined. We will discuss a little later where to get started in research and where ideas come from. However, generating research ideas at this point might seem intimidating. Below are some examples of research ideas we got from scanning articles on the website for *Psychology Today*:

- Topic 1

  Sleep and productivity

- Topic 2

  Religion and life expectancy

- Topic 3

  Friends and traveling

- Topic 4

  Creativity and drug use

Although we formed research ideas from exploring the website, these are not research questions. If you were to take any of these research topics above, you could go in one of a thousand different directions. For example, look at the first research idea from the previous page. We could examine how many factors related to sleep (the amount, the quality) could impact productivity.

On the other hand, a **research question** is a better-defined idea. Specifically, research questions are written generally as a structured sentence expressing some amount of clarity. In addition, a research question helps you to narrow your idea from being broad to something more specific. This is in stark contrast to a research topic which is broad in scope and is full of ambiguity. Hence, how would you take the aforementioned research topics and represent them in a research question? Below are some examples of how we might move those research topics into a specific research question.

Research Question: State a research idea in a clearly defined manner that is testable.

- Topic 1

  Does getting 8 hours of sleep increase productivity?

- Topic 2

  Do religious people have longer life expectancies?

- Topic 3

  What impact does traveling with friends have on the relationship?

- Topic 4

  Is creativity related to drug use in individuals?

The research questions above are far more direct and narrow than the topics we originally proposed. The research questions are stated in such a way that a project can be clearly identified and executed as opposed to the ambiguous nature of identifying a research topic.

We want to relate the concepts of research topics and questions to experiments conducted in the field of psychology. First, we will talk about the research of Albert Bandura. Possibly the most famous study conducted by Bandura (1965) was on observational learning. Bandura (1965) utilized a video that recorded adults playing with Bobo dolls in an aggressive manner. (FYI: A Bobo doll is a large inflated balloon that generally has a character like a clown on it and is filled with sand at the bottom so it stands upright.) Following the play, the adults' behavior was (a) positively reinforced with sweets, (b) punished with scolding or spanking, or (c) received no consequence.

© Knumina Studios, 2014. Used under license from Shutterstock, Inc.

This video was then shown to preschool children who observed the reinforcement, punishment, or no consequences condition. After viewing the video, the children were allowed to play in a room full of toys. In addition to all the toys, the room contained a Bobo doll. Results showed that the children who viewed the video with the adults receiving punishment following their interaction with the Bobo doll engaged in far less aggressive behaviors toward the doll than the other two groups (i.e., the reinforcement and no consequences). In Bandura's experiment, what was the research topic(s) and what was the research question?

As a reminder, a research topic is very broad and general in scope. The research topics in this experiment were observational learning, reinforcement, punishment, and children. All of these topics were present in the study. Yet, the research question for this experiment was more specific. This is because a research question provides some level of clarity and directionality to research. Thus, in this experiment, the research question was extremely detailed and thorough in its content: Does the type of reinforcement or punishment given to the model influence the observer's aggressive behaviors? It still encompasses the research topics, in addition to providing the readers (and researcher for that matter) with direction.

To further illustrate the point, here is another example. Elizabeth Loftus conducted one of the most influential studies in memory distortion and eyewitness recall over three decades ago. In her study, Loftus and Palmer (1974) showed a video of the two cars involved in a car wreck. After the video, Loftus and Palmer had people recall the events and then answer several questions. One of the questions asked the participants to estimate the speeds of the two cars. However, the groups of people received questions worded slightly differently. Loftus and Palmer asked one group, "About how fast were the cars going when they *hit* each other?" For other groups, they replaced the word *hit* with *smashed*, *collided*, *bumped*, and *contacted*. As you might have predicted, the type of verb used changed the participants' perceptions of speed. For this experiment, what were the research topic(s) and the research question?

For this experiment, the research topics were eyewitness recall, leading questions, and memory. These are very broad and can encompass a wide range of possible research ideas. However, the research question for this experiment was more detailed. Specifically, Loftus and Palmer's (1974) research question sought to determine if leading questions had long-term consequences on what a person remembers about an eyewitness event. Once more, this adds a level of clarity to the research project that the research topics alone do not. Now that we have discussed the difference between research topics and research questions, and have covered examples in psychological research, we can turn our attention to an earlier identified problem: Where do research ideas come from?

GETTING YOUR RESEARCH IDEA

We have just gone through two classic experiments in psychology, and although both had a large impact on their field, each researcher started at the same place: What am I going to investigate? Before the first participant is selected, methodology decided upon, and piece of data collected, all researchers must first develop an idea. One of the fundamental questions we routinely get from undergraduates surrounds this very concept. Students ask us questions including (a) what are we going to do a project on, (b) where do we get ideas from or how do I start a research project? Most research ideas are developed from one of the four areas: everyday experiences, functional problems, prior research, and theory.

The most basic place where ideas come from is **everyday experiences**. Generally, when asked by a student for help in coming up with an idea, we ask the student what interests him or her? By our nature, humans are curious about the world around us and we all enjoy explaining the things we experience (Piaget, 1954). For example, how many times have you walked by something and thought "why did that occur?" or "why did that person do that?" This is an excellent start for a research idea. Asking those questions have led to the development of psychology as a science and to some of the greatest discoveries in the field. After all, where would the field of psychology be if Hermann Ebbinghaus (1885) hadn't asked "why do we forget?" or Pavlov (1926) hadn't asked "why are those dogs salivating when they hear my footsteps?" or Loftus (1997) hadn't asked "are people's eyewitness accounts accurate?"

Everyday Experiences: Using experience from life to obtain a research idea.

You might be thinking it cannot be that simple. Those researchers we mentioned were big names with big brains. However, it is that simple. They all started out as a student like you. For example, all of you are planning on a career in the near future after graduation. So, how are you going to decide on which job you are going to take? This practical question could become a research question. In fact, one of our undergraduates asked this very question and designed a study to determine what factors contribute to a college student selecting a job. You can try this too. Think about a topic you find interesting from an aspect of everyday life. It could have to do with buying products, choosing where to eat, selecting a pet, or even asking why people behave in a certain way. Think about how that aspect of everyday life could become a research question.

Other times, research is born from people attempting to solve **functional problems**. Functional problems are real-world situation in which a solution is needed. For instance, researchers who developed medication to reduce the symptoms of depression were tackling a functional problem (i.e., depression). Previous researchers had identified the symptoms of depression, but these researchers decided to do something about this problem.

Functional Problems: Using real-world problems as a source for a research idea.

Likewise, a major problem in professional sports is the use of steroids. Recently, countless athletes in football, baseball, track and field, and other sports have been charged with anabolic steroid use. Therefore, it is no surprise that professional sports organizations spend millions and millions of dollars every year to combat this problem. Nearly all of this money is spent on research. This research is conducted to detect steroids, determine the results of steroid use, and develop effective ways to curb this use among athletes and teenagers in general. Thus, research is often born from the need to solve functional problems that exist in the world.

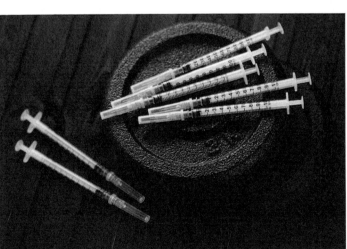

© Nickola_Che, 2014. Used under license from Shutterstock, Inc.

Have you ever read the last part of a scholarly research article? Generally, near the end of a journal article, the author(s) lists several possible extensions to the research presented in the manuscript. This is an excellent place to get new ideas for research. Often, people will take the recommendations of authors and proceed with the suggested research from this **prior research**. This will, in turn, produce additional research. Once you start doing research, any research you conduct will inevitably produce new ideas. In other words, research leads to more research. Throughout the research process, you will always think of an additional twist to your current research project. Although you may want to change your current idea, this is a time to write down your idea and use it for your next project.

For example, past work by Asch (1955) on conformity has led to years of research and published articles by many other people. You probably talked about Asch's (1955) studies on conformity in your General Psychology class, in which he presented people with a *standard line* and three *comparison lines*. Then, each participant had to verbally indicate which comparison line was equal to the standard line. The basic tenet is that people will conform (i.e., change their opinion or behavior in response to real or imagined pressure) in a social situation. In Asch's study, three-quarters conformed at least once by indicating a wrong response. This work led to Asch and others conducting additional research on why people conform, the causes of conformity, and how to reduce conformity.

Finally, many people develop research ideas by using a previous **theory** in a novel way. Take for instance the movie *A Beautiful Mind*. For those who are unfamiliar with this movie, it is a movie about a famous mathematician, Dr. John Nash, who develops a new theory about mathematical relationships often called the Nash equilibrium theory. The catch is that Dr. Nash has schizophrenia and battles with this illness throughout the movie. In real life, Dr. Nash's schizophrenia is under control and he is a brilliant mathematician. Originally, Dr. Nash's theory was used only sparingly and only in the field of mathematics. However, his theory was later applied to many different areas, including economics. It was this application in economics that won Dr. Nash a Nobel Prize many years later. Thus, it was due to the use of Nash's theory in a novel way that led to new research and applications.

In cognitive psychology, Information Integration Theory (IIT) has been applied to a number of topic areas. Developed by Norman Anderson (1979) in the 1960s and 1970s, IIT accounts for decisions made in a complex world. Anderson proposed people follow algebraic rules when making decisions. Specifically, IIT allows researchers to determine how people make decisions and the way they combine information about a decision to arrive at a choice. IIT has been used to determine how people make decisions in sports (Rulence-Pâques, Fruchart, & Dru, 2005), in social interactions (Christiansen, Kaplan, & Jones, 1999), on smoking and alcohol use (Hermand, Mullet, & Lavieville, 1997), and in groups (Graesser, 1990). Again, this is an example of a theory being used in a variety of different ways and not only within a specific area of psychology.

As can be seen, research ideas are everywhere. There is no set formula that should be used to develop a research idea. It is not a secret that only the extremely bright and intelligent are privileged to know. Rather, you as a potential researcher or consumer of research should be open to the idea that research can come from anywhere and everywhere. Just focus on the things you know and find interesting, and we guarantee a research question will develop.

CONDUCTING SEARCHES

Now that we have discussed ways to generate research ideas, it is time to explore how you would gather information on your selected topic. Not too long ago, researchers had to physically go to a library and search through a card catalog for information on their topic. Thankfully, the tools for these types of searches have been updated and can now be done over the Internet. Most universities have access to electronic databases where you can search for information on a given topic. In psychology, the most commonly accessed databases are PsycINFO and PsycARTICLES. Both of these databases have been developed and are maintained by APA. Each database has its advantages and disadvantages.

PsycINFO: PsycINFO is an abstract database maintained by APA containing over 3.6 million records dating back to the 1600s. It is called an abstract database because according to APA, it contains the abstracts or summaries from over 2,500 journals, books, book chapters, and dissertations. This database is the most comprehensive source for published psychological content. The biggest drawback to this database is that the information is not always available in full-text. However, PsycINFO contains all the information you will need to locate an article, including the authors, place of publication, and year of publication. Once an article is located by PsycINFO as being relevant to your search, it is then up to you to decide if you would like that source. Once you decide, you will need to get the article through your university library. Although this database does not always offer full-text, it does contain nearly every record on anything psychological in nature. Therefore, the odds of finding relevant information are extremely likely.

PsycINFO: Largest electronic psychological abstract database by APA.

PsycARTICLES: The other commonly accessed database for searching the psychological literature is PsycARTICLES. Unlike PsycINFO, PsycARTICLES only contains a relatively small number of records—according to APA, more than 179,000 in 97 journals. Like PsycINFO, PsycARTICLES does offer the abstract citation with all the relevant information. However, PsycARTICLES is known as a full-text database. Specifically, PsycARTICLES provides direct access to all the research articles contained within the database. Therefore, some researchers prefer searching through PsycARTICLES because of the convenience of having access to the entire article. The big disadvantage to using this database is the limited number of records it contains. With a small group of articles to search, you limit the likelihood of finding the information you may need.

PsycARTICLES: A full-text electronic psychological database by APA.

The Internet as a source: In addition to the aforementioned search engines, the Internet offers many more. Search engines on the **Internet** such as Google and Yahoo! are becoming an increasingly popular way to collect information. However, unlike PsycINFO and PsycARTICLES, the information on the Internet is not always verifiable or reliable. Simply, the information people find on the Internet is *not always* regulated. Anyone with access to a computer could potentially put anything on the Internet. When searching the Internet, you need to be careful about the quality of the information you are reading. For example, information from sites ending in .com or .net is often not regulated. These sites may put information on the Internet, but who is to say it is valid? Often people behind the sites are selling something, so you need to question the information presented. Some websites end

Internet: A worldwide, publicly accessible network containing vast amounts of information.

in .org. This ending usually represents sitesfor organizations or foundations. Many of these sites are nonprofit and are putting information on the Internet as a service to the public. However, it is important to be aware of the fact that the creators of websites can have agendas and may skew information presented to serve their needs. Websites may also end in .edu (like that of your university) and these are education websites. The information obtained here is for the most part considered legitimate. However, again there is little accountability for the information provided. Finally, some websites are .gov. These represent websites hosted by government agencies, which are generally reliable. The lesson about the Internet is simple. Although there is a wealth of information to be found, the validity (i.e., the accuracy of information) is not always high. If you find information on the Internet, it is always best to find the actual research the claims are based on in order to be sure the website is reporting information correctly.

STARTING A SEARCH

Everyone reading this book has conducted a search on the Internet for something. Usually, you just type in the topic and the Internet responds with millions of websites. If you were to conduct a search in one of the psychological databases, the same event would occur. The two biggest problems students encounter when searching for information is finding either too much or too little information. Each of these problems is easily remedied if you search properly. Specifically, when searching, you do not want to be too broad in your search or too narrow. Below is an example in which we will walk you through the process.

Let's say your research question for an upcoming class project is this: "Does viewing violent pornography influence men's attitudes toward women?" As we mentioned previously, many students get frustrated because they do not search properly. In this example, students will either do one of two things. First, they will type into their search engine (say PsycINFO) the word "pornography" (see Figure 6.1). This will yield a **large number of records** (or hits), over 1,900. No one really wants to sift through 1,900 + abstracts trying to find relevant information on a topic. Here, students are being too broad in their search. After this attempt, students usually take the extreme opposite approach. Specifically, students will input the entire research question into the search engine, "Does viewing violent

Large Number of Records: Occurs when a researcher uses terms in a search engine that are too broad.

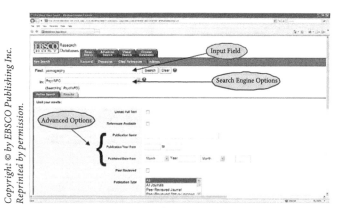

Copyright © by EBSCO Publishing Inc. Reprinted by permission.

Figure 6.1   View of Psycinfo Search Engine

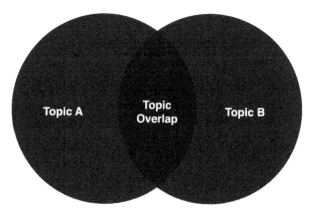

Topic A   Topic Overlap   Topic B

Figure 6.2   Search overlap

pornography influence men's attitudes toward women?" Not too surprisingly, the PsycINFO search returns with **0 records** (or hits). Too often, this is where we hear students indicate there is nothing on their topic. However, as we have indicated, this is a result of not searching properly.

So how do you search properly? For any search, you should first identify the main topic areas. In this case, the main topics are violent pornography and attitudes. It is not the topics individually that are of interest. Rather, it is the overlap (see Figure 6.2). By searching "attitudes" or "pornography" alone, you will get a large number of records, 380,172+ and 1,900+, respectively. However, it is the common ground between the two topics that contains the desired information. Therefore, by searching pornography *and* attitudes together, PsycINFO will only return those records that contain information on both pornography and attitudes, 495+ results. By simply adding the word *and*, you have narrowed your search considerably (see Figure 6.3). Yet, this search could be refined even further. Specifically, the type of pornography is vital in this research question: violent. Therefore, you can redo your search by adding violent to the search criteria. Now your search is for pornography AND attitudes AND violent. The result is you have narrowed your search to a little over 50 records having the search criterion you used (see Figure 6.4). This is a manageable number of records to search through and should give you an idea of what research has been done previously on your topic.

In addition to searching properly, you need to be flexible in the words you use when searching. Changing your search words such as "pornography" to "x-rated" can yield records your previous search did not include. Remember, there is always more than one way to identify a topic. You might use one set of terminology and someone else who has done work on your topic might use a different set of terminology. As a searcher, you need to be flexible and think of other ways to articulate your research question.

We have just gone through several concepts related to acquiring both your research topic and your research question. Once you have identified these factors, finding information is relatively straightforward. As soon as you have a research question and know what has been done on your topic, it is time to develop your hypotheses. The next section will walk you through this process.

Small Number of (or no) Records: Occurs when a researcher uses terms in a search engine that are too specific.

Using Synonyms: When conducting searches, you may need to think of a synonym for your research topic.

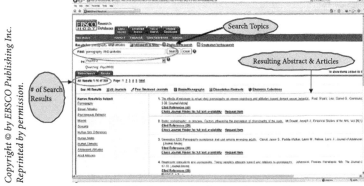

Copyright © by EBSCO Publishing Inc.
Reprinted by permission.

Figure 6.3 Search Window Results for Overlapping Topics

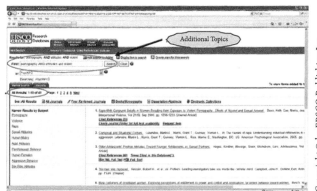

Copyright © by EBSCO Publishing Inc.
Reprinted by permission.

Figure 6.4 Search Window Results When Further Narrowing Topics

SECTION SUMMARY

- A *research topic* is a very broad idea or set of ideas that are ambiguous (pp. 102–104).

- A *research question* states your research idea in a clearly defined manner that is testable (pp. 103–104).

- Research ideas can be generated from (a) everyday experiences, (b) functional problems, (c) prior research, and (d) theories (pp. 104–107).

- Psychological databases such as PsycINFO and PsycARTICLES are great places to search for information on your research topic (p. 107).

- Internet resources can be helpful in finding information. However, the accuracy of these sources must be confirmed (pp. 107–108).

- When searching for previous research on a topic, make sure your topics are not too broad or too narrow (pp. 108–109).

GENERATING HYPOTHESES

How many of you grab a soft drink out of the vending machines before class or grab a cup of coffee before an early morning class? We remember taking a night class in graduate school that definitely required such a beverage to stay awake. We probably have all reached for a beverage with caffeine to keep us awake or "make it through" those days when we were extremely tired. If we wanted to test the idea that drinking caffeine actually helps to keep us awake, we would first need to form a research question. Our research question would be, "Does caffeine influence levels of alertness?" The next step for us to test the research question would be to generate hypotheses.

You might have been taught in elementary school that a hypothesis is an educated guess. We would like to elaborate on that definition by adding that a hypothesis is a statement about the relationship between variables.

Hypothesis: A statement about the relationship between variables.

In our example, we need **hypotheses** to make statements about the relationship between the variables of caffeine and alertness. More specifically, we need two hypotheses which are mutually exclusive and exhaustive. This means of our two hypotheses only one can be true *and* these hypotheses are the only two possibilities. Take a look at the two hypotheses below regarding the variables of caffeine and alertness.

Hypothesis 1: Caffeine *does not* have an influence on levels of alertness.

Hypothesis 2: Caffeine *does* have an influence on levels of alertness.

As you read Hypotheses 1 and 2, you will notice they are mutually exclusive. If Hypothesis 1 is correct, Hypothesis 2 can't be correct. If Hypothesis 2 is correct, Hypothesis 1 can't be correct. Furthermore, these hypotheses are the only possibilities.

When researchers go to test their hypotheses, they refer to Hypothesis 1 as the **null hypothesis**. The null hypothesis always states there is *no difference* or relationship among the scores of the dependent variables being studied. In other words, the independent variable has no influence on the dependent variable. In our example, the null hypothesis is stating the independent variable (i.e., caffeine) does not influence the dependent variable (i.e., levels of alertness). The null hypothesis is generally expressed in the following symbols.

Null Hypothesis: Hypothesis that states there is no difference between scores on the dependent variables.

Hypothesis 1 in symbols: $H_0: \mu_1 = \mu_2$

H_0 stands for the null hypothesis. The symbol μ stands for the mean of the population. Thus, this symbol means that the mean of population 1 *is equal to* the mean of population 2. In our example, we would state the mean levels of alertness of the population of individuals who consumed caffeine *is equal to* the mean levels of alertness of the population of individuals who did not consume caffeine. So, we are specifying who Group 1 is and who Group 2 is.

$$H_0: \mu_{\text{(participants who consumed caffeine)}} = \mu_{\text{(participants who did not consume caffeine)}}$$

It may seem awkward that the null hypothesis which states caffeine does not influence alertness uses the words "is equal to." However, reasoning through this helps to understand why this is the case. If caffeine does not influence alertness, people who consume caffeine have the same levels of alertness as people who do not consume caffeine.

Hypothesis 2 is referred to as the **research hypothesis** (or alternative). The research hypothesis always states the opposite of the null. This means the research hypothesis always states there *is a difference* on the scores of the dependent variables. In other words, there is an influence of the independent variable on the dependent variable. In our example, the research hypothesis is stating the independent variable (i.e., caffeine) does influence the dependent variable (i.e., alertness). The research hypothesis is generally expressed in the following symbols.

Research Hypothesis: Hypothesis that states there is a difference between scores on the dependent variables.

Hypothesis 2 in symbols: $H_1: \mu_1 \neq \mu_2$

H1 stands for the research hypothesis. The symbol μ stands for the mean of the population. Thus, this symbol means that the mean of population 1 *is not equal to* the mean of population 2. In our example, we would state the mean levels of alertness of the population of individuals who consumed caffeine *is not equal to* the mean level of alertness of the population of individuals who did not consume caffeine.

$$H_1: \mu_{\text{(participants who consumed caffeine)}} \neq \mu_{\text{(participants who did not consume caffeine)}}$$

It may seem awkward that the research hypothesis which states caffeine does influence alertness uses the words "is not equal to." However, reasoning through this helps to understand why this is the case. If caffeine does influence alertness, people who consume caffeine will have different levels of alertness as compared to people who do not consume caffeine.

Researchers have some options when selecting the research hypothesis. In the example above, we selected a **nondirectional research hypothesis**. A nondirectional hypothesis states the independent variable (i.e., caffeine) has an

Nondirectional Research Hypothesis: A hypothesis that does not make a prediction about the direction that the results will occur in.

influence on the dependent variable (i.e., alertness), but it does not give the specific direction the influence might have. In other words, it does not specify if caffeine will increase or decrease levels of alertness. If researchers wanted to be more specific in their research hypothesis, they could form a **directional research hypothesis**. A directional research hypothesis predicts a specific direction that the results will occur in. In our example, we could have predicted caffeine increases levels of alertness and the symbols would be as follows:

$$H_1: \mu_{(\text{participants who consumed caffeine})} > \mu_{(\text{participants who did not consume caffeine})}$$

This would mean that the participants who consumed caffeine had higher levels of alertness than the participants who did not consume caffeine. It is important to realize a researcher only has *one* research hypothesis. The researcher must pick from one of these three options: there is a difference (nondirectional), there is an increase in the dependent variable (directional), or there is a decrease in the dependent variable (directional).

To further illustrate the point, here is another example. Think back to the "Are You Equipped?" section at the beginning of this chapter, where your textbook authors were having a discussion about who is the better writer. The research question for this discussion would be, "Does textbook author influence writing quality?" In response to this question, John stated there is no difference in writing abilities. More specifically, John stated the textbook author who was writing the majority of the chapter (Jenn versus John) did not influence the writing quality. However, Jenn stated there is a difference in writing abilities and she is the better writer. More specifically, Jenn stated the textbook author who was writing the majority of the chapter (Jenn versus John) did influence the writing quality and Jenn's writing was of higher quality than John's writing.

In this example, who is stating the null hypothesis? In other words, we want to know who is stating that the independent variable (i.e., the authors of the textbook) does not influence the dependent variable (i.e., writing quality). If you said John, you are correct. John is stating Jenn's writing is equal to John's writing and this is expressed in symbols in the following way:

$$H_0: \mu_{(\text{Jenn's writing})} = \mu_{(\text{John's writing})}$$

On the other hand, Jenn is stating the research hypothesis that the independent variable (i.e., the authors of the textbook) does influence the dependent variable (i.e., writing quality). Jenn is stating that Jenn's writing is not equal to John's writing and this would be stated in symbols in the following way:

$$H_1: \mu_{(\text{Jenn's writing})} \neq \mu_{(\text{John's writing})}$$

When Jenn says the writing abilities are not equal (as in the symbols above), is she stating a nondirectional research hypothesis or a directional research hypothesis? If you said nondirectional, you are correct. Jenn is stating there is a difference in writing abilities but has not yet specified who is the better writer.

Next, Jenn specifies she believes she is the better writer and this would be expressed in symbols in the following way:

$$H_1: \mu_{(\text{Jenn's writing})} > \mu_{(\text{John's writing})}$$

Now when Jenn says her writing abilities are better than John's (as in the symbols above), is she stating a nondirectional research hypothesis or a directional research hypothesis? If you said directional, you are correct. Jenn is stating the specific direction she is predicting for the results.

YOU TRY IT!

We want you to practice generating null and research hypotheses. Below we have given you three research questions. For each, you are to (a) state the null hypothesis in words and in symbols, (b) state the research hypothesis in words and in symbols, and (c) say if your research hypothesis is nondirectional or directional.

1. On the TV show *How I Met Your Mother*, Barney Stinson proposed a theory called the "cheerleader effect." Barney's theory claims people look more attractive when they are part of a group than when they are alone. If we were to test the cheerleader effect, the research question would be, "Does context of an individual (in a group or alone) influence ratings of attractiveness?"

2. We have a graduate student who shared the following hypothesis. Our graduate student believes that you can determine a woman's arrogance by the size of her sunglasses. The research question for this example is, "Is there a relationship between size of sunglasses (regular versus extra-large) and a woman's arrogance?"

3. We are relatively young professors. Sometimes, our age works to our benefit in that we can relate well to our students. However, other times our age works against us. Occasionally, students might not realize that although we are young we still have expertise in our areas. This leads us to wonder if age of professor can have an influence on the class. The research question for this example is, "Does age of professor (young versus mature) influence students' participation in class?"

ANSWERS

Below are the answers to these practice exercises. Take a look at our answers and see how you did at generating null and research hypotheses.

1. In the cheerleader effect example, the first thing you need to do is reread the research question: Does context of an individual (in a group or alone) influence ratings of attractiveness?" When formulating the null hypothesis for this research question, be sure you are stating the independent variable (i.e., context of an individual) does not influence the dependent variable (i.e., ratings of attractiveness). Your null hypothesis could state, "Context of an individual does not influence ratings of attractiveness." It is also equally correct to word your null hypothesis in the following way: "There is no influence of context of an individual on ratings of attractiveness." Both of these wordings are correct because they mean the same thing (i.e., the independent variable does not influence the dependent variable). Your null hypothesis would be expressed in symbols in the following way:

$$H_0: \mu_{(group)} = \mu_{(alone)}$$

More specifically, these symbols mean ratings of attractiveness of the individual in a group are equal to ratings of attractiveness of the individual when alone. (Remember the null hypothesis, which states there is no influence of the independent variable on the dependent variable, uses the equal to sign in the equation.)

As you picked your research hypothesis, you had three options: (1) a nondirectional research hypothesis, (2) a directional research hypothesis with a prediction in one direction, and (3) a directional research hypothesis with a prediction in the opposite direction. Any of the three research hypotheses would have been correct. Let's further investigate each of these three hypotheses.

If you selected a nondirectional hypothesis, you might have said, "Context of an individual does influence ratings of attractiveness" or "There is an influence of context of an individual on ratings of attractiveness. This nondirectional hypothesis would be expressed in symbols as follows:

$$H_1: \mu_{(group)} \neq \mu_{(alone)}$$

These symbols mean ratings of attractiveness of an individual in a group are not equal to ratings of attractiveness when alone. If you formed a directional research hypothesis, you might have said, "Ratings of attractiveness will be higher in a group than alone," and this would be expressed in symbols as follows:

$$H_1: \mu_{(group)} > \mu_{(alone)}$$

Finally, if you had formed a directional research hypothesis in the opposite direction, you might have said, "Ratings of attractiveness will be higher when alone than in a group," and this would be expressed in symbols as

$$H_1: \mu_{(group)} < \mu_{(alone)}$$

By the way, psychologists have actually tested Barnye's theory. To lean more, read the work of Walker and Vul (2014).

2. In the sunglasses example, the research hypothesis was, "Is there a relationship between size of sunglasses (regular versus extra-large) and a woman's arrogance?" Your null hypothesis, stating that the independent variable of sunglass size does not predict the dependent variable of a woman's arrogance, could have been stated as, "The size of a woman's sunglasses is not related to her arrogance" or "There isno relationship between the size of a woman's sunglasses and her arrogance." The null hypothesis would be symbolized as follows:

$$H_0: \mu_{(regular)} = \mu_{(extra\text{-}large)}$$

This would mean that the arrogance level of a woman wearing regular-size sunglasses is equal to the arrogance level of a woman wearing extra-large sunglasses. Again, as you picked your research hypothesis, you were faced with the option of selecting a nondirectional research hypothesis or a directional research hypothesis. Your nondirectional research hypothesis would state, "The size of a woman's sunglasses is related to her arrogance" and would be symbolized as:

$$H_1: \mu_{(regular)} \neq \mu_{(extra\ large)}$$

This would mean that the arrogance level for a woman wearing regular-sized sunglasses is not equal to the arrogance level of a woman wearing extra-large sunglasses.

If you selected a directional research hypothesis, you could have stated, "A woman who wears regular-sized sunglasses is more arrogant than a woman who wears extra-large sunglasses"

$$H_1: \mu_{(regular)} > \mu_{(extra\ large)}$$

or that "A woman who wears extra-large sunglasses is more arrogant than a woman who wears regular-sized sunglasses."

$$H_1: \mu_{(regular)} < \mu_{(extra\ large)}$$

3. In the final example, the research hypothesis was, "Does age of professor (young versus mature) influence students' participation in class?" The null hypothesis would state, "Age of professor does not influence students' participation in class" or "There is no influence of age of professor on students' participation in class." In symbols, this would be stated as class participation of students with a young professor is equal to class participation of students with a mature professor:

$$H_0: \mu_{(young)} = \mu_{(mature)}$$

For the research hypothesis, you had three options. The nondirectional research hypothesis would state, "Age of professor does influence students' participation in class," represented in symbols as

$$H_1: \mu_{(young)} \neq \mu_{(mature)}$$

If you picked a directional research hypothesis, it would have stated either that "Young professors have more student participation in class than mature professors"

$$H_1: \mu_{(young)} > \mu_{(mature)}$$

or that "Mature professors have more student participation in class than young professors."

$$H_1: \mu_{(young)} < \mu_{(mature)}$$

How did you do? As you may have noticed above, your hypotheses might not have been worded exactly like ours. What is important, though, is that the meaning is the same. Ask yourself, does my null hypothesis say there is no influence of the independent variable on the dependent variable? If so, you are on the right track. Likewise, ask yourself, does my research hypothesis say there is an influence of the independent variable on the dependent variable? If so, you are on the right track. If you have a question about whether or not the hypothesis you generated is saying the same thing as ours, be sure to ask your professor.

We want to mention two final topics on generating null and research hypotheses before moving on. First, most of the time when you read research articles, the authors will state their research hypothesis and not mention the null hypothesis. This is because researchers are most interested in the research hypothesis and it is assumed that the reader knows the null hypothesis is the hypothesis being tested. Second, you may be wondering how to decide whether or not to use a nondirectional or directional research hypothesis. This is a great question, because the type of research hypothesis you select can influence the way you analyze your data. For right now, though, we will keep it simple. Unless you have a really good reason to believe your results will come out in a specific direction, you should use a nondirectional research hypothesis. However, if you are basing your research hypothesis on previous research, you might have enough evidence to suggest your results will come out in a specific direction and you should use a directional research hypothesis.

TESTING THE HYPOTHESIS

When you test your hypotheses, you are actually testing the null hypothesis. If your results are so extreme they could not likely be due to chance, then you can reject the null hypothesis and conclude that the independent variable did have an influence on the dependent variable. We will explain this in more detail in Chapter 14.

We also want to point out that results of a study are never used to *prove* a research hypothesis or a null hypothesis. Psychologists avoid saying results of an experiment prove a research hypothesis to be true. Rather, depending on the outcome, psychologists say either results *support* a research hypothesis or that the study is inclusive.

SECTION SUMMARY

- The *null hypothesis* states there is *no* difference between the groups of scores on the dependent variables (pp. 110–111).
- The *research hypothesis* states there *is* a difference between the groups of scores on the dependent variables (p. 111).
- Research hypotheses can be either directional or nondirectional (pp. 111–113).
  - A *nondirectional hypothesis* makes no specific prediction as to the direction the results will occur in (pp. 111–112).
  - A *directional research* hypothesis makes a specific prediction as to the direction the results will occur in (pp. 112–113).

Think about a time when you have been sick. Did it influence your ability to perform even the simplest of tasks let alone a full-time job? Research conducted by Smith, Tyrrell, and Willman (1987) sought to investigate this exact problem. Although we all know intuitively sickness can have a negative impact on human performance, Smith et al. decided to test this experimentally. Specifically, the researchers in this experiment wanted to know what influence the exposure to minor illness has on the efficiency of human performance. The researchers believed illness would negatively impact human performance. In order to test this hypothesis, Smith et al. infected people with influenza and the common cold. Following infection, the researchers kept the participants quarantined for 10 days while they studied the effects. The results indicated that while the cold affected eye–hand coordination, influenza affected only a person's ability to detect and respond to stimuli. In other words, there were differences between participants' performance before and after being infected.

© Ocskay Bence, 2014. Used under license from Shutterstock, Inc.

Questions

From this example, can you identify the following elements?

1. The research question.
2. The null hypothesis in symbols and words.
3. The research/alternative hypothesis in symbols and words.

Answers

1. In this experiment, the research question was, "What influence does the exposure to minor illness have on the efficiency of human performance?" To visit an earlier topic, the research topics were illness and human performance.

2. Hypothesis 1: Exposure to minor illness *does not* have an effect on human performance. The null hypothesis can be symbolized as

$$H_0: \mu_{(\text{before infection})} = \mu_{(\text{after infection})}$$

3. Hypothesis 2: Exposure to minor illness *does* have an effect on human performance (nondirectional).

   In this experiment, the researchers chose a directional research hypothesis in that they believed exposure to minor illness would have a negative effect on human performance. The nondirectional and directional hypotheses can be symbolized as follows:

The nondirectional hypothesis:

$$H_1: \mu_{(\text{before infection})} \neq \mu_{(\text{after infection})}$$

The directional hypotheses:

$$H_1: \mu_{(\text{before infection})} > \mu_{(\text{after infection})}$$

OR

$$H_1: \mu_{(\text{before infection})} < \mu_{(\text{after infection})}$$

CHAPTER SUMMARY

- A research topic and a research question are distinctly different. Everyone starts off with an idea in mind. This idea is usually not very well formed and quite ambiguous. When your research idea is in this form, it is a *research topic*. However, once you have refined this idea into a question that exhibits clarity and concreteness, you have developed a *research question* (pp. 102–104).

- Research ideas can be developed at anytime, in any place, and by anybody. Research ideas generally are developed from one of the four areas: (a) everyday experiences, (b) functional problems, (c) prior research, and (d) theory (pp. 104–107).

  - The most basic place that ideas can come from is *everyday experiences*. All throughout your daily life, questions can arise that lead to a research idea (p. 105).

  - Another area that can lead to a research idea is when someone tries to solve a *functional problem*. Research ideas are born from problems in the world because people search for a solution (p. 105).

  - Many times, research is an extension of *prior research*. One research study often generates new problems and ideas that are an excellent starting point for the development of a new research idea (p. 106).

  - Finally, new research ideas can be developed by taking a *theory* and applying it in a novel way (p. 106).

- Most searches in the field of psychology are conducted with search engines. The two most commonly accessed search engines are PsycINFO and PsycARTICLES® (pp. 107–108).

  - PsycINFO is a psychological database that contains abstracts (i.e., short summaries about the research). PsycINFO contains nearly 2.7 million citations dating back to the 1800s. Once a citation is found to be useful, you will most likely have to find the full-text article by visiting your university library (p. 107).

  - PsycARTICLES is a full-text psychological database. The advantage is that you do not have to go to your university library to get the article you find relevant. However, this database only contains citations from roughly 135,000 articles. This is far fewer than that of PsycINFO (p. 107).

- In addition to PsycINFO and PsycARTICLES as a source for finding information, you can use Internet search engines. However, information on the Internet is not always peer reviewed or verified for accuracy. If you are going to use the Internet, you need to make sure the information you obtain is accurate (pp. 107–108).

- When gathering information about your research idea, it is best to identify the underlying topics. Searching a topic that is too broad will yield too much information on your topic. However, by searching a topic that is too narrow, very little information will be obtained on your idea (pp. 108–109).

- A hypothesis is a statement about the relationship between two or more variables. When conducting research, you should state both your null hypothesis and your research hypothesis (p. 110).

  - A null hypothesis indicates there is *no* difference in scores on the dependent variables between groups in a study (pp. 110–111).

  - A research hypothesis indicates there *is* a difference in scores on the dependent variables between groups. A research hypothesis can be stated as either nondirectional (i.e., no direction is predicted) or directional (i.e., a direction is predicted) (pp. 111–113).

- Each hypothesis can also be represented symbolically (pp. 111–116).

  - Null hypothesis: $H_0: \mu_1 = \mu_2$

    where scores on variable 1 are equal to scores on variable 2 and they are not different (p. 111).

  - Research hypothesis: $H_1: \mu_1 \neq \mu_2$

    where scores on variable 1 are not equal to scores on variable 2 and differences exist (p. 111).

  - Directional research hypothesis: $H_1: \mu_1 > \mu_2$ Or $\mu_1 < \mu_2$

    where scores on variable 1 are greater or less than scores on variable 2 (pp. 111–112).

APA LEARNING GOALS LINKAGE

- **Goal 1. Knowledge Base in Psychology**

  You will demonstrate fundamental knowledge and comprehension of the major concepts, theoretical perspectives, historical trends, and empirical findings to discuss how psychological principles apply to behavioral problems.

  Sections Covered: Formulating a Research Question

  Explanation of the Goal: Although the main focus of this chapter was on hypothesis testing, we also learned about some of the classical research studies in the history of psychology. For example, we discussed the work of Bandura at the beginning of the chapter when differentiating between research topics and research questions. Later on, we covered how to get research ideas and mentioned Asch's work on conformity. Even if you have heard of these researchers before in an introduction course, it is helpful to revisit pivotal studies in the field from a research methods perspective.

- ## Goal 2. Scientific Inquiry and Critical Thinking

  You will demonstrate scientific reasoning and problem solving, including effective research methods.

  Sections Covered: Are You Equipped?, Formulating a Research Question, Generating Hypotheses, Are You Equipped Now?

  Explanation of the Goal: To conduct research, you must know how to locate and use relevant databases. The first part of this chapter was devoted to this topic. We explored how to use PsycINFO, PsycARTICLES, and the Internet as databases. The second part of the chapter was devoted to another essential skill in research, which is formulating testable research hypotheses. Specifically, we learned how to generate null and research hypotheses.

  Sections Covered: Are You Equipped?, Formulating a Research Question, Generating Hypotheses, Are You Equipped Now?

  Explanation of the Goal: This chapter opened with a discussion of research topics versus research questions. Knowing the difference between the two provided you with experience in approaching problems effectively by recognizing ill-defined and well-defined problems. Next, we used critical thinking to develop research ideas. These ideas can be obtained from everyday experiences, functional problems, prior research, and theory. Finally, we used critical thinking skills in generating multiple possible solutions to research questions when forming null and research hypotheses.

- ## Goal 3. Ethical and Social Responsibility in a Diverse World

  You will apply ethical standards to evaluate psychological science and practice and you will develop ethically and socially responsible behaviors for professional and personal settings in a landscape that involves increasing diversity.

  Sections Covered: Formulating a Research Question, Generating Hypotheses, Are You Equipped Now?

  Explanation of the Goal: We presented numerous examples of how psychological principles can relate to personal and social issues in everyday life. A few examples were violence and observational learning, memory distortions and eyewitness recall, and conformity. We also practiced forming research questions with everyday topics such as the relationship between human performance and sickness.

- ## Goal 4. Communication

  You will demonstrate competence in writing and in oral and interpersonal communication skills.

  Sections Covered: Formulating a Research Question

  Explanation of the Goal: APA states that psychology majors should be able to demonstrate information competence at each stage in the following process: (a) formulate a researchable topic that can be supported by database search strategies, (b) locate and choose relevant sources from appropriate media, and (c) use selected sources after evaluating their suitability. Furthermore, psychology students are expected to demonstrate these computer skills in using databases and searching the Internet for high-quality information. The information provided in the chapter on conducting searches will assist you in achieving the needed competence at each stage.

CHAPTER 7

Selection of Variables, Operational Definitions, and Measurement Issues

CHAPTER OUTLINE

Are You Equipped?

Selecting the Levels of Independent Variables

Measuring the Dependent Variable and Number of Dependent Variables

Operational Definitions

Types of Scales

Are You Equipped Now?

Chapter Summary

APA Learning Goals Linkage

ARE YOU EQUIPPED?

According to the website *Box Office Mojo* (2014), 73 out of the top 100 romantic movies of all time were released during the same six month period, October–March, in their respective years of release. Two questions may have popped into your mind: (1) Why do I need to know this? (2) Why are romantic movies released when it is predominately cold in the northern hemisphere? Recent research by Hong and Sun (2012) examined the relationship between temperature and preference for different movie genres. In particular, their research showed that in cold weather, people preferred romantic movies compared to other movie genres. Specifically, the researchers had 53 and 56 undergraduate students participate in 2 different studies. In the first study, the students were given either cold tea or hot tea to drink while evaluating several movies in different genres. At the end of the survey, students were asked to rate their interest in each of the movie genres as a whole. The procedure was exactly the same for the second study except instead of using tea to simulate temperature, the researchers placed participants in a cold (59–62 degrees Fahrenheit) or warm room (72–76 degrees Fahrenheit). The procedure was the same with the questioning taking place in the same manner. Here are the results:

- Participants in the cold drinking and cold room conditions showed a higher preference for romantic movies as compared to those in the warm conditions.
- Temperature did not impact participant's preference for other movie genres.

© Monkey Business Images, 2014. Used under license from Shutterstock, Inc.

As you read this example, you may be thinking about your own movie viewing habits. You may also be thinking about other variables that could have impacted the results of the study. However, for the purposes of this chapter, we would like to draw your attention to identifying the independent variable and the dependent variable. Remember from Chapter 5 that the independent variable is the variable thought to produce a change and the dependent variable is the variable that is being measured to look for this change. In this study, the researchers examined the relationship between temperature and preference for different movie genres. Therefore, the variable being measured for change was preference for different movie genres. Now, what variable was thought to influence preference for different movie genres? The answer is temperature.

As you go through this chapter, we also want you to keep in mind how the material relates to the APA goals for psychology majors. Specifically, this chapter will address the following goals:

- **Goal 2. Scientific Inquiry and Critical Thinking**

  You will demonstrate scientific reasoning and problem solving, including effective research methods.

- **Goal 3. Ethical and Social Responsibility in a Diverse World**

  You will apply ethical standards to evaluate psychological science and practice and you will develop ethically and socially responsible behaviors
  for professional and personal settings in a landscape that involves increasing diversity.

- **Goal 4. Communication**

  You will demonstrate competence in writing and in oral and interpersonal communication skills.

SELECTING THE LEVELS OF THE INDEPENDENT VARIABLE

Levels of the Independent Variable: The number of conditions for a specific independent variable.

So far, we have just been reviewing definitions we hope you already feel comfortable with. We now want to tell you how to select the **levels of the independent variable**. In the example above, there are two levels of the independent variable of temperature: There is level number one (i.e., cold) and level number two (i.e., warm). In this chapter, we are going to practice identifying the levels of an independent variable and discuss how to decide the number of levels that is needed for a given independent variable.

Think back to Chapter 6 where we looked at the research question, "Does caffeine influence levels of alertness?" In this research question, the independent variable was caffeine and the dependent variable was levels of alertness. We briefly discussed to actually test this research hypothesis you would need two groups: one group of participants would get a caffeinated beverage and the other group of participants would get a noncaffeinated beverage.

Group 1: Participants who would get a caffeinated beverage

Group 2: Participants who would get a noncaffeinated beverage

Then, you could compare the alertness levels of the two groups to see if there was a difference. If you were to really test this research question, your design would not be quite that simple. The reason is because you would probably need more than two levels of the independent variable. At present, the two levels are caffeine and no caffeine. However, you might want to consider varying the amount of the caffeinated beverage participants consume to see if there is a certain amount of caffeine participants need in their system before alertness levels are changed. You could have the following design:

Group 1: Participants who get 8 ounces of a caffeinated beverage

Group 2: Participants who get 24 ounces of a caffeinated beverage

Group 3: Participants who get no caffeine

You could then compare the levels of alertness of the three groups to see if there was a difference. It might be the case that it takes 24 ounces of a caffeinated beverage before we see an increase in alertness. The main point is by adding multiple levels of the independent variable you are better able to see the influence of that particular independent variable.

Here is another example. This idea came from a group of undergraduate students we worked with at Kansas State University. They wanted to know if the type of clothes a faculty member wore influenced students' perceptions of that faculty member's competence. In other words, do students perceive professors who wear dress clothes as more competent than professors who wear jeans? These students designed an experiment and had a professor guest lecture in two sections of General Psychology students. The guest professor wore dress clothes (nice dress slacks) to one section of General Psychology and casual clothes (blue jeans) to another section of General Psychology. In other words,

Group 1: One section of General Psychology with guest professor in dress clothes

Group 2: One section of General Psychology with guest professor in casual clothes

The General Psychology students were then asked to evaluate the guest professor and rate his or her competence in the discipline of psychology.

In this example, the research questions are as follows:

- What is the independent variable (i.e., what is being manipulated or thought to produce a change)?

    The independent variable is type of clothes, because it is what is being manipulated (or varied) in the experiment.

- How many levels of the independent variable are there?

    There are two levels of the independent variable: dress clothes and casual clothes.

- What is the dependent variable (i.e., what is being measured for change)?

    The dependent variable is competence of the guest professor. Thus, the competence of the guest professor is what is being measured and believed will change due to the independent variable.

The results were as follows. In short, the competence ratings depended on the sex of the guest professor. If the guest professor was a woman, she was judged to be equally competent wearing dress slacks as blue jeans. However, if the guest professor was a man, he was judged to be less competent when he wore blue jeans than when he wore slacks.

To further help you with understanding levels of the independent variable, here is another example. In this example, the research question was, "Does size of computer monitor influence reaction time?" John and some colleagues have tested if varying the size of a computer monitor (i.e., 17 inch, 19 inch, and 21 inch) will influence how quickly participants perform a task. John and his colleagues wanted to know if bigger computer screens would always lead to faster reaction time. They had three groups of participants.

Group 1: Participants who completed a task on a 17-inch computer monitor

Group 2: Participants who completed a task on a 19-inch computer monitor

Group 3: Participants who completed a task on a 21-inch computer monitor

They then compared the reaction times of participants in each of the three groups to see if there was a difference.

In this example,

- what is the independent variable?
- what are the levels of the independent variable?
- what is the dependent variable?

Here are the answers:

- The independent variable is the size of the computer monitor. It has three levels—17 inch, 19 inch, and 21 inch.
- The dependent variable is reaction time.

Results for this experiment found that bigger is not always better in terms of size of computer monitors. This research demonstrated the best size for a computer monitor is 19 inches. Believe it or not, 21 inches is actually too big and participants spend extra time turning their heads to look at all parts of the screen. (We bet Apple or Dell would not want these results to become well known.)

Here is one last example on identifying levels of independent variables. As you are reading the example, try to pick out the independent variable, its levels, and what is being measured. There are many different types of bosses in a workplace setting, and each boss has his or her own leadership style or way of treating employees. Some bosses treat all employees as equals and value the input of each employee (democratic leadership style), whereas other bosses treat employees as workers who do not have input in how things are done (autocratic leadership style). Researchers have been interested in knowing if leadership style of a boss (i.e., democratic versus autocratic) influences employees' satisfaction with their jobs.

In this example,

- what is the independent variable?
- what are the levels of the independent variable?
- what is the dependent variable?

Here are the answers:

- The independent variable is leadership style of a boss. It has two levels: democratic and autocratic.
- The dependent variable is employees' satisfaction with their jobs.

Before moving on to the topic of selecting dependent variables, we want to mention one more thing about selecting the levels of an independent variable. You may be wondering how does someone know how many levels is the correct amount to select. The answer is there is no magical number of levels for an independent variable. Sometimes, you start with levels that are far apart such as 8 ounces of a caffeinated beverage and 32 ounces of a caffeinated beverage. If there is a difference in these two levels, you could conduct another experiment with the levels of 16 ounces and 24 ounces to better understand the exact amount of caffeine needed to influence alertness.

YOU TRY IT!

It is now time for you to practice selecting levels of an independent variable. For the purposes of this example, we would like you to come up with three levels of the independent variable.

QUESTIONS

Here is your research question: "Does type of sport a student plays in college influence his or her class attendance rates?" Since you are going to pick the levels of the independent variable, we will save you some work and tell you the independent variable is type of sport and the dependent variable is class attendance rates. Now you need to think of at least three levels of the independent variable, type of sport. In other words, what are three different levels or types of sports that college students could play? Take a look at our answers below, after thinking about the question.

EXAMPLE 1:

IV: Type of sport

Levels of IV: football, baseball, and soccer

In Example 1, you would compare the attendance rates for students who played football, baseball, and soccer to see if a difference in attendance rates existed among the three sports.

EXAMPLE 2:

IV: Type of sport

Levels of IV: softball, basketball, and tennis

In Example 2, you would compare the attendance rates for students who played softball, basketball, and tennis to see if a difference in attendance rates existed among the three sports.

EXAMPLE 3:

IV: Type of sport

Levels of IV: cheerleading (yes we think it is a sport), rugby, and no sport

In Example 3, you would compare the attendance rates for students who were cheerleaders, played rugby, and did not belong to a sports team at all to see if a difference in attendance rates existed among the three. (Note: These three examples are not the only possibilities. There are many other different types of sports that you could have listed as levels of your independent variable and been correct.) In addition, although we only use three sports per example, you can have more than three levels of an independent variable. That choice is up to you and the ultimate goals of your study. So, how did you do?

SECTION SUMMARY

- An *independent variable* is the variable being manipulated in a study. It is believed to produce a change in the dependent variable (pp. 124–125).
- *Levels of the independent variable* are the number of conditions in an independent variable. All independent variables will have at least two conditions (i.e., the presence of a treatment and the absence of a treatment). However, an independent variable can have as many conditions as is necessary for the particular study you are conducting (pp. 124–128).
- A *dependent variable* is the variable being measured or observed for a change in a study. It is believed to change due to the impact of the independent variable (pp. 125–127).

MEASURING THE DEPENDENT VARIABLE AND NUMBER OF DEPENDENT VARIABLES

Universities across the country offer Supplemental Instruction (SI) for many historically difficult general education courses. SI is a program where a junior or senior student serves as a teaching assistant for an introductory level course by attending class regularly and holding study sessions outside of class time for students in the course. We both participated in this program a few years ago along with about 10 other faculty members. When we looked at the results, John had the most students who attend SI study sessions outside of class. As an SI program, we wanted to better understand how John was promoting SI to his students so we could do the same thing in the other classes. We could measure the way John's students responded to his promoting of SI (the dependent variable) in numerous ways. In other words, we were faced with a choice since there are different types of measures for a dependent variable. When conducting research, you too will be faced with this same choice in measuring your dependent variable. Measures of a dependent variable fall into one of the four groups: behavioral measures, attitudinal measures, cognitive measures, and physiological measures.

The first type of measure we have already mentioned. We could measure students' behavior, which would be called a **behavioral measure**. Behavioral measures focus on actions which are done or reported by a participant in a study. In this example, the behavioral measure would be the number of students who attended SI sessions outside of class. This measure could be based on actual attendance records (which it was in this study) or by asking participants to report their attendance for these sessions.

Another type of measure that we could take is an **attitudinal measure**. Attitudinal measures examine a person's belief, disposition, or feelings about a topic. In the SI example, we could survey the class to see if they had a positive or negative attitude (feeling) toward the use of the SI program. It is probably the case that John's students held a more positive (or favorable) attitude toward the SI program than students in other classes.

The third type of measure is a **cognitive measure**. Cognitive measures focus on a person's knowledge or mental ability (i.e., IQ testing). For the SI example, we could easily examine a cognitive measure. It could be the case that John's students knew more about the SI program. For example, his students may have known more facts about the program including on what days the outside study sessions met, where the outside study sessions met, and by how much attending SI sessions improved their exam grades.

Finally, we could measure the way John's students responded to how he promoted SI by taking a **physiological measure**. Physiological measures examine biological changes in a participant. It is possible that John's students were less stressed (lower heart rates, slower rates of breathing) at the idea of attending SI than students in other classes. Or, it could have been the case that his students were more focused during the SI session (less body movement) than in other classes.

We used this example to introduce and illustrate that when measuring a dependent variable there are many types of measures, such as behavioral, attitudinal, cognitive, and physiological that you can utilize. Let's look at another example on types of measures. Recently, we conducted research on how the social context of an audience influences perceptions of humor for racial jokes. Specifically, we wanted

Behavioral Measure:
A measure to investigate a person's behaviors.

Attitudinal Measure:
A measure assessing a person's attitudes to the topic.

Cognitive Measure:
A measure of one's mental ability or knowledge of a topic.

Physiological Measure:
Measures that are biological in nature (heart rate, pulse, blood pressure, etc.).

to know how the racial makeup of the audience influenced whether or not a racial joke is perceived to be humorous. For example, we had participants watch an African American comedian (e.g., Dave Chapelle) perform jokes about race relations and varied whether the audience is of mixed race, all Caucasian, or all African American. Next, we had participants watch a Caucasian comedian (e.g., Ralphie May) perform jokes about race relations and varied whether the audience is of mixed race, all Caucasian, or all African American. How could we measure perceptions of humor using behavioral, attitudinal, cognitive, and physiological measures?

For a behavioral measure, we could look to see if the participant laughed at the jokes in each kind of audience situation. For an attitudinal measure, we could see if the participant reported liking or not liking the comedian. We could measure the participant's knowledge or understanding of the jokes for a cognitive measure. Finally, we could measure the participant's pulse rate for a physiological measure while watching each comedian.

YOU TRY IT!

We want you to think of examples using behavioral, attitudinal, cognitive, and physiological measures. Pretend that you put together a 15-minute video presentation that highlights the benefits of attending a public college or university. You show this video to parents of high-school students. You want to measure if this video influences viewers' (i.e., parents) perceptions of public universities. How could you measure viewers' perceptions in each of the following ways: behavioral, attitudinal, cognitive, and physiological? After you have generated examples for each, take a look at our answers below.

ANSWERS

There are many possible answers to this question. Below, we have included some examples that we developed that could be used. However, remember this list is not exhaustive and you may have come up with something different.

a. **Behavioral measure:** One type of behavioral measure would be following up with viewers a few months later to see if they had requested information from a public university. Another type of behavioral measure would be following up with the viewers to see if their son or daughter had applied to or was now attending a public university.

b. **Attitudinal measure:** Measuring viewers' willingness to attend a public university themselves would be one type of attitudinal measure. A second type of attitudinal measure would be measuring viewers' willingness to send their son or daughter to a public university.

c. **Cognitive measure:** Measuring viewers' knowledge about facts related to public universities (e.g., average cost, faculty to student ratio, and resources available) would be an example of a cognitive measure.

d. **Physiological measure:** You could measure parents' biological response (e.g., heart rate, pulse) after having them imagine their child was attending a public university.

Again, these are just a few examples. You may have come up with other answers that were equally correct. If you are unsure about your answer, be sure to ask your professor.

In addition to the different types of measures (i.e., behavioral, attitudinal, cognitive, and physiological), the way you asses each can vary immensely based on your end goal for a study. Therefore, we want to mention some of the most popular assessments for a measure: percent correct, frequency of responding, and degree of response. Let's look at an example of each type of assessment method.

Percent Correct: In the example of SI from earlier section, we could assess what percentage of John's students were correct in knowing the days of the week study sessions were held on and the location. We could compare the percentage of students who were correct in John's class to the percentage of students who were correct about this same information in other classes. While this is a cognitive measure, we are assessing it using a percentage.

Frequency of Responding: In the humor research example above, we could assess how many of the participants responded to the comedians by laughing. We could classify this further by looking at the number of chuckles compared to the number of smiles. This would allow us to then compare the frequency of laughing across the audience conditions to determine if the racial makeup of the audience influences rates of laughing.

Degree of Response: In the humor research example above, we could assess how hard the participants laughed at the jokes. Specifically, we could assess the intensity of each laugh or the degree of body movement as a result of laughing. We could then compare how hard people laughed at the jokes across the audience conditions to determine if the racial makeup of the audience influences degree of laughing.

Before we move on to operational definitions, we want to mention a few more considerations about dependent variables. Similar to the levels of independent variables, you might be wondering how many dependent variables you should have. Again, there is not a magical number of dependent variables for a study. However, it can be beneficial to have more than one dependent variable. **Multiple dependent variables** allow you to see if you have converging results on a topic (remember this back from Chapter 4?). In addition to thinking about the number of dependent variables, you should also be cautious in selecting the difficulty level of the dependent variables. Sometimes, the task is too difficult for people to complete, causing scores to pile up at the bottom. If scores pile up at the bottom of the dependent variable, you will not be able to see the effect of the independent variable. This is known as a **floor effect**. The opposite can also happen. The task can be too easy causing results to pile up at the top of the distribution. This is known as a **ceiling effect.** One way to prevent floor and ceiling effects is to have your friend complete the task and give feedback on the difficulty level.

Jenn had a group of students in Iowa looking at how memories for traumatic events change over time. Her students surveyed people over their memories for the events surrounding Hurricane Katrina immediately after the event and a few weeks later. However, the questions on the survey were so difficult to answer that nobody did well at all. The students were then unable to see how memories change over time because people scored equally poorly on the task immediately after the event and a few weeks later. Therefore, we often recommend using preexisting scales because properties (validity and reliability) for these scales have already been established.

Percent Correct:
Average of correct responses to overall responses represented as a percentage.

Frequency of Responding:
A sum of the number of times a person/group responds to a question.

Degree of Response:
A measure of intensity of a response.

Multiple Dependent Variables: Most studies have more than one dependent variable. Having multiple dependent variables increases the amount of information collected.

Floor Effect: When scores fall primarily at the lower range of a response option.

Ceiling Effect: When scores fall primarily at the upper range of a response option.

© Pattie Steib, 2014. Used under license from Shutterstock, Inc.

QUESTION

Take a look at Figures 7.1 and 7.2. In these figures, we have fictitious grade distributions for a General Psychology class and an upper-level Physiological Psychology class. Can you identify which figure illustrates the floor effect and which illustrates the ceiling effect?

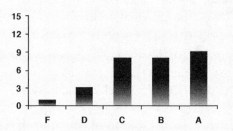

Figure 7.1   General Psychology   **Figure 7.2**   Physiological Psychology

ANSWER

Figure 7.2 of the upper-level Physiological Psychology class illustrates the floor effect. This is because the scores piled up at the bottom of the distribution, which in this case is the final grade. On the other hand, Figure 7.1 illustrates a ceiling effect with scores clustered at the top of the distribution.

SECTION SUMMARY

- The dependent variable can be measured in four different ways (pp. 128–130).
    - *Behavioral measures* are those measures that assess an individual's behavior (p. 129).
    - *Attitudinal measures* are those measures that assess an individual's attitudes toward the research topic of interest (p. 129).
    - *Cognitive measures* assess an individual's mental ability (p. 129).
    - *Physiological measures* are used to gather information that is biological in nature (p. 129).
- There are several different ways in which you can assess your dependent variable (pp. 130–131).
    - *Percent correct* is an average of correct responses to overall responses represented as a percentage (p. 131).
    - *Frequency of response* is a sum of the number of times a person or group responds to a question (p. 131).
    - *Degree of response* is a measure of the intensity of the response an individual has to a question (p. 131).

- For any study, most researchers use more than one dependent variable. This is done to collect more information as to the effect of the independent variable (p. 131).
- Sometimes, dependent variables that are used can experience either a ceiling or floor effect. A *ceiling effect* occurs when responses primarily fall on the upper limit of a response option. A *floor effect* is the opposite, in that scores primarily fall on the lower range of a response option (pp. 131–132).

OPERATIONAL DEFINITIONS

Do you watch any animated TV shows? If so, which one is your favorite? We admit that we have many favorites such as *Family Guy, American Dad,* and *Archer.* We have a fun assignment for you. Pick your favorite animated TV show and go watch it for 15 minutes. You read that correctly. We want you to go watch TV. While you are watching this 15 minutes worth of TV, take a piece of paper and pen with you and count the number of violent acts that you see. What you determine to be a violent act is up to you. We will be here when you get back.

So, how many violent acts did you find in the 15 minutes' worth of TV that you viewed? Do you think that we would have found the same number of violent acts if we were watching the TV show with you? We doubt it. But, why would we not have counted the same number of violent acts as you? Probably because we all have different definitions of a violent act. For example, if watching *Family Guy*, we would count Stewie tripping Brain as he goes down the stairs as a violent act. But you might not. This is because everybody has their own definition of violence.

It is important when we conduct research or read about research findings of others that we know how the variables are being operationally defined. Think about the following example. We read an article that reports a positive relationship between childhood aggression and viewing violent cartoons. Of course, we would want to know more about these results because we have two children who watch cartoons on weekends. Specifically, we would want to know what is meant by "violent cartoons." How was violence defined and measured? What is meant by childhood aggression? How was it defined and measured? In both these cases, we want to know the operational definitions of the variables. Sometimes, variables can be very broad in scope. Violence and aggression are two examples of broad variables that could encompass many different meanings. By knowing the **operational definition**, we can make a broad concept more specific.

> **Operational Definition:** Defines how a concept or idea will be measured.

The point is not to define the concept. Rather, the purpose of the operational definition is to define how the concept is measured. Simply, the intent of an operational definition is to get everyone in your study to think about the concept similarly, thereby making it easier to measure. Think back to the example using *Family Guy.* If we were to do this study, we would not define violence. As we said, everyone defines violence differently. Instead, we would look to clarify for participants what is considered a violent act for the purposes of the study. We could tell people those acts which involve at least some level of bloodshed are considered violent acts. This would narrow down the broad concept making it more specific so that participants are all on the same page. This will not only allow for better comparisons amongst participants but also provide others opportunity to replicate and extend research findings due to all participants using a concept similarly.

Sometimes, it is not easy to operationally define a variable. It may take time to think about what is exactly being manipulated or measured. However, it is important you do not skip over defining your variables. Without defining your variables, it will be very difficult to interpret results. Similarly, be sure to look for operational definitions of variables when you read research. In some cases, you may agree with the definitions the authors used, and in other cases, you may not. This will help you in interpreting the results.

Here is an example. Consider the following statement: College classroom performance can be increased by attending study sessions. You would want to know how "college classroom performance" and "study sessions" are operationally defined before you start investing time in attending the study sessions. What if it turns out that "college classroom performance" is defined as the number of times students participate in classroom discussions? Would you be willing to attend study sessions to increase your participation in discussions? Maybe not. But what if "college classroom performance" was defined as overall grade point average? Would you be willing to attend study sessions to increase your overall grade point average? The purpose of this example is to illustrate the importance of operational definitions. By knowing what is meant by "college classroom performance," you can determine how you will interpret the results.

SECTION SUMMARY

- In order to properly assess your variables, you must make sure that they are properly defined. An operational definition is used to define how a concept or idea will be measured (pp. 133–134).

TYPES OF SCALES

We would like for you to read the scenario below and tell us what you would do if you were in this situation.

Imagine that the United States is preparing for the outbreak of an unusual Asian disease, which is expected to kill 600 people. Two alternative programs to combat the disease have been proposed. Assume the exact scientific estimates of the consequences of the program are as follows:

- If Program A is adopted, 200 people will be saved.
- If Program B is adopted, there is a one-third probability that 600 people will be saved and a two-thirds probability that none will be saved.

Which program would you select? Would you select Program A or Program B? This scenario is from research conducted by Tversky and Kahneman (1981) and is a very famous study in cognitive psychology. They found that most people selected Program A (72% of participants) over Program B (28% of participants). The results support the idea that participants are risk averse. In other words, participants will select the for-sure option of Program A that saves 200 lives over the gamble of Program B. Did your choice of program indicate that you preferred the sure bet to the gamble?

The purpose of this example is to get you thinking about how researchers measure variables. Tversky and Kahneman (1981) decided to measure people's likelihood of selecting a program by having them essentially say "yes" or "no." By having participants say yes or no to the programs, they were using a nominal scale. A **nominal scale** is a scale used when participants select options that name things. Examples of nominal scales include ethnicity, religion, sex, and school classification. In all of these examples, the variable being measured is a category or name. For example, your school classification can be freshman, sophomore, junior, or senior,

© Doug James, 2014. Used under license from Shutterstock, Inc.

or your sex can be male or female. Nominal scales are beneficial when you want to gather information on the percentage of people who belong to, or who selected, a particular option (as Tversky and Kahneman did). However, it should be noted that there are limits to the type of statistical procedures that can be conducted with nominal scales, and therefore in these cases another scale should be selected (see a statistics book for more information).

Ordinal scales put items in order. Class rankings are examples of ordinal data. When you graduated from high school, you probably had a valedictorian and salutatorian. These were the students with the highest and second-highest grade point averages, respectively. When we were in graduate school, we were also ranked. At the end of every semester, we were given a class rank (e.g., 3rd out of 12) to let us know where we stood in relation to other graduate students in our class. A final example is the result of a National Association for Stock Car Auto Racing (NASCAR) race. It is typically reported which driver came in first, second, third, and so on. In Tversky and Kahneman's research, they could have used an ordinal scale instead of a nominal scale. Specifically, they could have changed the instructions and asked participants to rank their preferences by indicating their first choice and second choice. (Note: Ordinal scales are typically used when there are more than two items to rate. We are only using this two-item scenario to carry out the example from the beginning of this section and to illustrate that changing how the question is worded will change the type of scale you are using.)

Although ordinal scales provide information as to the order of preference, it does have drawbacks. Specifically, it does not tell you how far apart the options are or the distance between the options. For example, if John tells Jenn that Dale Earnhardt Jr. won the NASCAR race and Tony Stewart came in second, Jenn does not know by how much Dale Earnhardt Jr. won the race. Was it a close race or did Dale Earnhardt Jr. win by a good distance? Similarly, what does a ranking of 3rd out of 12 in a graduate course really mean? If the student ranked 3rd has a final course grade of 96% and the student ranked 10th has a final course grade of 93%, then there is not much difference between them. Thus, while ordinal scales can provide information on individuals' ranking, they do not provide information on the distance between the rankings. Another drawback is that similar to a nominal scale, the type of analysis that can be conducted with an ordinal scale is somewhat limited.

Nominal Scale:
Classification of data into one of the two or more categories.

Ordinal Scale:
Classification of data into an order or rank of magnitude.

Interval scales measure a variable on a scale assuming equal distance between the numbers. For example, each semester you probably complete evaluations about the courses for which you are currently enrolled. Students at our university do this too. In particular, students are asked to rate professors on a number of questions using a scale that goes from 1 to 5, where 1 is completely disagree and 5 is completely agree. In this example, the distance between 1 and 2 is assumed to be equal to the distance between 3 and 4, and so on. Likewise, in Tversky and Kahneman's research, they could have used an interval scale instead of a nominal scale. Specifically, they could have changed the instructions and asked participants to rate how likely they would be to adopt each program ranging from 1 (not very likely to adopt) to 100 (very likely to adopt).

A large percentage of psychological research uses interval scales because it lends itself to more advanced statistical procedures than nominal and ordinal scales. Yet, interval scales do not have a true zero value to represent the absence of a variable. Take temperature for example. Temperature is an interval scale. It has assumed equal distance between numbers. There is also zero degree on the temperature scale. However, zero degree in temperature does not represent an absence of temperature. In fact, we know after living in the Midwest that zero degree is very cold. Thus, the number zero is not representing the true amount of zero. Rather, the number zero is just an arbitrary number on the scale. If the variable you are measuring has a true zero value, the variable would use a ratio scale.

A **ratio scale** not only assumes equal distances between the numbers on the scale but also has a true zero value. We like to give the following example of how many time per week you exercise. The answer to the question could, in fact, be zero and indicate an absence of working out. Because there is a true zero, a person who works out eight times per week is working out twice as much as a person who works out four times per week. Can you think of how Tversky and Kahneman could have used a ratio scale? Remember, to use a ratio scale, an equal distance is assumed and an absolute zero is possible. Tversky and Kahneman could have a scale that ranges from 0 to 100, where 0 is equal to "would not adopt at all" and 100 is equal to "would definitely adopt" for each option.

YOU TRY IT!

We want you to practice writing questions and varying the response scales. First, here is a review of the types of scales.

> Nominal scales = name things, put into a category
> Ordinal scales = put things in order
> Interval scales = equal intervals
> Ratio scales = equal intervals, true zero value

PRACTICE 1

For Practice Problem 1, we will use the research question, "Are students satisfied with the advising process on their campus?" How could you measure student satisfaction with advising using a *nominal scale*?

ANSWER

You could ask students, "Are you satisfied with the advising you receive?" and students could respond "yes" or "no." We could then look at the percentage of students who responded yes and no. You might have a slightly different answer from ours and that is perfectly acceptable. Maybe you asked students, "Are you satisfied or not satisfied with the advising that you receive?" and students could respond "satisfied" or "not satisfied." In trying to determine if your answer is correct, just be sure that the way you asked the questions resulted in students responding on a scale that named something or put them into a category.

PRACTICE 2

For Practice Problem 2, we will use the research question, "What type of foods do college students prefer?" You are interested in the following types of food: pizza, lasagna, steak, chicken, and seafood. How could you measure food preferences using an *ordinal scale*?

ANSWER

You could give students the list of foods (pizza, lasagna, steak, chicken, and seafood) and ask the students to rate the foods from their most favorite to their least favorite (or from their least favorite to their most favorite). This would provide us with a ranking of food preferences. But remember that this ordinal scale would not tell us how far apart the preferences were. So, for example, you would not know by how much the student preferred the most favorite food of pizza to the second favorite food of steak.

PRACTICE 3

For Practice Problem 3, we will use the research question, "To what extent, do people prefer salty snacks?" How could you measure snack preference on an interval scale?

ANSWER

You could ask people to rate on a scale from 1 to 7 (with 1 indicating "do not prefer" and 7 indicating "greatly prefer") what type of snack they prefer. This interval scale would assume equal distance between the 7 numbers on the scale.

To what degree do you prefer salty snacks?

Do Not Prefer 1 2 3 4 5 6 7 Greatly Prefer

PRACTICE 4

For Practice Problem 4, we will use the research question, "How often do college students read books other than those assigned in classes?"

ANSWER

You could ask students the number of nonclass related books they have read in the past month. It is possible that the students have read zero books, and therefore a true zero exists. In addition, you would be able to say that someone who has read 10 books has read twice as many as someone who has read 5 books.

How did you do? If you found this exercise to be a little difficult that is normal. Wording questions to use different types of scales is part of survey construction that takes practice. The following "Are You Equipped Now?" section will help you at identifying types of scales rather than constructing them. You should find this much easier.

SECTION SUMMARY

- The way in which researchers measure their variables is important. There are four types of scales that can be used to properly measure a dependent variable (pp. 134–138):

- A *nominal scale* is used when data are classified into one of two or more categories (p. 135).

- An *ordinal scale* is used when data are classified into an order or rank of magnitude (p. 135).

- An *interval scale* is used when data are classified on a scale that assumes equal distance between numbers (p. 136).

- A *ratio scale* is used when data are classified on a scale that assumes equal distance and has a true zero value (p. 135).

ARE YOU EQUIPPED NOW?

In the early part of 2000, we began collecting data on the Olympics. Specifically, we took the approach of evaluating the amount of time people spent watching the Olympics, where they watched the Olympics, with whom they watched the Olympics, and what people got out of watching the Olympics. In order to investigate this topic and collect exploratory data, we designed a survey. Below is a list of questions directly from that survey for the Summer Olympics. Try and determine the type of data being collected from each question. In other words, is the scale being used nominal, ordinal, interval, or ratio?

1. What time of day did you primarily watch the Olympic Games?
   a. Morning   b. Afternoon   c. Evening   d. Late night

2. In general, where did you most often watch the Olympic Games?
   a. Your home
   b. Someone else's house
   c. Bar/Restaurant
   d. Other, please indicate _____

3. Among those who watched the sporting event with you, was at least one family member present?
   a. Yes   b. No

4. The events that I wanted to watch/see **should** have been covered more:

Strongly agree   1   2   3   4   5   6   7   Strongly disagree

5. I would like to have seen more coverage of **men's** sports:

Strongly agree   1   2   3   4   5   6   7   Strongly disagree

6. I would like to have seen more coverage of **women's** sports:

Strongly agree   1   2   3   4   5   6   7   Strongly disagree

7. Estimate the percentage of broadcasting time in Olympic coverage for each below (total equaling 100%):

_____ Opening ceremony/Closing ceremony

_____ Actual coverage of sporting event

_____ Summaries and highlights of events and competitions

_____ Commentator/analysis of sporting events

_____ Human interest stories about athletes

_____ Background stories about participating countries

_____ Background stories about past Olympics

_____ Stories about Australia and specific Olympic sites

8. Approximately how many hours of the Olympic coverage did you watch: _____

9. Take a moment to think about the events you watched. In the first column, check all those events that you watched during the Olympics. After completing that, go back and rank the ones that you checked; assign or give a rank of 1 for the event you most enjoyed.

☑	Rank		☑	Rank	
____	____	Men's Archery	____	____	Men's Sailing
____	____	Women's Archery	____	____	Women's Sailing
____	____	Men's Badminton	____	____	Men's Shooting
____	____	Women's Badminton	____	____	Women's Shooting
____	____	Baseball	____	____	Men's Soccer
____	____	Men's Basketball	____	____	Women's Soccer
____	____	Women's Basketball	____	____	Softball
____	____	Boxing	____	____	Men's Swimming
____	____	Men's Canoeing	____	____	Women's Swimming
____	____	Women's Canoeing	____	____	Men's Table Tennis
____	____	Closing Ceremony	____	____	Women's Table Tennis
____	____	Men's Cycling	____	____	Men's Tennis
____	____	Women's Cycling	____	____	Women's Tennis
____	____	Men's Diving	____	____	Men's Track and Field
____	____	Women's Diving	____	____	Women's Track and Field

	Men's Gymnastics	____ ____	Men's Triathlon
____ ____ Men's Gymnastics		____ ____	Men's Triathlon
____ ____ Women's Gymnastics		____ ____	Women's Triathlon
____ ____ Opening Ceremony		____ ____	Men's Volleyball
____ ____ Men's Rowing		____ ____	Women's Volleyball
____ ____ Women's Rowing			

ANSWERS

1–3

These questions all rely on a nominal scale. Each one of the questions asks participants to put themselves into a category. Whether that category is yes/no or asks about location of watching the Olympics with a predefined set of responses, each is a selected category.

4–6

The next three questions are all interval data. Here, participants are to rate themselves along a predetermined scale from 1 to 7. This scale assumes that between each number there is equal distance in value.

7–8

These two questions are ratio-scale questions. The participants can answer with any value they choose, even a zero value. It is the fact that this scale can have a true zero value that makes it a ratio scale.

9

The final question is both ordinal and nominal in scale. The participants are asked to select all that apply to them, which is a nominal scale (i.e., selecting yes or no). However, what makes the scale ordinal is the rank order of those selections that participants are asked to make. By putting a ranking to their data participants are using an ordinal scale.

CHAPTER SUMMARY

- An *independent variable* is the variable in a study that you are manipulating. You are manipulating this variable because you believe it will cause a change in the participant (pp. 124–125).

- The *levels of an independent variable* is the number of conditions that are being manipulated. All independent variables will have at least two levels. For example, the first level could be the presence of a manipulation or treatment. The second level could be the absence of a manipulation or treatment. Of course, an independent variable can have more than two levels, but it should always have at least two (pp. 124–128).

- A *dependent variable* is the variable that is being measured in a study. This is the variable that the researcher believes will change in response to the independent variable (pp. 125–127).
- Four different types of dependent variables are commonly used in psychology. The four types are behavioral measures, attitudinal measures, cognitive measures, and physiological measures. Depending on your design, you can use only one or all of these measures (pp. 128–130).
  - *Behavioral measures* are those measures that assess an individual's behavior (p. 129).
  - *Attitudinal measures* are those measures that assess an individual's attitudes toward the topic (p. 129).
  - *Cognitive measures* assess an individual's mental ability (p. 129).
  - *Physiological measures* are used to gather information that is biological in nature such as blood pressure, pulse, and so on (p. 129).
- In addition to deciding on the type of dependent variable that you will collect, you must also decide how you are going to assess each measure. Below are the three most common ways a dependent variable is assessed (pp. 130–131).
  - *Percent correct* is an average of correct response to overall responses represented as a percentage (p. 131).
  - *Frequency of response* is a sum of the number of times a person or group responds to a question (p. 131).
  - *Degree of response* is a measure of the intensity of the response an individual has to a question (p. 131).
- Good research will assess more than one dependent variable. By collecting data on more than one measure, you will maximize the likelihood of detecting a difference between the levels of your independent variable (pp. 131–132).
- In order to properly assess your variables, you must make sure that they are adequately defined. An *operational definition* is used to define how a concept or idea will be measured. It does not define the concept or idea but rather how it will be assessed (pp. 133–134).
- Once you have decided on the measure you will be taking and the way you want to assess each, you have to decide on the type of scale you want to use.
- There are four types of scales that can be used. Each collects information on a dependent variable in a different way (pp. 134–138). As a researcher, you must decide which scale is appropriate for your study.
  - A *nominal scale* is used when data are classified into one of the two or more categories (p. 135).
  - An *ordinal scale* is used when data are classified into an order or rank of magnitude (p. 135).
  - An *interval scale* is used when data are classified on a scale that assumes equal distance between numbers (p. 136).
  - A *ratio scale* is used when data are classified on a scale that assumes equal distance and a true zero value (p. 136).

- ## Goal 2. Scientific Inquiry and Critical Thinking

  You will demonstrate scientific reasoning and problem solving, including effective research methods.

  Sections Covered: Are You Equipped?, Selecting the Levels of Independent Variables, Measuring the Dependent Variables and Number of Dependent Variables, Operational Definitions, Types of Scales, Are You Equipped Now?

  Explanation of the Goal: In this chapter, we added to our understanding of the basic characteristics of the science of psychology by addressing the topic of selecting the levels of the independent variables. Next, we examined research methods used by psychologists. In doing so, we first listed how the dependent variables could be measured by behavioral, attitudinal, cognitive, and physiological means. Second, we covered the different ways to assess the dependent variables such as percent correct, frequency of responding, and degree of response and how the level of difficulty should be appropriate to avoid floor and ceiling effects. The importance of operational definitions as well as the types of scales (i.e., ordinal, nominal, interval, and ratio) concluded the chapter.

  Sections Covered: Are You Equipped?, Selecting the Levels of Independent Variables, Measuring the Dependent Variables and Number of Dependent Variables, Types of Scales, Are You Equipped Now?

  Explanation of the Goal: To help you enhance your critical thinking skills, you completed numerous exercises. In addition, to the "Are You Equipped" exercises at the beginning and the end of the chapter, you also completed "You Try It!" exercises for many of the sections in the chapter. These exercises required you to think critically as you selected the levels of an independent variable, generated ways to measure perceptions of parents after viewing a college recruitment video, and learned to write questions that have participants utilize the different types of psychological scales.

- ## Goal 3. Ethical and Social Responsibility in a Diverse World

  You will apply ethical standards to evaluate psychological science and practice and you will develop ethically and socially responsible behaviors for professional and personal settings in a landscape that involves increasing diversity.

  Sections Covered: Are You Equipped?, Selecting the Levels of Independent Variables, Measuring the Dependent Variables and Number of Dependent Variables, Operational Definitions, Types of Scales, Are You Equipped Now?

Explanation of the Goal: The material in this chapter can be applied easily to everyday life. In fact, we have used examples that apply to you and society in each section. It might not have surprised you that the psychological principles could be related to violence in cartoons, leadership styles, and factors that contribute to depression such as birth weight. However, you might have found it interesting that the material in the chapter could be applied to the Olympics, size of computer monitor, perceptions of humor, and results of a NASCAR race.

Sections Covered: Operational Definitions

Explanation of the Goal: Individual differences can influence beliefs, values, and interactions with others. In our discussion of operational definitions, we have illustrated how individual differences can influence the perception of violence. Thus, it is important as psychologists that we define how a concept or idea will be measured in a study.

• Goal 4. Communication

You will demonstrate competence in writing and in oral and interpersonal communication skills.

Sections Covered: Measuring the Dependent Variables and Number of Dependent Variables

Explanation of the Goal: APA recommends that students be able to communicate effectively in a variety of formats. Although we might typically think of communication in terms of oral and written forms, you will also need to be able to communicate and interpret quantitative visual aids accurately. To this end, you gained experience in interpreting graphical depictions of floor and ceiling effects. This skill will be important as a researcher in creating graphics to represent psychological findings and as a consumer in interpreting them.

Excerpts from APA Guidelines for the Undergraduate Psychology Major, Version 2.0, August 2013 *by the American Psychological Association. Copyright © 2013 by the American Psychological Association.*

CHAPTER 8

Selection and Assignment of Participants

CHAPTER OUTLINE

Are You Equipped?

Populations versus Samples

Probability Sampling Procedures

Nonprobability Sampling Procedures

Random Assignment to Conditions

Determining Sample Size

Power

Are You Equipped Now?

Chapter Summary

APA Learning Goals Linkage

ARE YOU EQUIPPED?

In 1963, Stanley Milgram published a research article in the *Journal of Abnormal and Social Psychology* that has become famous within the field of psychology. We are sure that you have heard about Milgram's research somewhere along the way, probably in General Psychology. Much discussion surrounding Milgram's research has focused on the question if the experiment was ethical to conduct. However, we are going to tell you about Milgram's research again. This time we want you to focus on how Milgram obtained participants for his experiment.

Danger
High voltage

© Pepj, 2014. Used under license from Shutterstock, Inc.

Milgram's research came from looking at how blind obedience can be destructive. Milgram reflected on the people killed in concentration camps by soldiers who were being obedient to an authority figure. Milgram wanted to study this obedience experimentally.

Milgram obtained his sample in the following way: "The subjects were 40 males between the ages of 20 and 50, drawn from New Haven and the surrounding communities. Subjects were obtained by a newspaper advertisement and direct mail solicitation." Participants who responded to the newspaper advertisement or the mail solicitation believed they were participating in an experiment on memory and learning.

Participants arrived two at a time. One participant was an individual obtained from the procedure described above and the other participant was actually a confederate involved in the research experiment who was a trained actor. Participants were told the researchers were investigating the role of punishment on learning. Participants drew from a hat to see who would be the teacher and who would be the student. However, the drawing was fixed so the true participant was always the teacher and the trained actor was always the learner. The learner was then strapped to an instrument believed to provide electric shock (in reality the learner never received any shocks). In the other room, the teacher faced an instrument allowing them to administer shock ranging from 15 to 450 volts. The teacher was instructed to give the student a shock for each incorrect response given and to increase the shock level for each subsequent mistake. Milgram wanted to see if participants would administer shock for incorrect responses and how many volts of electricity they would administer. Results indicated two-thirds of participants administered the full 450 volts! In addition, no participants refused to administer shock before 300 volts. As mentioned earlier, the learner did not receive any shocks. Rather, the trained actors played the teacher taped recorded response to each level of shock. Milgram reported that nobody could have predicted the obtained results. These results provide very interesting information as to human nature. As you are reading this chapter on how to obtain samples, think about what procedure Milgram used to obtain his sample. Also, consider the advantages and disadvantages of the sampling procedure Milgram utilized.

As you go through this chapter, we also want you to keep in mind how the material relates to the APA goals for psychology majors. Specifically, this chapter will address the following goals:

- **Goal 1. Knowledge Base in Psychology**

  You will demonstrate fundamental knowledge and comprehension of the major concepts, theoretical perspectives, historical trends, and empirical findings to discuss how psychological principles apply to behavioral problems.

- **Goal 2. Scientific Inquiry and Critical Thinking**

  You will demonstrate scientific reasoning and problem solving, including effective research methods.

- **Goal 3. Ethical and Social Responsibility in a Diverse World**

  You will apply ethical standards to evaluate psychological science and practice and you will develop ethically and socially responsible behaviors for professional and personal settings in a landscape that involves increasing diversity.

- **Goal 4. Communication**

  You will demonstrate competence in writing and in oral and interpersonal communication skills.

POPULATION VERSUS SAMPLE

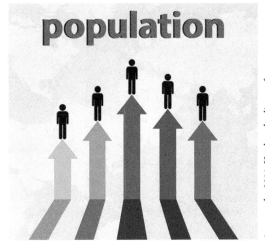

© sosogulz, 2014. Used under license from Shutterstock, Inc.

When we conduct research, we are interested in studying **populations** of people. We might want to know how men and women best lose weight or how children respond to different types of parenting styles. In these examples, we are interested in different populations. In the first example, men and women are the populations of interest. In the second example, children are the population of interest. So, if we were to try to answer these research questions, how would we go about testing the population? Would it be possible to test all people belonging to the population? In other words, could we logistically survey *all* men and women or *all* children? Probably not. However, we can still determine answers to the research questions by surveying a sample of the population. A **sample** is a group of people representative of the population who are selected to participate in the research.

PROBABILITY SAMPLING PROCEDURES

There are many different sampling techniques or ways to go about selecting individuals from the population. The two main procedures are probability sampling and nonprobability sampling. With a **probability sampling procedure**, individuals from the population have a known probability (or chance) of being selected. We will discuss the use of four types of probability sampling procedures: simple, systematic, stratified, and cluster. With a nonprobability sampling procedure, each individual does not have a known chance of being selected to participate. Examples of nonprobability sampling procedure include: convenience, snowballing, and quota. To better understand probability sampling procedures, consider the following example.

Parking is a hot topic on our campus. It feels as though every student complains about the parking situation and lack of spaces available. It causes students to be late for class and puts them in a bad mood. What if our university decided to better understand students' attitudes toward the parking situation? The population of interest would be all university students who have parking permits (the university would not be interested in how students who are parking without registered permits feel). In this situation, we would have a list of individuals in the population and therefore a probability sampling technique could be used. We could get a list from the controller's office of students in our population.

If we used a **simple probability sampling** procedure, each individual with a registered parking pass would have an equal probability of being selected to complete the study. We would then use an unbiased method of selecting people from the list. This could be putting all the names in a hat and randomly drawing out 100 names. We could also use a random number table to select individuals from the list. A random number table is a table of numbers usually produced by a computer program. Numbers are presented in rows and columns. In a random number table, the numbers are always random no matter whether you view them as a row, column, or diagonally. Thus, the numbers listed have no symmetrical or discernable order.

Population: The entire group of individuals in which you are interested in studying.

Sample: A smaller group of individuals that is representative of the larger population.

Probability Sampling Procedure: A procedure where individuals from the population have a known probability (or chance) of being selected for a study.

© Rob Wilson, 2014. Used under license from Shutterstock, Inc.

© James Steidl, 2014. Used under license from Shutterstock, Inc.

In order to use a random number table, you would give all individuals a number ranging from 1 to the total number of participants you have in your population. Next, you would pick a random spot on the table and select respondents with matching numbers from the table. Therefore, if you had started at Column F, Row 6 from Table 8.1, you would begin by selecting the 24th individual in your population for inclusion in your study. You would continue this process until you have a large enough sample. This is just one example of how the table can be used. Many computer programs (such as Excel or SPSS) can produce a table for use in a given experiment.

By any of these methods, each student with a registered parking pass (the population of interest) is equally likely to be selected to participate in the study. However, would it be an unbiased method to have the first 100 people who paid for parking permits this academic year to be our sample? Ask yourself, if we use only the first 100 students, then do all students have an equal chance of being selected? The answer is no. Taking the first 100 students who get parking permits to be the sample is a **biased sample**. A biased sample may produce different results. This is because students who are the first ones to buy their parking permits are probably also the ones who will arrive to campus early everyday to ensure a good parking spot. Thus, the students arriving early and getting good parking spots would not be representative of all students and their parking experiences.

Simple Probability Sampling: All individuals in a population have an equal probability of being selected.

Biased Sample: A sample in which not everyone in the population has an equal or known chance of being selected.

Sampling with Replacement: Individuals are selected one at a time with each individual being replaced before the next is sampled. Here, each selection has exactly the same probability of being selected.

Sampling without Replacement: Individuals are selected and are not replaced before the next is sampled. Here, the probability of being selected changes with each removal.

TABLE 8.1   Random Number Table Created in Excel.

		A	B	C	D	E	F	G	H	I	J
	Column										
	1	394	904	979	468	121	380	438	147	197	592
	2	666	297	139	512	989	308	478	680	782	834
	3	402	792	805	885	102	538	22	585	519	925
	4	413	371	472	788	268	537	70	550	669	473
Row	**5**	38	641	24	18	409	815	837	535	568	259
	6	1	820	702	456	695	24	956	839	543	240
	7	293	535	128	498	159	503	651	354	530	713
	8	405	577	208	783	632	183	294	138	647	134
	9	911	255	141	383	688	923	739	749	557	782
	10	816	561	818	312	267	748	335	760	437	373

From *Statistical Power Analysis for the Behavioral Sciences* by Jacob Cohen. Copyright © 1988 by Taylor & Francis. Reprinted by permission.

With the simple probability sampling procedure, we can sample with replacement or without replacement. Think back to the method of putting names in a hat. After we draw out the first name, we can either put the name back in the hat before drawing the second name (with replacement) or put the name to the side and not put it back in the hat (without replacement). If you use the simple probability **sampling procedure with replacement**, it is possible the same person could be selected more than once. However, each person in the population would have an equal probability of being selected. If you **sampled without replacement**, then the probability of being selected would change with the removal of each individual.

Researchers can decide if it is acceptable for a person to be selected more than once depending on the nature of the study.

Another type of probability sampling is **systematic probability sampling**. In this technique, we would select individuals from a list in a systematic manner (i.e., selecting every *k*th person). For example, we would select every 10th person on the list. This would give us a sample of 600 students (assuming there are 6,000 students in the population). If we wanted a smaller sample, we could select every 100th person on the list. This would give us a sample of 60 students. Systematic sampling gives us an unbiased sample in an efficient manner.

An additional type of probability sampling procedure is stratified. In a **stratified probability sampling** procedure, you begin by identifying subgroups (or strata) and then randomly sample from the subgroups. When it comes to the issue of parking on a college campus, can you think of subgroups of students whose membership to the group might influence their attitudes toward parking? We can think of a few important subgroups to consider. The first subgroup is day students (students who attend classes primarily during the day) and the second subgroup is night students (students who attend classes primarily at night). At least on our campus, day students have a much more difficult time finding parking spaces than night students. Therefore, we might want to sample from these subgroups in such a way that the numbers in the subgroup reflect the numbers in the population. In other words, if our population is composed of 80% day students and 20% night students, then our sample should be of a similar composition. We would identify our subgroups of day and night students and sample from each subgroup in an unbiased manner. Other subgroups that might be important to identify are students who live on-campus and students who live off-campus. It might be the case that students who live on-campus do not have problems with parking and students who live off-campus do have problems with parking. If you selected to use these subgroups, you would identify the students in each subgroup and sample in an unbiased manner from each.

Cluster sampling is the last type of probability sampling. In a cluster procedure, we would identify naturally occurring clusters of individuals within a population. Then, we would randomly select individuals from the clusters of individuals to be included in the sample. In our study on students' attitudes toward parking on campus, we could identify many clusters of students: for example, those who park on the north side of campus and the south side of campus. We would need to be sure that the same student does not participate twice. Specifically, it could occur that one student varies his or her parking pattern and parks on both the north and the south side of campus given one's classes on a particular day. In this case, we would want this student to only participate one time.

It is important to note that following these unbiased sampling procedures described previously does not guarantee an unbiased sample. In other words, an unbiased sampling procedure has the possibility of producing a biased sample. However, this possibility is highly unlikely. In addition, the benefit of using a random sampling technique or procedure increases the external validity of the design.

© stoonn, 2014. Used under license from Shutterstock, Inc.

Systematic Probability Sampling: Random sampling in which a systematic approach is used.

Stratified Probability Sampling: A probability sampling technique where a researcher begins by identifying subgroups (or strata) and then randomly samples from each subgroup.

Cluster Sampling: Involves identifying naturally occurring clusters of individuals from the population to select from to be included in the sample.

It is time for you to practice the four types of probability sampling procedures (i.e., simple, systematic, stratified, and cluster) using the following example. **HeyTell®** is an app for smart phones allowing users to send voice messages to friends and family instantly. HeyTell® thus allows you to send text messages without typing the message and this can be faster and safer than the traditional text message. HeyTell® wants to measure customer satisfaction with the product for those individuals with registered accounts. They are particularly interested in how frequently the app is used by specific age groups (young adults and adults) and in different areas of the country (rural and urban). We want you to explain how you would sample the population of all customers with each of the four types of probability sampling procedures. You try it and then compare your results with our answers below.

Simple

If we were to use a simple probability sampling procedure, we would need a list of all customers with a registered HeyTell® account. We could then use a random number table or put all the names in a box and draw names. This would give us our sample of customers selected from the population in an unbiased manner.

Systematic

In a systematic sampling procedure, we would select participants for the sample in a systematic way. One way would be to get an alphabetical list of all registered customers and select every 50th customer on the list.

Stratified

The two target age groups (young adults and adults) could be our subgroups. We would need a list of customers in each age group and then we would randomly select customers from each of the two groups.

Cluster

Finally, with a cluster procedure, we would identify naturally occurring groups in the population. We could identify clusters of customers such as those who live in different areas of the county, rural and urban. As before, we would want to be sure that no single customer participated more than once.

Before moving on to the topic of nonprobability sample procedures, we want to try one more example of probability sampling procedures with you. Our local obstetrics and gynecology (OBGYN) office had received many complaints. The complaints were mainly about poor office organization and extremely long waits (which were especially undesired for the pregnant clients). The doctors decided to hire a new office manager, reorganize how the office was run on a day-to-day basis, and schedule office visits in a different fashion. For the purposes of this example, we want you to pretend the doctors want to find out how the clients are responding to this new system. The doctors do not have time to survey all their clients (the population of interest), so they decided to take a sample. The doctors are also interested in how the pregnant clients are responding to the changes because these clients compose a large percentage of their repeat business. How could the doctors take a simple, systematic, stratified, and cluster sample? When you have thought about each, compare your answers to ours below.

Simple

If we wanted to construct a sample using a simple probability procedure, we could get a list of all the clients and use a random method to select our sample from the population.

Systematic

For the systematic probability sample, we would take our alphabetical list and select the participants for the sample in a systematic (regular and methodical) manner. This could be selecting every 25th client on the list.

Stratified

The subgroups of importance to our doctors are the pregnant and nonpregnant clients. We could get a list of all the pregnant clients and nonpregnant clients and randomly select from each. In this case, we would want to have more clients selected from the pregnant subgroup because the doctors are very interested in their responses.

Cluster

Clusters of individuals from our population could be found in the waiting room of the doctor's office or on the maternity floor of the hospital. We would select which of the clusters we wanted to survey and do so.

SECTION SUMMARY

- *Probability sampling procedures* are used to ensure every individual within a population has a known probability or likelihood of being selected for a study. There are four types of probability sampling procedures (pp. 147–151).
- With *simple probability sampling*, all individuals in a population have an equal probability of being selected (pp. 147–149).
- With *systematic probability sampling*, a random sample taken in a systematic approach is used (p. 149).
- *Stratified probability sampling* is a sampling technique where a researcher begins by identifying subgroups (or strata) and then randomly sample from each subgroup (p. 149).
- *Cluster probability sampling* involves identifying clusters of individuals from the population. These clusters are then sampled to obtain the sample (p. 149).

NONPROBABILITY SAMPLING PROCEDURES

If a probability sampling procedure is not possible, a **nonprobability sampling procedure** can be used. In these procedures, *not all* individuals within the population of interest have an equal or known likelihood of being selected. These nonprobability sampling procedures include convenience, snowballing, and quota. **Convenience** nonprobability sampling (sometimes referred to haphazard) involves using participants who are readily available or who will volunteer to participate. Many experiments in psychology are conducted on General Psychology students.

Nonprobability Sampling Procedure: A procedure where not all individuals within the population of interest have an equal likelihood or known probability of being selected.

Convenience Sampling: A procedure which involves using those participants who are readily available or will volunteer to participate.

© mangostock, 2014. Used under license from Shutterstock, Inc.

© I5M, 2014. Used under license from Shutterstock, Inc.

Those students are readily available and volunteer to participate to receive partial course credit or a monetary stipend. **Snowballing** is when you select initial participants who meet some set of criteria and then acquire other participants through a referral from your initial participants. Jenn used a snowballing procedure when she was in graduate school. Jenn was conducting research on married couples. She selected people to participate who met the criteria of being married. These married couples then gave Jenn the names of married couples they knew who would also be interested in participating. Her sample grew in size as a snowball grows when you add more snow to it.

The last nonprobability sampling procedure is **quota**. In quota sampling, you select a convenience sample is comprised of subgroups similar in number to the population. You could recruit General Psychology students to form a sample matching the population (all university students) in terms of percentage of students for each ethnic group. If Caucasian students make up 53% of the student population, then a quota sampling procedure would have a sample with 53% Caucasian participants. The disadvantage to all nonprobability sampling procedure is an increased likelihood of a biased sample. The biased sample can occur due to the self-selecting process of the procedure. In other words, individuals who self-select to participate could be different in nature than individuals who do not self-select. Ways to minimize this disadvantage will be discussed later.

Snowballing: A procedure where a sample is acquired by a referral process among similar individuals.

Quota Sampling: A convenience sample is selected that is comprised of subgroups similar in number to the population.

YOU TRY IT!

Instagram has become very popular. We are currently investigating how popular Instagram is among college students and differences in how men and women use the product. Help us with our study by answering the question. Then, compare your ideas on obtaining the sample with the answers below.

QUESTIONS

Explain how we could obtain our sample using the following procedures: (1) convenience, (2) snowballing, and (3) quota.

1. Convenience: You might have recommended that in the convenience procedure we post the opportunity to our General Psychology students to participate in the experiment.

2. Snowballing: You might have recommended for the snowballing procedure. We find students who use Instagram, survey them, and

ask if they know other students who use Instagram might be willing to participate.

3. Quota: Finally, with the quota procedure you might have recommended we get a convenience sample, paying attention to the numbers of individuals that comprise the subgroups. For example, we would want to be sure our sample was comprised of the same percentage of men and women who use the product.

SECTION SUMMARY

- The alternative to probability sampling procedures is using *nonprobability sampling* procedures. In this type of procedure, not all individuals within the population of interest have an equal likelihood or known probability of being selected, and biases may be a problem (pp. 151–153).
    - A *convenience sample* involves using those participants who are readily available or who will volunteer to participate (pp. 151–152).
    - A *snowballing sampling* procedure is where a sample is acquired by a referral process among similar individuals (p. 152).
    - A *quota sample* is similar to stratified sampling, where subgroups are identified which are similar in number to the population. However, this is a nonrandom sample (p. 152).

RANDOM ASSIGNMENT TO CONDITIONS

We mentioned previously many studies in psychology (and other social sciences) use the nonprobability sampling technique of a convenience sample by having General Psychology students as participants. You might wonder if using a convenience sampling procedure creates a biased sample. This is a good question because it certainly could. Nonprobability sampling procedures can cause threats to external validity. However, no matter whether you use a probability or nonprobability sampling procedure, it is always a good idea to use **random assignment** of participants to the treatment condition. This will control for threats to internal validity.

Take, for instance, the following example. Students in our Research Methods class want to know if listening to classical music improves academic performance. This is known as the Mozart effect and students in psychology are always interested in the topic, especially with the popularity a few years ago of the Baby Einstein series. The Research Methods class decides they need two groups of participants. Group 1 will listen to Mozart and Group 1 will not listen to music. Jenn tells the Research Methods class they can use her 8 a.m. and 10 a.m. sections of General Psychology classes and she will offer extra credit to those students willing to serve as participants. This is a nonprobability sampling technique, because the Research Method class is merely using students who are readily available and willing to volunteer. Next, General Psychology students wanting to participate could come to the research lab one afternoon and be randomly assigned to treatment conditions. For example, they could then be divided into two groups by flipping a coin. However, would it be random assignment to flip a coin and assign an entire class to the

Random Assignment: A procedure in which a selected participant has an equal probability of being placed into each group of a study.

treatment conditions? In other words, can we randomly assign the 8 a.m. class to one group and the 10 a.m. class to the other group? Although this may seem like an easy alternative, it is not a random process. This is because the classes differ as a whole. At our institution, students who register on time fill up the 10 a.m. classes, while students who wait until the last minute are stuck registering for the 8 a.m. classes. This means the two groups are not the same (are not equal) prior to the introduction of the variable of interest. It is important then that each student, not the class as a whole, be randomly assigned.

YOU TRY IT!

We want you to get comfortable with using random assignment. Read the following paragraph about a recent Stanford study by Dr. Dena Bravata and colleagues (2007). We would like for you to help us decide how to do our similar study.

A Stanford study recently found that pedometers help people stay active. A pedometer is a small device that counts the number of steps you take per day. (You might remember that not too long ago McDonald's gave away pedometers when you purchased salads.) Results indicated that those wearing pedometers increased physical activity by about 2,000 steps (equivalent to one mile) per day. We want to replicate this study with our General Psychology students. We will offer those students willing to participate in the study extra credit (and an alternative for extra credit for those not wanting to participate in research). We will have two groups of participants. One group of participants will wear pedometers allowing them to see the number of steps taken per day, and another group will wear pedometers not allowing them to see the number of steps taken per day. In this situation, how would you assign the participants to each of the two groups?

You probably decided to randomly assign participants to the two groups. Did you flip a coin, use the random number chart, or come up with another unbiased method of your own? We would like to mention one last word on random assignment before we change topics. It is not always possible to use random assignment. For example, a recent study in the news conducted by Dartmouth researchers found that rural patients are diagnosed earlier for colorectal and lung cancer than urban patients (Paquette & Finlayson, 2007). In this study, it would not be possible to randomly assign participants to being urban patients or rural patients. However, if you cannot randomly assign participants to the conditions, you can be sure to control for other factors across the two groups. In the study described above, the researchers controlled for factors such as age, race, gender, marital status, income, and education level.

SECTION SUMMARY

- *Random assignment* is the procedure in which a selected participant has an equal probability of being placed into each group of a study (pp. 153–154).

DETERMINING SAMPLE SIZE

One of the most difficult questions to answer when you are conducting a study is regarding the number of participants needed; in other words, "How big of a sample do I need?" Simply, there is no one way to determine sample size completely. Often, people rely on past precedent and do what others have done.

Sample size, the number of individuals participating in a study, is important to consider because you want to know how much data need to be collected to see a change in the dependent variable, if one truly exists. No one wants to collect more data than are needed to demonstrate the independent variable "worked." Fortunately, there is a known relationship between the sample size of a study and the ability of statistical tests to determine an effect. This relationship is known as power and is thus an important piece to the puzzle.

Sample: The number of individuals needed or selected for a study.

POWER

The probability of rejecting the null hypothesis when it is indeed false or the probability of accepting the alternative when it is true is the definition of **power**. In other words, we want to know the probability of seeing an effect when there is really an effect to be seen. As mentioned earlier, there is a positive correlation between power and sample size in that as one increases so does the other. So, should we just sample a large number of people to obtain high power? The answer is no. As you increase your sample size, other factors increase as well, such as time and money. Therefore, we try to achieve sufficient power while minimizing sample size. Cohen (1965) recommended the baseline for power be 0.80. Cohen indicated this level was sufficient enough to decrease the probability of a Type II error or failing to reject the null hypothesis when it is indeed false. (We will learn about Type I and Type II Errors later in Chapter 14.)

Power: The probability of rejecting the null hypothesis when it is indeed false.

In addition to determining sample size through power, you must also consider the effect size of the study. The **effect size** is the amount of overlap between populations. Specifically, effect size speaks to the magnitude of the treatment. The larger the overlap between the populations, the smaller the difference on the dependent variable. Contrarily, the smaller the overlap between the populations, the greater the difference on the dependent variable. Effect size can be determined by looking at previous research and be calculated post hoc. When estimating effect size, we rely on past research where effect size is noted to make a determination for our study. By using the combination of desired power and effect size, a researcher can easily narrow in on the needed sample size. For example, look at Table 8.2. This is a table of the relationship between power and effect size. If you were conducting a study where you wanted to obtain power of 0.80 and past research had shown your variables should yield an effect size of 0.60, then you would need only 18 participants. Typically, you would want power to be at least 0.80 to indicate you had sufficient strength in rejecting the null hypothesis when it is indeed false.

Effect Size: The amount of overlap between populations.

TABLE 8.2 Power Table.

		Effect Size								
		0.10	0.20	0.30	0.40	0.50	0.60	0.70	0.80	0.90
	0.25	167	42	20	12	8	6	5	4	3
	0.50	385	96	42	24	15	10	7	6	4
	0.60	490	122	53	29	18	12	9	6	5
	0.67	570	142	63	34	21	14	10	7	5
Power	**0.70**	616	153	67	37	23	15	10	7	5
	0.75	692	172	75	41	24	17	11	8	6
	0.80	783	194	85	46	28	18	12	9	6
	0.85	895	221	97	52	32	21	14	10	6
	0.90	1047	259	113	62	37	24	16	11	7
	0.95	1294	319	139	75	46	30	19	13	8
	0.99	1828	450	195	105	64	40	27	18	11

From *Statistical Power Analysis for the Behavioral Sciences* by Jacob Cohen. Copyright © 1988 by Taylor & Francis. Reprinted by permission.

SECTION SUMMARY

- The number of individuals needed or selected for a study is known as the *sample size* (p. 155).

- The probability of rejecting the null hypothesis when it is indeed false is known as *power* (p. 155).

- The amount of overlap between populations is known as *effect size* (p. 155).

ARE YOU EQUIPPED NOW?

At the beginning of this chapter, we reviewed Milgram's research on obedience. As our last activity for this chapter, we want to replicate Milgram's research. (By the way, Milgram's research has been replicated lately while controlling for ethical concerns.) For our replication study, we will use the students at our university as the population. Therefore, we have a known list of all people within the population. We would like for you to explain how you could use the four probability sampling techniques and three nonprobability sampling techniques to get our sample.

Probability Sampling Procedures

a. Simple: If we wanted to use a simple probability procedure, we could get list of all students at the university. We would then put the names in a big box and pull out 50 names of students to serve as participants.

b. Systematic: For the systematic procedure, we would again need a list of all university students. We would then select every 120th participant to get 50 names of students to serve as participants.

c. Stratified: We would identify the subgroups and randomly sample from the subgroups. Our subgroup could be sex and we would randomly sample from the men and women attending the university.

d. Cluster: The cluster procedure involves identifying clusters of students. These clusters might come from students who are from different parts of the state or those who live in different dormitories on campus. After identifying clusters of students to participate in the study, we would want to be sure that each student participates only one time

Nonprobability Sampling Procedures

a. Convenience: If we wanted to use a convenience sampling technique, we would use students enrolled in our classes (say our General Psychology classes). We would offer extra credit to those students willing to participate.

b. Snowballing: When using the snowballing procedure, we would go to the cafeteria and ask students, who we know, to participate in the study. We would then ask these students if they had friends who might also be willing to participate.

c. Quota: When using the quota procedure, we would want the subgroups in our sample to be numerically similar to subgroups in the population. Our sample would come from General Psychology classes and our subgroups (sex, day versus night student, and ethnicity) would be equivalent to that of the population.

CHAPTER SUMMARY

- A *population* is the entire group of people from which the results of a study are generalized. On the other hand, a *sample* is a smaller group that is representative of the larger population (p. 147).

- When conducting a study, it is not always feasible to use the entire population. Therefore, researchers use samples. There are two types of procedures that you can use: probability sampling and nonprobability sampling. *Probability sampling* ensures that everyone in the larger population has a known probability of being selected for the study. In contrast, *nonprobability sampling* is used when everyone in the larger population does *not* have a known probability of being selected for the study (pp. 147–154).

- There are four common types of probability sampling. These four types can be used to ensure participants in a larger population have an equal or known probability of being selected for a study (pp. 147–151).

  - In *simple probability sampling*, all individuals in a population have an equal probability of being selected. You can use this type of probability sampling with or without replacement (pp. 147–149).

    - In sampling with replacement, individuals are sampled one at a time, with each individual being replaced before the next is sampled. Here, each person has exactly the same probability of being selected (p. 149).

    - In sampling without replacement, individuals are sampled and are not replaced before the next is sampled. Here, the probability of being selected changes with each removal (p. 149).

- In *systematic probability sampling*, a random sample taken in a systematic approach is used (p. 149).
- *Stratified probability sampling* is a sampling technique where a researcher begins by identifying subgroups (or strata) and then randomly samples from each subgroup (p. 149).
- *Cluster probability sampling* involves identifying clusters of individuals from the population. These clusters are then included in the sample (p. 149).

- Nonprobability sampling does *not* ensure all members of the larger population have an equal or known probability of being selected for a study. Many times, it is not possible to sample all members. Therefore, a more commonly used alternative to the four types of probability sampling are the three types of nonprobability sampling (pp. 151–153).
  - A *convenience sample* involves using those participants who are readily available or who will volunteer to participate (pp. 151–152).
  - A *snowballing sampling* procedure is where a sample is acquired by a referral process among similar individuals (p. 152).
  - A *quota sample* is similar to stratified sampling, where subgroups are identified. However, this is a nonrandom sample (p. 152).

- One way to reduce bias to internal validity is by *randomly assigning* individuals in the sample to conditions. We take the individuals in our sample and give each one an equal chance of being assigned to one of the two or more levels of the independent variable (pp. 153–154).

- Deciding how many individuals to use in a study is not a simple task. In other words, sample size is the number of individuals that participate in a study. Sample size is a function of power and effect size. If you know the desired power for a study and the effect size that can be achieved, you can use a power table to determine the sample size that you need (p. 155).
  - *Power* is represented by a probability ranging from 0 to 1 (p. 155).
  - The amount of overlap between populations is known as effect size. Effect size estimates are determined by looking at past research (p. 155).

APA LEARNING GOALS LINKAGE

- ### Goal 1. Knowledge Base in Psychology

  You will demonstrate fundamental knowledge and comprehension of the major concepts, theoretical perspectives, historical trends, and empirical findings to discuss how psychological principles apply to behavioral problems.

  Sections Covered: Are You Equipped?

  Explanation of the Goal: Psychological research today has been greatly influenced by key experiments from the past. One such experiment in the history of psychology was that of Milgram's on obedience. This chapter opened with an overview of Milgram's 1963 experiment with special attention given to how individuals were recruited for participation.

- **Goal 2. Scientific Inquiry and Critical Thinking**

  You will demonstrate scientific reasoning and problem solving, including effective research methods.

  Sections Covered: Are You Equipped?, Populations versus Samples, Probability Sampling Procedures, Nonprobability Sampling Procedures, Random Assignment to Conditions, Determining Sample Size, Power, Are You Equipped Now?

  Explanation of the Goal: As we proceed through the textbook, we are learning more about the basic research methods utilized by psychologists. This chapter focused on how individuals are selected for participation in psychological research and how the participants can be assigned to treatment conditions. In order to discuss these topics, the chapter began with a discussion on the difference between populations and samples. Next, we outlined probability and nonprobability

  sampling procedures, articulating the strengthens and weaknesses of each sampling method. It is essential to recognize how biases may shape design, and therefore this chapter included information on biased samples and the use of random assignment to treatment conditions to reduce systematic differences. Finally, we equipped you to interpret basic statistical conclusions through the topics of determining sample size, effect size, and power.

  Sections Covered: Are You Equipped?, Probability Sampling Procedures, Nonprobability Sampling Procedures, Random Assignment to Conditions, Are You Equipped Now?

  Explanation of the Goal: This chapter was unique in that the "You Try It!" exercises all required you to generate multiple possible solutions to a problem. For example, you were asked to explain how to utilize the types of probability sampling procedures in obtaining a sample from a high school and how to utilize the types of nonprobability sampling techniques in obtaining a sample to study text messaging. Thus, your critical thinking skills were needed in creatively deciding how to solve a situation by using different approaches.

- **Goal 3. Ethical and Social Responsibility in a Diverse World**

  You will apply ethical standards to evaluate psychological science and practice and you will develop ethically and socially responsible behaviors for professional and personal settings in a landscape that involves increasing diversity.

  Sections Covered: Are You Equipped?, Probability Sampling Procedures, Nonprobability Sampling Procedures, Random Assignment to Conditions, Are You Equipped Now?

Explanation of the Goal: As with almost every chapter in the textbook thus far, we have applied psychological principles to everyday examples. In this chapter, we included examples of text messaging, parking on college campuses, and the use of pedometers. However, we also took time to examine how ethically complex situations can arise when psychological principles are applied to societal issues. Specifically, Milgram conducted his research on obedience to understand the issue facing society of how individuals committed such violent acts to other humans in concentration camps. However, designing an experiment to understand human behavior like obedience is not simple and involves many ethical considerations.

- **Goal 4. Communication**

  You will demonstrate competence in writing and in oral and interpersonal communication skills.

  Sections Covered: Power

  Explanation of the Goal: In continuing to improve your ability to communicate quantitative information, we included in this chapter a section on appropriate statistical analyses needed for interpretation purposes. Power and effect size are both needed to interpret measurements and thus we supplied information on the conventionally accepted levels for both.

CHAPTER 9

Controls and Threats to Internal Validity

CHAPTER OUTLINE

Are You Equipped?

Control

Threats to Internal Validity

Minimizing Threats

Are You Equipped Now?

Chapter Summary

APA Learning Goals Linkage

ARE YOU EQUIPPED?

Do you ever watch *American Idol*? Your textbook authors must admit that we have been avid fans of the show since the very first season. We will even DVR *American Idol*, so we do not miss a single episode. If you are not a fan of the show, let us tell you about its basic format. Singers compete on stage one at a time and then a panel of "expert" judges weigh in on their performances. At the end of the show, the voting lines open and the audience can call, text, or go online to vote for their favorite singer. Each week, the singer with the fewest votes is kicked off the show. The process sounds harmless and fair to the performers. However, we have noticed that we tend not to form our own opinions until the judges have given theirs. Basically, we wait until we hear what the judges are saying before we decide on if we liked the performance of the singer. Do you think there is a potential problem with the judges throwing in their two cents? In other words, does this method influence how viewers vote?

© s_bukley, 2014. Used under license from Shutterstock, Inc.

If you think this method could influence how people perceive the performance of the contestants and how people vote, we would agree with you. You can think of this example as an experiment with the viewers as participants and the judges as researchers. By giving their "expert" opinions, the judges (or researchers) are subtly communicating to the viewers (or participants) how they should behave. This could be a problem. We will describe in this section of the textbook why researchers should be careful not to influence participants' responses and avoid biasing the results.

As you go through this chapter, we also want you to keep in mind how the material relate to the American Psychological Association's goals for psychology majors. Specifically, this chapter will address the following goals:

- **Goal 2. Scientific Inquiry and Critical Thinking**

  You will demonstrate scientific reasoning and problem solving, including effective research methods.

- **Goal 3. Ethical and Social Responsibility in a Diverse World**

  You will apply ethical standards to evaluate psychological science and practice and you will develop ethically and socially responsible behaviors for professional and personal settings in a landscape that involves increasing diversity.

CONTROL

As discussed in Chapter 5, an experiment involves many variables, including an independent variable and a dependent variable. Researchers devote a substantial amount of time in selecting these two variables and deciding how they will be defined and measured. However, it is important to be aware of other variables with the potential to influence (and potentially bias) research findings. Extraneous variables and nuisance variables are two examples. **Extraneous variables** are variables not controlled for in the experiment that may have an effect on the dependent variable. However, when a variable varies systematically with the independent variable, making it difficult to determine the effect of the independent variable, it is said to be confounding. **Nuisance variables** are unwanted variables that can influence all groups of participants, causing the results to be less clear. We are going to give you examples for each to demonstrate these definitions and illustrate how these variables can influence the interpretation of results from an experiment. Let us start by reading the example below from a news story.

Extraneous Variables:
Variable that is not controlled for in the experiment that may have an effect on the dependent variable.

Nuisance Variables:
A variable that is not controlled for in the experiment that influences all participants in the same manner.

The news headline reads, "Study Suggests Possible Link between TV Viewing and Autism in Children." This news article describes research conducted at Cornell University by Michael Waldman examining rain, cable TV subscriptions, and autism. Researchers looked at two factors leading them to their conclusions about TV viewing and autism in children. First, the researchers looked at autism rates in counties of California, Oregon, and Washington. Results indicated that as rainfall increased, so too did rates of autism, and conversely as rainfall decreased, so too did rates of autism. The researchers found this interesting because prior research conducted by U. S. Bureau of Labor Statistics reported children watch more TV when it is raining. Second, the researchers looked at the percentage of households with cable TV subscriptions in the states of California and Pennsylvania. Results indicated that as cable TV subscriptions increased, so too did rates of autism, and, conversely, as cable TV subscriptions decreased, so too did rates of autism. The researchers combined these two results to conclude that there is a link between watching TV and autism. The researchers further justified this link by stating they can think of no other obvious factor correlated with both rain and cable TV subscriptions, except TV viewing.

From this example, can you think of an extraneous variable that could be influencing the interpretation of the results? In other words, is there another variable besides TV viewing that relates to cable TV subscriptions and rain? Here are a few hints:

1. You are looking for a variable the researchers did not mention controlling for in their results.
2. You are looking for a variable that potentially varies with both cable TV subscriptions and rain amounts.

Answer

We think a possible extraneous variable is population size. Our reasoning is as follows. As the population size increases in a particular area, the number of cable TV subscriptions also increases. Therefore, it is more likely that a city with 100,000 residents will have more cable TV subscriptions than a city with 2,500 residents. Similarly, as population size increases, the number of children within that area increases. The more children there are in an area, the more likely it is that cases of autism will be found in that area. Here is an example to understand this argument using fictitious data. Pretend that in any given city, children comprise 10% of the population. So, in a city of 100,000 people, there will be 10,000 children. Similarly, in a city of 2,500 people, there will be only 250 children (see Figure 9.1a). Therefore, as population size increases, the number of children increases. This works the same for rates of autism. Let's say for simplicity sake, that 1 out of every 100 children is diagnosed with autism. In the larger city with 10,000 children, there would be 100 cases of autism, and in a smaller city with 250 children, there would be 2.5 cases of autism (see Figure 9.1b). Thus, the larger city will exhibit more cases of autism (100 versus 2.5) and more cable TV subscriptions, not due to TV viewing but due to population size. Furthermore, the possibility exists that the counties receiving the most rain are also the counties with the most residents. Thus, we cannot confidently conclude that TV viewing (which occurs most frequently when it rains) causes autism. This is because the extraneous variable of population size varies with cable TV subscriptions, number of children with autism in a given area, and possibly counties receiving the most rain.

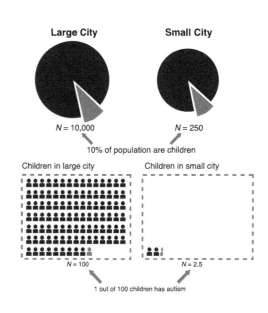

Now that we have seen how extraneous variables can make it difficult to determine the effect of the independent variable in an experiment, let us discuss nuisance variables. Like extraneous variables, nuisance variables are important to consider when interpreting research findings. Specifically, nuisance variables are variables that are not controlled for in the experiment that influences all participants in the same manner. It is important to note the similarities and differences between extraneous variables and nuisance variables. Typically, both extraneous variables and nuisance variables are unwanted. This means research findings can be influenced by both extraneous variables and nuisance variables in unwanted ways. Furthermore, we are not normally interested in the effect of extraneous and nuisance variables, except to understand how it might be influencing our research results. However, extraneous variables and nuisance variables are also different. Extraneous variables vary with the independent variables (so it is different between groups), whereas nuisance variables are the same for all groups.

This next example on nuisance variables comes from our own research on social media sites like Facebook. In the spring of 2007, we recruited participants for an experiment on "Student Internet Usage" with no mention made of friend networking sites. We were interested in how many students use friend networking sites and how many students do not use friend networking sites, and therefore, we did not mention friend networking sites in the title of the experiment so all students would participate in the experiment. Our results were very interesting and did demonstrate friend networking sites were popular among our students. In fact, 87.1% of participants indicated having either a MySpace or a Facebook account and 74.3% of participants had accounts in both sites. We also were surprised at the amount of time students spend per day on their accounts. We found students reported spending an average of 1.46 hours on their accounts and 1.10 hours on others' accounts. Finally, we were shocked at the average number of friends students reported having linked to their account. Specifically, the mean number of friends linked was 235.51.

Next, we designed a survey to gather more information about friend networking sites. Now that we know college students are using friend networking, it is important to understand why some college students use friend networking sites while other college students do not. Specifically for students who are using friend networking sites, we wanted to know what needs are being met for students by interacting with friends in this venue. We had our survey complete and were set to administer it in the beginning of the fall semester. However, we realized there could be a potential problem with that plan. Specifically, our original data were collected at the end of the spring semester and we are thinking about collecting data at the beginning of the fall semester. How could time of the year (spring semester versus fall semester) be a nuisance variable for us? In other words, how could the time of the year when we ask students about their usage of friend networking sites make the results less clear?

We think time of the year might be a nuisance variable for the following reasons. The data we will collect will primarily be from college freshmen. It is possible students do not create (or even learn about) friend networking sites until they have been in college a semester. Therefore, the data we collected in the spring would show how popular friend networking sites are for college students, but data collected in early fall on college freshmen might more accurately describe the high-school students' use of friend networking sites. Thus, time of the year is an unwanted variable. We are not interested in how usage of friend networking sites varies with the seasons (although that could be true) and we are also not interested in how popular these sites are among high-school students (although that might warrant future research). We just want to know in general how college students use friend networking sites. In order to do so, we must be aware of nuisance variables (like time of the year) that might make our results less clear.

An important take-home message from these examples of extraneous variables and nuisance variables is that research should be designed so it controls for as many variables as possible. Although we might not normally think of control as a good thing, with regard to research, control can be a positive. When you read research findings or hear them presented in the media, you should ask yourself if the research experiment was designed to control for extraneous and nuisance variables. However, if the research was not designed to control for these variables, be sure to ask yourself how this might have influenced the results. Maybe it does not significantly influence the results or maybe it does, like in the examples of TV viewing and autism discussed earlier.

SECTION SUMMARY

- When designing and conducting research, you must take into account variables that can potentially influence and/or bias results (pp. 162–165).
- Two types of variables that could potentially influence and/or bias results are as follows:
    - *Extraneous variables* are variables not controlled for in the experiment and vary with the independent variables (p. 162).
    - *Nuisance variables* are variables not controlled for in the experiment that influences all participants in the same manner (p. 162).

THREATS TO INTERNAL VALIDITY

As mentioned in Chapter 5, internal validity is being able to say with confidence that the independent variable caused the observed change in the dependent variable. Now, whether you are going to conduct your own research or you are consuming research findings presented in the media, you should be aware of threats to internal validity. Threats to internal validity are threats to saying that the manipulated variable (i.e., the independent variable) caused the change in the measured or observed variable (i.e., the dependent variable). In other words, a threat means something else could have caused the change observed besides the variable that was manipulated. Campbell and Stanly (1969) outlined threats to internal validity many years ago. In order to help you determine if any threats to internal validity are present in an experiment, you can ask yourself the following 10 questions. Depending on your answers, you will know if threats to internal validity are an issue.

- **Question 1**: Could the change in the dependent variable be due to an event beyond the researcher's control?

When an event beyond the researcher's control can explain the change in the dependent variable, **history** is a threat to internal validity. Let us pretend the U. S. Department of Agriculture does regular surveys on mature Americans to see what

History: An event beyond the researcher's control that can explain the change in the dependent variable.

concerns they have with foodborne illnesses. You hear on the news one night that mature Americans are now 50 times more likely to worry about Mad Cow disease than they were 5 years ago. You happen to remember there was an outbreak of Mad Cow disease last year (at around the same time the data were collected). It is possible the increase in concern over Mad Cow disease is partially due to the recent outbreak. This is an example of history being a threat to internal validity. The outbreak of Mad Cow disease was an event beyond the researcher's control, yet it influenced the results.

YOU TRY IT!

Here is another example for you to try. Not too many years ago, there was an outbreak of salmonella in peanut butter. Imagine you were conducting a study evaluating the safety of peanut butter use in family households for a major peanut butter producer. Would this salmonella outbreak have an impact on your results?

If you asked people before and after this outbreak how safe peanut butter was to eat, you might see a change in response immediately after the outbreak. Specifically, after the outbreak of salmonella, people would probably report peanut butter was less safe to eat than they would have reported before the outbreak. In this example, the change in the dependent variable (peoples' perceptions of the safety of peanut butter) is partially influenced by the recent outbreak of salmonella. In conclusion, always ask yourself if events going on beyond the researcher's control could have influenced the way participants responded in the experiment.

- **Question 2:** Could the change in the dependent variable be due to internal changes within the participant that have occurred over time?

Maturation: The change in the dependent variable is due to internal changes within the participants over time.

If so, **maturation** could be a threat to internal validity. Maturation means the change in the dependent variable is not only due to the independent variable but also due to internal changes within the participant that occurred over time. For example, when our oldest daughter was younger, she greatly enjoyed playing hide-and-seek. Unfortunately, she was not very good at the game because she was very egocentric. Egocentrism is the inability to see another person's point of view. When we would play hide-and-seek, she would hide under a small end table that had a short tablecloth. She was easy to find because her feet would inevitably be sticking out from under the tablecloth. From her point of view, she could not see us (i.e., she only saw the back of the tablecloth) and therefore we could not see her. Yet, when we found her quickly, she would become quite upset and insist that we had cheated. We cannot tell you how many countless hours we worked trying to get her to understand that her feet were out in the open. After several months of working with her, one day she pulled her feet under the tablecloth. Of course, we did not find her quickly and became concerned. After all, she was always so easy to spot. However, we eventually found her under the table cloth and naturally assumed that we were great hide-and-seek teachers. However, shortly after this episode we began to realize that it had nothing to do with us and that rather it was a result of a change in her internal state. She was maturing and outgrowing egocentrism. Although we deeply wanted to believe that it was our teaching (independent variable) that caused the change in her egocentrism (dependent variable), it was more than likely the effects of maturation. Therefore, you should always ask yourself if a change in the observed behavior (dependent variable) is due to your manipulation (independent variable) or just an internal change within the participant. Now, you try one on your own.

YOU TRY IT!

Many colleges and universities offer a freshman seminar/introduction to college class to prepare and equip students for college life. In these freshman seminar classes, instructors work with incoming students on a variety of topics such as time management, money management, and study skills. Because colleges and universities put a great deal of money into these classes, they want to know if the freshman seminar classes (the independent variable) have an influence on students' attitudes and behaviors (the dependent variable). This is commonly measured by conducting a survey at the end of the first year about information covered in the classes. Could there be a problem with this methodology related to maturation?

As you may have guessed, before concluding the freshman seminar class was responsible for the changes demonstrated on the survey, we must consider the fact that the students matured over time. In other words, the changes at the end of the year could be due to students' maturation during that time period. Think about your first year in college. You probably encountered many challenges and experiences that required you to grow up. Being away from parents for the first time, managing your own money, and figuring out a class schedule that works for you are just a few examples of activities that may have led to your own maturation. Therefore, it may not be the freshman seminar class itself causing the change in the student, but the fact that the student is growing up and maturing. In sum, be sure to ask yourself if changes within the individual due to the participant simply maturing may have caused the change in the dependent variable. This is an important threat to internal validity to consider with research on children, whose internal states are constantly changing and developing.

- **Question 3:** Could the change in the dependent variable be due to extreme scores moving toward the mean?

This is an example of a threat to internal validity known as **regression to the mean**. In regression to the mean, the change in the dependent variable is not due to the independent variable, but due to extreme scores moving toward the mean. Let's take a look at an everyday example. Have you ever noticed that two extremely attractive people can have an average-looking or unattractive child? Or, have you ever noticed that two extremely unattractive people can have an average-looking or attractive child? (As a disclaimer, we believe that all children are cute, especially our own!) However, if you think about this example, you will realize you have seen this before. This is an example of regression to the mean. Think about this example with attractiveness on a scale ranging from not at all attractive to very attractive. Two very attractive people (e.g., the extreme scores) have a less attractive child (e.g., regression toward the mean), or two very unattractive people (e.g., extreme scores) have an attractive child (e.g., regression to the mean).

Regression to the Mean: The change in the dependent variable is due to extreme scores moving toward the mean on later measures.

For those of you needing a less controversial example of regression to the mean, think about playing a video game. Have you ever played a video game breaking the all-time high score only to find that you were never able to duplicate that performance? This is another example of regression to the mean. You will most likely always follow up any extreme score (i.e., your all-time high score) with regression to the mean (i.e., a lower score). Therefore, anytime in research results where participants with extreme scores have subsequent scores which have moved up or down, be sure to ask yourself if the change was due to the independent variable or regression to the mean? This is an important threat to consider when individuals score very high or low on a first test and in the opposite direction on a second test. The change in performance could be due to regression toward the mean rather than a change in any variable.

- **Question 4:** Could the change in the dependent variable be due to how the participants were selected or assigned to groups?

Selection: Change in the dependent variable is due to how participants were selected for the experiment or how they were assigned to groups.

If **selection** of participants is a threat to internal validity, the change in the dependent variable could be due to how the participants were selected for the experiment or how they were assigned to groups. Here is an example from our own campus. All over the campus, blasted on signs and coffee mugs are the results of a survey on the number of alcoholic beverages students at our university consume when they drink. In fact, as we write this example, we are looking at a coffee mug that states, "Most university students make healthy choices. 69% have 0–4 drinks when they drink." Our university is not alone in advertising such results. We remember a similar slogan from our graduate university. However, there is a lot to consider when you look at these results. We will ignore the issues all together as to whether or not this is a healthy choice or whether or not participants are in fact telling the truth. Instead, just think about how the participants were selected for the survey. In other words, where did they come from or how were they selected? Were participants selected depending on if they lived on- or off-campus? Were all the participants in a sorority or fraternity? Were nontraditional age students included in the survey? Were men and women equally sampled? Did they only sample those students over the age of 21? It is possible that the answers to these questions might change the results. For example, do you think that members of a Greek affiliation drink more or less than the average college student? If they do drink different amounts compared to other college students, then having too many or too few Greek-affiliated students in the survey could bias the results. It is important to ask yourself if all students had the opportunity to be selected for the study and, if appropriate, were participants randomly assigned to treatment groups. If participants were *not* randomly selected/ assigned and a convenience sample was used (e.g., whatever students walked by the university cafeteria), selection could be a threat to internal validity.

- **Question 5:** Could the change in the dependent variable be due to participants systematically dropping out of the experiment?

Attrition: Participants systematically drop out of an experiment, thus changing the experimental results.

Attrition occurs when participants systematically drop out of an experiment and therefore change the results of the experiment. We can use the Atkins diet as an example. In case you are not familiar with this diet, the Atkins diet involves eliminating all carbohydrates from your diet (i.e., breads and starches). We decided to give the diet a try ourselves because some of our friends had lost weight successfully using it. However, the diet was not as successful for us. Not because it did not work per se, but because we dropped out or stopped the diet. (Although we enjoyed the meats and cheeses, we greatly missed breads and, of course, chocolate.) Think of a research experiment designed to test which diet is best at helping people lose weight: Atkins, Jenny Craig, or Weight Watchers. The results could show that the average weight lost on Atkins was 6 pounds per week and on Jenny Craig and Weight Watchers was 2 pounds per week. Based on such fictitious results, we might all start the Atkins diet immediately. However, you must ask yourself if the results in weight loss are due to the independent variable (type of diet) or participants systematically dropping out of the experiment. It could, in fact, be the case that a significant number of participants on the Atkins diet dropped out. Maybe 8 of the 10 people on the Atkins diet dropped out of the experiment leaving only 2 participants the diet really worked for in the group. On the other hand, the dropout rate for the Jenny Craig and Weight Watchers groups was much lower (e.g., only one dropout per condition), and therefore contained participants with varying degrees of weight-loss success. Thus, it is important to ask yourself if participants are dropping out of a study in a manner that might influence the results. If the answer is yes, attrition could be a threat to internal validity.

© Jenn Huls, 2014. Used under license from Shutterstock, Inc.

- **Question 6:** Could the change in the dependent variable be due to participants' familiarity with the test?

Testing is a threat to internal validity when the change in the dependent variable is not due to the independent variable, but rather is due to the participant becoming more familiar with the test or testing procedures. In academic settings, this is why instructors give practice quizzes or why students take practice SATs and ACTs. In sports, athletes run drills or practice plays over and over. In short, you get better at something when you practice it. Think about the example below on testing as a threat to internal validity. We both teach classes that historically students do not normally enjoy taking (Research Methods, Statistics, and Physiological Psychology). It happens occasionally that a student who is in one of our classes has previously taken the class from another instructor either at our institution or another. The repeater students will comment that the class is so much easier with us as instructors. Now, we might want to believe that we are such great instructors that student learning (the dependent variable) has drastically improved because of us (the independent variable). However, it is probably more likely that the increase in student learning (dependent variable) is due to testing (practice or familiarity). Specifically, the student has become familiar with the course material as well as how material in the course will be tested. Therefore, practice and familiarity can, at least partially, explain the increase in student learning we hear students reporting. When reading about research findings, be sure to ask yourself if the participant improved from the first test to the second test because of practice.

Testing: Change in the dependent variable is due to the participants becoming more familiar with the test or testing procedures.

- **Question 7:** Could the change in the dependent variable be due to participants in one group talking to participants in another group?

Typically, in research we have more than one group of participants. For example, one group of participants is given one level of the independent variable and the

Diffusion of Treatment:
Change in the dependent variable is due to participants in different groups communicating with each other.

Instrumentation: Change in the dependent variable is due to how the dependent variable was measured.

second group of participants is given a second level of the independent variable. Therefore, the participants in the two groups are given different instructions and different treatment levels. Similarly, in teaching, we sometimes teach two sections of the same course. This is a great opportunity to try different teaching strategies or different activities. The different teaching strategies serve as the independent variable and student learning serves as the dependent variable. We have used a similar situation to test teaching methods and student learning. For example, in the past we each taught two sections of General Psychology and played jeopardy with our students the class period before the exam. Traditionally, we have offered five points bonus on the exam to the winning team, four points to the second place team, and two points to all students who attended class the day we played jeopardy. However, we noticed that students were not studying for jeopardy because they were happy just receiving the two bonus points. We wanted to create an environment where students had studied prior to arriving to class on the day of jeopardy. One semester, we changed our approach so one section of our General Psychology classes was treated in the traditional manner (as described above), while the other section was told that the wining team would receive five bonus points and the second place team would receive four bonus points. There would be no bonus points for other students. We wanted to see if the bonus points offered (independent variable) would influence students' preparedness for the game (dependent variable). This worked as predicted for the first exam. The students in the traditional form of bonus points were not as prepared as students in the new format of bonus points. However, for the second exam this trend did not persist. Students in both sections were arriving to jeopardy unprepared. It turns out that students in the two classes were talking and assumed that they would all receive the two bonus points just for attending class on the jeopardy day. In other words, **diffusion of treatment** conditions had occurred. Be sure changes in the dependent variable are not due to participants in different groups communicating with each other. If they are communicating, this shared information could cause a change in the dependent variable.

- **Question 8:** Could the change in the dependent variable be due to changes in how the dependent variable was measured?

When a change in how the dependent variable was measured can explain the change in the dependent variable, **instrumentation** is a threat to internal validity. Pretend that we told you to go watch an episode of the *Simpsons* and count the number of violent acts that you see. You could even pick an episode of *The Family Guy* or *American Dad*. Now, pretend even further that we asked your friend to also watch the same episode you were watching and count the number of violent acts they saw. Do you think at the end of the episode that you and your friend would have counted a similar number of violent acts? Probably not. But, why not? The reason is you and your friend probably have different definitions of violence. Therefore, you may count Homer trying to choke Bart as a violent act, but your friend may not. Having an operational definition (see Chapter 7) would allow you and your friend to measure violent acts in the same way. Similarly, it is important for researchers to be sure that the dependent variable is always measured in exactly the same way. Changes in how the dependent variable is measured from one occasion to the next can produce a change in the dependent variable itself, as well as the interpretation of the results for the study.

- **Question 9:** Could the change in the dependent variable be due to the participant's expectation that change will occur?

Sometimes, just thinking a change will occur is enough to produce a change. This is known as a **placebo effect**. At our undergraduate university, a famous (or infamous) study had been conducted demonstrating the placebo effect. Well, let us clarify that it was famous only within our university and some of the details have probably been distorted as the story has been verbally passed along. Apparently, several years before we arrived at the university, a professor and a few psychology students designed an experiment to see if expectations alone really could change behavior. The psychology students recruited participants for an experiment to examine the effects of alcohol consumption on reaction time. Participants were given Jell-O shots to consume before participating in experiments where reaction time was measured. The students genuinely believed they were consuming Jell-O shots containing alcohol and their behavior in the experiments demonstrated this with impaired reaction time, slurred speech, and so on. However, to the participant's surprise, the Jell-O shots were not made with alcohol. In fact, it was just plain, regular Jell-O. When the participants were debriefed and told that the Jell-O contained no alcohol, some participants were in disbelief and actually refused to drive home until they had time to "sober up." This is a great example of how the participant's expectations (thinking the Jell-O shots contained alcohol) can influence the dependent variable (reaction time). You can imagine that this is an important threat to control for when testing the effectiveness of a new drug. Therefore, be sure participants' expectations are not influencing their behavior.

© Charles Knox, 2014. Used under license from Shutterstock, Inc.

- **Question 10:** Could the change in the dependent variable be due to the researcher's hypotheses or the participant's hypotheses?

If participants believe they should act or behave in a certain way during an experiment or if a researcher somehow communicates to participants how they should act or behave, **demand characteristics** could be a threat to internal validity. Demand characteristics are various hints and cues that participants use to tell them how the researcher wants them to behave, or at least how they think the researcher wants them to behave. If participants are responding to these demand characteristics, rather than the independent variable, this could explain the changes in the dependent variable. Think about the *American Idol* example in the "Are You Equipped?" section at the beginning of the chapter. By giving their expert opinions on contestants' performances, the judges are communicating to the audience how we should vote. Sometimes, on *American Idol*, this is done very subtly by the judges reminding the audience that it is a singing competition and not a popularity contest or by reminding the audience to vote for contestants who have given consistently good performances. However, other times, the message is not so subtle. But no matter how this is done, the audience sometimes respond to the judges (demand characteristics) rather than the performances (the independent variable).

Be sure to keep in mind that in a laboratory experiment, researchers purposely do not tell participants how to respond nor are participants being bad by trying to figure out how they should act. It is only natural for participants to try to figure out the experiment and, in some cases, try to help the researcher by acting the way they think they should. Likewise, the researcher should never purposely bias results by treating participants in such a way that his or her hypothesis is confirmed. However, researchers are human only and this can occur without them knowing it. In short, research should be designed to prevent demand characteristics from changing the dependent variable.

MINIMIZING THREATS

If you are thinking there must be ways to control for threats to internal validity, you are correct. In later chapters, we will discuss how threats to internal validity can be controlled for based on the research design that is used. However, we do want to mention in this section two simple techniques that can control many of the threats to internal validity. The two simple techniques are the use of a double blind study and the use of a placebo as a control.

When conducting research, a researcher can have a single or double blind study. In a **single blind study**, the participant has no knowledge of which group he or she has been assigned to—only the researcher knows. Although it is advantageous that the participant does not know which group he or she has been assigned to, there is a drawback. Specifically, the threat of demand characteristics may affect your study results. However, in a **double blind study** neither the participant nor the researcher interacting with the participant knows which experimental group the participant has been placed into. Thus, you reduce the likelihood of the participant or experimenter behaving in a way that can influence the study, because neither knows which group the participant is in.

The other type of basic control is the use of a placebo. A **placebo** is an inert substance that mimics the independent variable but has no effect. Think back to the threat we discussed called the placebo effect. The participants who received regular Jell-O were receiving a placebo (i.e., it had no effect). However, they still displayed a behavior change. Without the use of the placebo, researchers would not have been able to identify the internal threat of a placebo effect.

In addition to the aforementioned controls, think back to the beginning of the chapter when we discussed techniques. At the beginning of the chapter, we were discussing how controlling for extraneous variables and nuisance variables is a good thing. Hopefully, now you can see that controlling for threats to internal validity is also a good thing to do. We will investigate other controls in later chapters.

Single Blind Study: A study in which the participant has no knowledge of which experimental group he or she may be participating within–only the researcher knows.

Double Blind Study: An experiment in which neither the participant nor the researcher knows which experimental group the participant has been placed into.

Placebo: An inert substance that has no effect.

SECTION SUMMARY

- When an event beyond the researcher's control explains the change in the dependent variable, *history* is a concern (pp. 165–166).
- *Maturation* occurs when internal changes in the participant cause the change in the dependent variable (pp. 166–167).
- In *regression to the mean*, the change in the dependent variable is not due to the independent variable but due to extreme scores moving toward the mean on later measures (pp. 167–168).

- In *selection*, the change in the dependent variable is due to how the participants were selected for the experiment or how they were assigned to groups (p. 168).

- *Attrition* occurs when participants systematically drop out of an experiment and therefore change the results of the experiment (pp. 168–169).

- *Testing* is a threat to internal validity when the change in the dependent variable is not due to the independent variable, but rather due to the participant becoming more familiar with the test or testing procedures (p. 169).

- *Diffusion of treatment* occurs when changes in the dependent variable are due to participants in different groups communicating with each other (pp. 169–170).

- When a change in how the dependent variable was measured can explain the change in the dependent variable, *instrumentation* is a threat to internal validity (p. 170).

- Sometimes, just thinking a change will occur is enough to produce a change. This is known as a *placebo effect* (p. 171).

- If participants believe they should act or behave in a certain way during an experiment or if a researcher somehow communicates to participants how they should act or behave, *demand characteristics* could be a threat to internal validity (pp. 171–172).

- A *single blind study* is a study where the participant does not know which experimental group he or she has been placed into, but the researcher knows (p. 172).

- A *double blind study* is a study where neither the participants nor the researcher interacting with the participants knows which experimental group the participant has been placed into (p. 172).

- A *placebo* is an inert substance that has no effect (p. 172).

ARE YOU EQUIPPED NOW?

A popular news channel summarized research findings stating that "Acupuncture may ease hip and joint pain from osteoarthritis, the most common type of arthritis." The news source went on to describe the experiment conducted by Witt and colleagues in the following way. More than 3,500 participants from Germany with osteoarthritis of the hip and/or knee participated in the experiment. Most participants were in their early 60s. In addition, 11% of participants reported having acupuncture in the year prior to the experiment. Upon arriving to the experiment, participants were asked to select which joint (i.e., the hip or the knee) was producing the most pain and then to rate that pain on the provided scale. Of the participants, around 3,200 participants received acupuncture treatments during a 3-month time period and about 300 participants served as a control group (i.e., they were put on a waiting list and received no treatment). Results indicated that about a third of participants in the group receiving the acupuncture treatments reported less pain as compared to their initial visit and an increase in overall quality of life. However, only 6% of participants in the control group reported a decrease in pain and an increase in quality of life.

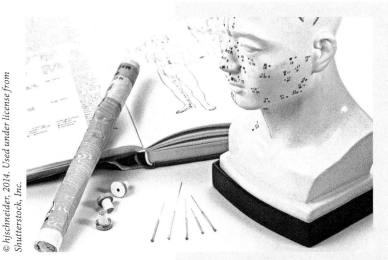

© hjschneider, 2014. Used under license from Shutterstock, Inc.

This article was a very compelling one. We might even be tempted to tell everyone we know with osteoarthritis that they should run out and receive acupuncture treatments. However, you have just learned about threats to internal validity. In other words, you have learned about factors that might be a threat to saying that the independent variable (i.e., acupuncture treatments) caused the change in the dependent variables (i.e., perceived pain and quality of life). Think about the 10 questions presented in this chapter. Could any of these be threats to internal validity? If so, explain. (Hint: As you read through the questions and look for threats to internal validity, we want you to focus on factors that were very likely to be threats to internal validity. Sometimes, for example, a factor might be a possible threat to internal validity, but one that is highly unlikely. Do not include such a factor in your list.)

Answer

When we looked through the 10 questions, we found 6 factors that could be threats to the internal validity of the experiment. They are maturation, regression to the mean, selection, attrition, placebo effect, and demand characteristics. We will explain why below.

- *Maturation* means the change in the dependent variable is not only due to the independent variable but also due to internal changes within the participant that occurred over time. It is possible that the decrease in pain reported by participants was not due to the acupuncture treatments alone, but due to an internal change that occurred within the participant over the 3-month time period. It might have been possible in milder cases of osteoarthritis for the pain to ease over time by itself. For example, maybe the seasons changed during the 3-month time period and the change in temperatures helped to alleviate some of the pain. If this occurred, the decrease in pain reported by participants would be due to maturation rather than the independent variable (acupuncture treatments).

- In *regression to the mean*, the change in the dependent variable is not due to the independent variable, but due to extreme scores moving toward the mean. It is our hypothesis that the participants who received the acupuncture treatments were in pain, not just minor discomfort. We think this for two reasons. First, we would have to be in severe pain to sign up for an experiment that used a treatment that may or may not work. Second, participants were instructed to select the joint that caused the most pain. Both of these factors create a situation that would cause participants at the beginning of the experiment to rate the pain as very high. If the pain is rated on the upper end of a pain scale on the first occasion, subsequent ratings after treatment could inherently go down, creating regression to the mean.

- If *selection* of participants is a threat to internal validity, the change in the dependent variable could be due to how the participants were selected for the experiment. In this experiment, no information was given about how participants were selected to participate. For example, no information was given regarding how participants were recruited or if a financial stipend was given to participants. However, we are most concerned with a self-selection problem. Participants who believed the acupuncture treatments would relieve pain are those who self-selected to participate in the experiment. In other words, those participants with osteoarthritis who agreed to participate could somehow be different from those participants with osteoarthritis who did not participate. Specifically, those individuals who did not think acupuncture treatments would work did not participate in the experiment. To support our hypothesis that selection could be a threat to internal validity, the article even stated that about 11% of participants had already received acupuncture in the year before the experiment, potentially demonstrating that participants open to the idea in the first place participated in the study.

- *Attrition* occurs when participants systematically drop out of an experiment and therefore change the results of the experiment. Attrition could have been a threat to internal validity in the current experiment. For example, what if some participants did not believe that the acupuncture treatments were working for them? They may have decided to drop out of the experiment before it ended. This would leave a greater number of participants remaining in the experiment who believed the acupuncture treatments were decreasing their pain. Thus, at the conclusion of the experiment, the acupuncture treatments could look more effective in relieving osteoarthritis pain because those participants the acupuncture treatments did not work for had dropped out of the experiment.

- Sometimes just thinking a change will occur is enough to produce a change. This is known as a *placebo effect*. Remember, participants in this study were experiencing enough pain that they were actively searching for relief. It may be such that the participants wanted so strongly for this new treatment to alleviate their pain that they experienced pain relief. Therefore, it may not be the effectiveness of the independent variable (acupuncture treatment), but the expectation the participant held for the effectiveness of the independent variable that led to a decrease in pain.

- *Demand characteristics* are various hints and cues that participants use to tell them how the researcher wants them to behave, or at least how they think the researcher wants them to behave. It is possible that during the acupuncture treatments the doctors interacting with the participants could have given various cues that caused the participants to believe the treatments would help. This seems only logical. The doctors participating in this study certainly believed in the effectiveness of acupuncture to relieve pain associated with osteoarthritis. If they did not, they would not be willing to administer this treatment. Therefore, it is only natural to believe that their positive attitudes toward acupuncture treatments might be conveyed to the participants in the experiment. And, it is this positive attitude that the participants could have used to determine the manner in which they should behave (i.e., experiencing the relief of pain).

How did you do? Did you find the same threats to internal validity that we did? Did you find other threats to internal validity that we did not? If so, bring them up to a friend or your professor and discuss them.

CHAPTER SUMMARY

- Control is at the heart of all research. Researchers need to make sure there are not unaccounted-for variables in a study that could influence or bias results (pp. 162–165).
- Two common types of variables that can lead to biased results are extraneous and nuisance variables:
    - *Extraneous variables* are variables not controlled for in the experiment that vary with the independent variables (p. 162).
    - *Nuisance variables* are not controlled for in the experiment that influences all participants in the same manner (p. 162).
- When conducting a study, a researcher needs to consider threats to internal validity. *Internal validity* is ensuring the observed change in behavior/mental process is due to the variable(s) that is/are being manipulated. However, there are factors that can threaten internal validity in a study (pp. 165–172).
    - For each, the observed change might not be due to the independent variable but rather due to an unaccounted-for aspect.
        - *History*—change due to outside events during the study (pp. 165–166).
        - *Maturation*—change due to internal changes in the participant (pp. 166–167).
        - *Regression to the mean*—change due to the extreme scores moving toward the mean on later measures (pp. 167–168).
        - *Selection*—change due to how the participants were selected for the experiment or how they were assigned to groups (p. 168).
        - *Attrition*—change as a result of participants dropping out of a study systematically (pp. 168–169).

- *Testing*—change due to the participant becoming more familiar with the test or testing procedures (p. 169).

  - *Diffusion of treatment*—change due to participants in different groups communicating with each other (pp. 169–170).

  - *Instrumentation*—change due to how the dependent variable was measured (p. 170).

  - *Placebo effect*—change due to participants thinking/believing a change will occur (p. 171).

  - *Demand* characteristics—change due to participants believing they should act or behave in a certain way during an experiment or if a researcher somehow communicates to participants how they should act or behave (pp. 171–172).

- It is better to use a *double blind study* as opposed to a *single blind study*. A double blind offers the benefit of neither the researcher nor the participant knowing which group the participant has been placed into (p. 172).

- A *placebo* is an inert substance that has no effect (p. 172).

APA LEARNING GOALS LINKAGE

- **Goal 2. Scientific Inquiry and Critical Thinking**

  You will demonstrate scientific reasoning and problem solving, including effective research methods.

  Sections Covered: Are You Equipped?, Control, Threats to Internal Validity, Minimizing Threats, Are You Equipped Now?

  Explanation of the Goal: This chapter adds to our knowledge of research methods in numerous ways. To begin, information was provided on limitations to inferences that can be drawn from research designs. The first example of this was provided at the beginning of the chapter when we observed how nuisance and extraneous variables can influence outcomes. The second example was later in the chapter when we scrutinized how single versus double blind studies can lead to different outcomes in a study, thereby changing the inferences that are drawn. We also addressed how to select and apply appropriate methods to maximize internal validity. In order to do so, we outlined threats to internal validity that should be avoided or minimized. These measures are taken in research design so that alternative explanations for the findings can be reduced. Finally, through our discussion of threats to internal validity such as selection of participants, demand characteristics, and placebo effect, we recognized how personal biases may shape the research process.

  Sections Covered: Are You Equipped?, Control, Threats to Internal Validity, Are You Equipped Now?

Explanation of the Goal: Critical thinking involves weighing support for conclusions and using the scientific method to solve problems related to behavior and mental processes. The exercises in this chapter were designed to practice these skills of critical thinking. In particular, you were often asked to evaluate how conclusions from a study might be limited due to threats to internal validity. This uses the critical thinking skill of weighing support for conclusions. You also practiced controlling for threats to internal validity to answer questions on important topics like the relationship between TV viewing and rates of autism. This exemplifies the critical thinking skill of using the scientific method to solve problems related to behavior and mental processes.

- ## Goal 3. Ethical and Social Responsibility in a Diverse World

You will apply ethical standards to evaluate psychological science and practice and you will develop ethically and socially responsible behaviors for professional and personal settings in a landscape that involves increasing diversity.

Sections Covered: Are You Equipped?, Control, Threats to Internal Validity, Are You Equipped Now?

Explanation of the Goal: When psychological principles are applied to key societal issues, the inferences drawn become crucial. As social scientists, we must be very cautious when drawing conclusions on topics (e.g., autism, health-care options) that influence the public. This chapter also illustrated how relaxing activities like watching *American Idol* and using social networking sites are not exempt from relating to psychological concepts.

Sections Covered: Threats to Internal Validity, Are You Equipped Now?

Explanation of the Goal: Individual differences can influence behavior and mental processes and thus the outcome of a study. Through our coverage of threats to internal validity, we saw how changes within an individual over time, maturation, can influence psychological findings. Awareness of this topic allows threats to be minimized and consequently the number of alternative explanations reduced.

Excerpts from APA Guidelines for the Undergraduate Psychology Major, Version 2.0, August 2013 *by the American Psychological Association. Copyright © 2013 by the American Psychological Association.*

Types of Designs

Part 4

CHAPTER 10

Between Subjects Designs

CHAPTER OUTLINE

Are You Equipped?

Introduction to Between Subjects Designs

Factors to Consider

Ways to Minimize Disadvantages

Are You Equipped Now?

Chapter Summary

APA Learning Goals Linkage

ARE YOU EQUIPPED?

A recent study by Dong and Wyer (2014) conducted several experiments to examine the impact of social characteristics in a social interaction. Specifically, in their first experiment, they had participants listen to an audiotaped conversation between a male and a female. Participants were to imagine themselves as the speaker of the same sex and then to either (1) form an impression of the opposite speaker or (2) think of the impression the other speaker was forming of them in terms of how long the conversation lasted. The researchers wanted to know how perceived duration impacted social interactions.

In this example, the independent variable would be impression. It would have two levels: impression of the opposite speaker and impression formed by the opposite speaker. The dependent variable would be perceived duration of the conversation. If you were the researchers and had 50 participants who had volunteered for your study, how would you go about deciding how the participants would be exposed to the two levels of the independent variable?

© bikeriderlondon, 2014. Used under license from Shutterstock, Inc.

There is more than one correct answer to this question. However, in this chapter we are going to focus on one way to expose participants to the levels of the independent variable. Specifically, we will discuss between subjects designs. It just so happens that the researchers of the above study used a between subjects design. This means that one group of participants was allowed to form impressions of the opposite speaker, while the other group of participants was allowed to think about the impression the opposite speaker had formed of them. Next, participants in both groups completed a survey about the conversation they had. Results indicated that there was no difference in perceived time when the participants focused under either condition.

What makes this a between subjects design? This is a between subjects design because the participants only received one of the levels of the independent variable. The participants either formed an impression of the opposite speaker or thought about the impression the opposite speaker was forming of them. But, the participants never served under both conditions. In this chapter, we will talk more about between subjects designs and discuss advantages and disadvantages of its use in research.

As you go through this chapter, we also want you to keep in mind how the material relates to the American Psychological Association's goals for psychology majors. Specifically, this chapter will address the following goals:

- **Goal 1. Knowledge Base in Psychology**

  You will demonstrate fundamental knowledge and comprehension of the major concepts, theoretical perspectives, historical trends, and empirical findings to discuss how psychological principles apply to behavioral problems.

- **Goal 2. Scientific Inquiry and Critical Thinking**

  You will demonstrate scientific reasoning and problem solving, including effective research methods.

We will relook at these goals at the end of the chapter.

INTRODUCTION TO BETWEEN SUBJECTS DESIGNS

In this chapter, we are going to begin by building on a concept that we introduced to you in Chapter 7. Specifically, we are talking about levels of an independent variable. We introduced this topic to you with the example of temperature and preference for movie genres. The two levels of the independent variable temperature were cold and warm. Next, we discussed the example of caffeine influencing levels of alertness. In that example, we had three levels of the independent variable: no caffeine, 8 ounces of a caffeinated beverage, and 24 ounces of a caffeinated beverage. In other words, the levels of the independent variable are the specific conditions of that variable. When you have levels of an independent variable, a decision must be made as to how participants will be exposed to those levels. There are different ways this can be done. This chapter will focus on one way.

The first way participants can be exposed to the levels of the independent variable is through a between subjects design. This can also be referred to as a between participants design or an independent group design. In a **between subjects design**, your research participants will be exposed to only one level of the independent variable. Thus, your participants will serve only in one group and would never be exposed to more than one condition of your independent variable.

Between Subjects Design: Participants will be exposed to only one level of the independent variable.

In the experimental temperature and movie preference study described in Chapter 7, the temperature was the independent variable. Participants were placed under a condition where they were made either cold or warm. The warm condition was defined as drinking warm tea or being placed in a room with the temperature set between 72 and 76 degrees Fahrenheit. While, the cold condition was defined as drinking cold tea or being placed in a room with the temperature set between 59 and 62 degrees Fahrenheit. For this study, participants could be placed into only one of the two groups. Furthermore, participants could not be in both groups at the same time. This would make the independent variable of temperature a between subjects variable.

In Chapter 7, we also used a between subjects design to see if caffeine influenced levels of alertness. We had three groups of participants: participants who received 8 ounces of a caffeinated beverage, participants who received 24 ounces of a caffeinated beverage, and participants who received no caffeine. In this example, a total of 30 participants were exposed to only one of the three levels. There was never a participant who was exposed to more than just one condition.

Take a look at Table 10.1. This is known as a **research matrix**. It is a visual representation of a research design.

Research Matrix: A visual representation of a research design.

TABLE 10.1 Research matrix.

No Caffeine	8 Ounces	24 Ounces
10 participants	10 participants	10 participants

Another example from Chapter 7 was also a between subjects design. Remember John's research on monitor size and reaction time? He had three groups of participants too. Each group was exposed to a different monitor size and the reaction times were measured. Here is what this research design would look like visually (Table 10.2).

TABLE 10.2 Research matrix for monitor size.

17 inch	19 inch	21 inch
25 participants	25 participants	25 participants

We know we have only just started this chapter, but we want to see how you are doing. Here are some questions for you to try regarding John's study on monitor size. Pretend you are a researcher working with John on the study.

QUESTIONS

1. You want to give every participant in the study a piece of paper with the contact information of the researchers. How many pieces of paper will you need or how many total participants do you have?

2. Your friend Joe wants to know about your study because he is thinking of participating. Tell Joe how many groups it is possible for him to participate in as per the design.

ANSWERS

1. If you wanted to give each participant a piece of paper with the researchers' contact information, you would need 75 pieces of paper. This is because 25 + 25 + 25 = 75. In other words, there are three groups with 25 participants in each yielding a total of 75 participants.

2. You would tell Joe that it would be possible for him to be assigned to one of the three groups. Joe would be allowed to use the 17-inch, 19-inch, or 21-inch monitor. However, he would not get to use more than one of the monitor sizes due to the type of research design being used.

A CLASSIC RESEARCH EXAMPLE

Now that we have looked at some examples from Chapter 7, we want to take a look at a classic research experiment within the field of psychology that also decided to use a between subjects design for one of the independent variables. This study was conducted in 1973 by researchers Darley and Batson titled, "*From Jerusalem to Jericho: A study of situational and dispositional variables in helping behavior.*"

As you might be able to gather from the title, the researchers got their research idea from the Bible, in particular the Good Samaritan parable. The researchers set out to design a study to examine the influence of situational and personality variables on helping behavior. The variable that we want to mention in this chapter is the independent variable, degree of hurry.

The participants used in this experiment were Princeton Theological Seminary students. The participants began the experiment in one building and were then asked to go to another building for the second part of the study. The participants then passed a "victim" placed by the researchers between the two buildings. The victim was slumped in a doorway and coughed twice and groaned as the participants passed. The independent variable was the degree to which the participants were instructed to hurry to the other building (i.e., high-hurry, intermediate-hurry, and low-hurry) and the dependent variable was the amount of help offered to the victim.

This is, in fact, how Darley and Batson exposed participants to the independent variable. Participants in the first group were told they were running late and the research assistant in the next building would be waiting for them (high-hurry). Participants in the second group (the intermediate group) were told the research assistant was ready for them and they could go to the next building. Finally, the last group of participants under the low-hurry condition were told it would be a few minutes before the research assistant would be ready for them in the next building, but to go ahead and head over. In case you are wondering about the results, the researchers found that participants who were under the high-hurry condition were the least likely to offer help to the victim.

YOU TRY IT!

QUESTION

Based on what you have learned to this point, can you determine how the independent variable of hurry was used as a between subjects variable?

ANSWER

The independent variable was a between subjects variable because participants were exposed to only one of the three levels. This means that a given student/participant could have served under the high-hurry, intermediate-hurry, or low-hurry condition. However, students would not have served under more than one condition.

CONTEMPORARY RESEARCH EXAMPLES

Although Darley and Batson's design was used in the 1970s, it does not mean that this type of design is outdated. In fact, researchers continue to use between subjects designs to investigate current topics of interest. Take for example a research study by Barlett, Harris, Smith, and Bonds-Raacke. This study was published in 2005 with the purpose of determining whether action figures contribute to negative body image in young adult men who handled them. Barlett was interested in this idea because previous research had examined the relationship between girls' body image and playing with Barbie dolls that have unrealistic figures. For Barlett's study, the independent variable was muscularity of action figures handled and the dependent variable was body image. The study had three groups of male participants.

Group 1: This group served as the control group. The group did not handle any action figure. The group only received measures of body image to complete.

Group 2: This group was one of the experimental groups. This group manipulated highly muscular action figures. After handling the highly muscular action figures, the participants completed the body images measures.

Group 3: This group was the second experimental group. This group manipulated moderately muscular action figures. After handling the moderately muscular action figures, the participants completed the body image measure.

Below you will find a visual representation of the research design (see Table 10.3).

TABLE 10.3   Research matrix for Barlett, Harris, Smith, and Bonds-Raacke (2005).

Control	Experimental 1	Experimental 2
No action figures	Highly muscular figures	Moderately muscular figures
32 participants	22 participants	28 participants

As you can see from the visual representation, there were a total of 82 participants. Each participant received only one level of the independent variable and thus would have been assigned to only one of the three groups. Results did find participants in the experimental group that handled the highly muscular action figures had a decrease in body esteem after handling the action figures. Barlett has continued to investigate the influence of media on users. In a more recent study, Barlett, Harris, and Bruey (2008) examined the influence of the amount of blood in a violent video game on aggression, hostility, and arousal. The amount of blood was the independent variable and the dependent variables were aggression, hostility, and arousal.

Participants were randomly assigned to one of the four groups. Each group of participants played a video game for 15 minutes (*Mortal Kombat: Deadly Alliance*). However, the blood level varied for each of the groups. For Group 1, the blood level was set on maximum. For Group 2, the blood level was set on medium. For Groups 3 and 4, the blood levels were set to low and no, respectively (see Table 10.4). After playing the violent video game, participants completed measures of aggression, hostility, and arousal.

This too was a between subjects design. Participants served in one of the four groups. In other words, participants would have been exposed to high, medium, low, or the no blood condition.

TABLE 10.4   Research matrix for Barlett et al. (2008).

Group 1	Group 2	Group 3	Group 4
Maximum Blood	Medium Blood	Low Blood	No Blood

Results indicated there were differences in hostility and physiological arousal based on the amount of blood level the participant was exposed to in the video games. Specifically, participants in the maximum and medium blood levels had a significant increase in both hostility and physiological arousal. However, participants in the low blood and no blood levels did not have a significant change in these dependent variables.

There are both advantages and some drawbacks to the between subjects design. Before we discuss them, we want to tell you about one more contemporary research study that utilized a between subjects variable. This study was developed on the observation that men and women often disagree about the meaning of women's nonverbal cues. Farris, Treat, Viken, and McFall (2008) wanted to see if this was in fact the case. Men and women participants were asked to view photo images of women for varying amounts of time. After viewing the images, the participants were asked to place the photos into one of the four categories: friendly, sexually interested, sad, or rejected. The researchers then compared the accuracy of responses for men and women. Results indicated men were more likely than women to misidentify friendly targets as indicating sexual interests and to misidentify sexually interested targets as indicating friendliness.

This was a between subjects design. The researchers were interested in if men and women were equal in their ability to judge women's nonverbal cues. The between subjects variable was participants' sex. This is a between subjects design because the participants were either men or women. The participants could not be both and therefore were in either one of the two levels of the variable of sex.

We used this example to bring up the variable of sex (or gender) of the participants. Sex is an example of a subject variable which is always a between subjects variable. Anytime researchers are interested in comparing responses of men to women, you have a between subjects variable. There are other variables that by nature are between subjects variables. In Chapter 8, we mentioned a study that examined the relationship between where one lives (urban or rural location) and when a specific form of cancer is diagnosed. For this research, the independent variable was where one lives and it had two levels, urban or rural. Participants either lived in an urban or rural setting. However, the participants could not live in both. Hence, this would be another example of a variable which is between subjects. Can you think of any others? If so, mention them to your professor and see if you are correct.

© MaxyM, 2014. Used under license from Shutterstock, Inc.

SECTION SUMMARY

- A *between subjects design* occurs when participants in a study are exposed to only one level of the independent variable (pp. 182–187).
- A *research matrix* is a visual representation (in table form) of your research design (p. 183).

FACTORS TO CONSIDER

When using a between subjects design, you will need to consider factors such as the advantages and disadvantages of this approach. In order to accomplish this, we are going to do several things. First, we will discuss the advantages and disadvantages of this type of design listed in Figure 10.1. Next, we will examine these within the context of two research experiments we already discussed in this chapter. Finally, we will let you practice with an example. Take a look at Figure 10.1. Keep in mind, just because there are more reasons listed in as advantages than as disadvantages, this does not make this design the best one for all research experiments. You will see in later chapters other research designs have numerous benefits as well.

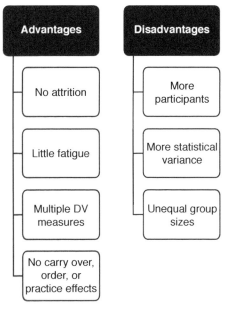

Advantages	Disadvantages
No attrition	More participants
Little fatigue	More statistical variance
Multiple DV measures	Unequal group sizes
No carry over, order, or practice effects	

Figure 10.1 Advantages and disadvantages of a between subjects design.

Attrition: Participants dropping out of a study or not returning to complete additional parts to a study.

Statistical Variance: The degree of spread among data when surrounding the mean.

Carryover Effect: These occur when the effects of a prior treatment conditions influence subsequent treatment conditions.

Order Effect: Effects of a study are due to the participants experiencing the same order of presentation of the levels of the independent variable.

Advantages to the between subjects design include the fact you do not have to worry about **attrition** (e.g., participants not retuning for a second part of the experiment and dropping out); little fatigue; the opportunity to collect multiple dependent measures because of available time; and no **carryover, order,** or **practice effects**. The downsides to this design include the fact that you will need more participants, you will have more **statistical variance** (making it more difficult to see differences between groups), and your groups could be unequal in size. We want to explain how these pros and cons could have influenced researchers' decisions to select a between subjects design in experiments we discussed previously. The first experiment we will look at again is the one by Barlett et al. (2005), examining the influence of action figures on body image of males. Recall this experiment had three groups of participants. The first group served as a control group by participants not handling any action figures and completing measures on body image. The second group was the first experimental group, handling highly muscular action figures before completing the body image measures. The final group was the second experimental group which handled moderately muscular action figures before completing the scales. The design for this study had many benefits. First, the researchers did not have to require participants to come back to the experiment a second time (possibly on another day) to complete another level of the independent variable. Because the participants completed their one level of the independent variable within the 1-hour time frame, the researchers did not have to consider the issue of attrition. Second, the researchers did not have to worry about the participants becoming tired and fatigued, thus influencing participants' performance. Participants under the two experimental conditions were required to handle the action figures for a maximum time period of 45 minutes. This amount of time would not result in participants being severely tired. Third, because the participants were only under one of the three conditions, there was additional time to collect more than one dependent variable. In fact, the researchers had participants' complete three scales to measure body image. This included self-esteem, body esteem, and body satisfaction. Finally, the researchers were not concerned about carryover, order, or practice effects.

A **carryover effect** is when the effect of a treatment condition is literally carried over into a second treatment condition. For example, if participants completed the first experimental condition of handling highly muscular action figures first and the second experimental condition of handling moderately muscular action second, you would wonder about the possibility of a carryover effect. This is because after handling the highly muscular action figures, the male participant's body image would decrease. As the male participant started the second condition and handled the moderately muscular action figures, his body image would still be decreased due to the first condition. In this situation, we would be unable to determine if the decrease in body image under the second condition was actually due to the moderately muscular action figures or the highly muscular action figures. This is because it is difficult to undo what a participant has already seen or done. An **order effect** could have occurred if participants completed all three levels of the independent variable and always completed them in the same order. You would not be able to determine if the condition caused the influence on the dependent variable or the order of the presentation. For example, scores on body image may always decrease under the third condition presented. This may be due to the fact that participants are ready to complete the experiment and go home. Therefore, it would be difficult to determine if the third condition alone decreased scores or it was just the fact that it was the third (and last) condition of the experiment that led to the experiment. Finally, the researchers did not have to consider in their design the fact that participants could improve their performance on subsequent trials and so **practice effects** were a nonissue.

Even with these numerous benefits, the researchers did have a few cons to consider when they selected their approach. First, by using a between subjects design, the researchers needed more participants. Instead of 25 participants being exposed to all three levels of the independent variable, the researchers needed at least 75 participants to have a minimum of 25 participants in each of the three levels. Second, because different participants served under each of the three conditions, there needed to be a greater difference in the treatment effect for the results to be significant. Had it been the same participants in each of the three levels, the within group differences would have been reduced and the difference between the levels would not need to be as great. Finally, the researchers had to be careful when gathering data to ensure that the groups were relatively close in numbers.

There were similar advantages and disadvantages to using a between subjects design when used in the later research conducted by Barlett et al. (2008), examining the effect of the amount of blood in a violent video game on aggression, hostility, and arousal. Participants were randomly assigned to one of the four groups. Each group of participants played a video game for 15 minutes. However, the amount of blood varied for each of the groups. For Group 1, the blood level was set on maximum. For Group 2, the blood level was set on medium. And, for Groups 3 and 4, the blood levels were set to low and no, respectively. After playing the violent video game, participants completed measures of aggression, hostility, and arousal.

© Sean D, 2014. Used under license from Shutterstock, Inc.

Practice Effect:
Participants improve performance due to subsequent experiences on the same task.

Benefits of this design include participants did not have to return for a second (or third) part of the study and therefore did not have the opportunity to drop out. Second, participants only played the video game for 15 minutes (rather than 60 minutes if they had been in all four levels of the independent variable). Since this time span was brief, the researchers did not have to consider fatigue as a variable influencing aggression, hostility, and arousal. Also, since the participants served only in one level of independent variable requiring 15 minutes, the participants had time to complete three dependent measures. Third, participants' exposure to one treatment condition did not influence their response to another treatment condition. In other words, no influence was carried over to another condition. Similarly, the order of presentation did not influence responses and participants did not improve over time as they completed four conditions. The disadvantages, however, included the need for more participants to have a minimum number under each of the four conditions, more statistical variance, and the possibility of unequal group sizes.

Think back to the research experiment by Darley and Batson on level of hurry and helping behavior. This research experiment had three groups of participants. Participants in the first group (the high-hurry group) were told they were running late and the research assistant in the next building would be waiting for them. Participants in the second group (the intermediate group) were told the research assistant was ready for them and they could go to the next building. Finally, the last group of participants under the low-hurry condition was told it would be a few minutes before the research assistant would be ready for them in the next building, but to go ahead and head over.

QUESTION

Can you describe one advantage of this between subjects design for Darley and Batson and one disadvantage?

ANSWER

There is not just one correct answer to this question. In fact, you could have selected any of the reasons listed in the table we previously discussed. However, probably the most obvious disadvantage is Darley and Batson had to recruit more participants for the between subjects design they utilized than if the participants had served under all three of the conditions. Yet, this disadvantage is outweighed by numerous advantages. Preventing a carryover effect was a huge advantage for this being a between subjects design. This prevented the helping behavior from being influenced by the previous treatment condition. It takes time in becoming comfortable with thinking critically about the advantages and disadvantages of research designs. After you complete Chapter 11 (which is also on types of research designs), this type of thinking about pros and cons to research designs will get easier with practice.

SECTION SUMMARY

- Between subjects designs have several advantages which make it an appealing design to use. Advantages include no attrition; very little participant fatigue; the collection of multiple dependent variables; and no order, carryover, or practice effects (pp. 187–190).

    - When participants drop out of studies or fail to complete all parts of a study, it is known as *attrition* (p. 188).

    - A *carryover effect* occurs when a prior treatment condition from an experiment influences current or future treatment conditions (p. 188).

    - If all participants experience the same order of treatment conditions in an experiment, then any obtained results may be due to the order and not the conditions themselves. This is known as an *order effect* (p. 188).

    - An improvement in performance by a participant on subsequent stimuli independent of the variable being manipulated is known as a *practice effect* (p. 189).

- Even though between subjects designs have several advantages, there are disadvantages to using this methodology. Disadvantages include the use of a large number of participants and higher statistical variance between conditions (pp. 187–189).
  - *Statistical variance* is the degree of spread among scores from the mean of the group of scores. This can make it more difficult to deter mine if group differences exist (p. 188).

WAYS TO MINIMIZE DISADVANTAGES

It is possible to minimize the disadvantages of the between subjects design we previously described. If you know you are going to use a between subjects design, you could reduce the number of levels of the independent variable (if possible). This way you might need only three groups instead of four groups. Reducing the number of groups you need will, in turn, reduce the number of participants you need. You can also reduce statistical variance by randomly assigning participants to the groups and using sound methodology. Finally, it is a fairly simple task to keep track of the number of participants in each group as you collect data. The number of participants in each group does not have to be exactly the same. However, it should be fairly close.

We would like to mention one final note before wrapping up this chapter. You may be wondering how to decide when to use a between subjects design. This will depend on the specific variables you are interested in and how easily the disadvantages can be overcome for your particular study. It could be the case that you need to employ a different research design. We will talk about within subjects designs and factorial designs in the next two chapters, respectively.

ARE YOU EQUIPPED NOW?

Dr. Rosebud Roberts with the Mayo Clinic in Rochester, Minnesota, conducted the following study, which was summarized on Health Orbit.com. Roberts collected data on 2,050 individuals between the ages of 70 and 89, through interviews, examinations, and cognitive tests. Results indicated 15% of the sample exhibited mild cognitive impairment. Dr. Roberts also found that men were one and a half times more likely than women to exhibit cognitive impairment.

In this design, the subject variable was sex of participants and the dependent variables were performance on interviews, examinations, and cognitive tests used to assess cognitive impairment.

QUESTION
Why did Dr. Roberts use a between subjects design in this experiment?

ANSWER
We hope this was a relatively easy "Are You Equipped Now" section. Dr. Roberts used a between subjects design because the participants were either men or women. The participants could not be both and therefore were only exposed to one level of the independent variable.

CHAPTER SUMMARY

- A *between subjects design* occurs when participants in a study are exposed to only one level of the independent variable. Therefore, participants participate in only one group of the study (pp. 182–187).

- A r*esearch matrix* is a visual representation (in table form) of your research design. Typically, a research matrix allows a participant to "see" the type of treatment each group will receive in a research study (p. 183).

- Between subject designs have several *advantages* which make it an appealing design to use. Advantages include no attrition; very little participant fatigue; the collection of multiple dependent variables; and no order, carryover, or practice effects (pp. 187–190).

    - When participants drop out of studies or fail to complete all parts of a study, it is known as *attrition* (p. 188).

    - Since participants in this methodology are exposed to only one level of the independent variable, they are less likely to be fatigued in completing the experiment (p. 188).

    - A between subjects design allows multiple dependent variables to be collected in a study due to the participants only being under one treatment condition (p. 188).

    - A *carryover effect* occurs when a prior treatment condition from an experiment influences current or future treatment conditions (p. 188).

    - If all participants experience the same order of treatment conditions in an experiment, then any obtained results may be due to the order and not the conditions themselves. This is known as an *order effect* (p. 188).

    - An improvement in performance by a participant on subsequent stimuli independent of the variable being manipulated is known as a *practice effect* (pp. 188–189).

- Even though between subjects designs have several advantages, there are *disadvantages* to using this methodology. Disadvantages include the use of a large number of participants and higher statistical variance between conditions (pp. 187–189).

    - In order to obtain sufficient sample sizes for the levels of the independent variable, more participants are used. Specifically, a relatively equal number of participants have to be utilized for each treatment condition, which increases the number of participants as compared to designs where each participant goes through all treatment conditions (p. 188).

    - *Statistical variance* is the degree of spread among scores from the mean of the group of scores. This can make it more difficult to determine if group differences exist (p. 188).

- **Goal 1. Knowledge Base in Psychology**

  You will demonstrate fundamental knowledge and comprehension of the major concepts, theoretical perspectives, historical trends, and empirical findings to discuss how psychological principles apply to behavioral problems.

  Sections Covered: Are You Equipped?, A Classic Research Example, Contemporary Research Examples, Are You Equipped Now?

  Explanation of the Goal: In each of the aforementioned sections, we have presented research examples by which we have illustrated the use of between subjects designs. These examples have been chosen to help you apply the psychological principles in this chapter to personal, social, or organizational issues. For example, in the section "Contemporary Research Examples," we discussed how between subjects designs have been used to study the relationship between violent video games and aggression. Given the prevalence of these games in our society, it has become important to apply our knowledge in research design to this social issue. Without the application of psychological principles to this issue, we are left with an inability to determine the scientific impact that violent video games may have on aggression.

- **Goal 2. Scientific Inquiry and Critical Thinking**

  You will demonstrate scientific reasoning and problem solving, including effective research methods.

  Sections Covered: Introduction to Between Subject Designs, Factors to Consider, Ways to Minimize Disadvantages

  Explanation of the Goal: As a psychology major, you will be expected to explain different research methods commonly used within the field. The between subjects design discussed in this chapter is a popular methodology. In articulating the strengths and limitations of the between subjects design, we also introduced major research concepts such as attrition; fatigue; and carryover, order, and practice effects. By knowing the advantages and disadvantages of this design, you will be able to select and apply appropriate methodologies to answer your research questions.

  Sections Covered: Are You Equipped?, You Try It!, Are You Equipped Now?

Explanation of the Goal: After explaining the concepts in this chapter, we have tested your knowledge and comfort level with the material. In particular, we have asked you to evaluate problems and generate a solution to that problem. To generate solutions, you need to have an open but critical mind and link the problem to the specific material learned. This allowed you to select the best solution to the problem. It is through the use of critical thinking skills that we can investigate areas of interest such as differences between men and women in (a) cognitive impairments with age and (b) ability to judge women's nonverbal cues.

Excerpts from APA Guidelines for the Undergraduate Psychology Major, Version 2.0, August 2013 *by the American Psychological Association. Copyright © 2013 by the American Psychological Association.*

CHAPTER 11

Within Subjects Designs

CHAPTER OUTLINE

Are You Equipped?

Introduction to Within Subjects Designs

Factors to Consider

Matched Subjects Designs

Are You Equipped Now?

Chapter Summary

APA Learning Goals Linkage

ARE YOU EQUIPPED?

Back in the late 1980s and early 1990s, the soda wars were in full force. In particular, the Pepsi Cola Co. and the Coca Cola Co. were competing for the crown of top soda producers. Although both companies had several variations of sodas, the two main rivals for this crown were each company's number one brand, Pepsi and Coke, respectively. To determine the overall champion, the Pepsi Cola Co. went around the country with a contest known as "The Pepsi Challenge" (you can still go to the YouTube and find the old commercials). During the challenge, participants would have the opportunity to taste a sample of cola from each contender, Pepsi and Coke. Once the participant had tasted each of the contenders, he or she would then make a judgment about which one tasted better. Typically, these taste tests occurred at events with large crowds surrounding a Pepsi Co. booth. Not too surprisingly, the results of the Pepsi Co. challenge indicated a vast majority of people preferred the taste of Pepsi over Coke. In fact, this led the Pepsi Co. to make several commercials in which they showed people choosing Pepsi over Coke followed by crowds cheering. However, the interesting aspect of this story is, whether the Pepsi Cola Co. intended it or not, they were utilizing a popular research methodology.

© Givaga, 2014. Used under license from Shutterstock, Inc.

For this methodology, there was one independent variable (i.e., type of cola). The independent variable had two levels, Coke and Pepsi. The dependent variable for this methodology was the judgment of which cola tasted better. Now think about how the participants were exposed to the two levels of the independent variable. Was this procedure a between subjects design as described in the previous chapter or something a little different? This methodology is different from the between subjects design we discussed in Chapter 10. Probably, the most obvious difference is that participants were exposed to all levels of the independent variable and not just one level. This is known as a within subjects design and will be the focus of this chapter.

As you go through this chapter, we also want you to keep in mind how the material relates to the American Psychological Association's goals for psychology majors. Specifically, this chapter will address the following goals:

- **Goal 1. Knowledge Base in Psychology**
  You will demonstrate fundamental knowledge and comprehension of the major concepts, theoretical perspectives, historical trends, and empirical findings to discuss how psychological principles apply to behavioral problems.
- **Goal 2. Scientific Inquiry and Critical Thinking**
  You will demonstrate scientific reasoning and problem solving, including effective research methods.

INTRODUCTION TO WITHIN SUBJECTS DESIGNS

This chapter will build on information regarding the levels of an independent variable that we discussed in Chapters 7 and 10. Specifically, we will be discussing the use of a **within subjects design**. A within subjects design is a methodology in which each participant is exposed to all levels of the independent variable. This is very different from the previous chapter on the between subjects design in which participants were exposed to only one level of the independent variable. Within subjects designs are also referred to as repeated measures designs (or within participant designs). This is because the participants literally repeat the dependent measures under all the conditions of the independent variable.

Within Subjects Design:
Design in which participants are exposed to all levels of the independent variable.

EXAMPLES FROM CHAPTER 7

As we did in the last chapter, let us go back and look at an earlier example to help explain this topic. Think about the study John conducted on monitor size. In that study, John wanted to determine if monitor size (independent variable) had an effect on performance (dependent variable) within a microworld simulation. For that example, there were three groups of participants and three different monitor sizes, 17 inch, 19 inch, and 21 inch. This study used a between subjects design, where each participant was exposed to only one of the three levels of the independent variable (monitor size). This is represented visually in Figure 11.1.

Design	17 inch	19 inch	21 inch
Between Subjects	25 participants	25 participants	25 participants

Fig 11.1   Research matrix for a between subjects design.

In reality, John et al. carried out a different methodology. The methodology consisted of a within subjects design and not a between subjects design. Rather than having three separate groups each experience working on a different size monitor, this study had one group of individuals experience working on all three monitor sizes. Thus, the size of the monitor was a within subjects variable. The research matrix resembled what is in Figure 11.2.

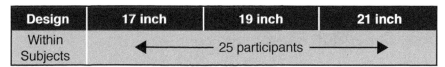

Fig 11.2   Research matrix for a within subjects design.

What you need to remember is in a within subjects design, each participant is exposed to all levels of the independent variable. Therefore, each person in this study was exposed to all three types of monitor size (i.e., 17, 19, and 21 inches). So, 25 total participants were needed. This is a smaller number than the 75 participants needed for a between subjects design.

In addition to John's monitor study, we also discussed in a previous chapter a study on caffeine and alertness. We explained how each of the participants was given 0, 8, or 24 ounces of a caffeinated beverage. Again, this is an example of a between subjects design because each participant was exposed to only one level of the independent variable. However, this study could have been conducted as a within subjects design. In order to change this study to a within subjects design, what needs to be done?

If you said that each participant should be exposed to all levels of the independent variable, you were correct. In order to conduct this study as a within subjects design, each participant would have his or her alertness tested after receiving 0, 8, and 24 ounces of a caffeinated beverage. Therefore, there would be only one group of participants receiving all three levels of the independent variable (caffeine).

YOU TRY IT!

Pretend that you are a research assistant working on John's study about monitor size using a within subjects design. Before data collection begins, you will need to answer the questions below.

QUESTIONS

- You want to give every participant in the study a piece of paper with the contact information of the researchers. This is in case the participants have questions after the study is complete. How many pieces of paper will you need? In other words, how many total participants do you have?

- Your friend Sara wants to know about your study because she is thinking of participating. Tell Sara how many conditions she will be exposed to.

ANSWERS

1. If you wanted to give each participant a piece of paper with the researcher's contact information, you would need only 25 pieces of paper. This is because you have only one group of 25 participants.

2. You would tell Sara that she would be exposed to a total of three conditions. Specifically, Sara would use the 17-, 19-, and 21-inch monitors because of the within subjects design.

A CLASSIC RESEARCH EXAMPLE

Classic research experiments within the field have utilized within subjects designs. For example, in an experiment Stroop (1935) wanted to know what would occur when a person was presented a color word (e.g., red) written in an incongruent ink color (e.g., green). In order to test the effects on an individual, Stroop developed three types of stimuli that can be seen below. The first type of stimuli consisted of color words printed in black ink. The second type of stimuli consisted of color words printed in an ink different from the color expressed by the word's semantic meaning. The final stimuli consisted of blocks in different colors. Stroop conducted two different experiments with these stimuli. The independent variable in each experiment was the type of stimuli to which the participants were exposed. The dependent variable was the amount of time it took for the participants to complete the task.

The first experiment involved a comparison between Stimuli 1 and Stimuli 2. Specifically, Stroop had two levels to the independent variable (task type). In this experiment, the time to complete the task was the dependent variable and was measured by how quickly the participants could correctly read the word in each stimuli.

In the second experiment, a comparison between Stimuli 2 and Stimuli 3 was made. Again, Stroop had two levels to the independent variable (task type). However, the dependent variable was measured by how quickly the participants could name the colors in each of the stimuli. If you are wondering what Stroop's results were, we are going to tell you in the next section.

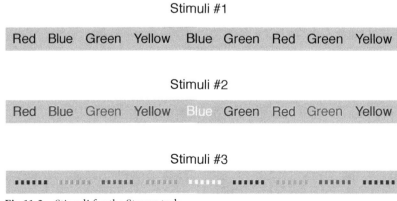

Fig 11.3 Stimuli for the Stroop task.

QUESTION

We want you to think about how to conduct these two experiments discussed above using a within subjects design. Specifically, how would you conduct a within subjects experiment to make a comparison between the levels of the independent variable in the first experiment? And, how would you conduct a within subjects experiment to make a comparison between the levels of the independent variable in the second experiment? Also, do you have a hypothesis about the results Stroop obtained?

ANSWER

Here is what Stroop did. For the first experiment, Stroop had a group of participants read the words for Stimuli 1 (black ink) and Stimuli 2 (incongruent ink). Participants in this experiment would be exposed to both sets of stimuli (e.g., both levels of the independent variable). Interestingly, results showed no difference between these two types of stimuli in terms of reaction time. Participants did not show a difficulty in reading the color words when printed in black or in a color inconsistent with the semantic meaning of the word.

In the second experiment, Stroop had a group of participants indicate the color of the ink used for each word (Stimuli 2) and for each set of blocks (Stimuli 3). The participants were to say the color independent of the word that was written for Stimuli 2 and indicate the color of the set of blocks. Again, participants in this experiment would be exposed to both sets of stimuli (levels of the independent variable). Unlike the first experiment, results for the second experiment showed a large difference between Stimuli 2 and Stimuli 3 in terms of reaction time. Specifically, participants had a difficult time saying the color of the ink for Stimuli 2 as compared to saying the color of the ink for Stimuli 3 leading to longer reaction times. Stroop reasoned that the automatic response of reading was interfering with the identification of the printed word's ink color.

Stroop's study has seen many variations since its original publication almost 80 years ago. In fact, researchers have used some version of the Stroop Task in over 700 research experiments. The most common replication occurs with the second experiment. This experiment shows the usefulness of a within subjects research design. However, the within subjects research design is not only a tool of the past but also one that is quite useful to researchers today.

CONTEMPORARY RESEARCH EXAMPLES

Recently, researchers chose to conduct a within subjects research design to examine music preference while playing computer games (Tamir, Mitchell, & Gross, 2008). This study was a within subjects design with the independent variable of music condition. The within subjects variable had three levels: angry, exciting, and neutral. Tamir et al. (2008) wanted to see what impact the music had on the participants playing the computer games. Participants in the experiment were exposed to all three levels of the music condition while they were playing the same computer games. The research matrix for this study looked like the one given in Figure 11.4.

IV	Angry Music	Exciting Music	Music
	All Participants Experience Each Music Type		

Fig 11.4   Research matrix for Tamir et al. (2008).

As you can see from the matrix, every participant played a computer game while listening to all three types of music: angry, exciting, and neutral. We will discuss this study in more detail and provide the results in Chapter 12. At that time, we will tell you more about the research design and the findings.

YOU TRY IT!

We have explained several different studies to you in this chapter, each one using a within subjects design. In a recent study, researchers wanted to determine if the type of scenario given influenced a participant's adjustment from an anchor (Janiszewski & Uy, 2008). An anchor in psychology has very little to do with a boat and how to keep it from moving in a body of water. Rather, when speaking of an anchor and adjustment, psychologists are usually referring to the work by Tversky and Kahneman (1974). This is a psychological heuristic in which people use a starting point (an anchor) as the basis to make judgments about a given scenario (adjustment).

In their experiment, Janiszewski and Uy (2008) had 43 participants read 10 scenarios in which they wanted to determine the impact of the scenario type on the anchoring and adjustment of the participants. The researchers anchored the participants by supplying the retail price for a product. A scenario in this study read similar to the one below:

> Imagine that you have just earned your first paycheck as a highly paid executive. As a result, you want to reward yourself by buying a large-screen, high-definition plasma TV. As you browse through a store, you see a plasma TV from Sony that you like because of its attractive carbon-fiber finish. Its WEGA 50-inch screen has been rated by a panel of electronics experts as the "clearest and sharpest in the market today, because of a new technology that doubled its resolution and increased it contrast ratio to 4,000:1.
>
> If you were to guess the plasma TV's actual cost to the retailer (i.e., how much the store bought it for), what would it be? Because this is your first purchase of a plasma TV, you have very little information with which to base your estimate. All you know is that it should cost less than the retail price of $5,000. Guess the product's actual cost. This electronics store is known to offer a fair price. Most of their items are priced very close to their actual cost because they compete on volume. The only reason that this particular plasma TV is expensive is that it uses a new technology and the picture quality is outstanding. So the actual cost would be only slightly less than $5,000.

Participants made ratings for 10 scenarios. Specifically, participants provided ratings of a plasma TV, as described above, and the following items: beach house, beverage, cheese, context-free, basketball, figurine, Hummer, pen, and pet rock (see Figure 11.5).

QUESTION

Why was this a within subjects design? What were the participants exposed to that lead you to this conclusion?

ANSWER

Because the independent variable is scenario type, there were 10 levels of the independent variable. Typically, most independent variable do not reach double digits like this study. A visual representation of this design is provided below. The 43 participants in this study received all levels of the independent variable. This means that each participant read and made judgments on all 10 scenarios that were available.

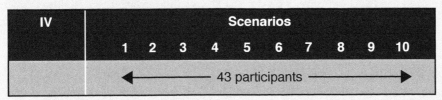

Fig 11.5   Sample research matrix for Janiszewski and Uy (2008).

SECTION SUMMARY

- A *within subjects design* occurs when participants in a study are exposed to all levels of the independent variable. This design is also known as a repeated measures design or within participants designs (pp. 195–201).

FACTORS TO CONSIDER

So far in this chapter, we have presented you with several classic and contemporary examples of within subjects designs. However, as with any research design, there are advantages and disadvantages of the use of a within subjects designs. We will discuss the advantages and disadvantages of within research designs that are listed in Figure 11.6. After which, we will use examples from this chapter to illustrate how each advantage and disadvantage could influence a design. Let us begin by looking at Figure 11.6.

There are two main advantages to using a within subjects design. The first advantage is the use of a small number of participants in your study. Unlike a between subjects design, where there are different groups of participants for each level of the independent variable, within subjects designs have only one group of participants.

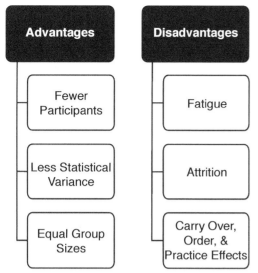

Advantages	Disadvantages
Fewer Participants	Fatigue
Less Statistical Variance	Attrition
Equal Group Sizes	Carry Over, Order, & Practice Effects

Fig 11.6 Advantages and Disadvantages of Within Subjects Designs.

Statistical Variance: The degree of spread among data surrounding the mean.

For example, see Figures 11.7 and 11.8. Imagine you were conducting an experiment where you had an independent variable with four levels and you desired to have 30 people complete each level. If you were to conduct the experiment as a between subjects design, then you would have four groups (each representing a level of the independent variable) with 30 participants in each group. This would yield a total sample size of 120 participants. However, if you conducted this study as a within subjects design, then you would have one group with 30 participants, each experiencing all four levels of the independent variable.

Thus, a within subjects design can greatly reduce the number of participants you need for a given study. This is important to consider when conducting research with special populations, where the recruitment of participants may be difficult.

The second advantage to a within subjects design is that these designs have less statistical variance. **Statistical variance** occurs in part because of differences between participants. For example, participants arrive to experiments with varying education levels, intelligence levels, prior knowledge, and so on. However, in a within subjects design, these differences are reduced because the same participants are exposed to each level of the independent variable. This is extremely beneficial because a researcher can see how the change in the independent variable influenced a participant's score on the dependent variable. This is a distinct advantage over a between subjects design. A within subjects design reduces the variance (or differences between people), making it easier to see differences in the levels of the independent variable. Finally, a within subjects design has the advantage of each level of the independent variable having group sizes that are equal. The same participants partake in each condition, so you do not have to worry about conditions having unequal numbers.

Design					
Between Subjects	30	30	30	30	Total: 120

Fig 11.7 Between subjects design.

Design	Level 1	Level 2	Level 3	Level 4	
Within Subjects	← Same 30 participants for each level →				Total: 30

Fig 11.8 Within subjects design.

Fatigue: Occurs when participants become tired during an experiment.

However, there are some disadvantages to using a within subjects design. The first disadvantage is the development of **fatigue** in participants. Unlike a between subjects design, where participants are exposed to only one level of the independent variable, participants in a within subjects design are exposed to all levels of the independent variable. Therefore, by the end of the experiment, participants can become fatigued. The more levels (conditions) that a within subjects design has, the more likely it is that a participant can get tired of taking part in the study. This can easily influence scores on the dependent variables, because participants begin to lose focus. Often, this leads to another disadvantage, attrition.

Attrition occurs when participants withdraw from or drop out of a study before it has ended. Here is an example of attrition you might have noticed. A researcher is looking to assess the impact of using a new teaching technology. On the first day of a class, the researcher takes measurements about the new teaching technology using all 50 students in the class. The researcher then plans to take other measurements at the midpoint and at the end of the semester. However, as is the case in many college classes, the student population drops during the semester.

Therefore, the researcher collects data on only 36 students at the midpoint and only 28 students at the end of the study. Rather than having 50 participants in his or her study, the researcher now has full data for only 28 students. This is a perfect example of how attrition can influence the results obtained. Specifically, we would not hear about the new technology from the students who dropped out of the class. Participants systematically dropping out of the experiment (or, in this example, the class) causes attrition to influence the interpretation of the results. The students dropping out of the class may be the ones who are struggling with the new teaching technology. This would leave primarily those students in the class who liked the new technology.

© bikeriderlondon, 2014. Used under license from Shutterstock, Inc.

Attrition: Participants dropping out of a study or not returning to complete additional parts to a study.

The other major disadvantages are **carryover**, **order**, and **practice effects**. These effects were covered in Chapter 10. However, we have included a short review here. A carryover effect occurs when the effect of a treatment condition is literally carried over into a second treatment condition. An order effect occurs when a participant completes all levels of the independent variable and always completes them in the same order. This is a problem because a researcher would not be able to determine if the different levels of the independent variable caused the influence on the dependent variable or if it was the order of the presentation. Finally, a practice effect occurs when a participant improves his or her performance on subsequent trials of a study. Be sure to refer back to Chapter 10 if you would like specific examples of each.

WAYS TO MINIMIZE DISADVANTAGES

Although within subjects designs come with disadvantages, there are ways to minimize and even negate these problems. The best way to fight fatigue is not to expose your participants to all levels of the independent variable in one sitting. Rather, it might be beneficial for researchers to have the participants complete part of a study in the first session and finish the second part at another time. This can also aid in reducing any practice effect that may occur between trials in an experiment. However, this suggestion should be balanced with the likelihood of increasing attrition.

Attrition can be combated with the offer of an incentive for participation in a study. For example, when John was in graduate school, he conducted several 8-week longitudinal studies. John retained participants in the study by the use of money. By offering a financial incentive, participants were more willing to come back and participate because there was a benefit to them personally. There are some special ethical considerations with the use of financial incentives. For more information on ethics, refer to Chapter 3.

Carryover Effects: These occur when the effects of a prior treatment conditions influence subsequent treatment conditions.

Order Effects: Effects of a study are due to the participants experiencing the same order of presentation of the levels of the independent variable.

Practice Effects: Participants improve performance due to subsequent experiences on the same task.

Lastly, carryover and order effects are usually reduced by **counterbalancing** conditions between subjects. Rather than always presenting the conditions in the same order, a researcher changes the order such that all combinations are possible in a study. This will allow a researcher to observe any effect which may be a result of the order of the conditions. For example, a researcher has a within subjects design in which there were four levels of the independent variable, A, B, C, and D. The researcher presents to all participants the four conditions in the same order (i.e., A–D). The results of this study showed there was a difference between level A and level D. Can the researcher be sure that A and D are truly different? Not necessarily because it could be the case that the participants experienced fatigue, carryover, or order effects that led to A and D being different. Specifically, it could be the case that D is always different because of the position in the experiment and not the actual condition. Rather, had the researcher used counterbalancing (see Figure 11.9), he or she could be confident that any differences between the levels are because of the independent variable and not the order in which the levels were presented.

	Combination 1	**Combination 2**	**Combination 3**	**Combination 4**
Subject 1	Condition A	Condition B	Condition C	Condition D
Subject 2	Condition B	Condition C	Condition D	Condition A
Subject 3	Condition C	Condition D	Condition A	Condition B
Subject 4	Condition D	Condition A	Condition B	Condition C

Fig 11.9   Sample counterbalancing with four levels of the independent variable.

YOU TRY IT!

We have discussed the advantages and disadvantages to within subjects designs and we want you to practice identifying these factors. Take a look at the scenario below.

A professor wants to investigate the impact of different types of studying habits on an algebra test. She decides to conduct a within subjects design in which she has 25 General Psychology students as participants. The professor has four levels to her independent variable: no studying, studying with the aid of notes only, studying with the aid of the textbook only, and studying with the aid of notes and a textbook. Her study involves each of the 25 participants spending 2 hours in each condition followed by a 30-minute algebra task. The professor conducts this study on a Saturday, making sure that each participant receives the same order for each level of the independent variable. In addition, the same exam was given after each condition so that the researcher was able to compare scores. Surprisingly, her results indicated that students did best in the no studying condition followed by conditions two, three, and four.

Questions

1. Do you believe not studying is the best method? If not, what are some possible limitations to this within subjects design which could have led to these odd results?

2. How would you conduct this study to minimize disadvantages?

1. The researcher's results could be because of the participant fatigue or an order effect. The design required the participants to complete 2 hours in each of the four conditions, followed by four 30-minute exams. This would mean that each participant would participate for 10 total hours. By the end, the participants might not care about the test and put down any answer to be done. In this case, the participant's fatigue in the study influenced the last condition. In addition, each participant followed the same order. So, an order effect could have taken place in which the last condition received the poorest score because of its position and not the actual level of the independent variable (Figure 11.10).

Participant	Condition 1	Condition 2	Condition 3	Condition 4
1	No studying	Studying with the aid of notes only	Studying with the aid of the textbook only	Studying with the aid of notes and a textbook
2	Studying with the aid of notes only	Studying with the aid of the textbook only	Studying with the aid of notes and a textbook	No studying
3	Studying with the aid of the textbook only	Studying with the aid of notes and a textbook	No studying	Studying with the aid of notes only
4	Studying with the aid of notes and a textbook	No studying	Studying with the aid of notes only	Studying with the aid of the textbook only

Fig 11.10 Example of counterbalancing for You Try It!

2. There are ways to conduct the study such that you minimize disadvantages. First, rather than having each level of the independent variable conducted in succession on one day, we would suggest spacing out the study over several weeks. Although your level of attrition may be impacted, this would limit any fatigue and carryover effects. In addition, we would recommend offering some kind of incentive to make sure participants complete all parts of the study. This would minimize attrition. Next, we would reduce the study time from 2 hours to 1 hour and use different versions of the algebra test. This would help to both reduce the impact of fatigue and reduce the practice effect. Lastly, we would use counterbalancing to reduce the likelihood of order effects.

SECTION SUMMARY

- Within subjects designs have several advantages that make it an appealing design to use. Advantages include few participants, less statistical variance, and equal group sizes (pp. 201–203).
  - By having each participant partake in each level of the independent variable, you reduce the number of participants needed (pp. 201–202).
  - *Statistical variance* is the degree of spread among scores from the mean of the group of scores. A within subjects design reduces this variance making it easier to determine if differences exist among the levels of the independent variable (pp. 201–202).
  - The group sizes are equal because each participant is exposed to all levels of the independent variable (pp. 201–202).
- Even though within subjects designs have several advantages, there are disadvantages to using a within subjects design. These include attrition, carryover, order, and practice effects (pp. 202–203).
  - Participants are more likely to become tired in a within subjects design and suffer from *fatigue* because they are exposed to all levels of the independent variable (p. 203).
  - When participants drop out of studies or fail to complete all parts to a study, this is known as *attrition* (p. 203).
  - A *carryover effect* occurs when a prior treatment condition from an experiment influences present or future treatment conditions (p. 203).
  - If all participants experience the same order of treatment conditions in an experiment, any obtained results may be because of the order and not the conditions themselves. This is known as an *order effect* (p. 203).
  - An improvement in performance by a participant on subsequent stimuli independent of the variable being manipulated is known as a *practice effect* (p. 203).
- *Counterbalancing* conditions between participants is a good way of minimizing order and carryover effects. Counterbalancing involves making sure all combinations of order of presentation occur in a study (pp. 203–204).

MATCHED SUBJECTS DESIGN

Matched Subjects Designs: A methodology where participants are matched on a particular characteristic before being assigned to the different levels of the independent variable.

Sometimes, it is not feasible to conduct a within subjects design even though you may want to because of its advantages. However, a similar design, which retains many of the within subjects design advantages, is a **matched subjects designs**. A matched subjects design is a type of research methodology in which participants are matched on a particular characteristic before being assigned to the different levels of the independent variable. In other words, instead of having the same participant complete all levels of the independent variable (as you would in a within subjects design), you would match or pair participants so that each level of the independent variable has a different but characteristically similar participant. This matching of participants across levels of an independent variable affords you the benefit of a within subjects design without having the same participant in each condition. Therefore, you can compare dependent variables across the conditions as if you had conducted a within subjects design.

To illustrate the matched subjects design, we will walk you through an example. You want to know how successful children are in school based on the amount of homework given. The independent variable would be the amount of homework given and its levels could be *meets requirements* and *exceeds requirements*. The dependent variable would be the children's scores on the end of grade tests. One factor which might influence these findings is the children's excitement about school work in general. So, you match the children on their excitement level. In order to do this, you must test their base level of excitement. After getting the scores, you rank order the children in terms of highest excitement level to lowest. Next, you take the scores of the first two children with the highest scores, randomly assigning each to one of the two groups (meets or exceeds). Subsequently, you take the next two children with the highest scores and match them before placing them into one of the two groups. You continue this process until all children are matched and assigned to the two homework groups. This is how a matched subjects design works. In essence, you have made sure each group is equal in terms of the matched variable you have chosen (i.e., each group has the same number of high-and low-level excitement children). You should be able to detect results between the groups because you have reduced the effect of individual differences, just as you would had you used a within subjects design.

As you may have figured out, matched subjects designs also come with disadvantages. The introduction of an additional step, the matching step, can become time consuming. Depending on the intricacy of the match, you may have to spend additional time and, possibly, resources to ensure the match is complete. When considering this design, you will need to think about the limitations of making the match in comparison to the benefit offered by controlling for the variable.

ARE YOU EQUIPPED NOW?

Have you ever watched the show *Mythbusters*? *Mythbusters* is a show on the Discovery Channel in which two guys, Jamie and Adam, attempt to debunk myths which exist in the world. Although this show is intended to be for entertainment, there is a lot of science that goes into the busting of myths. For each myth, the guys set up a study or experiment in which they test the details of the myth. During the third season of the show, the guys set out to debunk "Seasickness Cures." Many people get easily seasick or motion sick. There are a number of cures, some urban myths, which can be used to get rid of seasickness. Jamie and Adam decided to look at the five most common cures to seasickness: homeopathic tongue tingle (a spray you squirt under your tongue), wrist straps, ginger pills, acupuncture, and the use of over-the-counter pharmaceuticals. The type of cure in this case was the independent variable and the level of sickness was the dependent variable. If you were to conduct this as a within subjects design, how would you do it? And, what would be the biggest disadvantage you might face with this study?

There are a number of ways to conduct this study. However, as long as each person was exposed to all levels of the independent variable (the cures), you conducted the study correctly. The Mythbusters actually utilized a within subjects design to test these cures. Specifically, Jamie and Adam developed a model of NASA's seasickness chair, in which a chair rotates in a circle at seven revolutions per minute and a blindfolded participant sits in the chair. During the rotation of the chair, the participant is to lean his or her head forward, back, and to the left and right, touching tennis balls on the chair. This is to simulate seasickness. The *Mythbusters* had two participants who were exposed to all levels of the independent variable. Results showed that the ginger pills and the over-the-counter pharmaceuticals were the most effective at preventing seasickness (although the pharmaceuticals made the participants extremely drowsy). In addition, as you may have figured out, the biggest disadvantage in this study was that the participants were getting sick during each condition. However, it is not the getting sick that was the disadvantage but rather, attrition the desire to quit the experiment.

Therefore, the *Mythbusters* might have been better served using a matched subjects design for this experiment. By matching subjects on their susceptibility to seasickness and attempting to get them sick only once (i.e., five matched subjects exposed to only one level of the independent variable), the *Mythbusters* might have been more merciful to their participants. However, we doubt it would have made good television.

CHAPTER SUMMARY

- A *within subjects design* occurs when participants in a study are exposed to all levels of the independent variable. It is also known as a repeated measures design and within participants design (pp. 195–201).
- Within subjects designs have several advantages which make it an appealing design to use. Advantages include fewer participants, less statistical variance, and equal group sizes (pp. 201–203).
  - By having each participant partake in each level of the independent variable, you reduce the number of participants needed (pp. 201–202).
  - *Statistical variance* is the degree of spread among scores from the mean of the group of scores. A within subjects design reduces this variance, making it easier to determine if differences exist among the levels of the independent variable (pp. 201–202).
  - Since each participant is exposed to all levels of the independent variable, the group sizes are equal (pp. 201–202).
- Even though within subjects designs have several advantages, there are disadvantages to using a within subjects design. These include attrition, carryover, order, and practice effects (pp. 202–203).
  - Since each of the participants is being exposed to all levels of the independent variable, they are more likely to tire in the study and suffer from *fatigue* (p. 203).

- When participants drop out of studies or fail to complete all parts to a study, this is known as *attrition* (p. 203).

- A *carryover effect* occurs when a prior treatment condition from an experiment influences current or future treatment conditions (p. 203).

- If all participants experience the same order of treatment conditions in an experiment, then any obtained results may be because of the order and not the conditions themselves. This is known as an *order effect* (p. 203).

- An improvement in performance by a participant on subsequent stimuli independent of the variable being manipulated is known as a *practice effect* (p. 203).

- *Counterbalancing* conditions between participants is a good way of minimizing order and carryover effects. Counterbalancing involves making sure that all combinations of order of presentation occur in a study (pp. 203–204).

- A *matched subjects design* occurs when participants are matched on a particular characteristic before being assigned to the different levels of the independent variable. This type of design is an alternative methodology to a within subjects design without many of the disadvantages (pp. 206–207).

APA LEARNING GOALS LINKAGE

- **Goal 1. Knowledge Base in Psychology**

  You will demonstrate fundamental knowledge and comprehension of the major concepts, theoretical perspectives, historical trends, and empirical findings to discuss how psychological principles apply to behavioral problems.

  Sections Covered: Introduction to Within Subjects Designs

  Explanation of the Goal: Stroop's research conducted in 1935 is a classic in the field of psychology. In one of the experiments, participants were asked to read the words displayed in black ink and incongruent ink. In the second experiment, participants indicated the color of the ink used for each incongruent word and for each set of blocks. These experiments were included in this chapter as Stroop utilized a within subjects design and exposed participants to all levels of the independent variable within the experiments.

  Sections Covered: Are You Equipped?, Introduction to Within Subjects Designs, Are You Equipped Now?

  Explanation of the Goal: The examples from this chapter that applied to everyday life were both novel and continuations from previous chapters. New examples included the Coke versus Pepsi dual presented at the opening and the *Mythbusters'* testing of motion sickness remedies presented at the end. Monitor size and reaction time and caffeine and alertness were reexamined in the context of within subjects designs.

- ## Goal 2. Scientific Inquiry and Critical Thinking

  You will demonstrate scientific reasoning and problem solving, including effective research methods.

  Sections Covered: Are You Equipped?, Introduction to Within Subjects Designs, Factors to Consider, Matched Subjects Designs, Are You Equipped Now?

  Explanation of the Goal: Within subjects designs and matched subjects designs are two types of research methods. In this chapter, we examined these two methods and the types of questions and hypotheses associated with each. In addition, we articulated the strengths of the within subjects design (i.e., fewer participants, less statistical variance, and equal group sizes) and the limitations (i.e., fatigue, attrition, carryover, order, and practice effects). In the coverage of reducing limitations, special attention was given to the use of counterbalancing.

  Sections Covered: Are You Equipped?, Introduction to Within Subjects Designs, Factors to Consider, Are You Equipped Now?

  Explanation of the Goal: You engaged in critical thinking in this chapter by approaching problems effectively. Specifically, you were asked to design studies so that participants were exposed to all levels of the independent variable. We practiced this skill with classic and contemporary research examples. In addition, you utilized creative thinking when you were asked to improve the design of studies so that disadvantages because of the nature of the within subjects design would be minimized.

CHAPTER 12

Factorial Designs

CHAPTER OUTLINE

Are You Equipped?

Introduction to Factorial Designs

Results of Factorial Designs

Are You Equipped Now?

Chapter Summary

APA Learning Goals Linkage

ARE YOU EQUIPPED?

This preview is a little different from previous chapters. We will not be asking you to try something new. Rather, we will be telling you about something new. Specifically, we are going to introduce a new type of research design.

A recent study by Dommeyer (2008) examined what factors influence whether or not people respond to a mail survey. In other words, are there factors that can influence if a person responds to a survey that he or she received in the mail? Dommeyer wanted to know if the attractiveness of the researcher in a cover letter would influence people's response to the mail survey. Dommeyer also wanted to know if the sex of the researcher (male or female) in the cover letter would influence people's response to the mail survey.

This quasi-experimental study described above was a factorial research design. It was a factorial research design because it had more than one independent variable. The first independent variable was attractiveness of the researcher in the cover letter. This independent variable had two levels: attractive and not attractive. The second independent variable (or subject variable in this case) was sex of the researcher in the cover letter. It also had

two levels: male and female. Participants in this experiment would have received one of the four cover letters. The first cover letter had an attractive female researcher. The second cover letter had an unattractive female researcher. The third and fourth cover letters had an attractive male researcher and an unattractive male researcher, respectively. These four cover letters can be viewed in a research matrix as shown in Table 12.1.

TABLE 12.1 Factorial design research matrix.

	IV #2 Level 1	IV #2 Level 2
IV #2 **Level 1**	Attractive Female	Attractive Male
IV #2 **Level 2**	Unattractive Female	Unattractive Male

This experiment would be referred to as a 2 × 2 between subjects factorial research design. In this chapter, we will discuss why this experiment is a factorial research design. We will also discuss how to understand a research matrix. Finally, we will discuss three types of factorial research designs. These are between subjects, within subjects, and mixed subjects factorial research designs.

As you go through this chapter, we also want you to keep in mind how the material relates to the American Psychological Association's goals for psychology majors. Specifically, this chapter will address the following goals:

- **Goal 1. Knowledge Base in Psychology**

  You will demonstrate fundamental knowledge and comprehension of the major concepts, theoretical perspectives, historical trends, and empirical findings to discuss how psychological principles apply to behavioral problems.

- **Goal 2. Scientific Inquiry and Critical Thinking**

  You will demonstrate scientific reasoning and problem solving, including effective research methods.

- **Goal 4. Communication**

  You will demonstrate competence in writing and in oral and interpersonal communication skills.

INTRODUCTION TO FACTORIAL DESIGNS

Before we begin this chapter, we should tell you the results of Dommeyer's (2008) study. The only variable that influenced people's response to the survey was the sex of the researcher. Interestingly, people were more likely to respond to a mail survey if the researcher was a female than a male.

In this chapter, we are going to discuss different types of factorial designs. Factorial designs are important to cover in a research methods course because many psychological studies employ them. **Factorial research designs** have more than one independent variable. If you think back to the examples we have covered previously, the examples had only one independent variable. However, there were generally two or three levels of the independent variable. Take, for example, sex of participant as a variable. Sex has two levels (male and female). It is also a between subjects variable. Another example we have discussed was size of computer monitor. It had three levels (i.e., 17 inch, 19 inch, and 21 inch). This chapter will focus on research designs which have more than one independent variable and each independent variable will typically have two or three levels.

A factorial research design can be one of the three types. It can be a completely **between subjects factorial research design**. In this situation, all of the independent variables in the research design are between subjects variables. Participants are, therefore, exposed only to one level of each of the independent variables (think back to Chapter 10). Next, there is a completely **within subjects factorial research design**. In this situation, each of the independent variables in the research design is a within subjects variable. Hence, participants are exposed to all levels of each of the independent variables (think back to Chapter 11). Finally, you could have a **mixed subjects factorial research design**. In this situation, not all of your independent variables would be of the same type. You might have one between subjects variable and one within subjects variable. To help better illustrate these three types of factorial designs, we will now walk you through examples of each.

BETWEEN SUBJECTS FACTORIAL DESIGNS

In Chapter 10, we talked about the research study on situational and dispositional variables in helping behavior. At the time, we presented the results to you of one of the between subjects variables. It was the variable of hurry. As you might recall, the variable of hurry had three levels: high, intermediate, and low. Participants were assigned to one of these three levels. Results indicated that participants in the high-hurry condition were least likely to help the person they passed by on their way from one building to the next. In actuality, this study conducted by Darley and Batson (1973) had a second independent variable. Remember how in the experiment participants began the experiment in one building and then were asked to go to another building for the second part of the study? Well, participants were told that when they arrived at the second building they would be giving a 3-to-5-minute talk based on the message of a passage that they received. The second independent variable was the message of the passage. It had two levels. The levels were task-relevant condition (i.e., these participants were to give a talk on professions of seminary students) and helping-relevant condition (i.e., these participants were to give a talk on the Good Samaritan parable from the Bible). This second variable of message was a between subjects variable. This is because participants were assigned to only one of the two conditions.

Up to this point, we have just been reviewing information on between subjects variables that we covered in Chapter 10. However, if we combine the two independent variables into one study, we can discuss our new topic of this chapter. Specifically, Darley and Batson (1973) used a between subjects factorial research design. It was a between subjects factorial research design because it had more than one independent variable. Participants in the experiment would have actually been assigned to one of the six conditions. These six conditions can be viewed in the research matrix in Table 12.2. This research matrix illustrates a 3 × 2 between subjects factorial research design.

Factorial Research Design: A research design which uses more than one independent variable.

Between Subjects Factorial Research Design: A research design in which all independent variables are between subjects.

Within Subjects Factorial Research Design: A research design in which all independent variables are within subjects.

Mixed Subjects Factorial Research Design: A research design in which not all of the independent variables are of the same type (i.e., one independent variable is between subjects and the other within subjects).

TABLE 12.2 **Research matrix for "Jerusalem to Jericho" study.**

	IV #2 Level 1	IV #2 Level 2
IV #1 Level 1	High hurry Helping relevant	High hurry Task relevant
IV #1 Level 2	Intermediate hurry Helping relevant	Intermediate hurry Task relevant
IV #1 Level 3	Low hurry Helping relevant	Low hurry Task relevant

YOU TRY IT!

We know we have just started this chapter, but we want to see how you are doing. Below are a few questions based on the research matrix above. Try them out.

QUESTIONS

1. Why is this a factorial research design?
2. Why is this a between subjects factorial research design?
3. What does the 3 stand for in the 3 × 2 design?
4. What does the 2 stand for in the 3 × 2 design?
5. How do you determine how many total conditions there are in this study?

ANSWERS

1. This is a factorial research design because it had more than one independent variable. Specifically, it had two independent variables: hurry and message.

2. This is a between subjects design because both of the independent variables were between subjects variables. The first variable, hurry, was a between subjects variable with participants being assigned to only one of the three conditions. The second variable, message, was also a between subjects variable with participants being assigned to only one of the two conditions. In any between subjects design, participants are only assigned to one level of each of the independent variables.

3. In this particular design, the 3 represents the three levels of the first independent variable of hurry. The three levels were high, intermediate, and low.

4. The 2 represents the two levels of the second independent variable, message. The two levels were task relevant and helping relevant. In a factorial research design, researchers discuss the design by using this standard format. If the research design has two independent variables,

the format would be _____ × _____. The number of levels of the first independent variable goes in the first blank and the number of levels of the sec ond independent variable goes in the second blank. By theway, when you say this format, the "×" reads as "by." So, you would say a "3 by 2 design" (not "3 times 2 design").

5. You can figure out how many total conditions there are by multiplying the number of levels of each of the independent variables. In this case, we had 3 times 2, which equals 6 (i.e., high hurry/task relevant, intermediate hurry/task relevant, low hurry/task relevant, high hurry/helping relevant, intermediate hurry/helping relevant, and low hurry/helping relevant).

How did you do? Some of the questions that we asked you over the research study were ones we had not talked about yet. Therefore, if you did not know the answers to these questions, do not worry. We will practice these again later.

Next, we want to tell you about another study that was also a between subjects factorial research design. This was a 2 × 2 between subjects factorial design. Based on this little amount of information, you already could answer many questions including the following:

- *Why is this a factorial research design?*

- *What does the first 2 represent in the 2 × 2 design?*

- *What does the second 2 represent in the 2 × 2 design?*

- *How many total conditions are there?*

You could even answer these questions without knowing the exact names of the independent variables. However, we want to tell you more about the study. The researchers Brescoll and Uhlmann (2008) wanted to know if men and women were judged the same for expressing similar emotions in the workplace. Participants in this experiment watched a video of a job candidate. The job candidates were being interviewed while sitting at a table. The job candidates were describing an incident in which they and a colleague lost an important account and how it made them feel. The first independent variable was sex of job candidate. Sex had two levels—male and female. This was a between subjects variable because participants were either male or female. The second independent variable was emotion displayed. Emotion displayed had two levels—anger and sadness. This was also a between subjects variable. So, participants viewed one of the four job candidates. A research matrix is given in Table 12.3.

After viewing one of the four job candidates, the participants were asked many questions about the candidates, including how much they would pay them and their competence levels. Because both of the independent variables were between subjects variables, the overall research design was also between subjects. By now, you are probably getting the hang of between subjects designs. If you would like one last example, go back to the beginning of the chapter and read the "Are You Equipped?" section again.

TABLE 12.3 Sample research matrix for between subjects design.

	IV #2 Level 1	IV #2 Level 2
IV #1 Level 1	Male Anger	Male Sadness
IV #1 Level 2	Female Anger	Female Sadness

WITHIN SUBJECTS FACTORIAL DESIGNS

It is now time to talk about the second type of factorial research designs. This is a within subjects factorial research design. In this design, participants are exposed to all levels of the independent variables of interest. In Chapter 11, we talked about the research conducted by Tamir, Mitchell, and Gross (2008), and music preference while playing computer games. At that time, we told you about the within subjects variable of music condition. This independent variable had three levels of angry, exciting, and neutral. Participants in the experiment were exposed to all three levels of the music condition while they were playing computer games. However, this was just one of the independent variables the study actually investigated. Another independent variable of interest was type of game. Type of game had two levels: confrontational and nonconfrontational. The researchers wanted to know if the type of computer game, in addition to the type of music, influenced performance. By adding this second variable, we now have a 3 × 2 within subjects factorial research design. If we were to think about this design visually, it would look like the research matrix in Table 12.4. However, keep in mind that because this is a within subjects design, all participants would at some point be in each of the six conditions.

Before we move on and discuss the last type of factorial research design, we want to talk about one more example of a completely within subjects factorial research design. This next study was adapted from Desrumaux, De Bosscher, and Léoni (2009) to determine how evaluating a job applicant varies by the applicant's gender and physical appearance. For our purposes, we are going to focus on two of the independent variables, making this a 2 × 2 within subjects design.

TABLE 12.4 Research matrix for Tamir, Mitchell, and Gross (2008).

	IV #2 Level 1	IV #2 Level 2
IV #1 Level 1	Angry Nonconfrontational	Angry Confrontational
IV #1 Level 2	Exciting Nonconfrontational	Exciting Confrontational
IV #1 Level 3	Neutral Nonconfrontational	Neutral Confrontational

Before we tell you more about this experiment, we want to see what you can already figure out based on the little information we have given you. Try these questions.

QUESTIONS

1. Why is this a factorial research design?
2. How many levels does the first independent variable have?
3. How many levels does the second independent variable have?
4. How many total conditions will there be in the research matrix?

ANSWERS

1. This is a factorial research design because it has more than one independent variable.
2. The first independent variable has two levels. You can tell this because the standard format for a factorial research design is ____ × ____, where the number of levels for the first independent variable is in the first blank.
3. The second independent variable also has two levels. You can tell this because the standard format for a factorial research design is ____ × ____, where the number of levels for the second independent variable is in the second blank.
4. This research matrix will have four conditions. You can figure this out because 2 × 2 = 4.

Now, we will tell you more about the research design. The first independent variable was the gender of the applicant and the two levels were male and female. The second independent variable was the physical appearance of the applicant. The two levels were attractive and unattractive. Both of these variables were within subjects variables, meaning that participants were in all of the four conditions represented visually in Table 12.5.

TABLE 12.5 Sample research matrix for a within subjects factorial design.

	IV #2 Level 1	IV #2 Level 2
IV #1 **Level 1**	Male Attractive	Male Unattractive
IV #1 **Level 2**	Female Attractive	Female Unattractive

Specifically, participants viewed four resumes. Characteristics on the resume, such as age, marital status, interests, and work experience, were kept constant across the conditions. However, the picture presented with the resume was varied. The four pictures were attractive male, unattractive male, attractive female, and unattractive female. After viewing each resume with the accompanying picture, participants rated the applicants on numerous factors including hireability. Results indicated that although gender had no influence on ratings of hireability, physical appearance did. As predicted, the attractive applicants were more likely to be hired than the unattractive applicants.

MIXED SUBJECTS FACTORIAL DESIGNS

Finally, there are mixed subjects factorial research designs. In a mixed subjects factorial research design, the independent variables are not all of the same type. In other words, some variables are between subjects and others are within subjects. Therefore, the design is mixed in terms of the types of variables. We want to tell you about two research studies that used a mixed subjects design.

The first study was conducted by Cameron and Rutland (2006). The purpose of the study was to determine if extended contact through story reading in school could reduce children's prejudice toward the disabled. This was a 3 × 2 mixed subjects design. The first independent variable was type of extended contact. It had three levels. The levels were neutral, decategorization, and "intergroup." In other words, the children heard stories that portrayed friendships between disabled and nondisabled children. In some of the stories, there was no emphasis placed on the individual qualities of the children (neutral). In other stories, the qualities were emphasized little (decategorization) or stressed (intergroup). Participants were placed into one of the three conditions. The children heard neutral, decategorization, or "intergroup" stories.

The second independent variable was time of interview. It had two levels. The levels were preextended contact and postextended contact. This was a within subjects variable, meaning that all children were interviewed before and after the extended contact. When you have a mixed subjects design, you still determine the total number of conditions in the same way. For the study we have just described, you would have 3 × 2 = 6.

How would you draw the research matrix? Give it a try and compare your matrix to our matrix given in Table 12.6.

TABLE 12.6 Research matrix for Cameron and Rutland (2006).

	IV #2 Level 1	IV #2 Level 2
IV #1 Level 1	Neutral Precontact	Neutral Postcontact
IV #1 Level 2	Decategorization Precontact	Decategorization Postcontact
IV #1 Level 3	"Intergroup" Precontact	"Intergroup" Postcontact

Remember that the second independent variable is a within subjects variable, so all children complete the precontact and postcontact conditions. Results of this study showed the extended contact did lead to more positive attitudes toward the disabled, especially for the intergroup condition.

The second mixed subjects design we want to discuss was conducted by Janiszewski and Uy (2008). We will describe the first of the five studies conducted. In Chapter 11, we told you about one of the independent variables that the researchers used. This was the within subjects variable of scenario. Specifically, participants in this experiment all read 10 scenarios and then estimated a number based on the information given in the scenario. The 10 scenarios were the following: beach house, beverage, cheese, context free, basketball, figurine, Hummer, pen, pet rock, and plasma TV. When we talked about this experiment in Chapter 11, it may have seemed strange to have participants estimate numbers in these 10 scenarios. However, now we are going to tell you about the second independent variable used in the experiment and the task will make more sense.

The researchers' second independent variable was type of anchor. This was a between subjects variable with three levels. The three levels were rounded anchor, precise under anchor, and precise over anchor. Participants were assigned to one of the three levels. The researchers wanted to know if precise or rounded anchors influenced judgments of numbers. An example might make this research design clearer. In the context-free scenario, participants read something like the following: "There is a number saved in a file on this computer. It is slightly less than ____.

TABLE 12.7 Sample research matrix for a mixed subjects design.

	IV #2 Level 1	IV #2 Level 2	IV #2 Level 3	IV #2 Level 4	IV #2 Level 5	IV #2 Level 6	IV #2 Level 7	IV #2 Level 8	IV #2 Level 9	IV #2 Level 10
IV #1 Level 1	Rounded Beach house	Rounded Beverage	Rounded Cheese	Rounded Context-free	Rounded Basketbal	Rounded Figurine	Rounded Hummer	Rounded Pen	Rounded Pet rock	Rounded Plasma TV
IV #1 Level 2	Precise under Beach house	Precise under Beverage	Precise under Cheese	Precise under Context-free	Precise under Basketball	Precise under Figurine	Precise under Hummer	Precise under Pen	Precise under Pet rock	Precise under Plasma TV
IV #1 Level 3	Precise over Beach house	Precise over Beverage	Precise over Cheese	Precise over Context-free	Precise over Basketball	Precise over Figurine	Precise over Hummer	Precise over Pen	Precise over Pet rock	Precise over Plasma TV

Can you guess the number?" In the rounded condition, the _____ would have been a number such as 5,000. In the precise under, the _____ would have been a number such as 4,989, and in the precise over, the _____ would have been a number such as 5,012. This was a mixed subjects design because the independent variables were not all of the same type. The first independent variable of scenario was a within subjects variable and the second independent variable of anchor type was a between subjects variable. The results found that participants in the rounded condition gave larger adjustments than the two precise conditions. If you like to think about things visually, the research matrix for this design is given in Table 12.7.

SECTION SUMMARY

- A *factorial research design* is a design where there is more than one independent variable. Typically, a factorial research design has two or three independent variables with each variable having multiple levels (pp. 212–213).

- In a *between subjects factorial research design*, there is more than one independent variable. However, since this design is between subjects, participants are exposed only to one level of each independent variable. In this design, the number of groups of participants is determined by multiplying the total number of levels for each variable (i.e., 3 × 2 design yields 6 distinct groups, each receiving one level of each independent variable) (pp. 213–216).

- In a *within subjects factorial research design*, there is more than one independent variable. However, since the design is within subjects, participants are exposed to all levels of each independent variable. In this design, you have one group of participants who experience all treatment conditions (pp. 216–218).

- In a *mixed subjects factorial research design*, there is more than one independent variable. However, in this design both between and within subjects variables are used (pp. 218–220).

RESULTS OF FACTORIAL DESIGNS

We want to briefly mention how to understand the results of a factorial research design. The benefit of a factorial design (no matter what type) is that you can get the answer to three questions with just one experiment. You can find out (a) if there was an influence of the first independent variable on the dependent variable(s), (b) if there was an influence of the second independent variable on the dependent variable(s), and (c) if the influence of the first independent variable depended on the second independent variable.

MAIN EFFECTS

Finding out if each of the independent variables influenced the dependent variable(s) is referred to as a **main effect**. There could be a main effect for each independent variable that you have in a factorial research design. We will talk about main effects using the 2 × 2 between subjects factorial design from the preview of this chapter. In this study, the researchers wanted to know if attractiveness of the researcher in the cover letter (IV #1) and sex of the researcher in the cover letter (IV #2) influenced response rates from mail surveys. To begin, the researcher would have looked for a main effect for the first independent variable of attractiveness. Let's call the first independent variable A. When you are looking for a main effect of A, you need to ignore B (in this case, sex). Put another way, you will look at A while collapsing across B. Take a look at Table 12.8. If we were looking to see if attractiveness had an influence on the number of responses received, we would compare all of the responses from participants who received the letter from the attractive researcher to all of the responses from participants who received the letter from the unattractive researcher. The X in the table represents the mean number of responses received. Therefore, we would need to average across the male and female conditions to determine the mean number of responses for the attractive researcher and for the unattractive researcher.

Main Effect: Determining if an independent variable has had an effect on the dependent variables while ignoring or collapsing across the other independent variables in the factorial research design.

TABLE 12.8 Example of the main effect for independent variable A.

	Male	Female	
Attractive			X
Unattractive			X

Subsequently, we would look to see if there was a main effect of B. In other words, we want to know if sex of researcher in the cover letter influenced response rate while ignoring or collapsing across attractiveness. In Table 12.9, the X again represents the mean number of responses. We would need to average across the attractive and unattractive conditions to determine the mean number of responses for the male and female researchers.

TABLE 12.9 Example of the main effect for independent variable B.

	Male	Female
Attractive		
Unattractive	*X*	*X*

We can look to the study by Darley and Batson (1973) for another example. The researchers wanted to know if the independent variable of hurry (high, intermediate, and low) and the independent variable of message of passage (task relevant and helping relevant) influenced willingness to help.

To begin, the researchers would have looked for a main effect for the first independent variable of hurry. When you are looking for a main effect of A, you need to ignore B (message). Put another way, you will look at A while collapsing across B. Take a look at Table 12.10. If we were looking to see if hurry had an influence on willingness to help, we would compare the willingness to help from participants in the high, intermediate, and low conditions. The *X* in the table represents the mean number of people willing to help. So, we would need to average across the task-relevant and helping-relevant conditions to determine the mean helping response for the high, intermediate, and hurry levels.

TABLE 12.10 Main effect for Darley and Batson's (1973) independent variable 1.

	Task relevant	Helping relevant	
High hurry			*X*
Intermediate hurry			*X*
Low hurry			*X*

Next, we would look to see if there was a main effect of B. In other words, we want to know if message of passage influenced willingness to help while ignoring or collapsing across hurry. In Table 12.11, the *X* again represents the mean number of responses. So, we would need to average across the hurry conditions to determine the mean number of responses for the task-relevant and helping-relevant conditions.

TABLE 12.11 Main effect for Darley and Batson's (1973) independent variable 2.

	Task relevant	Helping relevant
High hurry		
Intermediate hurry		
Low hurry		
	X	*X*

INTERACTIONS

The final question a factorial design answers is if the influence of the first independent variable depends on the influence of the second independent variable. This is referred to as an **interaction**. In an interaction, you obtain results that would not have been produced from either independent variable alone. These results literally tell you how your independent variables interact with one another. We like to have students think about interactions using the following example. We want to know how sex and exercise condition influence weight lost. Our first independent variable is the subject variable of sex of participant (male and female), and our second independent variable is exercise condition (exercise, peer support, and control) as is displayed by the matrix in Table 12.12. To begin, we would look for main effects of A and B to see if sex and exercise condition each had an influence on weight lost. It is probably the case that men lose more weight than women. This could be determined by evaluating the difference between X_{Women} and X_{Men}. And, it is also probably the case that exercise yields the most weight lost. This can be determined by evaluating the difference between $X_{Exercise}$, $X_{Peer\ support}$, and $X_{Control}$.

Interaction: Occurs when the effect of one independent variable depends on another independent variable.

TABLE 12.12   Research matrix for interaction.

	IV #2 Male	IV #2 Female	
IV #1 Exercise			X
IV #1 Peer support			X
IV #1 Control			X
	X	X	

However, could we say the best way to lose weight if you are female is to engage in exercise? The answer to this question is no. To answer that question, we would also want to know if the independent variables interacted together in some way on the dependent variable. For example, it could be the case that women will lose more weight with peer support than men, and men will lose more weight with exercise than women. In order to make this determination, we must now evaluate each of the six conditions to see where differences exist and not average across independent variables. If this concept is still a little unclear, don't worry. We will return to this idea of factorial interactions in a later chapter.

© Sebastian Duda, 2014. Used under license from Shutterstock, Inc.

SECTION SUMMARY

- A *main effect* is the effect an independent variable had on the dependent variables in a given research design (pp. 221–222).
- An *interaction* occurs when the effect on the independent variables for a given study is due to the other independent variables in that study (p. 223).

ARE YOU EQUIPPED NOW?

Let us see how you are doing with all the material we have discussed in this chapter. We will describe part of an experiment we have not previously told you about. As you read about the experiment, keep looking for the independent variables and you will be able to answer our questions. (Hint: There are two independent variables.)

Researchers at the Center for AIDS Intervention Research conducted an experiment with 207 individuals taking HIV medications (Catz, Kalichman, Benotsch, Miller, & Suarez, 2001). Participants were randomly assigned to read one of the six vignettes. The vignettes varied by medical situation and physician prescription action. For medical situation, participants were randomly assigned to one of the three levels. In the first medical situation, participants were informed that the HIV viral load had increased. In the second medical situation, participants were informed that the HIV viral load had decreased. In the third medical situation, participants were informed that the HIV viral load had remained the same. For physician prescription action, participants were randomly assigned to one of the two levels. The first action was a medication change, while the second action was continued monitoring. After reading one of these vignettes, participants rated their affective anticipated response (i.e., how they would predict they would feel if these were their test results).

QUESTIONS

1. Why was this a factorial research design?
2. What was the first independent variable?
3. What was the second independent variable?
4. What type of factorial research design was this (i.e., between, within, or mixed)?
5. What does the research matrix look like?

ANSWERS

1. This was a factorial research design because there was more than one independent variable. In fact, there were two independent variables.
2. The first independent variable was medical situation. This independent variable had three levels. The three levels were increased viral load, decreased viral load, and no change. This was a between subjects variable because the participants were randomly assigned to be in only one of the three levels.

3. The second independent variable was physician prescription action. It had two levels. The levels were medication change and continued monitoring. This was a between subjects variable because the participants were randomly assigned to be in only one of the two levels.

4. It is a between subjects factorial design because both of the independent variables are between subjects variables.

5. The research matrix looks like the one shown in Table 12.13.

TABLE 12.13   Research matrix.

	IV #2 Level 1	IV #2 Level 2
IV #1 Level 1	Increased viral load Medication change	Increased viral load Continued monitoring
IV #1 Level 2	Decreased viral load Medication change	Decreased viral load Continued monitoring
IV #1 Level #3	No change in viral load Medication change	No change in viral load Continued monitoring

CHAPTER SUMMARY

- A *factorial research design* is a design where there is more than one independent variable. Typically, a factorial research design has two or three independent variables, with each variable having multiple levels. Rarely do factorial designs have more than three variables. This is because if the researcher manipulated too many variables, he or she would be unable to tell which independent variable was producing the observed change in the dependent variable (pp. 212–213).

- In a *between subjects factorial research design*, there is more than one independent variable. However, since this design is between subjects, participants are exposed only to one level of each independent variable. In this design, the number of groups of participants is determined by multiplying the total number of levels for each variable (pp. 213–216).

  - For example, in a research design with an independent variable that has three levels and another independent variable with two levels, there are a total of six distinct conditions. However, participants would be placed into only one of the six conditions as the study is a between subjects factorial design (p. 215).

- In a *within subjects factorial research design*, there is more than one independent variable. However, since the design is within subjects, participants are exposed to all levels of each independent variable. In this design, you have only one group of participants who experience all treatment conditions (pp. 216–218).

- For example, in a research design with an independent variable that has three levels and another independent variable with two levels, there are a total of six distinct conditions. Each participant would participate in all six distinct conditions as the study is a within subjects factorial design (p. 216).

- In a *mixed subjects factorial research design*, there is more than one independent variable. Specifically, in a mixed design there are between and within subjects variables (pp. 218–220).

  - For example, in a research design with a between subjects independent variable that has three levels and another within subjects independent variable with two levels, there are a total of six distinct conditions. The participants would participate in only one of the levels of the first independent variable but all of the levels of the second independent variable (p. 219).

- A *main effect* is the effect an independent variable has on the dependent variables in a given research design. In other words, this evaluates the impact of manipulating a single independent variable while ignoring or collapsing across all other independent variables (pp. 221–222).

- An *interaction* occurs when the effect on the independent variables for a given study is dependent upon other independent variables in that study. In other words, this evaluates whether the presence of each independent variable has an effect on the other independent variables as seen by a change in the dependent variable (p. 223).

APA LEARNING GOALS LINKAGE

- **Goal 1. Knowledge Base in Psychology**

  You will demonstrate fundamental knowledge and comprehension of the major concepts, theoretical perspectives, historical trends, and empirical findings to discuss how psychological principles apply to behavioral problems.

  Sections Covered: Are You Equipped?, Introduction to Factorial Designs, Results of Factorial Designs, Are You Equipped Now?

  Explanation of the Goal: Factorial research methods can be applied to personal, social, and organizational issues. In fact, every section in this chapter contained an example of a factorial design that was related to understanding thoughts and behaviors of individuals in everyday life situations. Applying psychological principles to common situations allowed us to understand why men's and women's emotions are judged differently in the workplace and how we can work to reduce prejudice behavior.

- **Goal 2. Scientific Inquiry and Critical Thinking**

  You will demonstrate scientific reasoning and problem solving, including effective research methods.

  Sections Covered: Are You Equipped?, Introduction to Factorial Designs, Results of Factorial Designs, Are You Equipped Now?

Explanation of the Goal: This chapter introduced us to different types of factorial research designs. First, we talked about between subjects factorial research designs. This is a research design where all independent variables are between subjects variables. The second factorial design we covered was the within subjects factorial research design. In this case, all of the variables are within subjects variables. Another research design, mixed subjects factorial design, occurs when not all independent variables are of the same type. As factorial designs are very common in psychological research, it is imperative they are included in a discussion of research methods. In addition to types of research designs, this chapter furthered our knowledge in interpreting basic statistical conclusions related to factorial designs with information given on main effects and interactions of variables.

Sections Covered: Are You Equipped?, Introduction to Factorial Designs, Are You Equipped Now?

Explanation of the Goal: Psychologists recognize that human behaviors and mental processes are complex. As a result, the research methods utilized must take into account how multiple factors might be influencing an individual. You engaged in critical and creative thinking by completing exercises in this chapter, which required you to design studies to understand the influence of these multiple factors.For example, we discussed how the gender of a job applicant and the physical appearance of a job applicant can both contribute to ratings of hireability. Similarly, we saw how more than one factor plays a role when an individual is deciding whether or not to help someone else.

- ## Goal 4. Communication

You will demonstrate competence in writing and in oral and interpersonal communication skills.

Sections Covered: Are You Equipped?, Introduction to Factorial Designs, Results of Factorial Designs, Are You Equipped Now?

Explanation of the Goal: Quantitative communication skills are needed to exhibit factorial research designs in a graphical form. Consequently, we practiced how to construct and interpret a research matrix to display information about the variables manipulated in a factorial design. We also used graphical information to illustrate how factorial designs tell us the influence each independent variable has on the dependent variable (main effect) and if the independent variables interact to produce a result on the dependent variable (interaction).

CHAPTER 13

Single Case Designs

CHAPTER OUTLINE

Are You Equipped?

An Introduction to Single Case Designs

Why Use Single Case Designs?

Conducting Single Case Designs

Limitations of Single Case Designs

Are You Equipped Now?

Chapter Summary

APA Learning Goals Linkage

ARE YOU EQUIPPED?

In the early 1920s, two researchers took a child under the age of one and used classical conditioning techniques to condition an emotional response. Specifically, Watson and Rayner (1920) took a young child, *Little Albert*, and conditioned him to associate the appearance of a white rabbit with being scared. On its own, the rabbit did not elicit any response from Little Albert. However, in the experiment, the researchers paired the white rabbit with the hitting of a hammer on a metal bar (which naturally caused the child to become frightened). Within seven pairings of the white rabbit with the hammer and bar, Little Albert was conditioned; so each time he saw the white rabbit, he displayed a fearful response. Interestingly, this fear in Little Albert transferred over to anything white and fluffy. Although this is one of the most famous studies in psychology, many do not know that this was a specialized type of research design. Can you determine what is different about this study from many of the other studies we have discussed thus far?

What is unique about this design is that it involved only one participant. This type of design is known as a single case or a N = 1 design. The study by Watson and Rayner (1920) became one of the most important research findings in early psychology. And, unlike other designs in which numerous subjects are used, the researchers had a single participant. Yet, the impact on the field of psychology was significant. Watson and Rayner are not alone in their use of single case designs. Additional findings in the field of psychology were the result of single case designs. These designs will be the focus of our discussion in this chapter.

As you go through this chapter, we also want you to keep in mind how the material relates to the American Psychological Association's goals for psychology majors. Specifically, this chapter will address the following goals:

- **Goal 1. Knowledge Base in Psychology**

  You will demonstrate fundamental knowledge and comprehension of the major concepts, theoretical perspectives, historical trends, and empirical findings to discuss how psychological principles apply to behavioral problems.

- **Goal 2. Scientific Inquiry and Critical Thinking**

  You will demonstrate scientific reasoning and problem solving, including effective research methods.

- **Goal 3. Ethical and Social Responsibility in a Diverse World**

  You will apply ethical standards to evaluate psychological science and practice and you will develop ethically and socially responsible behaviors for professional and personal settings in a landscape that involves increasing diversity.

AN INTRODUCTION TO SINGLE CASE DESIGNS

Single Case Design:
A design focusing on a single participant, single group of participants, or a small group of participants.

Historically, a design in which the focus is on a (a) single participant, (b) small group of individuals, or (c) single group of participants was known as a single subject design (Shadish, Cook, & Campbell, 2002). Today, researchers refer to these types of designs as **single case designs**. We will examine specific examples later in the chapter. For now, it is important to know that the focus of a single case design is the individual. Specifically, researchers are attempting to show the impact an experimental condition has on a single participant. Often, these designs are mistaken as case studies. Remember from Chapter 4, a case study is an in-depth observation of an individual, animal, event, or treatment method. In truth, a case study is a type of single case design. However, not all single case designs are case studies.

The field of psychology has used single case designs from the beginning. In fact, one of the earliest users of single case designs was Wilhelm Wundt, regarded by most as the *father of psychology*. Wundt developed a technique known as introspection, which is a type of single case methodology. In his methodology, a single participant was trained to become consciously aware of his or her inner thoughts and feelings. Wundt believed this was the best way to explore the human mind. From participants' reported experiences, Wundt attempted to extrapolate a picture of the working mind. Although Wundt used several individuals in his research with introspection, his work focused on the individual and his or her own personal experience. This type of methodology does not sample from a large population as do many of the designs we have discussed thus far. Rather, the individual is the focus of interest.

Early on, the area in which single case designs were utilized the most was in behavioral psychological research. For example, we have already discussed the study with Little Albert, in which conditioning was used to elicit an emotional response. Furthermore, researchers such as Pavlov and Skinner used single case designs to explore classical and operant conditioning. Today, researchers are using single case designs to explore work in clinical, counseling, educational, cognitive, physiological, and other applied research setting in psychology.

One of the earliest research experiments on child development involved the use of a chimpanzee named Gua. Gua was raised by two researchers, Winthrop Kellogg and Luella Kellogg (1933). The Kelloggs were interested in how life experiences with the environment impacted early-stage development. Therefore, the Kelloggs decided to raise Gua side by side with their own infant child for nine months. Over the time period, the researchers systematically assessed the differences between their human child and the adopted chimp. The results showed that much of the early experiences that Gua was afforded resulted in a modification of traditionally instinctive behaviors. Specifically, Gua showed great maturation in nearly all areas of development including speech comprehension. The only exception was in the area of speech production.

© MongPro, 2014. Used under license from Shutterstock, Inc.

QUESTIONS

1. Why is this considered to be a single case design?

2. What is the independent variable the Kelloggs were manipulating? In other words, what was the experimental manipulation the Kelloggs were trying to show had a direct impact on development?

ANSWERS

1. The use of the single chimp makes this an example of a single case design. All the data collected and conclusions that the Kelloggs (1933) developed from their study centered on their systematic observation of a single participant, Gua. The study focused on the chimp and how her behavior changed over a 9-month period.

2. The independent variable the researchers were trying to manipulate was the early-life experiences with the environment. Specifically, the Kelloggs (1933) wanted to see if manipulating the early experiences with the environment had a direct impact on the chimp's rate of development. As it turned out, this was indeed the case, with Gua maturing at a quick rate.

Interestingly, one of the theorized reasons as to why the study was stopped was the Kelloggs' own infant son began developing many characteristics of the chimp. This would only further strengthen the Kelloggs' claim of early-life experiences that can modify development. For many years, this study was the basis for illustrating how maturation is impacted by learning. Again, what is unique about this study is the results were obtained by examining the change in a single participant and was not achieved with a large group of participants.

Although we have started this chapter by illustrating the impact and usefulness of single case designs, these types of designs cannot be used carte blanche. Rather, these designs are preferred by researchers when large group designs using inferential statistics are not possible or desired. Specifically, in large group designs, the researchers rely on averages across all participants which can lead to individual differences becoming masked within the data. However, single case designs focus solely on detecting these differences within the individual (or small group).

Previously, we mentioned the prevalence of single case designs in a number of areas in psychology. However, single case designs are most likely to occur in three specific situations. The first situation is in clinical research where a patient with a specific disorder is the focus of interest. Referring back to the beginning of this chapter, this case would be an example of a single case design that focuses on a single participant. Second, single case designs are preferred when investigating unique or specialized populations where large numbers either (a) do not exist or (b) access is limited. These populations might include using

Fortune 500 CEOs (Chief Executive Officers), government officials (i.e., senators), or experts in a given domain for a research study. This is an example of a single case design with a small group of individuals. Finally, single case designs are useful in group or team research, where the single unit of analysis is the group or team. In particular, single case research is often used when examining juries or business work teams where the jury or work team itself is the single case. This is an example of a single case design focusing on a single group of participants.

SECTION SUMMARY

- Single case designs are a special classification of research designs where the focus is on a
  - single participant,
  - small group of individuals, or
  - single group of participants (pp. 230–232).
- Single case designs are most likely to occur
  - in clinical research,
  - with specialized or unique populations where large numbers (a) do not exist or (b) access is limited, and
  - in group or team research (pp. 231–232).

WHY USE SINGLE CASE DESIGNS?

Until now, we have only introduced and made suggestions about when to use a single case design. However, it is important to know why it may be appropriate to use a single case design and what the benefits are to using a single case design over other types of designs. Surprisingly, the use of a single case design has nothing to do with limiting the amount of data collected. Instead, there are two main reasons to use a single case design:

- Single case designs can have high internal validity.
- Single case designs avoid problems with obtaining control groups.

First, single case designs can have high internal validity (see Chapter 5). Internal validity is the power of a design to isolate the independent variable as being responsible for any experimental effects. Thus, single case designs are good at showing that any manipulation of the independent variable had an impact on the dependent variable. This allows the researcher to establish practical significance between variables. For example, everyone knows that when you deprive someone of water, they become dehydrated. However, what does "become dehydrated" actually mean? This is a generalization of what happens. Rather, in a single case design, you would take a single participant and deprive him or her of water. This would give you a first-hand glimpse as to the practical relationship between water and the specific impact it has on a participant. Ethically, you could not do this experiment, but it is a great example of what is meant by establishing a practical relationship. Therefore, with single case designs, individual effects are not masked by group averages as they can be in a large participant designs. Instead, you directly see the impact of the independent variable on the dependent variable, thereby establishing the exact relationship between those variables.

Second, single case designs avoid problems with obtaining control groups. As with most experiments in which a researcher manipulates a variable, you have two groups: a control and an experimental group. However, in a single case design, the participant of interest serves as his or her own control group and, therefore, acts as his or her own baseline for comparison. This is similar to a within subjects design in which the participants act as a control by participating in all levels of the independent variable. Thus, there is no need for a second group for comparison. Rather, a researcher observes behavior before and after the introduction of the independent variable.

YOU TRY IT!

Arguably, the most important research on memory occurred back in the late 1800s. Herman Ebbinghaus (1885) was a pioneer in human memory research. In order to investigate human memory, Ebbinghaus devised a set of experiments in which he was the participant. His research focused on how quickly humans learn information. In his experiments, Ebbinghaus developed lists of nonsense syllables. These lists would consist of multiple consonant–vowel–consonant groups such as JEZ, FIQ, and YOT. Next, he would learn the same list of syllables at two different occasions, with varying time intervals in between. He would then learn the list again, noting how long it took to learn the list each time. From this difference in time (i.e., the first time to learn and the second time to learn), Ebbinghaus was able to calculate what he called a *savings*. For example, when learning a list for the first time, it took Ebbinghaus an average of 952 seconds. When relearning that list 19 minutes later, it took him an average of 452 seconds. This yields a savings of 57% of the information. Ebbinghaus repeated this experiment with different lists for intervals of 19 minutes, 1 hour, 8.8 hours, 24 hours, 48 hours, 6 days, and 31 days (levels of his independent variable). Using these different times between tests, Ebbinghaus was able to illustrate a forgetting curve. The curve shows retention of information drops, the most within the first 20 minutes and then gradually flattens out over several days. See Figure 13.1 for a visual representation.

QUESTIONS

1. What makes this study a single case design?
2. Why does Ebbinghaus' study have high internal validity?
3. When did Ebbinghaus serve as the control group in the study?

ANSWERS

1. The only participant in Ebbinghaus' study was himself. He served as the control group to establish a baseline and then served in the experimental group by varying the time period between sessions.

2. Ebbinghaus' study could have had high internal validity because he was able to demonstrate how time influenced learning and retention of information. By developing the forgetting curve, he was able to empirically show how his independent variable (time) had an impact on his dependent variable (learning). Specifically, because Ebbinghaus served in both the control and the experimental group, thereby reducing any threats to internal validity (see Chapter 9).

3. Again, Ebbinghaus' use of himself as his participant allowed other researchers to see first hand the relationship between the variables in his study. He served as the control group in the study during the initial phase of learning. The learning of the list the first time was the control condition. At this point, the independent variable of time had not been introduced. Therefore, the initial learning phase served as the control for the study.

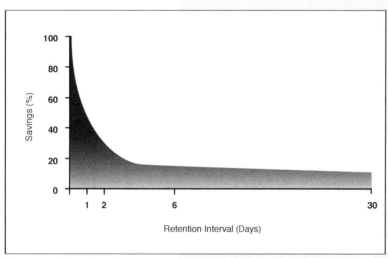

Fig 13.1   Ebbinghaus forgetting curve

SECTION SUMMARY

- Single case designs can have high internal validity (pp. 232–233).
- Single case designs avoid problems with obtaining control groups (pp. 232–233).

CONDUCTING SINGLE CASE DESIGNS

There are several ways in which you can develop and carry out a single case design. In other words, there are specific types of methodologies used in single case designs. We are going to discuss the three most common types of methodologies used in single case design research: (a) AB or pretest–posttest designs, (b) ABA or reversal designs, and (c) multiple baseline designs.

AB DESIGNS (PRETEST–POSTTEST)

Thus far, we have mentioned this design several times in this chapter without actually giving it a name. An **AB design** (Figure 13.2), also known as a pretest–posttest design, involves taking measurements before and after the administering of an independent variable. For example, when testing a new drug for schizophrenia, the researchers would take an initial baseline assessment of the symptoms (A) after which the researchers would administer the drug for a certain period. Then, the researchers would bring the participant back following that period and conduct a follow-up assessment of the symptoms (B).

AB Designs: A methodology where measurements are taken before and after the administering of an independent variable.

This type of design occurred in the research by Ebbinghaus (1885). He attempted to learn the information as quickly as he could, thereby establishing a baseline (A). Then, he administered the independent variable (time) followed by a follow-up session of learning (B). However, the use of an AB design does not always allow the research to fully see the impact of the independent variable. There are other designs which are better able to show the impact of the independent variable on a participant.

Baseline Measurement (**A**) ➡ IV ➡ Follow-up Measurement (**B**)

Fig 13.2 AB design.

ABA DESIGNS (REVERSAL DESIGNS)

Remember, the purpose of a single case design is to detect the impact of an independent variable. With an AB design, this is accomplished by looking at the change from point A to point B. However, the most powerful present methodology to show the impact of the independent variable in single case designs is the **ABA or reversal design** (Figure 13.3). This methodology initially proceeds just like an AB design. However, once information after the independent variable is collected (B), the independent variable is then removed. At this point, the participant is exposed to a time period (same amount as the independent variable) where nothing occurs in terms of manipulation. After that time is up, the researcher conducts another measurement (A). Once the independent variable is removed, the participant should return to a baseline state. Thus, the third assessment is also called measure (A).

ABA Designs: A methodology where measurements are taken before and after the administering of an independent variable as well as after the removal of the independent variable.

| Baseline Measurement (**A**) ➡ IV ➡ Follow-up Measurement (**B**) ➡ Removal ➡ Baseline Measurement (**A**) |

Fig 13.3 ABA design.

For example, Kuoch and Mirenda (2003) conducted a single case study in which they looked at the influences of a social story on the behavior of autistic children. A social story is a story used to teach specific social skills as an alternative to a problem behavior (i.e., problems with sharing toys). Kuoch and Mirenda used an ABA design to assess the impact of the social story on specific behavioral problems. During the initial baseline phase, the researchers would observe the participant in certain problem situations and record the number of behavioral problems (A). Following the initial baseline, the intervention stage was administered (B). In this stage, the researchers would read to the participant a social story before a problem situation was presented. Afterward, the researcher would count the number of behavioral responses the participant displayed in the corresponding problem situation. Finally, the researchers removed the use of the social story and collected data in a follow-up baseline (A). This is a great example of the use of an ABA design in single case research. Interestingly, participants' behavior was permanently changed following the intervention. In particular, the initial baseline results showed higher numbers of behavioral problems as compared to the follow-up baseline. Even with the usefulness of an ABA design, instances exist when it is not possible to conduct an ABA design. Reasons for not using an ABA design usually fall into two categories, ethical concerns or feasibility concerns. The first category deals with the ethical consequences of removing an independent variable after it has had a positive effect. For example, if a researcher developed a new drug that cured cancer in his or her patient, is it ethical of that researcher to withdraw the drug just to see if the patient's health will return to baseline? Should the researcher go through a reversal, knowing that it could increase the chances that the patient would develop cancer again? The answer is obviously no. Therefore, an ABA design could not be used in this particular case. The other category surrounds the feasibility of truly removing the independent variable. In particular, it may not be possible to fully remove the effects of the independent variable, thereby reverting the participant's behavior to baseline. This often happens in research where the independent variable involves learning or the development of skill. In these situations, the removal of a learned skill is not practical, resulting in the participant being unable to revert to his or her baseline performance. This category was evident in the example used earlier, where Kuoch and Mirenda (2003) had participants who did not revert (or reverse) to their initial baseline performance.

MULTIPLE BASELINES

A multiple baseline design is a stronger version of an AB or ABA design since it allows researchers to determine the impact of certain threats to internal validity. Researchers use this type of design to ensure that the change that is seen is due to the independent variable and not something else. When using **multiple baseline designs**, researchers have a small number of participants receive the independent variable at varying times. This allows the researcher to see how outside events might influence the participant.

For example, over the past few years, middle schools have been grappling with educating students about bullying. Imagine a new program that has been developed to educate these students. However, since this program is still unproven, a county superintendent chooses to conduct a study. The superintendent selects three schools in his or her county to participate in the study. In order to minimize outside effects and fully determine the likelihood of the program to be successful, the superintendent decides to use a multiple baseline methodology. Specifically, the superintendent introduces the program in each school at varying times. The following results are based on reported incidences of bullying by students (see Figure 13.4). The first school in this program received the program after 4 weeks of classes, the second school after 8 weeks of classes, and the third school after 12 weeks of classes. As can be seen from the results, all schools showed similar levels of baseline bullying activity. However, immediately following the introduction of the program, incidences of bullying changed in all schools. These results show that the program had an effect. The researcher (in this case, the superintendent) can argue that the program led to the change and the change was not because of outside influences such as a history effect or maturation (threats to internal validity).

Multiple Baselines Designs: A methodology where researchers have a small number of participants receive the independent variable at varying times.

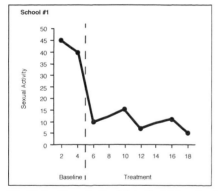 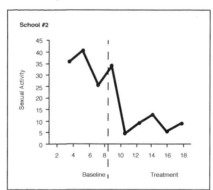 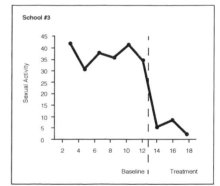

Fig 13.4   Hypothetical data for high-school intervention

We are looking to conduct a single case design. We want to look at the influence of mental imagery on performance in elite athletes. Mental imagery occurs when a person mentally rehearses events in his or her mind before performing them in reality. We have a small population of elite swimmers who have never used mental imagery. Since this is a small and specialized population, we know that we will be using a single case design. What type of methodology would you use to conduct a study on this topic—an AB design, an ABA design, or a multiple baseline approach?

ANSWERS

1. You could have conducted this research study using any of the aforementioned designs. For this study, an AB design would collect data for the initial baseline (A) of swimming performance. This would then be followed by the administering of the independent variable of mental imagery techniques and the collection of data again on swimming performance (B).

2. If you chose to conduct an ABA design, you would follow the same procedure as the AB design. However, after the administering of the mental imagery techniques, you would remove that independent variable before collecting the follow-up baseline on swimming performance (A). The key here is the removal of the mental imagery techniques before assessing swimming performance a second time.

3. Casby and Moran (1998) used this approach when studying this exact topic. They used a multiple baseline approach with four swimmers. Each swimmer was assessed for varying amounts of time to establish baseline performance followed by the administering of the independent variable of mental imagery. Results showed that regardless of when the independent variable was implemented, none of the swimmers significantly improved their performance. Therefore, the researchers concluded that the use of mental imagery had no direct impact on performance.

© Maridav, 2014. Used under license from Shutterstock, Inc.

SECTION SUMMARY

When conducting single case designs, several methodologies can be used.

- *AB designs* are also known as pretest–posttest designs. These designs involve taking measurements before (A) and after the introduction of the independent variable (B) (pp. 235–236).
- *ABA designs* are also known as reversal designs. In this methodology, measurements are taken before (A), after the introduction of the independent variable (B), and after the removal of the independent variable (A) (pp. 235–236).
- A *multiple baseline design* involves introducing the independent variable in a study at varying times to a small group of participants. With this design, the participants all experience a varying amount of time in the baseline and treatment conditions (p. 237).

LIMITATIONS OF SINGLE CASE DESIGNS

Even with all of the benefits that can be gained by using a single case design, there are several limitations to these types of designs. First, because single case designs use within subject methodologies, the design faces the same limitations that we discussed in Chapter 12. These include carryover, order, and practice effects. In addition, with single case designs, a researcher has to be very aware of fatigue or over evaluation/assessment influencing the participant. Specifically, since there is a single participant whom the researcher is directing the attention toward, the participant become less cooperative faster as compared to being a participant in a larger study.

However, the most glaring limitation to single case designs has to do with the generalizability of the results to large populations. While single case designs have high internal validity, they have low external validity. In other words, single case designs cannot be used to predict behavior beyond the participant or small group within the study. This is a major limitation. Nonetheless, many (if not most) single case designs are only useful to the participant or small group being studied and are not concerned with generalizing to a larger population. Therefore, single case designs are very useful to advancing knowledge when used appropriately.

Each year, there are major transitions that occur for sports teams within the season. One of the most notable of these transitions occurs in the National Basketball League (NBA) with the start of the free agency period. During this time of the year, organizations compete for the opportunity to trade for a high value player that can improve their team's chances of winning the NBA title. Often, when a team trades for a player, it is with the understanding that the player will only be a part of the team for a short period (usually through the end of the current season). It is also during this part of the season when many sports pundits ask the question, will the player have a positive impact on the team? Typically, this positive impact is measured in terms of wins and losses through the remaining schedule and the team's final outcome for the season. Once the season is over, these organizations then have to make a decision to keep or release these players.

QUESTIONS

Can you explain how this event in the NBA season could be an example of a single case design? Specifically, can you identify the participants, the independent variable, and the type of methodology used here?

ANSWERS

In this example, the participants are the teams which have acquired a player and the independent variable is the acquired player. This may seem counterintuitive but the addition of a player is what is being manipulated in this scenario (i.e., the presence on the team or the absence). If you said that the approach being used was an AB design, you are partially right. Actually, this single case design would be using a multiple baselines approach. The methodology follows like an AB design with a baseline assessment (A) and the administering of the treatment (B). However, since the participants are the different teams, this becomes a multiple baseline approach. Specifically, several teams may acquire a player (the independent variable) at different times during the free agency period. This allows each team to have a varying amount of time to establish a baseline before the independent variable is administered (i.e., the acquisition of a new player). With this approach, the answer to the question of impact on a team could be seen.

CHAPTER SUMMARY

- A *single case design* focuses on a (1) single participant, (2) single group of participants, or (3) small group of participants (pp. 230–232).
- Single case designs are most likely to occur in three areas (pp. 231–232):
  - Single case designs are most popular when conducting clinical research (pp. 231–232).
  - Single case designs are used when investigating specialized or unique populations where large numbers (1) do not exist or (2) access is limited due to availability (pp. 231–232).

- Finally, single case designs are used in research investigating group or team research where the group or team is the focus (e.g., jury studies) (pp. 231–232).
- Single case designs have several advantages:
    - Single case designs have been shown to have high internal validity (pp. 232–233).
    - Single case designs avoid problems with obtaining control groups (pp. 232–233).
- When conducting single case research, there are several methodologies to explore:
    - *AB designs* are also known as pretest–posttest designs. These designs involve taking measurements before (A) and after the introduction of the independent variable (B) (p. 235).
    - *ABA designs* are also known as reversal designs. In this methodology, measurements are taken before (A), after the introduction of the independent variable (B), and after the removal of the independent variable (A) (pp. 235–236).
    - A *multiple baseline design* involves introducing the independent variable in a study at varying times to a small group of participants. With this design, the participants all experience a varying amount of time in the baseline and treatment conditions (p. 237).

APA LEARNING GOALS LINKAGE

- **Goal 1. Knowledge Base in Psychology**

    You will demonstrate fundamental knowledge and comprehension of the major concepts, theoretical perspectives, historical trends, and empirical findings to discuss how psychological principles apply to behavioral problems.

    Sections Covered: Are You Equipped?, An Introduction to Single Case Designs, Conducting Single Case Designs

    Explanation of the Goal: Many psychological studies in the history of the field used a single case design. The chapter started with a single case design conducted by Watson and Rayner to condition fear in a child. Ebbinghaus experimented with forgetting with only himself as a participant. We also mentioned the work of Wundt, often considered the father of psychology, and the Kelloggs, who were interested in early developmental experiences. These examples demonstrate that the individual is a relevant level of analysis within the field.

- **Goal 2. Scientific Inquiry and Critical Thinking**

    You will demonstrate scientific reasoning and problem solving, including effective research methods.

    Sections Covered: Are You Equipped?, An Introduction to Single Case Designs, Why Use Single Case Designs, Conducting Single Case Designs, Limitations of Single Case Designs, Are You Equipped Now?

Explanation of the Goal: Single case designs focus on a single participant, single group of participants, or small group of participants. In this chapter, we introduced you to this design, along with the different types of single case designs commonly used (AB designs, ABA designs, and multiple baseline designs). We articulated the strengths and limitations of the design in the corresponding sections on advantages and disadvantages of the approach. One major limitation was regarding the ability to generalize conclusions from single case designs to other populations. By discussing this limitation, you gained the skills needed to recognize how individual differences may influence the applicability of research findings.

Sections Covered: Are You Equipped?, Introduction to Single Case Designs, Why Use Single Case Designs, Conducting Single Case Designs, Are You Equipped Now?

Explanation of the Goal: The exercises that you completed in this chapter entailed recognizing the use of single case designs in classical (e.g., Ebbinghaus and Kelloggs) and current research examples (e.g., mental imagery and swimmers). You then used critical thinking skills to explain how the designs of the studies yielded both advantages and disadvantages.

- **Goal 3. Ethical and Social Responsibility in a Diverse World**

You will apply ethical standards to evaluate psychological science and practice and you will develop ethically and socially responsible behaviors for professional and personal settings in a landscape that involves increasing diversity.

Sections Covered: Are You Equipped?, Introduction to Single Case Designs, Why Use Single Case Designs, Conducting Single Case Designs, Are You Equipped Now?

Explanation of the Goal: To begin, we identified appropriate applications of psychology in solving problems at the beginning of the chapter when we outlined how different areas of psychology all use single case designs. The examples provided continued to relate to societal issues such as autism and applying psychological principles to personal issues such as mental imagery for swimmers.

Sections Covered: Limitations of Single Case Designs

Explanation of the Goal: APA states that psychology majors should recognize and respect human diversity. In the section on the limitations of single case designs, we learned to anticipate how psychological explanations may vary across populations.

Hypothesis Testing Continued and Interpreting Results

Part 5

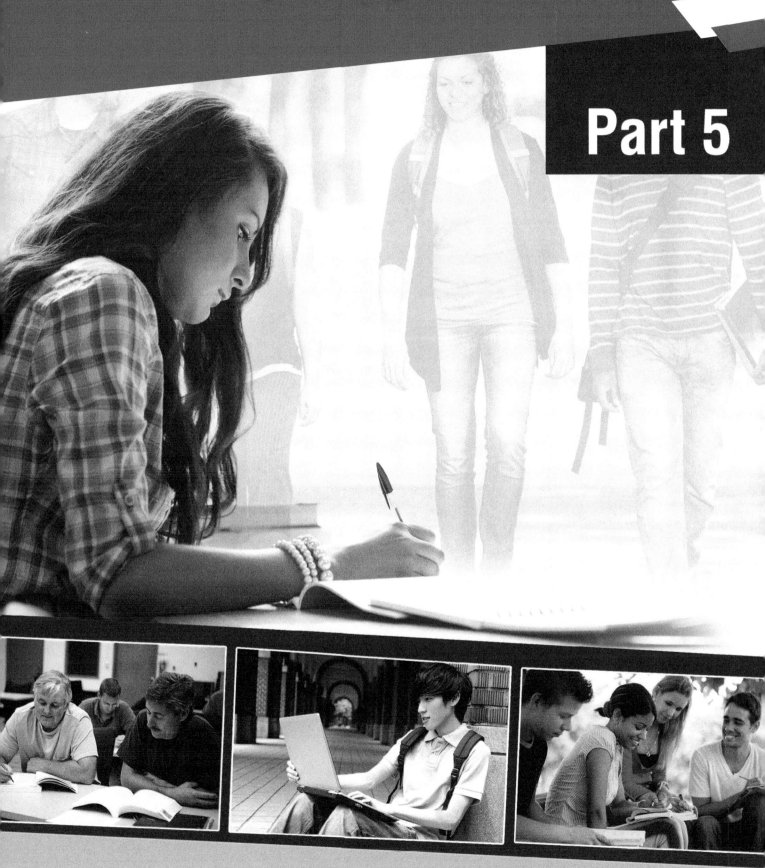

CHAPTER 14

Hypothesis Testing Revisited and Interpreting Results

CHAPTER OUTLINE

Are You Equipped?

Examining the Results—Rejecting the Null or Failing to Reject the Null Hypothesis

Introduction to Interpreting Statistical Results

Are You Equipped Now?

Chapter Summary

APA Learning Goals Linkage

ARE YOU EQUIPPED?

Researchers Dunn, Huntsinger, Lun, and Sinclair (2008) conducted a study to explain how individuals interpret gift giving in new acquaintance situations. The researchers obtained their participants from another study that had paired members of the opposite sex and that required them to engage in social interactions for fewer than 5 minutes. Afterwards, the researchers separated these new acquaintances and asked them to rank order their own preferences for $20 gift cards to 12 stores and restaurants. Participants were then asked to select a gift card for their new acquaintance and were told their new acquaintance would be doing the same for them. Participants were informed that they had a small chance of actually winning the gift card in a lottery. Next, the participants were told what gift card their new acquaintance had selected for them. However, in reality, the researchers randomly assigned participants to receive either a good gift card (the participant's first choice) or a bad gift card (the participant's 11th choice). After learning what their new acquaintance had selected for them, participants completed a survey and indicated how similar they were to the acquaintance in terms of interests and ways they spend their free time.

© Eman Design, 2014. Used under license from Shutterstock, Inc.

The researchers had predicted that men and women would respond differently to receiving good and bad gifts from new acquaintances. The results indicated that women reported the same degree of similarity between themselves and the new acquaintances, whether they received a good gift or a bad gift. Men, on the other hand, reported different levels of similarity between themselves and the new acquaintances based on the type of gift. Specifically, men reported higher levels of similarity after receiving a good gift and lower levels of similarity after receiving a bad gift.

In Chapter 6, we introduced the topic of hypothesis testing and discussed how researchers design experiments to answer questions. Dunn et al. (2008) conducted a study to test a hypothesis. The null hypothesis was that men and women would not be different in how they responded to the good and bad gifts, whereas the research hypothesis was that men and women would differ in how they responded. We want to add to your knowledge of hypothesis testing by discussing how researchers decide whether to reject the null hypothesis or fail to reject the null hypothesis. Dunn et al. would reject the null hypothesis because they found differences in how men and women responded to the gift selected. In this chapter, you will learn how to look at statistical outcomes for a study and decide the appropriate action in regard to the null hypothesis.

As you go through this chapter, we also want you to keep in mind how the material relates to the American Psychological Association's goals for psychology majors. Specifically, this chapter will address the following goals:

- **Goal 2. Scientific Inquiry and Critical Thinking**

  You will demonstrate scientific reasoning and problem solving, including effective research methods.
- **Goal 4. Communication**

  You will demonstrate competence in writing and in oral and interpersonal communication skills.

EXAMINING THE RESULTS: REJECTING THE NULL OR FAILING TO REJECT THE NULL HYPOTHESIS

Previously, we introduced the concept of hypothesis testing. In this chapter, we will be revisiting this topic and adding to your understanding of hypothesis testing. In particular, we will discuss how a researcher decides whether the null hypothesis should be rejected or not at the conclusion of the study. In order to provide continuity, we will start by reviewing some of the earlier examples.

CHEERLEADER EFFECT REVISITED

In Chapter 6, we discussed the cheerleader effect proposed by the character Barney Stinson on the TV show *How I Met Your Mother*. Barney's theory claims that people look more attractive when they are part of a group than when they are alone. In this example, we formed the research questions: "Does context of an individual (in a group or alone) influence ratings of attractiveness?" and "Can you remember how to identify each in words and symbols?"

The null hypothesis could be stated as: "Context of an individual does not influence ratings of attractiveness" or "There is no influence of context of an individual on ratings of attractiveness." In symbols, the null hypothesis would be represented as follows:

$$H_0: \mu_{(group)} = \mu_{(alone)}$$

The research hypothesis could be stated as: "Context of an individual does influence ratings of attractiveness" or "There is an influence of context of an individual on ratings of attractiveness." In symbols, the research hypothesis would be represented as follows:

$$H_1: \mu_{(group)} \neq \mu_{(alone)}$$

You could also form a directional research hypothesis where you hypothesize that attractiveness ratings will be higher when in a group than when alone. In this case, your directional research hypothesis could be stated as, "Ratings of attractiveness will be higher in a group than alone." In symbols, the directional research hypothesis would be represented as

$$H_1: \mu_{(group)} > \mu_{(alone)}$$

Once you have developed the appropriate hypotheses, you can conduct your study. The question then becomes, "What do we do once we have the results?" We mentioned at the end of Chapter 6 that researchers never say that they have *proved* a result. Rather, researchers are more likely to say the results support a particular hypothesis or the results are inconclusive. In order to make any causal inference about the results of a study, researchers have two options they must consider: to reject the null hypothesis or to fail to reject the null hypothesis.

In order to do this, researchers test the null hypothesis. The logic behind testing the null hypothesis is quite elegant. It is easier to disprove the null hypothesis than it is to disprove the research hypothesis. Therefore, researchers are looking to disprove the null hypothesis or the likelihood that the means of the groups are equal.

As we have mentioned, when researchers have conducted a study and analyzed their data, they have a decision to make regarding the null hypothesis. The researcher can either reject the null hypothesis or fail to reject the null hypothesis. If a researcher **rejects the null hypothesis**, the results have indicated that there is a statistically significant difference between the means of the groups (i.e., the means of the groups are not equal). If the researcher **fails to reject the null hypothesis**, the results have indicated that the means of the groups are equal (i.e., there is no difference in the means of the groups).

To determine if the groups are statistically different from one another, researchers perform statistical procedures and examine the level of significance. The **level of significance** is known as the alpha level (α) and is determined prior to conducting

Rejecting the Null Hypothesis: Indicates that there is a statistically significant difference between the means of the groups in the study.

Failing to Reject the Null Hypothesis: Indicates that there is not a statistically significant difference between the means of the groups in the study and that the means are equal.

Level of Significance: The level of significance is indicated by the alpha level (α).

an experiment. Alpha is the probability of obtaining data, assuming the null hypothesis is true. In psychological research, most researchers accept an alpha level of 0.05 as the desired level of significance.

The lower the *p*-value, the less likely the obtained differences in the results are due to chance and the more likely the obtained differences in the results are due to the manipulation of the study. If the *p*-value obtained from a study is less than the conventional alpha level of 0.05 (i.e., $p < 0.05$), we reject the null hypothesis. In other words, the results are so extreme that they are unlikely due to chance and have indicated a statistically significant difference between the means of the groups. If the *p*-value obtained from a study is greater than the conventional alpha level of 0.05 (i.e., $p > 0.05$), we fail to reject the null hypothesis. If a researcher fails to reject the null hypothesis, the results have indicated that there is not a statistically significant difference between the means of the groups. This does not imply the researcher has proved the null hypothesis. Rather, it just means the researcher is unable to reject it.

YOU TRY IT!

Below are two examples of research studies. We provide you with the research question and the results of the study. To complete this You Try It! you will need to use your knowledge gained from Chapter 6 in addition to the information covered thus far in the chapter. We would like for you to state (a) the null hypothesis; (b) the null hypothesis in symbols; (c) the research hypothesis, identifying if it is directional or nondirectional; (d) the research hypothesis in symbols; and (e) whether, based on the results, you should reject the null hypothesis or fail to reject the null hypothesis.

Questions

1. A researcher has designed a study to answer the question, "Do men or women drink more coffee?" The researcher conducts the study by observing the coffee consumption of men and women during a 1-week period. The researcher hypothesizes that men will consume *more* coffee than women. After the study is concluded, the researcher finds that there is no difference between men and women ($p > 0.05$).

2. You want to know whether typed or handwritten papers are graded differently by professors. So, you have professors read and evaluate papers of both types. You hope to show that there is a *difference* in the way typed and handwritten papers are evaluated. After the study is concluded, you find that there is a difference between typed and handwritten papers in the grades received. This result is statistically significant at the $p < 0.05$ level.

1. The null hypothesis for this question could be stated as, "There is *no* difference between the amount of coffee consumed by men and women." In symbols this would be represented as follows:

$$H_o: \mu_{(men)} = \mu_{(women)}$$

The research hypothesis in this study is a directional research hypothesis. This is evident by the researcher indicating men would consume *more* coffee than women would consume. The directional research hypothesis could be stated as, "Men will consume *more* coffee than women." In symbols,

$$H_1: \mu_{(men)} > \mu_{(women)}$$

Based on the results of this study ($p > 0.05$), the researchers would fail to reject the null. In other words, the results did not indicate a statistically significant difference between men and women in their consumption of coffee. In addition, the results were counter to what the researcher predicted.

2. The null hypothesis in this question could be stated as, "There is *no difference* in the evaluation of typed and handwritten papers." In symbols, this would be represented as follows:

$$H_o: \mu_{(typed\ papers)} = \mu_{(handwritten\ papers)}$$

The research hypothesis in this study is a nondirectional research hypothesis. This is evident by indicating that a difference should occur and not specifying which type of paper will receive higher grades. The nondirectional research hypothesis could be stated as, "There is a *difference* in the evaluation of typed and handwritten papers." In symbols,

$$H_1: \mu_{(typed\ papers)} \neq \mu_{(handwritten\ papers)}$$

Based on the results of this study ($p < 0.05$), you would reject the null hypothesis. Specifically, the results of the study showed a statistically significant difference in the evaluation of typed and handwritten papers.

TYPE I AND TYPE II ERRORS

Given the information presented so far, it would appear as though all you need to do is look at the *p*-value to determine whether to reject or fail to reject the null hypothesis. However, there is more to the decision. As can be seen from Table 14.1, there are four possible outcomes to a study. First, you can make the decision to reject the null when the null hypothesis is false. This would be a correct decision. The other correct decision would be to fail to reject the null when the null hypothesis is true. However, there are occasions when decision errors are made.

As can be seen from the table, there are times where you reject the null hypothesis when the null is, in fact, true. This is known as a **Type I Error**. This first type of error, Type I Error, occurs when a researcher finds the groups to be different when

Type I Error: It occurs when a researcher rejects the null when the null is in fact true.

they are really the same. The probability of making a Type I Error in an experiment is related to the level of the significance set at the beginning. Conventionally, there is a 5% chance or less of rejecting the null when it is, in fact, true. If the alpha level is set more stringent (0.01), the probability of committing the Type I Error is lower. There is a 1% chance or less of rejecting the null hypothesis when it is, in fact, true. Therefore, the lower the alpha level, the lower the probability that a researcher will commit a Type I Error. The second error that can be made is known as a **Type II Error**. A Type II Error occurs when a researcher fails to reject the null hypothesis even though the null hypothesis is false. This is a situation when the researcher finds the groups to be the same when they are really different. A Type II Error occurs when statistical power is low. In Chapter 8, we discussed about power. Power is the probability of rejecting the null hypothesis when it is indeed false or the probability of accepting the research hypothesis. The formula for power is represented by $1 - \beta$. The chances of committing a Type II Error are directly related to the power level of a study. The lower the power a study has, the greater the chance of committing a Type II Error. Likewise, the stronger the power a study has, the less the chance of committing a Type II Error. A more thorough review of power can be found in a statistic book.

	TABLE 14.1 Hypothesis testing conclusions.	
True state of affairs	**Researcher's decision**	
	Reject the null Hypothesis	**Fail to reject the null hypothesis**
Null hypothesis is true	Type I Error probability = α	Correct decision probability = $1 - \alpha$
Null hypothesis is false	Correct decision-probability = $1 - \beta$	Type II Error probability = β

Some examples will help in understanding Type I and Type II Errors. Just like researchers, juries can make two correct decisions. These would be to find an innocent person not guilty of a crime and to find a guilty person guilty of a crime. However, juries can also make decision errors. For example, a jury might find an innocent person guilty of a crime. Or, a jury might find a guilty person innocent of a crime. However, just as juries do not make decision errors on purposes, neither do researchers. Nor do only bad researchers make errors. Rather, the errors made by researchers are due to the use of probability in hypothesis testing.

ROLE OF REPLICATION

The last topic we would like to mention on hypothesis testing is the role that replication plays in research. The results and conclusions drawn from research studies must be verified. One of the best ways to ensure that a result is accurate and not a product of an error is by replicating the study. A study replication occurs when another researcher (or the same researcher) re-creates a study using the same methodology as used in the original study. Study replication allows researchers to verify results. If a study is replicated and the results are the same as the original, researchers can be confident that a decision error was not committed.

However, if a study is replicated and results are different from the original study, an error might have been committed. If this were to occur, the conclusions from the original study would need to be reevaluated. The next time you conduct a research study, think about conducting a follow-up study to ensure your results are not an error.

SECTION SUMMARY

- *Rejecting the null hypothesis* indicates that there is a statistically significant difference between the means of the groups in the study (pp. 246–249).

- *Failing to reject the null hypothesis* indicates that there is not a statistically significant difference between the means of the groups in the study and that the means are equal (pp. 246–249).

- The *level of significance* is indicated by the alpha level (α) (pp. 247–248).

  - Traditionally, psychologists accept an alpha level of 0.05 (p. 248).

  - If the obtained p-value in a study is less than the conventional alpha level, we reject the null hypothesis (p. 248).

  - If the obtained p-value in a study is more than the conventional alpha level, we fail to reject the null hypothesis (p. 248).

- When conducting research, there are four possible decision outcomes. The first two are to reject the null when it is false or to fail to reject the null hypothesis when it is true (pp. 249–250).

  - A *Type I Error* occurs when a researcher rejects the null hypothesis when the null is, in fact, true (pp. 249–250).

  - A *Type II Error* occurs when a researcher fails to reject the null hypothesis even though the null hypothesis is false (pp. 249–250).

INTRODUCTION TO INTERPRETING STATISTICAL RESULTS

Most psychology departments require that students take a course in research methods. This is because the skills and knowledge obtained through the course material are foundations for working in any area of psychology. At some universities, research methods and statistics are taught together in one course, while at other universities, the two subject areas are taught as different courses. Our goal for the next section is not to teach you how to conduct statistical procedures. Rather, we want to provide suggestions on how to draw conclusions when you read statistical outcomes. This information will benefit you no matter which approach your university takes to teaching research methods and statistics.

We will discuss two branches of statistics known as descriptive and inferential statistics. The purpose of descriptive statistics is to describe the data, whereas the purpose of inferential statistics is to allow you to draw conclusions about the population of interest from the sample used. In the following sections,, we will cover the common procedures for each of the two branches of statistics and the implications you should consider when interpreting them.

DRAWING CONCLUSIONS FROM DESCRIPTIVE STATISTICS

Descriptive Statistics:
Statistics used by researchers to describe data sets.

Measures of Central Tendency: Numbers that represent the scores in the data set.

Mean: The average of the scores in the data set.

Median: The number in the middle of a data set.

Mode: The most frequently occurring number in a data set.

Descriptive statistics are used by researchers to describe data sets. Specifically, descriptive statistics summarize data sets by providing numbers which are representative or typical of the set. This is helpful because most of the time you do not have access to a researcher's full data set. It is also a quick way to obtain an overview of the scores in the set.

A frequent way of summarizing a data set is to give measures of central tendency. **Measures of central tendency** are numbers that represent the scores in the data set. Three commonly used measures of central tendency are the mean, median, and mode. The **mean** is the average of the scores in the data set. To obtain the mean, you add up all the scores in the data set and divide by the total number of scores. The **median** can be found by arranging all the scores in the data set from highest to lowest (or lowest to highest) and locating the number in the middle. If there is an even number of scores in the data set, you will need to calculate the mean for the two numbers in the middle. The **mode** is the most frequently occurring number in the data set and it is possible to have more than one mode.

Here is a data set:

10, 20, 30, 40, 40, 50

To find the *mean*, you would add up the scores and divide by the total number of scores:

$$10 + 20 + 30 + 40 + 40 + 50 = 190$$

$$\frac{190}{6} = 31.66$$

To find the *median*, you arrange the scores from lowest to highest and locate the middle value.

10, 20, 30, 40, 40, 50

Note: Because there is an even number of scores, the average of the two numbers in the middle (30 and 40) is taken. The median is 35.

To find the *mode*, you look for the number that occurs most frequently. The mode for this example would be 40 because it is the only score that occurs more than once.

Normal Distribution:
A normal distribution of scores occurs when most scores cluster around the middle and few, but equal, numbers cluster on the extremes.

You can infer much about a data set by knowing if the mean, median, and mode are the same (or about the same). If these three measures are similar, the data set has a **normal distribution** (see Figure 14.1). You can see from the illustration that when a data set has a normal distribution, most of the scores cluster around the center. Few scores occur at the high and low ends of the distribution. One way to apply this concept is using the distribution of exam scores from a psychology course. If scores from the exam follow a normal distribution, it would mean that most of the students earned a C on the exam. Fewer students would have earned B's and D's and even fewer students would have earned A's and F's. Normal distributions are also symmetrical, meaning that there would be an equal number of high scores and low scores.

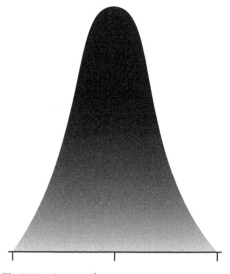

Fig 14.1   A normal curve

If you know that a data set has a normal distribution, there are conclusions you can draw about the scores. The first implication for any data set with a normal distribution is that most of the participants gave responses that fell in the middle of the distribution. It is also the case that extreme scores, in either direction, are less frequent. Therefore, any measure of central tendency would be a good representation for the data set. Specifically with a normal distribution, the mean, median, and the mode all are the same value. However, the conclusions that you draw about a data set change when the distribution is not normal. A distribution that is not normal is said to be skewed. A **skewed distribution** is one in which the most frequently occurring scores are not in the middle. In other words, the scores pile up at one end of the distribution or the other (see Figure 14.2a and b). With a skewed distribution, the mean, median, and mode are not the same.

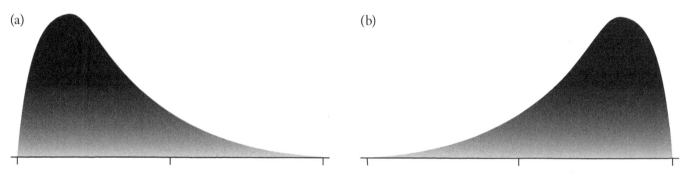

Fig 14.2   (a) Positively skewed. (b) Negatively skewed.

One issue to consider with a skewed distribution is which measure of central tendency best represents the data set. In their statistics book, Aron, Aron, and Coups (2009) provide a wonderful illustration of this situation by using data from Miller and Fishkin (1997), who surveyed male and female participants regarding how many partners they ideally wanted to have in the next three decades. If you compare responses of men and women by looking at the means, men (64.3) desired to have a far greater number of partners than did women (2.8). However, Aron et al. point out that because the data set is not normal, the mean is not the most representative number. This is because means are easily influenced by extreme scores. This occurred in the Miller and Fishkin data set because a few of the male respondents gave very high numbers in the thousands, thus increasing the mean. In this situation, it is helpful to look at the median. The median indicated that the score in the middle for both men and women was 1. Thus, looking at the mean or the median in this study can lead you to draw different conclusions about the number of partners that men and women want in the future. The take-home message is that when you see a skewed distribution, you have to be careful about conclusions that you make by looking at the mean. If there are extreme scores in the data set, the median might be the more representative score.

Skewed Distribution:
A distribution in which the most frequently occurring scores are not in the middle.

Before moving on to the topic of inferential statistics, we would like to briefly mention two measures of variability that can also be used to summarize data. These two measures are variance and standard deviation. Although variance provides information on the spread of scores in a set, standard deviation is used most frequently to provide information on how much scores vary from the mean. A large standard deviation would indicate that scores vary widely from the mean and are spread out in the data set. A small standard deviation would indicate that most scores are located around the mean. Knowing the amount of standard deviation can help to determine if the mean is a representative score for the data set.

CONCLUSIONS FROM INFERENTIAL STATISTICS

Inferential Statistics: Used to draw inferences about a population from the sample used.

One-Sample *t*-Test: Used to determine when a mean is significantly different from a constant.

Dependent *t*-Test: Used to determine if the mean difference between pairs is significantly different from zero.

Independent *t*-Test: Evaluates whether or not two means are significantly different from one another.

Inferential statistics are used so that inferences can be drawn about a population from the sample used. As we discussed earlier in this textbook, it is not feasible or practical to conduct research on entire populations. However, we can obtain a representative sample of individuals from the population of interest. We can then use inferential statistics to make generalizations about our population. Hence, inferential statistics allow us to make generalizations that go beyond our sample.

One of the most basic inferential statistics is the *t*-test. There are three types of *t*-test. The **one-sample *t*-test** is used to determine when a mean is significantly different from a constant. This constant can be obtained from previous research, chance level, or the midpoint on a scale. The **dependent or paired samples *t*-test** is used to determine if the mean difference between the pairs is significantly different from zero. The pairs for this *t*-test can be from repeated measures designs or matched subjects designs. Finally, the **independent *t*-test** evaluates whether or not means from two different groups are significantly different from one another.

The first issue to consider when a researcher uses a *t*-test is whether or not the researcher used the correct *t*-test when analyzing his or her data. Although there are similarities among the three *t*-tests, each one actually evaluates a different assumption. The correct *t*-test needs to be used for the specific application. For example, we would use a *t*-test if our university wanted to assess the effectiveness of a faculty development workshop. We could have students evaluate the same group of faculty members on their teaching before and after they attend the workshop. In order to determine if the workshop influenced the ratings, we would use a dependent samples *t*-test. This is because we have the following conditions: one independent variable with two levels, a repeated measures design, and an intervention. You would not use a one-sample or independent *t*-test. If you have not had statistics yet, you may not know when to use each of the *t*-tests. This is all right. The important thing to remember is that when you do learn the information, the first step in evaluating this inferential statistics is to ensure that the correct one was used.

The second issue to consider with the use of a *t*-test is the probability of committing a Type I Error (or rejecting the null hypothesis when it is, in fact, true). This is an issue to have in mind if the researcher uses more than one *t*-test. This is referred to as multiple *t*-tests. For each *t*-test conducted, the alpha level is at 0.05. However, with each additional *t*-test, the alpha level increases. For example, if you have two *t*-tests, the *p*-value would be 0.10 (i.e., 0.05 + 0.05 = 0.10). One way the researchers can reduce the probability of making a Type I Error when conducting multiple *t*-tests is to make the alpha level more stringent. Specifically, you take 0.05 and divide by the number of *t*-tests you plan to conduct. To be significant, each *t*-test should be less than the new *p*-value. In an example with five *t*-tests, you would take 0.05 and divide by five, which equals 0.01. Thus, for each *t*-test, the new alpha level would be 0.01. This process is known as the **Bonferroni correction**.

Another type of inferential statistics is **analysis of variance** (commonly abbreviated ANOVA). When you have one independent variable with three or more levels, you can use a one-way ANOVA. The results will tell you if there are differences between the levels, and follow-up analyses will tell you where the particular differences occurred. If you have more than one independent variable as with a factorial design, you could perform a more advanced ANOVA, allowing all variables to be examined. For example, if you had two variables, you would perform a two-way ANOVA and if you had three variables, you would perform a three-way ANOVA. These more complex ANOVAs can tell you if there are differences for each independent variable (main effects) and if the independent variables interact with one another (interactions).

If a researcher has conducted any type of ANOVA, he or she should provide you with some basic information to help you interpret the results. First, you should look to see if there were any missing data points and, if so, how the researchers handled the situation. Systematically missing data points would warrant further explanation. Second, you should look to see if there were outliers (or extreme scores) in the data set. As we discussed earlier, extreme scores can influence the shape of the distribution. This leads us to the third suggestion of assessing the shape of the distribution. If a distribution is severely skewed, it might not be possible to conduct inferential statistics without data transformation. Finally, you have to see if the variables being studied have a linear relationship.

In this brief section on drawing conclusions from inferential statistics, we have mentioned only a few common procedures. Many other inferential statistics are available to address particular research questions, such as Pearson correlations which examine the extent to which two variables are related. However, with each inferential statistics utilized, you should always be cautious when drawing conclusions. For example, with the Pearson correlation, you should not imply cause and effect, as the procedure provides information only on relationships between variables of interest. APA style recommends that for any inferential statistics used, the following information should be provided when it is possible: the sample size of each condition, means and standard deviations for each condition, the obtained statistical value, degrees of freedom, the obtained *p*-value, effect size, and confidence intervals.

Bonferroni Correction: The correction used when conducting multiple statistical tests to limit the possibility of making a Type I Error.

Analysis of Variance (ANOVA): Used when you have an independent variable with three or more levels or when you have multiple independent variables.

QUESTIONS

1. When we return exams in our classes, we find it beneficial to share with students information on the distribution of scores. We provide this information so that students will have an idea of how they scored on the exam in comparison to their peers. However, deciding which descriptive information to provide to the class is not always an easy decision. To illustrate this example, take a look at the graph given in Figure 14.3. These are modified grades from one of Jenn's statistics classes. For this data set, the mean is 77, the mode is 92, and the median is 86. If you were the professor of the class, do you think sharing the mean scores on the exam with the class is a representative score of the data set? Why or why not?

2. If a researcher is conducting a study and wants to perform a series of seven *t*-tests to evaluate the research hypotheses, what would you recommend the alpha level to be for each test? Why would you recommend this level?

3. We found a news report that summarized research findings from Lawlor, Timpson, Harbord, and Leary (2008). These researchers were looking at the relationship between a mother's weight during pregnancy and the child's fat mass at the age of 9 or 11. The researchers predicted that the more a mother weighed during pregnancy, the higher the fat mass would be in the child. Such findings would support the developmental over nutrition hypothesis, which states that overeating during key developmental times has an influence on the offspring. The results of the study found that (a) prepregnancy maternal weight (BMI) was positively associated with the child's fat mass and (b) the relationship between maternal BMI and the child's fat mass was stronger than the relationship between paternal BMI and the child's fat mass. This study reported on the *relationships* between variables. If you are drawing conclusions from these results, what caution should you have in mind?

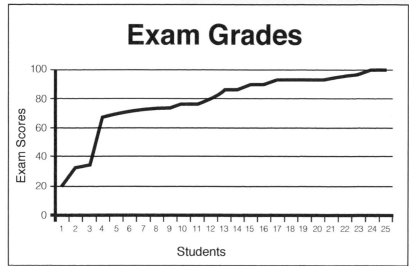

Fig 14.3   Hypothetical exam grades

1. In looking at the distribution of scores on the exam, we would argue that the mean would not be the most representative number. If the class was given only the mean of 77, it might be inferred that most students earned a C. However, this is not the case at all. By providing students with the mode of 92 and the median of 86, students get a better picture of the distribution of scores. It is actually the case that most students did well in the exam, with a few low scores pulling down the mean. This example relates back to the section on drawing conclusions from descriptive statistics. Our purpose in using this example was to illustrate how knowing if a distribution is skewed or normal aids in interpreting the scores.

2. If a researcher is conducting multiple *t*-tests, the alpha level should be more conservative. In this situation, the researcher should take 0.05 and divide by 7, equaling the new alpha level of 0.007. This procedure, known as the Bonferroni correction, reduces the likelihood of committing a Type I Error or rejecting the null hypothesis when it is in fact true.

3. The results from Lawlor et al. (2008) on maternal BMI and child's fat mass are very interesting and have implications for the biological basis of weight. However, the inferential statistics used provides information only on relationships. Thus, you should not infer cause and effect.

© baldyrgan, 2014. Used under license from Shutterstock, Inc.

STATISTICAL SIGNIFICANCE VERSUS PRACTICAL SIGNIFICANCE

At the beginning of this chapter, we discussed when to reject the null hypothesis and when to fail to reject the null hypothesis. When we reject the null hypothesis, we are saying that the results are statistically significant and the differences observed are not due to chance or error. It is important now to bring up the distinction between statistical significance and practical significance. This is because not all results that are found to be statistically significant are of practical use in the everyday world. For example, you could survey 1,000 undergraduate students and ask them if they preferred to have class at 8:00 a.m. or 8:15 a.m. You might find that students significantly prefer starting class at 8:15 over 8:00. However, the practical use of this information might be limited for a university. Class might need to start on the hour so as not to interfere with the schedule for the remainder of the day. But, does the fact that students prefer to start class 15 minutes later really warrant a change? Many reviewers and editors are aware of the fact that large sample sizes can produce significant results despite relatively small differences between groups. Therefore, it is becoming a common practice for authors to explain how the results are of practical use in the field of psychology. For that reason, obtaining statistically significant results might not be the end goal after all. The ideal combination would be to find significant results that contribute to the field in a meaningful way.

SECTION SUMMARY

- *Descriptive statistics* are used by researchers to describe data sets (pp. 252–254).
  - *Measures of central tendency* are numbers that represent the scores in the data set (p. 252).
    - The *mean* is the average of the scores in the data set (p. 252).
    - The *median* is the number in the middle of a data set (p. 252).
    - The *mode* is the most frequently occurring number in a data set (p. 252).
  - A *normal distribution* of scores occurs when most scores cluster around the middle, and few, but equal, numbers cluster on the extremes (pp. 252–253).
  - A *skewed distribution* is one in which the most frequently occurring scores are not in the middle (pp. 252–253).
- *Inferential statistics* are used so as to draw inferences about a population from the sample used (pp. 254–257).
  - There are three types of *t*-tests (p. 254).
    - The *one-sample t-test* is used to determine when a mean is significantly different from a constant (p. 254).
    - The *dependent t-test* is used to determine if the mean difference between pairs is significantly different from zero (p. 254).
    - The *independent t-test* evaluates whether or not two means are significantly different from one another (p. 254).
    - *Bonferroni correction* can be used when multiple statistical tests are conducted. The correction is used to limit the possibility of making a Type I Error (p. 255).
    - *Analysis of variance* is used when you have an independent variable with three or more levels or when you have multiple independent variables (p. 255).
- In the field of psychology, many times researchers achieve results which are statistically significant. However, researchers should also be aware of the practical significance their results carry. In other words, does a statistically significant result have a practical impact on society (p. 257).

ARE YOU EQUIPPED NOW?

Researchers Feldman, Weller, Zagoory-Sharon, and Levine (2007) conducted a study to examine the relationship between a mother's oxytocin levels during and after pregnancy with bonding behaviors. Sixty-two women participated in this study. The participants took part in three assessments. The first assessment was during the first trimester, the second assessment was during the third trimester, and the final assessment was postpartum (after birth). At each session, blood was taken to measure oxytocin levels. At the final session, the women (a) completed questionnaires, (b) were videotaped for 15 minutes while interacting with the infants, and (c) were interviewed for at least half an hour regarding thoughts and behaviors. The researchers wanted to know if oxytocin levels were related to maternal behaviors (e.g., gaze, affect, touch, and vocalization), attachment, and checking behaviors. To begin, the researchers found no relationship between oxytocin levels and demographic factors. However, there were correlations between oxytocin levels in early pregnancy and maternal behaviors ($p < 0.05$), attachment ($p < 0.05$), and checking behaviors ($p < 0.01$) and there were correlations between oxytocin levels postpartum and maternal behaviors ($p < 0.05$), attachment ($p < 0.01$), and checking behaviors ($p < 0.001$). For the purposes of this activity, we briefly summarized the work of Feldman et al.. If you are interested in learning more about this study, we encourage you to read the full article. From the brief information we provided on the study, we would like you to apply the information that you learned in this chapter. Take a look at the following questions:

QUESTIONS

1. The researchers found no relationship between oxytocin levels and demographic factors. In this situation, would the researchers reject the null hypothesis or fail to reject the null hypothesis?

2. The researchers found correlations between oxytocin levels in early pregnancy and maternal behaviors ($p < 0.05$), attachment ($p < 0.05$), and checking behaviors ($p < 0.01$) and there were correlations between oxytocin levels postpartum and maternal behaviors ($p < 0.05$), attachment ($p < 0.01$), and checking behaviors ($p < 0.001$). In this situation, would the researchers reject the null hypothesis or fail to reject the null hypothesis?

3. Why might the researchers want to replicate their findings? (Hint: Be sure to address what replication prevents in your answer.)

4. In this article, the researchers provide results from inferential statistics on the relationship among variables. Referring to the section on drawing conclusions from inferential statistics, what is the one factor that you want to consider when interpreting correlational findings?

5. From Question 2, we see that the researchers found results of statistical significance. However, do you think the results were of practical significance? Why or why not?

ANSWERS

1. In this situation, you would fail to reject the null hypothesis. This is because there were no differences in oxytocin levels based on demographic factors.

2. For the relationship between oxytocin levels and bonding behaviors, the researchers would reject the null hypothesis. This is because the obtained p-value for each relationship was less than the conventional level of 0.05. This indicates that the results are so extreme that they are unlikely due to chance.

3. The researchers might want to replicate the findings in order to reduce the chance of making a decision error. If the results were consistent upon replication, the researchers could be confident that a Type I or Type II error was not committed.

4. You would want to be sure not to infer cause and effect. Rather, you can only conclude that these variables are related.

5. We believe that this study is of practical significance. In the discussion section of the article, the authors argue several compelling reasons as to why the results help to advance our understanding of parent-infant bonding behaviors. We encourage you to read what they had to say!

CHAPTER SUMMARY

- Upon the completion of a study, a researcher has one of two choices to make: rejecting the null hypothesis or failing to reject the null hypothesis (pp. 246–249).
  - *Rejecting the null hypothesis* indicates there is a statistically significant difference between the means of the groups in the study (pp. 246–249).
  - *Failing to reject the null hypothesis* indicates there is not a statistically significant difference between the means of the groups in the study and that the means are equal (pp. 247–248).
- The *level of significance* is indicated by the alpha level (α) (p. 248).
  - Traditionally, psychologists accept an alpha level of 0.05 (p. 248).
  - If the obtained *p*-value in a study is less than the conventional alpha level, we reject the null hypothesis (p. 248).
  - If the obtained *p*-value in a study is more than the conventional alpha level, we fail to reject the null hypothesis (p. 248).
- When conducting research, there are four possible decision outcomes. The first two are to reject the null or to fail to reject the null hypothesis. The other two are types of errors:
  - A *Type I Error* occurs when a researcher rejects the null when the null is, in fact, true (pp. 252–254).
  - A *Type II Error* occurs when a researcher fails to reject the null even though the null hypothesis is false (pp. 252–254).
- When evaluating the results, researchers use descriptive or inferential statistics (p. 251).
- *Descriptive statistics* are used by researchers to describe data sets (pp. 252–254).
  - *Measures of central tendency* are numbers that represent the scores in the data set (p. 252).
    - The *mean* is the average of the scores in the data set (p. 252).
    - The *median* is the number in the middle of a data set (p. 252).
    - The *mode* is the most frequently occurring number in a data set (p. 252).
  - A *normal distribution* of scores occurs when most scores cluster around the middle, and few, but equal, numbers cluster on the extremes (pp. 252–253).
  - A *skewed distribution* is one in which the most frequently occurring scores are not in the middle (pp. 252–253).

- *Inferential statistics* are used so that inferences can be drawn about a population from the sample used (pp. 254–257).
  - There are three types of *t*-tests (p. 254).
    - The *one-sample t-test* is used to determine when a mean is significantly different from a constant (p. 254).
    - The *dependent t-test* is used to determine if the mean difference between pairs is significantly different from zero (p. 254).
    - The *independent t-test* evaluates whether or not means from two different groups are significantly different from one another (p. 254).
  - *Bonferroni correction* can be used when multiple statistical tests are conducted. The correction is used to limit the possibility of making a Type I Error (p. 255).
  - *Analysis of variance* is used when you have an independent variable with three or more levels or when you have multiple independent variables (p. 255).
- In the field of psychology, many times researchers achieve results which are statistically significant. However, researchers should also be aware of the *practical significance* their results carry. In other words, does a statistically significant result have a practical impact on society (p. 257)?

APA LEARNING GOALS LINKAGE

- **Goal 2. Scientific Inquiry and Critical Thinking**

  You will demonstrate scientific reasoning and problem solving, including effective research methods.

  Sections Covered: Are You Equipped?, Examining the Results: Rejecting the Null or Failing to Reject the Null Hypothesis, Type I and Type II Errors, Introduction to Conclusions from Descriptive Statistics, Drawing Conclusions from Inferential Statistics, Statistical Significance versus Practical Significance

  Explanation of the Goal: In this chapter, we have introduced many basic statistical results and discussed ways to interpret these results. Furthermore, we have demonstrated how to evaluate the appropriateness of conclusions derived from psychological research, as was evident in the "Are You Equipped?" section on gift giving with new acquaintances. Finally, distinction is made between statistical significance and practical significance. This is especially important when interpreting results that might be statistically significant but of little practical importance (e.g., preference for class time).

  Sections Covered: Are You Equipped?, Examining the Results: Rejecting the Null or Failing to Reject the Null Hypothesis, Heinz Ketchup Example Revisited, Drawing Conclusions from Descriptive Statistics, Are You Equipped Now?

Explanation of the Goal: Throughout Chapter 14, we have worked on approaching problems effectively by generating multiple solutions. For example, we generated both null and research hypotheses in the "You Try It!" section on the Cheerleader Effect Revisited. We also used critical thinking skills when presenting hypothetical outcomes for a study. Specifically, we generated possible research outcomes when discussing types of errors. Likewise, we worked on using scientific evidence to resolve conflicting claims.

This was illustrated in the examples of gift-giving behaviors, gender differences in caffeine consumption, and mother's weight and child's fat mass.

- ## Goal 4. Communication

You will demonstrate competence in writing and in oral and interpersonal communication skills.

Sections Covered: Examining the Results: Rejecting the Null or Failing to Reject the Null Hypothesis, Type I and Type II Errors, Introduction to Interpreting Statistical Results, Drawing Conclusions from Descriptive Statistics, Drawing Conclusions from Inferential Statistics

Explanation of the Goal: For this goal, we have shown how to apply basic mathematical concepts and operations to support measurement strategies. First, this can be seen in our discussion of descriptive statistics. Descriptive statistics are used to describe data sets. Measures of central tendency, such as the mean, median, and mode, are common ways to describe research findings. From this information, you can draw conclusions about the shape of the distribution. Second, inferential statistics can be used to draw inferences about a population from the sample used. The *t*-tests and ANOVAs are examples of some basic inferential statistics presented in this chapter. Coverage of this information is needed so that you can accurately communicate your research findings to others and to allow you to effectively interpret and draw conclusions presented by other researchers.

Excerpts from APA Guidelines for the Undergraduate Psychology Major, Version 2.0, August 2013 *by the American Psychological Association. Copyright* © 2013 *by the American Psychological Association.*

CHAPTER 15

APA Style: Sixth Edition

CHAPTER OUTLINE

Are You Equipped?

An Introduction to APA-Style Writing

References

Are You Equipped Now?

Chapter Summary

APA Learning Goals Linkage

ARE YOU EQUIPPED?

Two of our former undergraduate students provided us with the reference list below used for a brief report on sleep. The students purposefully made some APA-style mistakes. Can you spot them?

Buboltz, W. C., Loveland, J., Jenkins, S. M., Brown, F., Soper, B., Hodges, J., & (2006). College Student Sleep: Relationship to Health and Academic Performance. College students: Mental *health* and coping strategies. Landow, Mery V. (Ed.); pp. 1–39. Hauppauge, NY, US: Nova Science Publishers, 2006.

Harrison, Y., & Horne, J. (2000). The impact of sleep deprivation on decision making: A review. *Journal of Experimental Psychology: Applied, 6*(3), 236–249.

Horne, J. A., Anderson, N. R., & Wilkinson, R. T. (1983). Effects of sleep deprivation on signal detection measures of vigilance: implications for sleep function. *Journal of Sleep Research & Sleep Medicine, 6*(4), 347–358.

Kellah, E. (2006). The Relationship of University Students' sleep habits and academic motivation. *NASPA Journal, 43*(3), 432–445.

Epstein, Lawrence, and Mardon, Steven. (2007). The Harvard Medical School Guide to a Good Night's Sleep. McGraw-Hill, New York, NY.

Schenck, Carlos, H. (208). Sleep: A Groundbreaking Guide to the Mysteries, the Problems, and the Solutions. Penguin Group New York, NY.

Amschler, D., & McKenzie, J. (2005). Elementary Students' Sleep Habits and Teacher Observations of Sleep-Related Problems. *Journal for School Health, 75, Issue 2*, 50–56.

In this chapter, we are going to talk about the standard format for writing within the field of psychology known as APA style. If you were not able to spot all the mistakes in the example above, you will be able to do so after reading this chapter. (We would like to thank Sabrina and Jorge for purposely formatting a reference section with mistakes for this introduction!)

As you go through this chapter, we also want you to keep in mind how the material relates to the American Psychological Association's goals for psychology majors. Specifically, this chapter will address the following goals:

- **Goal 2. Scientific Inquiry and Critical Thinking**

  You will demonstrate scientific reasoning and problem solving, including effective research methods.

- **Goal 3. Ethical and Social Responsibility in a Diverse World**

  You will apply ethical standards to evaluate psychological science and practice and you will develop ethically and socially responsible behaviors for professional and personal settings in a landscape that involves increasing diversity.

- **Goal 4. Communication**

  You will demonstrate competence in writing and in oral and interpersonal communication skills.

- **Goal 5. Professional Development**

  You will apply psychological content and skills to career goals and develop meaningful professional direction for life after graduation.

AN INTRODUCTION TO APA-STYLE WRITING

Writing within the field of psychology follows a standard form developed by the American Psychological Association (APA). APA created this format so that all authors could communicate their findings in the same manner. Think of how difficult it would be if each individual author in the field of psychology could decide the format of his or her manuscript! It can seem like a chore to learn the fine details of APA style (now on the sixth edition). However, we encourage you to hang in there. Once you learn the general format, you will appreciate how it simplifies communication for the field. This chapter is divided into two sections. The first section will cover the basic parts of a manuscript and the formatting for each. The second section will be devoted to referencing the works of others in APA style.

Most bodies of work in APA style contain the following: a title page, an abstract, an introduction to the topic, a methods section describing the research methods used, a results section containing the findings, a discussion of the work, and a reference list. In this chapter, we are going to discuss each of these sections briefly. For a detailed explanation, be sure to consult the *Publication Manual of the American Psychological Association, 6th Edition* (APA, 2010). For APA style, the preferred typeface is Times New Roman and the font size is 12 point. The standard margins are 1 inch all around and double spacing should be used throughout.

THE TITLE PAGE

The first page of a manuscript is the title page. You can see an example of a title page in the appendix. You will notice the title page has a title, a running head, an author byline, institutional affiliation of the author(s), author note (if desired), and page numbers beginning with 1. Below is a summary of each part of the title page:

- In the header of the title page, you will find the running head and page numbers. The running head is contained in the header, aligned left, and appears on all pages of the manuscript. The running head is a shortened version of the title and should be no more than 50 characters. The page number appears in the header and is aligned right. The title page is page number 1.

- The title should provide readers with the main topic of the manuscript. It is recommended that titles contain meaningful terms, as it will be shortened for the running head, and be no more than 12 words. The title is centered on the upper half of the page in uppercase and lowercase letters.

- On the line immediately following the title, you center the name of the author(s). The preferred format is first name, middle initial(s), and last name.

- On the following line, you list the affiliation of the author(s). The affiliation is typically a college or university.

- An author note can also be included on the title page. An author note has many purposes but the main purposes are to provide readers with the contact information for one of the authors and provide acknowledgments.

ABSTRACT

Although we are discussing the abstract early on in this chapter because it appears after the title page, your abstract should be the last part of the manuscript you write. You should write the abstract last because it provides a summary or overview of the entire manuscript. Most people will read the abstract through an electronic database to decide if they want to read the entire manuscript. Therefore, your abstract should be well written and accurately convey the contents of the manuscript. A good abstract is written as a report, stating the facts. In other words, an evaluative tone is not used. If your abstract is for an experiment or study, it should summarize your research question, participants, methods, results, and conclusions. Abstracts range in length from 150 to 250 words, so it is important to concisely summarize your work.

You should begin the abstract on a new page (immediately following the title page). Abstracts will have a header. In the header, the running head is aligned left and page number 2 is aligned right. The title, **Abstract**, is centered on the top line and written in uppercase and lowercase letters using boldface type. The abstract is written as one paragraph, with no indentation.

INTRODUCTION

The purpose of the introduction in a manuscript is to introduce the topic and place it in the context of research within the field. In short, the introduction provides readers with background information on a topic they may or may not know. Introductions typically follow an inverted triangle format. See Figure 15.1 for an illustration. Introductions follow the inverted triangle by starting off broad in scope and becoming narrower as they proceed.

Fig 15.1 The inverted triangle represents the way an introduction should be written

Introductions start with broad knowledge on the topics of interests. After introducing the reader to the topics of interest, the introduction moves on to discuss previous literature in the area. At this stage of the introduction, the triangle (below) begins to narrow. The introduction is now more focused and provides a concise overview of previous work. There are different ways you can summarize this previous work. For example, you could present the research chronologically, starting with the earliest publication date. However, the best way to structure this section is by topic. In other words, structure this part of the introduction so conceptually similar works are presented together. This allows the reader to know what work has been conducted in a particular area and the findings. Next, you present the reader with the specific problems with previous research or explain why additional research is needed. This information provides a transition for the reader. The transition allows the reader to begin thinking about what research could be conducted next. Finally, you end the introduction with the purpose of your study, your hypotheses, and a brief overview of the methods. If you have done a good job on the introduction, the reader will understand why your study is needed and the reasoning behind your hypotheses (see Table 15.1). If your introduction lacks smooth transitions or fails to "set up" the purpose of your study, readers can feel confused or feel the study does not significantly add to the body of knowledge on the topic. One strategy we recommend is to read your introduction and stop at the section immediately before the purpose. At this point, ask yourself if your study is the next logical extension to the previous work and if findings from your study would add a needed piece of information to the puzzle.

TABLE 15.1   Writing Your Introduction.
Outline of introduction

1. Introduction of Topic

2. Review of Previous Findings on Topic
  a. Chronological Order
  b. Topical Order

3. Explanation of Why Additional Research is Needed
  a. Problems/Inconsistencies
  b. Gaps in the Literature
  c. Tensions

4. Current Study
  a. How it Solves or Addresses Issues Brought Up in #3
  b. Hypothesis(es)
  c. Overview of Methods

Introductions are placed on a new page, with a running head. Specifically, introductions are placed on page 3 of a manuscript (the title page is number 1 and the abstract is number 2). You begin the introduction with the title of the manuscript on the top line. The title should be centered and written in uppercase and lowercase letters. The text of the introduction begins on the next line and new paragraphs are indented. The remaining sections of the manuscript (method, results, and discussion) follow the introduction but do not require a page break. When writing the introduction, be sure to use either past tense (e.g., "Raacke found that . . .") or present perfect tense (e.g., "Previous researchers have found that . . ."). Transitional devices keep the flow of the introduction smooth. These transitions can link statements (then, since), show cause and effect (therefore), or serve as addition links (moreover).

METHOD

The purpose of the method section is to provide readers with information on how you conducted your study. In fact, enough detail should be provided so that a reader could replicate (reproduce) your study if he or she desired. Besides replication purposes, providing details allows the reader to identify strengths or weaknesses in your methodology. The method section has two subsections, which describe the participants and the materials/procedure used. The first subsection, participants, provides the reader with information on the sample of participants. This includes sex, age, race/ethnicity, the total number of participants, the total number of participants in each condition, and, if available, information on sexual orientation and socioeconomic status. This description of the sample is needed so the reader can draw generalizations about the population of interest. The second section, materials and procedures, provides the reader with specific information on the materials needed to carry out the experiment and step-by-step instructions for the procedure. Although you need to describe materials such as the survey given to participants or equipment used to collect data, information on the computer software to analyze the data is not needed. When describing the procedure, be sure to include the following:

- The experimental design used (e.g., identify variables and type of design).
- Information on how the participants were selected.
- Information on how the participants were assigned to conditions.
- A description of any controls features used such as counterbalancing.
- A paraphrased version of the instructions given to participants.
- A step-by-step description of what participants did.

The method section is written in past tense or present perfect tense as is the introduction. When writing the method section, use a personal pronoun over the third person. For example, "We had participants complete the three surveys" is preferred over "The authors had participants complete three surveys." The method section utilizes many of APA's stylistic rules. This is because the method section contains numbers and the identification of groups of people. In general, you should use numerals for numbers 10 or higher and write out (express in words) number under 10. Anytime a number begins a sentence, it is written out. APA provides guidelines for the most appropriate terminology when referring to groups of people. For example, terms such as *lesbian, gay men,* and *bisexual individuals* are preferred over the term *homosexual. Blacks* and *African Americans* are currently both approved terms.

However, do not use hyphens for multiword names. Treat *black* and *white* as proper nouns and provide parallel labels (*Whites* and *Blacks*, not *Whites* and *African Americans*). Other acceptable terms include *American Indian, Native American, and Native North American.*

The word **Method** is centered on the page using boldface and written in uppercase and lowercase letters. The method section begins wherever the introduction ends. Thus, you do not begin the method sections on a new page. The subsections of the method section, participants and materials/procedures, are aligned left in boldface and written in uppercase and lowercase letters.

RESULTS

The results section allows you to present the findings of your study to readers. You present these findings by providing information on the descriptive and inferential statistics that were utilized. The results section also includes references to tables and figures that aid readers in understanding the findings. However, the results section is not the appropriate section to evaluate your hypotheses. This is saved for the discussion section. The results section begins with the word **Results** in boldface centered on the page, written in uppercase and lowercase letters.

We realize our discussion of the results section is very brief. However, depending on the instructor of your course, you may or may not cover statistics. If you do cover statistics and need to know how to reference specific procedures in APA style, consult the *Publication Manual* (APA, 2010).

DISCUSSION

After the results section, you will need to center the word **Discussion** in boldface using uppercase and lowercase letters. Do not begin a new page. When writing the discussion section, you are encouraged to use present tense. Every discussion section has standard components. First, you should briefly restate the purpose of your study. Even though this information is presented at the beginning of the manuscript, it is helpful to remind the reader. Second, you evaluate your hypotheses. In other words, discuss if your hypotheses were supported or not supported. If the hypotheses were not supported, provide some insights as to why this unexpected outcome may have occurred. Third, relate your findings to previous research in the field. This comparison usually involves work cited in the introduction section of your manuscript. However, it is acceptable to bring in new references that are relevant to your findings. A crucial component to the discussion section involves addressing potential limitations and shortcoming of your study. It may seem strange that you would want to draw the reader's attention to these issues. However, any skilled reader would pick up on the limitations that you mention and it is a good practice to acknowledge your own weaknesses. Remember no study is ever perfect, so there will always be something for you to discuss. At the end of your discussion, present readers with information regarding why your findings are important to the field (practical significance) and provide suggestions for future research.

TABLES AND FIGURES

Tables and figures are often used to simplify results that would be difficult to present in the results sections. Keep in mind that tables and figures should not duplicate information already given in the manuscript. The results section should instruct the reader to look at the tables and/or figure and also draw the reader's attention to the important information.

YOU TRY IT!

QUESTIONS

1. Why is it beneficial for the field of psychology (and most social sciences) to have an agreed-upon formatting style?
2. What are the main parts of a manuscript?
3. Why/how do you use an inverted triangle within the introduction?
4. What are the two subsections of the method section?
5. What are some important factors that your discussion section should address?

ANSWERS

1. First, it is beneficial for the field of psychology and other social sciences to have an agreed-upon formatting style because it brings simplicity to reading the works of others. Second, by using a standard style, readers know what to expect and where to look for information.
2. The main parts of a manuscript are as follows: title page, abstract, introduction, method, results, discussion, references, and tables/figures.
3. It is helpful to use an inverted triangle approach when writing an introduction because it allows the reader to see why the study was conducted. This approach starts off broad and introduces readers to the general topics. Next, the introduction begins to narrow in focus by presenting the reader with a summary of previous research in the area. Finally, the introduction specifies how the current study will contribute to the literature and the predicted hypotheses.
4. The two subsections of the method section are the participants and the materials/procedure.
5. Some important factors that your discussion section should address are evaluation of hypotheses, relation of results to previous research, limitations of current design, and future research ideas.

SECTION SUMMARY

There are eight main sections to an APA-style manuscript: (pp. 264–269)

- Title page
  - A title page includes a running head, page number, title, author name(s), and affiliations (p. 265).

- Abstract
  - A 150–250-word summarization of your entire article in block format (p. 265).
- Introduction
  - The purpose of the introduction in a manuscript is to introduce the topic and place the topic in the context of research within the field (pp. 266–267).
  - An introduction follows an inverted triangle format by starting off broad in scope and becoming narrower (pp. 266–267).
- Method
  - The purpose of the method section is to provide readers with information on how you conducted your study (pp. 266–268).
  - The method section includes information on the experimental design used, how the participants were selected, how the participants were assigned to conditions, a description of any controls features used such as counterbalancing, a paraphrased version of the instructions given to participants, and a step-by-step description of what participants did (pp. 266–268).
- Results
  - This section allows you to present the findings of your study to readers. You present these findings by providing information on the descriptive and inferential statistics that were utilized (p. 268).
- Discussion
  - This section is the part of your manuscript where you restate the purposes of your study, evaluate your hypotheses, relate the results to prior research, and discuss any limitations to your work (p. 268).
- References
  - The reference section is a list of all the work cited in the manuscript (p. 264).
  - Tables and figures (p. 269)
  - Tables and/or figures are located after the reference section and are a visual representation of results not reported in the manuscript (p. 269).

REFERENCES

APA style has many details regarding how to reference the works of others. In the remainder of this chapter, we will discuss how to cite a reference within the body of a manuscript and in the reference list. When you are writing a paper in psychology, it is very important to reference the sources that contributed to your work. This practice is important because it gives credit to previous authors for their contributions. When writing an introduction, for example, the bulk of the writing should be cited from sources. Only smaller portions of the introduction such as transitions and general statements of fact will not have references. This may sound strange. You might initially think that the bulk of your paper should be your own thoughts on an issue. However, the standard form in the field is to begin papers with a summary of what others have done on a given topic. Once you become accustomed to it, you will see how your own writing style comes through in the way in which you organize and talk about the work of others. Besides, discussing someone else's work or ideas without referencing them is considered plagiarism. Here are a few general guidelines about referencing within the text (i.e., within the body of the manuscript) and in a reference list (found at the end of a document):

- References cited in the text must appear in the reference list.
- References cited in the reference list must appear in the text.
- Only include sources that you actually used in the text in the reference section. This is different from bibliographies. Bibliographies can include suggestions for further reading on a topic.

WITHIN-TEXT CITATIONS

Nearly all of your references within the text will occur without quotes. The limited use of quotes is discussed in the next section. Most often, you will be explaining in your own words the ideas, theories, and research findings of others. Even though you are communicating this information using your own words, it is still necessary to cite the original source. There are three standard ways for citing a reference within the text of a manuscript. First, you can provide the last name of the author as part of the text, with the date of publication in parenthesis. A second option would be to give the author's last name, followed by a comma, and date of publication in parentheses at the end of a sentence or paragraph. A final approach is to give the date and author's name as part of the text.

- *Example 1*
  Raacke (2009) found that college students . . .
- *Example 2*
  It was found that college students study best at night (Raacke, 2009).
- *Example 3*
  In 2009, Raacke found that college students . . .

The three examples above illustrate the appropriate form when there is only one author. When there are two authors, you would cite both authors the first time the reference occurs and any subsequent references. Note that when both authors' last names are given in the text with the date in parentheses as in Example 1, the word "and" is inserted between the authors' last names. However, when the authors' last names and date of publication are given in parentheses as in Example 2, there is an ampersand (&) inserted between the authors' last names.

> - *Example 1*
>
>   Raacke and Bonds-Raacke (2009) found that college students . . .
> - *Example 2*
>
>   It was found that college students study best at night (Raacke & Bonds-Raacke, 2009).
> - *Example 3*
>
>   In 2009, Raacke and Bonds-Raacke found that college students . . .

When you have three to five authors, you should cite all the authors' last names and date of publication on the first citation of the reference. You would apply the same rules as above on using commas, the word "and," and the ampersand.

> - *Example 1*
>
>   Raacke, Bonds-Raacke, and King (2009) found that college students . . .
> - *Example 2*
>
>   It was found that college students study best at night (Raacke, Bonds-Raacke, & King, 2009).
> - *Example 3*
>
>   In 2009, Raacke, Bonds-Raacke, and King found that college students . . .

However, on subsequent references with three–five authors, only the first author's last name is given, followed by *et al.*

> - *Example 1*
>
>   Raacke et al. (2009) found that college students . . .
> - *Example 2*
>
>   It was found that college students study best at night (Raacke et al., 2009).
> - *Example 3*
>
>   In 2009, Raacke et al. found that college students . . .

When there are six or more authors, use the first author's last name followed by et al. for the first and all subsequent citations. These rules which apply to works by one to six or more authors will generally suffice. However, there are some special circumstances you might find helpful to know about. For example, it is not uncommon for one author to have multiple publications in the same year. To distinguish between the works, you follow the date of publication by the suffixes *a, b, c,* and so on. The suffixes appear in the reference list also (to be discussed in the next section). You assign the suffixes alphabetically by the first letter of the first word of the title. So, the letter *a* should be given to the reference with the first letter in the title that comes first in the alphabet.

- *Example 1*

  Bonds-Raacke and Raacke (2007a) found that using social net-working . . .

- *Example 2*

  Using social networking sites is related to self-esteem (Bonds-Raacke & Raacke, 2007b).

It is also common to cite two or more works within the same parentheses. When doing so, use semicolons to separate the references and list the works alphabetically by the first author's last name.

Example

Using social networking sites is related to self-esteem (Bonds-Raacke & Raacke, 2007; Burns, 2006; Thomas, 2009).

These two examples are not the only special circumstances you may encounter when writing a manuscript. You might need to arrange multiple works by the same author with different publication years in parentheses or differentiate in the text authors with the same last name or surname. Therefore, be sure to consult the *Publication Manual* (APA, 2010) when needed.

You will need to use quotations if you decide to replicate work from another author word for word. Keep in mind that direct quoting should be kept to a minimum and should be used only when the original wording could not adequately be expressed in your own words. Be sure your direct quotes are accurate in content, spelling, and grammar. If you are quoting a source and have fewer than 40 words included, the quotation is included as part of the text. Specifically, the material being quoted is surrounded with double quotation marks. The page number is given in the citation, in addition to author's last name, and date of publication.

- *Example 1*

  Bonds-Raacke (2009) stated that "couples taking college courses together reported an increase in satisfaction with college life" (p. 25).

- *Example 2*

  Results indicated that "couples taking college courses together reported an increase in satisfaction with college life" (Bonds-Raacke, 2009, p. 25).

Longer quotations, 40 or more words, are not included within the text. Rather, a block quotation format is used. This means you indent the entire quote five spaces from the left and do not use quotation marks. The authors and publication date can be provided either at the end of the quote with the pages numbers (Option 1) or at the beginning (Option 2). Examples are provided below to illustrate each option.

- *Option 1*

  The authors acknowledge the issue of the sample:

  > This study is not without limitations. To begin, the primary demographics of users were traditional age, first-year college students. It could certainly be the case that the identified dimensions for this sample would not be the same for users of friend networking sites with varying demographics. (Bonds-Raacke & Raacke, 2009, p. 25)

- *Option 2*

  Bonds-Raacke and Raacke (2009) acknowledge the issue of the sample:

  > This study is not without limitations. To begin, the primary demographics of users were traditional age, first-year college students. It could certainly be the case that the identified dimensions for this sample would not be the same for users of friend networking sites with varying demographics. (p. 25)

REFERENCE LIST

The reference list is found at the end of a manuscript and contains information on all of the sources cited within the text of the manuscript. The purpose of a reference list is to allow readers to locate the original work of the sources you cited. The reference list should be double-spaced and follow the hanging indent format. Furthermore, the word **References** should be centered in boldface at the top of a new page. The reference list is organized alphabetically by the last names of the first authors. Here are some other general guidelines for alphabetizing the list:

- If two different authors have the same last name, you alphabetize by the initials of the first name.

  Locklear, A. B. (2010).

  Locklear, D. E. (2009).

- As in within-text citations, if the same first author is cited in more than one reference, the references are listed from earliest date of publication, and if the same first author has more than one reference with the same date of publication, suffixes following the date are assigned alphabetically by the first word in the title.

  Hunt, A. B. (1992). Factors that predict academic success.

  Hunt, A. B. (1994a). American Indian academic challenges.

  Hunt, A. B. (1994b). Success rates of college students.

- Remember to use initials only for the first and middle names, as these are never written out in the reference list.

> Bonds-Raacke, J. M. (CORRECT)
>
> Bonds-Raacke, Jennifer Marie (INCORRECT)

- Prefixes such as *Mc* should be listed alphabetically by the literal spelling.

> McIntry, J. D. (1989).
>
> Morgan, A. D. (1998).

- If an author has a work published alone and is also the first author of another work with coauthors, the one author published work is listed first (even if multiple author work was published earlier).

> Morgan, A. D. (1998).
>
> Morgan, A. D., Bonds-Raacke, J. M., & Raacke, J. D. (1997).

- References with the same first author but different second author should be alphabetized by the last name of the second author.

> Morgan, A. D., Bonds-Raacke, J. M., & Smith, J. D. (1997).
>
> Morgan, A. D., Raacke, J. D., & Thomas, R. P. (1997).

TYPICAL SOURCES

The *Publication Manual* (APA, 2010) gives a thorough listing of types of sources and the appropriate way of listing them. However, the most commonly cited types of sources are periodicals (i.e., journals, newsletters, and magazines) and books. You can either read journal articles from the original journal or retrieve them through an electronic database, for example, in a PDF format.

If you read a journal article from the original journal, the appropriate form is as follows:

> Author, A. A. (xxxx). Title of journal article. *Title of Journal, volume number*(issue number), pp–pp.
>
> Raacke, J. D. (2010). College student perceptions of movies. *College Student Journal, 4*(2), 18–25.

In this example, we want to call your attention to the following elements:

- The first letter of the author's last name and the first and middle initials, are capitalized. The author's last name is followed by a comma with a period after each initial.
- The publication date is given in parentheses and followed by a period.
- For the periodical article title (i.e., title of manuscript), you capitalize only the first word of the title, any proper nouns, and any word appearing after a colon. The title is followed by a period.
- For the periodical title (i.e., title of journal), you capitalize important words in the name of the journal and italicize the name of the periodical.
- The periodical title is followed by a comma and then the volume number of the journal, which is also in italics. If available, the issue number can be added in parentheses but not in italics. The issue number is provided when a new issue of the journal begins with page one instead of continuing to number where the previous issue stopped. Please note that the issue number in the reference above was for example purposes only. Because, page numbers are not continuous from the previous issue for the *College Student Journal,* issue numbers are not included.
- Following either the volume, or the issue number if available, there is a comma.
- The reference ends with the inclusive page numbers of the article and a period.

Note that the same format is used with as many as seven authors. Commas are used to separate authors and to separate last names and initials. An ampersand is placed before the last author.

> Raacke, J. D., Bonds-Raacke, J. B., & Davis. S. (2010). College student perceptions of movies. *College Student Journal, 4,* 18–25.

If you read a journal article obtained through an electronic source such as in a PDF form, the format is the same with the addition of a digital object identifier (DOI) reference at the end. The DOI can be found on the first page of a journal article. It is most frequently located by the copyright information. It is not required that you include the retrieval date, unless you believe that the source of the information may change.

> Raacke, J. D., Bonds-Raacke, J. B., & Davis. S. (2010). College student perceptions of movies. *College Student Journal, 4,* 18–25. doi: 10.2000/456

Other frequently used sources are books and book chapters. If you are citing an entire book, the author is listed, followed by the date of publication, title of work, location of publisher, and publisher.

> Author, X. X. (xxxx). *Title of book.* Location: Publisher.
>
> Harris, R. J. (2009). *A look at media influences.* Manhattan, KS: Kansas State Press.

In this example, we want to call your attention to the following elements:

- The first letter of the author's last name and the first and middle initials are capitalized. The author's last name is followed by a comma with a period after each initial.
- The publication date is given in parentheses and followed by a period.
- For the book title, capitalize only the first letter of the first word and any proper nouns. Place the title in italics and follow the title with a period.
- Next, provide the location of the publishers. For within the United States, provide the city and state using official U.S. state abbreviations. For outside the United States, provide the city and country. After the state or country, use a colon.
- Finally, give the name of the publisher. Words such as "Publishers" or "Company" do not need to be included.
- Close the element with a period.

If you are referencing a specific chapter within an edited book, use the following format:

Author, A. B. (xxxx). Title of book chapter. In A. Editor and B. Editor (Eds.), *Title of book* (pp. XX–XX). Location: Publisher.

Bonds-Raacke, J. M. (2006). Gender portrayals in Disney movies. In R. Harris and J. Shanteau (Eds.), *Media portrayals* (pp. 25–40). Manhattan, KS: Kansas State Press.

In this example, we want to call your attention to the following elements:

- The first letter of the author's last name and the first and middle initials are capitalized. The author's last name is followed by a comma with a period after each initial.
- The publication date is given in parentheses and followed by a period.
- For the chapter title, capitalize only the first letter of the first word and any proper nouns and follow the title with a period.
- Use the word "In" preceding the editors' names. When listing the editors' names, provide the initial for the first name, followed by a period, and provide the whole last name. Use (Ed.) or (Eds.) followed by a comma.
- Place the title of the book in italics, capitalizing the first letter of the first word and any proper nouns.
- In parentheses, use the abbreviation pp. and provide inclusive page numbers followed by a period. The pages numbers are not in italics.
- Next, provide the location of the publishers. For within the United States, provide the city and state using official U.S. state abbreviations. For outside the United States, provide the city and country. After the state or country, use a colon.
- Finally, give the name of the publisher. Words such as "Publishers" or "Company" do not need to be included.
- Close the element with a period.

Again, we have only provided you with a brief introduction on how to reference materials in the reference list. If you run across a situation that we have not addressed, be sure to look it up. With practice, using the *Publication Manual* (APA, 2010) becomes easy.

YOU TRY IT!

QUESTIONS

1. When citing a source within the body of a manuscript, you have three standard options to pick from. The first option is to provide the last name of the author in the text and the date of publication in parenthesis. What are the other two options?

2. When you have three authors, how is the reference cited the first time and on subsequent citations?

3. How do you decide when to use a direct quote within the text and when to use a block quotation format?

4. If an author has a work published alone and is also the first author of another work with coauthors, which work is listed first on the reference page?

When referencing a journal, what elements of the reference are in italics?

ANSWERS

1. The other two options for referencing a citation are to (a) give the author's last name, followed by a comma, and date of publication in parenthesis at the end of a sentence and (b) provide both the author's name and date as part of the text.

2. When you have three authors, the last names of all three authors are listed on the first citation. However, on subsequent citations, only the last name of the first author followed by *et al.* is listed.

3. A direct quote is used when there are fewer than 40 words. However, when there are 40 or more words, a block quotation is used.

4. If an author has a work published alone and is also the first author of another work with coauthors, the one author work is listed first (no matter what the publication date).

5. When referencing a journal, the title of the journal and the volume number (not issue number) are in italics.

SECTION SUMMARY

- Referencing the work or ideas of others is important (pp. 271–278).
- Within-text citations
  - There are three standard ways for citing a source within the body of a manuscript (pp. 271–273).
  - When you have a source with one or two authors, information on both authors is given at each citation. However, if there are three–five authors, information on all authors is provided only on the first citation. Finally, when there are six or more authors, information is provided only on the first author for all citations (pp. 273–274).
  - Direct quotations should be kept to a minimum and block quotes are used with longer quotes (pp. 273–274).

- Reference list
  - Reference lists contain information to locate all sources cited in your manuscript (pp. 274–275).
  - Reference lists are organized alphabetically by the last name of the first author (pp. 274–275).

- Typical sources
  - The most commonly cited sources are periodicals and books (pp. 275–277).
  - Each type of source is cited using a standard format (pp. 274–275).

ARE YOU EQUIPPED NOW?

Now that we have covered some of the rules of writing in APA-style it is time to practice! Go back to the Are You Equipped from the beginning of this chapter. In that section, two of our students had prepared a reference list and your job was to look for the APA-mistakes. Try this exercise again.

To show you the APA-mistakes, we inserted comments on the next page. We decided that inserting comments might be helpful to you. This is because with technological advances it is not uncommon for reviewers to provide feedback to authors in this manner. Thus, it is helpful to have experience with these tools. We also provided the corrected version so that you can see the final product.

To begin, the works cited in the reference section should be in alphabetical order. This is not the case here when the first reference starts with the letter B and the last reference starts with the letter A!

For the title of an article, only the first letter of important words or words following a colon is in caps. This also the case for the words Sleep, Health, Academic, and Performance.

The title of the book is in italics and only the first letter of key words is in caps.

After the article title, the editor information is given.

The ampersand should be placed before the last author.

Buboltz, W. C., Loveland, J., Jenkins, S. M., Brown, F., Soper, B., Hodges, J., **&** (2006). College **S**tudent Sleep: Relationship to Health and Academic **Performance**. College students: Mental *health* and coping strategies. Landow, Mery V. (Ed.); **pp** . 1-39. Hauppauge, NY, US: Nova Science **Publishers** , **2006**

Following the title of the edited book, the page numbers are given in parenthesis.

The word "Publishers" is not needed.

The year of publication is already given.

Harrison, Y., & Horne, J. (2000). The impact of sleep deprivation on decision making: A review. *Journal of Experimental Psychology: Applied, 6 (3),* 236-249.

The issue number should not be included because page numbers are continuous from previous issue.

There needs to be a space before the letter A.

Horne, J.**A** ., Anderson, N.R., & Wilkinson, R. T. (1983). Effects of sleep deprivation on signal detection measures of vigilance: implications for sleep function. *Journal of Sleep Research & Sleep Medicine, 6 (4),* 347-358.

The " I " in implications should be in caps because it follows a colon.

The issue number should not be included because page numbers are continuous from previous issue.

In the title of a journal article, only the first letter of important words is in caps. This is also the case for University and Students.

Kellah, E. (2006).The **R**elationship of University Students' sleep habits and academic motivation. NASPA Journal, 43 **(3),** 432-445.

The issue number should not be included because page numbers are continuous from previous issue.

First names are not used. Only the first letter of the first name is given.

Epstein, **Lawrence** , and Mardon, Steven. (2007). The Harvard Medical School **G**uide to a Good Night's Sleep. **McGraw** -Hill, New York, NY.

In the title of a journal article, only the first letter of important words is in caps. This is also the case for the words Good, Night's, and Sleep.

The location of the publication comes before the name of the publishers.

First names are not used.

The title of the book should be in italics.

Only the first letter of key words are in caps. This also is the case for the words Guide, Mysteries, Problems, and Solutions.

Schenck, **Carlos** , H. (208). **Sleep** : A **G**roundbreaking Guide to the Mysteries, the Problems, and the Solutions. Penguin **Group** New York, NY

There should be a colon before the location of the publishers.

Only the first letter of key words are in caps.

Amschler, D., & McKenzie, J. (2005). **Elementary** Students' Sleep Habits and Teacher Observations of Sleep-Related Problems. *Journal for School Health, 75,* **Issue** *2,* 50-56

The issue number is given in parenthesis following the volume number. The word "issue" is not used. In addition, the issue number should not be included because page numbers are continuous from previous

CHAPTER SUMMARY

- There are eight main sections to an APA-style manuscript (pp. 264–269):
  - Title page
    - A title page includes a running head and page number, title, author name(s), and affiliations (p. 265).
  - Abstract
    - A 150–250-word summarization of your entire article in block format (p. 265).
  - Introduction
    - The purpose of the introduction in a manuscript is to introduce the topic and place the topic in the context of research within the field (pp. 266–267).
    - An introduction follows an inverted triangle format by starting off broad in scope and becoming narrower (pp. 266–267).

- Method
  - The purpose of the method section is to provide readers with information on how you conducted your study (p. 267–268).
  - The method section includes information on the experimental design used, how the participants were selected, how the participants were assigned to conditions, a description of any controls features used such as counterbalancing, a paraphrased version of the instructions given to participants, and a step-by-step description of what participants did (p. 267–268).
- Results
  - The results section allows you to present the findings of your study to readers. You present these findings by providing information on the descriptive and inferential statistics that were utilized (p. 268).
- Discussion
  - The discussion section is the part of your manuscript where you restate the purposes of your study, evaluate your hypotheses, relate the results to prior research, and discuss any limitations to your work (p. 268).
- References
  - The reference section is a list of all the work cited in the manuscript (p. 264).
- Tables and figures
  - Tables and/or figures are located after the reference section and are a visual representation of results not reported in the manuscript (p. 269).
- Referencing the work or ideas of others is important (pp. 271–278).
  - Within-text citations
    - There are three standard ways for citing a source within the body of a manuscript (pp. 271–273).
    - When you have a source with one or two authors, information on both authors is given at each citation. However, if there are three–five authors, information on all authors is provided only on the first citation. Finally, when there are six or more authors, information is provided only on the first author for all citations (pp. 273–274).
    - Direct quotations should be kept to a minimum and block quotes are used with longer quotes (pp. 273–274).
  - Reference list
    - Reference lists contain information to locate all sources cited in your manuscript (pp. 274–275).
    - Reference lists are organized alphabetically by the last name of the first author (pp. 274–275).
  - Typical sources
    - The most commonly cited sources are periodicals and books (pp. 275–277).
    - Each type of source is cited using a standard format (pp. 275–277).

- ### Goal 2. Scientific Inquiry and Critical Thinking

You will demonstrate scientific reasoning and problem solving, including effective research methods.

Sections Covered: Introduction, Discussion

Explanation of the Goal: As we have shown, when writing an introduction it is important to keep this goal in mind. First, when summarizing research in the introduction section, you must carefully evaluate conclusions drawn from psychological research. These conclusions are used to guide and direct the current research and consequently need to be reported correctly. Second, we showed that in the discussion section of a paper, the conclusions drawn about the methodology and results are important. This is because the discussion section allows you to generalize research findings and mention possible limitations to the study.*Sections Covered:* Introduction, Discussion, Review

Explanation of the Goal: There have been several instances in this chapter where you have engaged in critical thinking. For example, when writing an introduction to a paper, you must identify the components of arguments from various sources. As an author, you need to be able to evaluate the conclusions, assumptions, and gaps in the literature that are related to your chosen topic of research. Furthermore, the use of critical thinking is seen in the discussion of a paper. Specifically, you develop sound arguments based on reasoning and evidence from your methodology and results to make concttlusions and inferences about your work.

- ### Goal 3. Ethical and Social Responsibility in a Diverse World

You will apply ethical standards to evaluate psychological science and practice and you will develop ethically and socially responsible behaviors for professional and personal settings in a landscape that involves increasing diversity.

Sections Covered: Within-text Citations

Explanation of the Goal: The importance of this goal can be seen in our discussion of the use of quotes and perils of plagiarism. Specifically, we wanted you to recognize the necessity of ethical behavior in all aspects of science and practice of psychology and how this relates to writing in the field.

Sections Covered: Methods

Explanation of the Goal: As psychology majors, it is important that you recognize sociocultural and international diversity. This awareness is particularly important in the method section of a manuscript. When describing the participants in a study, it is necessary to interact effectively and sensitively with participants of diverse backgrounds, abilities, and cultural perspectives.

- **Goal 4. Communication**

  You will demonstrate competence in writing and in oral and interpersonal communication skills.

  Sections Covered: Introduction, Methods, Results, Discussion, Tables and Figures

  Explanation of the Goal: Throughout this chapter we have worked on using APA style effectively to communicate to an audience. In particular, we have demonstrated the need for professional writing conventions in the use of proper grammar, audience awareness, and formality in writing in APA style. We have also stressed the importance of exhibiting quantitative literacy and the application of basic mathematical concepts when writing the results section of a manuscript. Lastly, we have stressed the importance of providing rationale for information displayed in tables and figures in a manuscript.

- **Goal 5. Professional Development**

  You will apply psychological content and skills to career goals and develop meaningful professional direction for life after graduation.

  Sections Covered: An Introduction to APA-Style Writing

  Explanation of the Goal: This chapter is directly related to this goal. We have demonstrated the importance of APA-style writing to the field of psychology. This understanding of how to communicate within psychology will be expected whether you choose to pursue a graduate-level degree or choose to immediately work in the field after receiving your undergraduate degree. By developing this skill, writing in APA style, you will be making relevant strides to achieving any career goal related to the field of psychology.

Running head: PARENTIFICATION AND RELATED OUTCOMES   1

Childhood Parentification Associated with Negative Versus Positive Outcomes in Adulthood

Brittney Black, Katharine Lindberg, Alysja Garansi, & Merry Sleigh

Winthrop University

Author Note:

Correspondence may be addressed to: Dr. Merry J. Sleigh, Department of Psychology, 135 Kinard Building, Winthrop University, Rock Hill, SC 29733, Email: sleighm@winthrop.edu

Abstract

Childhood parentification has been linked to many negative outcomes in adulthood and few positive outcomes. The goal of this study was to further explore whether specific types of parentification link to positive outcomes not investigated in previous research. Participants (30 men and 70 women) completed the Parentification Questionnaire and responded to a series of positive and negative statements by indicating how much the statement described them. Results revealed that all three aspects of parentification (instrumental, emotional, and perceived unfairness) were associated exclusively with adverse outcomes. However, emotional parentification and perceived unfairness were linked to many more adverse outcomes than was instrumental parentification. These findings suggest children who take on adult responsibilities are vulnerable to negative outcomes in adulthood such as negative self perceptions, loneliness, and anxiety.

Keywords: parentification, negative, positive, outcomes, instrumental, emotional

Childhood Parentification Associated with Negative Versus Positive Outcomes in Adulthood

Parentification occurs when children take on adult responsibilities during a time when it is developmentally inappropriate for them to do so (Wells & Jones, 2000). This phenomenon is prevalent in society (Hooper, 2007) and seen across cultures (e.g., Shih, Wu, & Lin, 2010; Titzmann, 2012). There are two primary types of parentification, emotional and instrumental. Emotional parentification occurs when children provide emotional support to other family members, such as having parents confide in them. Instrumental parentification occurs when children take on family tasks that are typically done by adults, such as washing clothes or caring for siblings. Parentification often co-occurs with perceptions of unfairness in the home, and these perceptions are conceptualized as a sub-set of parentification (Jurkovic, Thirkfield, & Morrell, 2001). Typically, the children who are taking on the adult role are aware of the atypical nature of the home situation and believe it to be unfair, leading to feelings of resentment. Parentification develops during childhood, and can continue into adult life, with both negative and positive outcomes for children (Carroll & Robinson, 2000; Hooper, Marotta & Lanthier, 2008; Jurkovic et al., 2001; Peris, Goeke-Morey, Cummings, & Emery, 2008; Wells & Jones, 2000).

Several factors are believed to have a causal with parentification. For example, family unpredictability, parental alcoholism, poor parental health, and marital conflict are linked to parentification (Burnett, Jones, Blwise, & Ross, 2006; Godsall, Jurkovic, Emshoff, Anderson, & Stanwyck, 2004; Hooper, DeCoster, White, & Voltz, 2011; Kelley et al., 2007; Peris et al., 2008). Some of these factors exert a stronger influence than others. For example, Carroll and Robinson (2000) found children of workaholics and children of alcoholics both had the potential for parentification; however, the children of workaholics experienced significantly higher levels of parentification than children of alcoholics. The most likely explanation is that workaholic parents are physically absent from the home to a greater degree than an alcoholic parent, who is more likely to be emotionally absent. Children without a parent in the home are more likely to have to take on adult responsibilities. In sum, not only are there many factors leading to parentification, these factors may have differential impacts.

In addition to being multi-causal, parentification is linked to multiple negative outcomes. Castro, Jones, and Mirsalimi (2004) found a positive relationship between childhood parentification and the impostor phenomenon, defined as not believing in one's self or abilities. Children who experienced parentification and the impostor phenomenon felt as if they lacked uniqueness, talent, and the ability to meet others' demands. The experience of childhood parentification also has been linked to feelings of shame in adulthood (Wells & Jones, 2000). Shame-prone individuals feel badly about themselves; instead of focusing on correcting bad behaviors, they are paralyzed by self-blame. Even more serious, parentification has been linked to a variety of pathologies such as eating disorders, mood disorders, substance abuse disorders, and personality disorders (Hooper et al., 2011), as well as overall mental health symptomology (Hooper & Wallace, 2010). Taken in conjunction, these findings suggest childhood parentification can lead to a range of negative adult outcomes.

Despite these adverse associations, previous research has revealed some positive outcomes linked to parentification. Hooper et al. (2008) found people who experienced parentification have the potential for posttraumatic growth. Specifically, these adults are likely to show increased resiliency, an improved ability to respond to life's challenges in a positive and constructive manner. However, even in this study, the level of growth was considered minimal and emotional parentification was simultaneously linked to distress. Focusing specifically on instrumental parentification has yielded more consistent positive findings. Thirkield (2002) demonstrated childhood instrumental parentification predicted greater interpersonal competence in adulthood. Similarly, instrumental parentification in the form of caring for siblings was linked to psychosocial adjustment instead of maladjustment (Fitzgerald, Schneider, Zinzow, Jackson, & Fossel, 2008).

The current theory to explain these positive outcomes is that successfully handling adult responsibilities, such as caring for siblings as children, may elicit feelings of self-efficacy (Fitzgerald et al., 2008). This theory would explain why instrumental parentification, which is characterized by children taking responsibility for adult chores, has been linked to more positive outcomes than parentification in general. Further support for this theory comes from Williams and Francis (2010) who argued that children with an internal locus of control may be shielded from the negative effects of parentification while still gaining benefits. People with an internal locus of control, who feel personally in control of life events, are more likely to take credit for their accomplishments and thus experience self-efficacy.

The relationship between parentification and positive outcomes can be complicated. For example, Hooper, Doehler, Jankowski, and Tomek (2012) found that adolescents with alcoholic parents were less likely to have alcohol problems themselves if they were experiencing parentification, a seemingly positive outcome. At the same time, parentification was linked to an increase in depressive symptoms for adolescents with alcoholic parents. In other words, parentification was a buffer for one adverse outcome and a moderator for the other.

In sum, past research suggests childhood parentification is linked to some positive and many negative adult outcomes. Because much of the previous research has assumed and examined adverse outcomes, Hooper et al. (2008) argued for a more thorough examination of potential positive outcomes. Thus, the goal of this study was to further examine how the different aspects of parentification link to a series of positive and negative adult behaviors, with the intention of identifying positive associations previously uninvestigated. We hypothesized instrumental parentification would be linked to more positive outcomes in comparison to emotional parentification and perceptions of unfairness. We also hypothesized emotional parentification and perceptions of unfairness would be linked to more negative outcomes. Last, we hypothesized participants high in all types of parentification would show a stronger desire for a stable career and income than participants low in parentification, in an effort to overcome the instability of growing up in a parentification environment.

Method

Participants

Participants were 30 men and 70 women, with a mean age of 20.29 ($SD = 3.69$) enrolled in a southeastern university. Fifty-seven percent of participants were Caucasian, 31% were African-American, and the remainder represented other ethnicities. Thirty-eight percent of participants were the oldest child in their families, 38% were youngest children, 14% were middle children, and the remainder was only children. The average family income reported by participants was $72,000 ($SD = $51,000$). Participants were given extra credit for participation and all participation was voluntary.

Materials and Procedure

Instrumental and emotional parentification and perceived fairness in participants' childhood homes were measured with a modified Parentification Questionnaire (Hooper & Wallace, 2010). The original Parentification Questionnaire was a 30 item, self-report measure developed by Jurkovic and Thirkield (1998). Hooper and Wallace (2010) focused on 21-items that loaded on three constructs (instrumental parentification, emotional parentification, and perceived fairness), and demonstrated this modified scale as a reliable measure of

parentification; Cronbach's alpha coefficients were over .80 for all scales (instrumental

parentification = .81, emotional parentification = .82, perceived fairness = .88).

A "Perceptions of Fairness" score (POF), an "Emotional Parentification" score (EPS),

and an "Instrumental Parentification" score (IPS) were computed for each participant by

following Hooper and Wallace's (2010) instructions to reverse score specified items and then

calculate the mean for the relevant questions on each dimension. A higher POF score indicated

that participants perceived a greater sense of unfairness in their childhood home. For IPS and

EPS, a higher score indicated more experience with the particular type of parentification.

Instrumental parentification included five items such as, "I often did the family's

laundry" and "My parents expected me to help discipline my siblings." Emotional parentification

included seven items such as, "At times I felt I was the only one my mother or father could turn

to" and "In my family I often made sacrifices that went unnoticed." Perceived fairness included

nine items such as, "My parents often tried to get me to take their sides in conflicts" and "It often

seemed that my feelings weren't taken into account in my family." Participants rated how true

each statement was of them on a five-point Likert scale with 1 representing "Strongly Disagree"

and 5 representing "Strongly Agree." The higher the score for each sub-scale, the more of that

specific type of parentification the participants experienced in their childhood homes.

A series of statements were also created to reflect both positive and negative adult

outcomes. These outcomes were selected by having the four authors of this study, who were

familiar with the published literature on this topic, independently generate a list of psychological

outcomes with the potential to be linked to parentification. Variables investigated in previous

studies or variables appearing on only one list were eliminated. From the remaining items, 19 were selected to represent positive outcomes (e.g., self-confidence, practical, organized, emotionally open to others) and 15 were selected to represent negative outcomes (e.g., anxiety, loneliness, harsh self-evaluation, pessimistic view of the future). A larger number of positive outcomes were selected because previous research focused more heavily on negative outcomes and to meet Hooper et al.'s (2008) request for more efforts to link parentification to positive outcomes. Participants rated how much each outcome matched their adult experiences on a five-point Likert scale with 1 representing "Strongly Disagree" and 5 representing "Strongly Agree." The higher the score, the more the specific outcome characterized the participant.

Participants were asked to respond to two questions related to their future career plans. One question asked participants to estimate their future income with an open-ended response. A second question asked participants to rank four life outcomes: getting married, having children, making money, and having a successful career (1 represented "Most important" and 4 represented "Least Important"). Participants were also asked to indicate to which family members they felt emotionally close. Participants could select as many options as desired from mother, father, some of my siblings, and all of my siblings. Last, participants provided demographic information including their grade point average and family income of the home in which they were raised. Participants were surveyed in group settings. Participants responded first to the parentification questions followed by the positive and negative statements. Demographics were assessed last.

Results

The relationships among the sub-scales were examined using Pearson's correlations. Emotional parentification and instrumental parentification were positively correlated, $r(93) = .55$, $p < .01$. POF was positively correlated with both instrumental, $r(90) = .38$, $p < .01$, and emotional parentification, $r(96) = .68$, $p < .01$. These correlations, revealing medium to large

effect sizes, among the sub-scales are consistent with previous research (e.g., Hooper & Wallace,

2010).

The negative outcomes selected for this research project were positively correlated,

providing one reliability check. To cite but a few examples, anxiety was positively correlated

with harsh self-evaluations, $r(97) = .41$, $p < .01$, and a pessimistic view of the future, $r(96) =$

.27, $p < .01$. Loneliness was positively correlated with a pessimistic view of the future, $r(96) =$

.24, $p < .05$, difficulty relying on others, $r(97) = .43$, $p < .01$, and difficulty expressing emotions,

$r(97) = .25$, $p < .015$.

Relations with IPS

Bivariate correlations were conducted to examine possible relationships between the IPS

and parentification statements. The higher the IPS, the less participants viewed themselves as

practical, $r(93) = -.24$, $p < .05$, and organized, $r(93) = -.21$, $p < .05$. The higher the IPS, the

more participants liked to solve their own and others' problems, $r(91) = .30$, $p < .01$, and the

lower their grade point average, $r(86) = -.29$, $p < .01$. These correlations represent small effect

sizes and are depicted in Table 1.

Relations with EPS

Bivariate correlations were conducted to examine possible relationships between the EPS

and parentification statements. The higher the EPS, the lower the participants' self-esteem, $r(99)$

$= -.38$, $p < .01$, the less confidence they had in their abilities, $r(99) = -.26$, $p < .05$, and the less

attractive participants rated themselves, $r(98) = -.28$, $p < .01$. The higher the EPS, the more

anxious participants rated being, $r(99) = .43$, $p < .01$, and the more alone participants felt, $r(96)$

$= .43$, $p < .01$. A higher EPS was positively correlated with participants feeling uncomfortable expressing their emotions, $r(97) = .26$, $p < .01$, and finding it difficult to rely on others, $r(97) = .34$, $p < .01$. A higher EPS was negatively correlated with being emotionally open to others, $r(99) = -.28$, $p < .01$, and being comfortable working with others, $r(99) = -.22$, $p < .05$. Participants with a higher EPS were more likely to evaluate themselves harshly, $r(97) = .27$, $p < .01$, hold a pessimistic view of the future, $r(96) = .22$, $p < .05$, and have spent time in therapy, $r(97) = .38$, $p < .01$. The higher the EPS, the more participants saw themselves as taking care of other people, $r(97) = .39$, $p < .01$, and desired to solve their own and others' problems, $r(97) = .23$, $p < .05$. These relations reveal both small and medium effect sizes and are depicted in Table 1.

Relations with POF

Bivariate correlations were conducted to examine possible relationships between the POF and parentification statements. The higher the POF, the lower the participants' self-esteem, $r(96) = -.51$, $p < .01$, the less confidence they had in their abilities, $r(96) = -.37$, $p < .01$, and the less attractive participants rated themselves, $r(95) = -.32$, $p < .01$. The higher the POF, the more anxious participants rated being, $r(96) = .35$, $p < .01$, the more participants agreed that they held themselves back from doing things, $r(94) = .21$, $p < .05$, and the more alone participants felt, $r(93) = .49$, $p < .01$. A higher POF was positively correlated with participants feeling uncomfortable expressing their emotions, $r(94) = .35$, $p < .01$, and finding it difficult to rely on others, $r(94) = .43$, $p < .01$. A higher POF was negatively correlated with being emotionally open to others, $r(96) = -.27$, $p < .01$. Participants with a higher POF were more likely to evaluate themselves harshly, $r(94) = .33$, $p < .01$, hold a pessimistic view of the future, $r(93) = .22$, $p <$

.05, and have spent time in therapy, $r(94) = .30$, $p < .01$. These relations reveal primarily medium effect sizes and are depicted in Table 1.

Additional Findings

Bivariate correlations were conducted to examine possible relationships between IPS, EPS, POF, and statements related to participant's future success. The lower the family income, the higher the IPS, $r(85) = -.27$, $p < .05$, the higher the EPS, $r(90) = -.23$, $p < .05$, and the higher the POF, $r(89) = -.26$, $p < .05$. The higher the POF, the more income participants expected to have in their future career, $r(74) = .23$, $p < .05$. Emotional and instrumental parentification did not predict expected income; however the higher the EPS, the more important having a successful career was to the participant, $r(92) = -.23$, $p < .05$. These relations reveal small effect sizes and are depicted in Table 1.

Next, ethnicity and sex differences were explored. African-American and Caucasian participants were compared using an independent t-test. These two groups did not differ on any of the parentification sub-scales. Similarly, there were no sex differences on parentification sub-scale scores.

Finally, relationships between parental closeness and the parentification scales were assessed. Participants who were close to their mothers were compared to participants who reported not being close to their mothers. Participants who were close to their mothers had lower POF, $t(93) = 6.49$, $p < .01$; EPS, $t(95) = 2.14$, $p < .05$, and IPS, $t(90) = 2.34$, $p < .05$. Participants who were close to their fathers were compared to participants who reported not being close to their fathers. Participants who were close to their fathers had lower POF, $t(93) = 4.02$, $p < .01$, and EPS, $t(95) = 2.51$, $p < .05$.

Discussion

We hypothesized instrumental parentification would be associated with more positive outcomes than would emotional parentification and perceptions of fairness. This hypothesis was not supported. Adults who had experienced instrumental parentification viewed themselves as less practical and less organized. In other words, instrumental parentification was negatively associated with these two positive outcomes. These participants also reported lower college GPAs, another negative outcome. One possible explanation is that participants who, as children, were expected to take on adult responsibilities rebelled against that in adulthood, choosing to be less practical and less organized. Another possibility is that these adults were comparing themselves to a high, perhaps unachievable, standard that had been created during childhood for them and as adults they found themselves failing to meet the standard; thus, they perceived themselves as being less organized and practical. The participants could have also been less organized and less practical because of watching parents who portrayed these traits making it a learned behavior.

Adults high in instrumental parentification also were more likely to feel the need to solve their own problems and those of others. This pressure may be directly related to their childhood experience of being responsible for the care of others. Perhaps children who are raised in a situation where they are responsible for others incorporate that sense of responsibility into their adult identity. Although being responsible is a healthy trait, feeling as though others' problems are yours to solve can be unhealthy and overwhelming.

We also hypothesized emotional parentification would be primarily associated with negative outcomes. This hypothesis was supported. Emotional parentification was associated with a variety of adverse outcomes such as negative self-perceptions, anxiety, social discomfort, pessimism, and time spent in therapy. Hooper et al. (2008) also found emotional parentification to be strongly linked to negative adult outcomes such as distress. Emotional parentification may affect children's self-perception, as well as their view of others, leading to negative outcomes related to self and relationships. These children may not have been able to develop a healthy self-image and coping strategies as a result of being distracted by the emotional needs of their parents. In addition, these children may not have had role models in their lives with healthy self-images and coping strategies to learn from, which could increase their likelihood to adopt the unhealthy self-images and coping strategies of individuals around them.

Participants who experienced high levels of perceived unfairness in their childhood exhibited similar characteristics to participants high in emotional parentification. POF was highly correlated with emotional parentification. Perhaps the overlap in adverse outcomes reflects the fact that participants who experienced emotional parentification simultaneously perceived their home situation to be unfair.

Overall, the three sub-scales were linked to negative adult outcomes; however, instrumental parentification was associated with fewer negative outcomes than emotional parentification and perceptions of fairness. This pattern somewhat matches previous research in which positive adult outcomes were more likely to be linked to instrumental parentification than to emotional parentification or perceptions of fairness (e.g. Fitzgerald et al., 2008; Thirkield, 2002). A current theory is that instrumental parentification leads to feelings of self-efficacy (Fitzgerald et al., 2008). Our study provides some support for this theory, as participants high in instrumental parentification did have some negative perceptions of their abilities; however, they did not view themselves as incompetent across all realms.

Hooper (2007) suggested parentification could be better understood in the context of attachment theory, where parentification serves to interfere with healthy attachment between the parent and child. Emotional parentification and perceived unfairness may be particularly detrimental to the parent-child relationship, as they both contain an emotional element. Instrumental parentification, in contrast, is more about practical matters, such as getting dinner on the table and has even been linked to increased interpersonal competence (Thirkield, 2002). Our data provide support for the idea that parentification interferes with healthy parent-child attachment as proposed by Hooper (2007). We found that participants who had a close relationship with their mothers had lower rates of all types of parentification. Participants who had a close relationship with their fathers were less likely to have perceived unfairness and emotional parentification.

Previous research linked parentification to lower income (Burton, 2007). Our findings matched, with all types of parentification being linked to lower family income. We hypothesized that participants high in parentification would desire a stable career, an assumption that was partially supported by the data. Participants who scored higher on perceived unfairness expected to have a higher career income, while participants who experienced higher levels of emotional parentification felt that it was important to have a successful career. Instrumental parentification was not associated with career goals. One possible explanation is that participants who experienced emotional parentification and perceived unfairness valued a steady income and a stable job as a result of the poverty and burdens they experienced as a child.

This study had limitations. The sample was drawn from college students; adults who experienced extreme parentification may not be enrolled in college and thus not have the opportunity to participate in parentification studies. Another limitation is that the Parentification

Questionnaire requires participants to recall childhood experiences, a method that is subject to some level of inaccuracy and bias. Both of these limitations are characteristic of the research in this domain with few exceptions (e.g., Hooper et al., 2012).

Overall, parentification was linked to negative rather than positive outcomes in adulthood. Emotional parentification and perceptions of unfairness in the childhood home were associated with more negative outcomes than was instrumental conditioning. An increased understanding of parentification may lead to the development of strategies to combat the negative experiences in early childhood, such as counseling techniques, positive mentors and role models, and training to identify situations where parentification is occurring. One timely application might be to military families where one or both parents are deployed, leaving the children to take on increased household responsibilities. Future researchers may want to examine whether the effectiveness of specific intervention strategies depends on the cause of the parentification.

References

Burnett, G., Jones, R., Bliwise, N. G., & Ross, L. T. (2006). Family unpredictability, parental alcoholism, and the development of parentification. *American Journal of Family Therapy, 34,* 181-189. doi:10.1080/01926180600550437

Burton, L. (2007). Childhood adultification in economically disadvantaged families: A conceptual model. *Family Relations, 56,* 329-345. doi:10.1111/j.1741-3729.2007.00463.x

Carroll, J. J., & Robinson, B. E. (2000). Depression and parentification among adults as related to parental workaholism and alcoholism. *The Family Journal: Counseling and Therapy for Couples and Families, 8,* 360-367. doi:10.1177/1066480700084005

Castro, D. M., Jones, R. A., & Mirsalimi, H. (2004). Parentification and the imposter phenomenon: An empirical investigation. *The American Journal of Family Therapy, 32,* 205-216.

Fitzgerald, M. M, Schneider, R. A, Zinzow, H. M., Jackson, J., & Fossel, R. V. (2008). Child sexual abuse, early risk, and childhood parentification: Pathways to current psychosocial adjustment. *Journal of Family Psychology, 22,* 320-324. doi:10.1037/0893-3200.22.2.320

Godsall, R. E., Jurkovic, G. J., Emshoff, J., Anderson, L., & Stanwyck, D. (2004). Why some kids do well in bad situations: Relation of parental alcohol misuse and parentification to children's self-concept. *Substance Use and Misuse, 39,* 789-809. doi:10.1081/JA-120034016

Hooper, L. M. (2007). The application of attachment theory and family systems theory to the phenomena of parentification. *The Family Journal, 15*, 217-223. doi:10.1177/1066480707301290

Hooper, L. M., DeCoster, J., White, N., & Voltz, M. L. (2011). Characterizing the magnitude of the relation between self-reported childhood parentification and adult psychopathology: A meta-analysis. *Journal of Clinical Psychology, 67*, 1028-1043. doi:10.1002/jclp.20807

Hooper, L. M., Doehler, K., Jankowski, P. T., & Tomek, S. E. (2012). Patterns of self-reported alcohol use, depressive symptoms, and body mass index in a family sample: The buffering effects of parentification. *The Family Journal, 20*, 164-178. doi:10.1177/1066480711435320

Hooper, L. M., Marotta, S. A., & Lanthier, R. P. (2008). Predictors of growth and distress following childhood parentification: A retrospective exploratory study. *Journal of Child and Family Studies, 17*, 693-705. doi:10.1007/s10826-007-9184-8

Hooper, L. M., & Wallace, S. A. (2010). Evaluating the parentification questionnaire: Psychometric properties and psychopathology correlates. *Contemporary Family Therapy, 32*(1), 52-68. doi:10.1007/s10591-009-9103-9

Jurkovic, G. J., & Thirkield, A. (1998). Parentification Questionnaire (Available from G.J. Jurkovic, Department of Psychology, Georgia State University, University Plaza, Atlanta, GA 30303).

Jurkovic, G. J., Thirkfield, A., & Morrell, R. (2001). Parentification of adult children of divorce: A multidimensional analysis. *Journal of Youth and Adolescence, 30*, 245-257. doi:10.1023/A:1010349925974

Kelley, M. L., French, A., Bountress, K., Keefe, H.A., Schroeder, V., Steer, K., Fals-Stewart, W., & Gumienny, L. (2007). Parentification and family responsibility in the family of origin of adult children of alcoholics. *Addictive Behaviors, 32*, 675-685. doi:10.1016/j.addbeh.2006.06.010

Peris, T. S., Goeke-Morey, M. C., Cummings, E. M., & Emery, R. E. (2008). Marital conflict and support seeking by parents in adolescence: Empirical support for the parentification construct. *Journal of Family Psychology, 22*, 633-642. doi:10.1037/a0012792

Shih, F. M., Wu, L. C., & Lin, S. H. (2010). A correlational study on parentification, self-differentiation, and health for students in senior high and vocational high schools in Taiwan. *Bulletin of Educational Psychology, 41*(1), 823-846.

Titzman, P.F. (2012). Growing up too soon? Parentification among immigrant and native adolescents in Germany. *Journal of Youth and Adolescence, 41*, 880-893. doi:10.1007/s10964-011-9711-1

Thirkield, A. (2002). The role of fairness in emotional and social outcomes of childhood filial responsibility. Unpublished doctoral dissertation, Georgia State University, Atlanta, GA. (UMI No.3036391).

Wells, M., & Jones, R. (2000). Childhood parentification and shame-proneness: A preliminary study. *The American Journal of Family Therapy, 28*(1), 19-27. doi:10.1080/019261800261789

Williams, K., & Francis, S. E. (2010). Parentification and psychological adjustment: Locus of control as a moderating variable. *Contemporary Family Therapy: An International Journal, 32*, 231-237. doi:10.1007/s10591-010-9123-5

Table 1

Adult outcomes associated with parentification sub-scale scores

Outcomes and Variables	Parentification Sub-scales		
Positive Outcomes	IPS	EPS	POF
Self-esteem		-.38	-.51
Self-confidence		-.26	-.37
Attractive		-.28	-.32
Practical	-.24	-.26	
Organized	-.21		
Emotionally open to others		-.28	-.27
Comfortable working with others		-.22	
Negative Outcomes			
Experiencing anxiety		.43	.35
Feelings of loneliness		.43	.49
Find it hard to rely on others		.34	.43
Difficulty expressing emotions		.26	.35
Harsh self-evaluations		.27	.33
Pessimistic view of the future		.22	.22
Participated in therapy		.38	.30
See myself always taking care of others		.39	
Often try to solve my own problems as well as others' problems	.30	.23	
Hold back from doing things I want to do			.21
Career Variables			
Family income	-.27	-.23	-.26
GPA	-.29		
Expected income			.23
Importance of career		.23	

*Presented correlations significant at p < .05

REFERENCES

Aeschbach, D., Cutler, A. J., & Ronda, J. M. (2008). A role for non-rapid-eye-movement sleep homeostasis in perceptual learning. *Journal of Neuroscience, 28,* 2766–2772. doi:10.1523/JNEUROSCI.5548-07.2008

Amdur, R. (2003). *The institutional review board member handbook.* Boston, MA: Jones and Bartlett Publishers.

American Psychological Association. (2002). Ethical principles of psychologists and code of conduct. *American Psychologist, 57,* 1060–1073. doi: 1060-1073 10.1037//0003-066X.57.12.1060.

Anderson, N. H. (1979). Algebraic rules in psychological measurement. *American Scientist, 67,* 555–563.

Aron, A., Aron, A., & Coups, E. (2009). *Statistics for psychology* (5th ed.). Upper Saddle River, NJ: Prentice Hall.

Asch, S. E. (1951). Effects of group pressure upon the modification and distortion of judgment. In H. Guetzkow (Ed.) *Groups, leadership and men.* Pittsburgh, PA: Carnegie Press.

Asch, S. E. (1955). Opinions and social pressure. *Scientific American, 193,* 31–35.

Bandura, A. (1965). Influence of models' reinforcement contingencies on the acquisition of imitative responses. *Journal of Personality and Social Psychology, 1,* 589–595.

Barlett, C. P., Harris, R. J., & Bruey, C. (2008). The effect of the amount of blood in a violent video game on aggression, hostility, and arousal. *Journal of Experimental Social Psychology, 44,* 539–546.

Barlett, C., Harris, R., Smith, S., & Bonds-Raacke, J. (2005). Action figures and men. *Sex Roles, 53,* 877–885.

Baum, C. (Producer), & Shyer, C. (Director). (1991). *Father of the bride* [Motion Picture]. USA: Touchstone Pictures.

Biederman, I., Yue, X., & Davidoff, J. (2009). Representation of shape in individuals from a culture with minimal exposure to regular, simple artifacts: Sensitivity to nonaccidental versus metric properties. *Psychological Science, 20,* 1437–1442. doi: 10.1111/j.1467-9280.2009.02465.x

Bonds, J. M., & Nicks, S. D. (1999). Sex by age difference in couples applying for marriage. *Psychological Reports, 84,* 42–44.

Bonds-Raacke, J. M., Cady, E. T., Schlegel, R., Harris, R. J., & Firebaugh, L. (2007). Remembering gay/lesbian television and film characters: Can Ellen and Will improve heterosexuals' attitudes towards homosexuals? *Journal of Homosexuality, 53,* 19–34.

Bonds-Raacke, J. M., & Raacke, J. D. (2007). The relationship between physical attractiveness of professor and students' ratings of professor quality. *Journal of Psychiatry, Psychology, and Mental Health, 1,* 1–7.

Bravata, D. M., Smith-Spangler, C., Sundaram, V., Gienger, A. L., Lin, N., Lewis, R., … Sirard, J. R. (2007). Using pedometers to increase physical activity and improve health: A systematic review. *Journal of the American Medical Association, 298,* 2296–2304. doi: 10.1186/1471-2458-9-309.

Brescoll, V. L., & Uhlmann, E. L. (2008). Can an angry woman get ahead?: Status conferral, gender, and expression of emotion in the workplace. *Psychological Science, 19,* 268–275.

Bushman, B. J., & Anderson, C. A. (2001). Media violence and the American public: Scientific facts versus media misinformation. *American Psychologist, 56,* 477–489. doi: 10.1037//0003-066X.56.6-7.477

Cameron, L., & Rutland, A. (2006). Extended contact through story reading in school: Reducing children's prejudice toward the disabled. *Journal of Social Issues, 62,* 469–488.

Casby, A., & Moran, A. (1998). Exploring mental imagery in swimmers: A single-case study design. *Irish Journal of Psychology, 19,* 525–531.

Catz, S. L., Kalichman, S. C., Benotsch, E. G., Miller, J., & Suarez, T. (2001). Anticipated psychological impact of receiving medial feedback about HIV treatment outcomes. *AIDS Care, 13,* 631–635.

Christiansen, N. D., Kaplan, M. F., & Jones, C. (1999). Racism and the social judgment process: Individual differences in the use of stereotypes. *Social Behavior and Personality, 27,* 129–144.

Cohen, J. (1965). Some statistical issues in psychological research. In B. B. Wolman (Ed.), *Handbook of clinical psychology.* New York, NY: Academic Press.

Costello, E. J., Worthman, C., Erkanli, A., & Angold, A. (2007). Prediction from low birth weight to female adolescent depression. *Archives of General Psychiatry, 64,* 338–344.

Cowan, N. (2010). The magical mystery four: How is working memory capacity limited, and why? *Current Directions in Psychological Science, 19,* 51–57. doi: 10.1177/0963721409359277

Cox, D. S., Cox, A. D., Sturm, L., & Zimet, G. (2010). Behavioral interventions to increase HPV vaccination acceptability among mothers of young girls. *Health Psychology, 29,* 29–39.

Curtiss, S. (1977). *Genie: A psycholinguistic study of a modern-day "Wild Child."* New York, NY: Academic Press.

Darley, J. M., & Batson C. D. (1973). "From Jerusalem to Jericho": A study of situational and dispositional variables in helping behavior. *Journal of Personality and Social Psychology, 27,* 100–108.

Desrumaux, P., Bosscher, S. D., & Léoni, V. (2009). Effects of facial attractiveness, gender, and competence of applicants on job recruitment. *Swiss Journal of Psychology, 68,* 33–42.

Dommeyer, C. J. (2008). The effects of the researcher's physical attractiveness and gender on mail survey response. *Psychology & Marketing, 25,* 47–70. doi: 10.1002/mar.20198

DeNoon, D. (2006, October 20). Study suggests possible link between TV viewing and autism in children. *FoxNews.com.* Retrieved from http://www.foxnews.com

Drews, F. A., Pasupathi, M., & Strayer, D. L. (2008). Passenger and cell phone conversations in simulated driving. *Journal of Experimental Psychology: Applied, 14,* 392–400. doi: 10.1037/a0013119

Dunn, E. W., Huntsinger, J., Lun, J., & Sinclair, S. (2008). The gift of similarity: How good and bad gifts influence relationships. *Social Cognition, 26,* 469–481.

Durán, R. J. (2009). Legitimated oppression: Inner-city Mexican American experiences with police gang enforcement. *Journal of Contemporary Ethnography, 38,* 143–168.

Dye, M. W. G., Green, S., & Bavelier, D. (2009). Increasing speed of processing with action video games. *Current Directions in Psychological Science, 18,* 321–326. doi: 10.1111/j.1467-8721.2009.01660.x

Ebbinghaus, H. (1885/1913). *Memory. A contribution to experimental psychology.* New York, NY: Teachers College, Columbia University.

Eissenberg, T., Panicker, S., Berenbaum, S., Epley, N., Fendrich, M., Kelso, R., Penner, L., & Simmerling, M. (2004). IRBs and psychological science: Ensuring a collaborative relationship. Available online at http://www.apa.org/research/responsible/irbs-psych-science.aspx

Farris, C. Treat, T. A., Viken, R. J., & McFall, R. M. (2008). Perceptual mechanisms that characterize gender differences in the decoding of women's sexual intent. *Psychological Science, 16,* 348–354

Feldman, R., Weller, A., Zagoory-Sharon, O., & Levine, A. (2007). Evidence for a neuroendocrinological foundation of human affiliation plasma oxytocin levels across pregnancy and the postpartum period predict mother-infant bonding. *Psychological Science, 18,* 965–970.

Farrelly, P. (Producer), Farrelly, B. (Producer), Wessler, C. B. (Producer), Thomas, B. (Producer), Farrelly, P. (Director), & Farrelly, B. (Director). (2000). *Me, myself, & Irene* [Motion Picture]. USA: 20ᵗʰ Century Fox.

Gazdzinski, S., Kornak, J., Weiner, M. W., & Meyerhoff, D. J. (2008). Body mass index and magnetic resonance markers of brain integrity in adults. *Annals of Neurology, 63,* 652–657. doi: 10.1002/ana.21377 annals of neurology

Gentile, D. A. (2009). Pathological video game us among youth 8 to 18: A national study. *Psychological Science, 20,* 594–602. doi: 10.1111/j.1467-9280.2009.02340.x

Gerbner, G., & Gross, L. (1976). Living with television: The violence profile. *Journal of Communication, 26,* 172–199.

Grinter, R. E. & Palen, L. (2002). Instant messaging in teenage life. *Proceedings of the ACM conference on computer supported cooperative work* (pp. 21–30.) NY: ACM Press. Retrieved February 2ⁿᵈ, 2009 from http://www.cc.gatech.edu/~beki/Publications.html.

Harris, R. J. (2004). *A cognitive psychology of mass communication* (4ᵗʰ ed.). Mahwah NJ: Lawrence Erlbaum Associates.

HealthOrbit (2008, April 1). Longer work days leave Americans nodding off on the job. *HealthOrbit.com.* Retrieved from http://www.healthorbit.com

HealthOrbit (2008, April 9). Overweight kids have fewer cavities, new study shows. *HealthOrbit.com.* Retrieved from http://www.healthorbit.com

HealthOrbit (2008, April 17). Men more likely to have problems with memory and thinking skills. *HealthOrbit.com.* Retrieved from http://www.healthorbit.com

Hermand, D., Mullet, E., & Lavieville, S. (1997). Perception of the combined effects of smoking and alcohol on cancer risks in never smokers and heavy smokers. *Journal of Health Psychology, 2,* 481–491.

Howard, R. (Producer), Grazer, B. (Producer), & Howard, R. (Director). (2001). *A beautiful mind* [Motion Picture]. USA: Universal Studios.

Janiszewski, C., & Uy, D. (2008). Precision of the anchor influences the amount of adjustment. *Psychological Science, 19,* 121–127.

Johnson, P. M. & Kenny, P. J. (2010). Dopamine D2 receptors in addiction-like reward dysfunction and compulsive eating in obese rats. *Nature Neuroscience, 13,* 635–641. doi:10.1038/nn.2519

Jones, M. H., & Estell, D. B. (2007). Exploring the Mozart effect among high school students. *Psychology of Aesthetics, Creativity, and the Arts, 1*, 219–224.

Kellogg, W. N., & Kellogg, L. A. (1933). *The ape and the child: A study of environmental influence upon early behavior.* Oxford, England: Whittlesey House.

Kopycka-Kedzierawski, D. T., Auinger, P., Billings, R. J., & Weitzman, M. (2008). Caries status and overweight in 2 to 18 year old US children: Findings from national surveys. *Community Dentistry and Oral Epidemiology, 36*, 157–167. doi: 10.1111/j.1600-0528.2007.00384.x

Kuoch, H., & Mirenda, P. (2003). Social story interventions for young children with autism spectrum disorders. *Focus on Autism and Other Developmental Disabilities, 18*, 219–227.

Landis, C. (1924). Studies of emotional reactions. *Comparative Psychology, IV*, 447–509.

Larson, S. G. (2003). Misunderstanding margin of error. *The Harvard International Journal of Press/Politics, 8*, 66–80. doi: 10.1177/1081180X02238785

Lawlor, D. A., Timpson, N. J., Harbord, R. M., & Leary, S. (2008). Exploring the developmental overnutrition hypothesis using parental–offspring associations and FTO as an instrumental variable. *PLoS Medicine, 5*, 484–493.

Lewin, T. (2009, October 24). No Einstein in your crib? Get a refund. *The New York Times.* Retrieved from http://www.nytimes.com

Lilienfeld, S. O., Lynn, S. J., Ruscio, J., & Beyerstein, B. L. (2010). *50 great myths of popular psychology: Shattering widespread misconceptions about human behavior.* Malden, MA: Wiley-Blackwell.

Linnau, K. F., & Mann, F. A. (2003). Doll's head "Bezoar": Complete craniocervical dislocation causing bowel obstruction. *American Journal of Roentgenology, 180*, 986.

Loftus, E. F., & Palmer, J. C. (1974). Reconstruction of automobile destruction: An example of the interaction between language and memory. *Journal of Verbal Learning and Verbal Behavior, 13*, 585–589.

Loftus, E. F. (1997). Repressed memory accusations: Devastated families and devastated patients. *Applied Cognitive Psychology, 11*, 25–30.

McConnell, J. V., Cutler, R. L., & McNeil, E. B. (1958). Subliminal stimulation: An overview. *American Psychologist, 13*, 229–242.

Middlemist, R. D., Knowles, E. S., & Matter, C. F. (1976). Personal space invasions in the lavatory: Suggestive evidence for arousal. *Journal of Personality and Social Psychology, 33*, 541–546.

Milgram, S. (1963). Behavioral study of obedience. *Journal of Abnormal and Social Psychology, 67*, 371–378.

Miller, L. C., & Fishkin, S. A. (1997). On the dynamics of human bonding and reproductive success: Seeking windows on the adapted-for human-environmental interface. In J. Simpson & D. T. Kenrick (Eds.), *Evolutionary social psychology* (pp. 197–235). Hillsdale, NJ: Erlbaum.

O'Neil, J., Steele, G., Huisingh C., & Smith, G. A. (2008). Escalator-related injuries among older adults in the United States, 1991–2005. *Accident Analysis & Prevention, 40*, 527–533.

Ong, A. D., & Weiss, D. J. (2000). The impact of anonymity on responses to "sensitive" questions. *Journal of Applied Social Psychology, 30*, 1691–1708.

Paquette I., & Finlayson S. R. (2007). Rural versus urban colorectal and lung cancer patients: Differences in stage at presentation. *Journal of the American College of Surgeons, 205*, 636–41. doi:10.1016/j.jamcollsurg.2007.06.196

Pavlov, I. (1928). *Lectures on conditioned reflexes.* New York, NY: International Publishers.

Piaget, J. (1954, 1981). *Intelligence and affectivity: Their relationship during child development.* Palo Alto, CA: Annual Review, Inc.

Publication manual of the American psychological association (6th ed.). (2010). Washington D.C.: American Psychological Association.

Raacke, J. D., & Bonds-Raacke, J. M. (2008). MySpace and Facebook: Applying the uses and gratifications theory to exploring friend-networking sites. *CyberPsychology and Behavior, 11,* 169–174.

Reitman, I. (Producer & Director). (1984). *Ghostbusters* [Motion Picture]. USA: Sony Pictures Incorporated.

Rosenthal, R. (1994). Science and ethics in conducting, analyzing, and reporting psychological research. *Psychological Science, 5,* 127–134.

Rothbaum, B. O., Hodges, L. F., Anderson, P., Price, L., & Smith, S. (2002). 12-month follow-up of virtual reality and standard exposure therapies for the fear of flying. *Journal of Consulting and Clinical Psychology, 70,* 428–432.

Rulence-Pâques, P., Fruchart, E., Dru, V., & Mullet, E. (2005). Algebraic rules in sport decision-making. *Theory and Decision, 58,* 387–406.

Shadish, W. R., Cook, T. D., & Campbell, D. T. (2002). *Experimental and quasi-experimental designs for generalized causal inference.* Boston, MA: Houghton Mifflin.

Smith, A. P., Tyrrell, D. A. J., & Willman, J. S. (1987). Selective effects of minor illness of human performance. *British Journal of Psychology, 78,* 183–188.

Stroop, J. R. (1935). Studies of interference in serial verbal reactions. *Journal of Experimental Psychology, 18,* 643–662.

Tamir, M., Mitchell, C., & Gross, J. J. (2008). Hedonic and instrumental motives in anger regulation. *Psychological Science, 19,* 324–328.

Taveras, E. M., Rifas-Shiman, S. L., Oken, E., Gunderson, E. P., Gillman, M. W. (2008). Short sleep duration in infancy and risk of childhood overweight. *Archives of Pediatric Adolescence Medicine, 162,* 305–311. doi: 10.1001/archpedi.162.4.305.

The Women's Conference (2010). *We honor Dr. Jane Goodall.* Retrieved from http://www.womensconference.org/dr-jane-goodall/

Tversky, A., & Kahneman, D. (1974). Judgment under uncertainty: Heuristics and biases. *Science, 185,* 1124–1131.

Tversky, A., & Kahneman, D. (1981). The framing of decisions and the psychology of choice. *Science, 211,* 453–458.

Vivian, J. (2008). *The media of mass communication* (9th Ed.) Boston, MA: Allyn & Bacon.

Watson, J. B. & Raynor, R. (1920). Conditioned emotional reactions. *Journal of Experimental Psychology, 3,* 1–14.

Weis, R., & Cerankosky, B. C. (2010). Effects of video-game ownership on young boys' academic and behavioral functioning: A randomized, controlled study. *Psychological Science, 21,* 463–470. doi: 10.1177/0956797610362670

Witt, C. M., Jena, S., Brinkhaus, B., Wegsheider, K. & Willich, S. N. (2006). Acupuncture in patients with osteoarthritis of the knee or hip: A randomized, controlled trial with an additional nonrandomized arm. *Arthritis & Rheumatism, 54,* 3458–3493. doi: 10.1002/art.22154

Worth Publishers (Producer). (2002). *The frontal lobes and behavior: The story of Phineas Gage* [DVD]. Available from Worth Publishers.

Worth Publishers (Producer). (2002). *Life without memory: The case of Clive Wearing* [DVD]. Available from Worth Publishers.

Zarkadi, T., Wade, K. A., & Stewart, N. (2009). Creating fair lineups for suspects with distinctive features. *Psychological Science, 20,* 1448–1453. doi: 10.1111/j.1467-9280.2009.02463.x

GLOSSARY

A

AB design   A methodology where measurements are taken before and after the administering of an independent variable.

ABA design   A methodology where measurements are taken before and after the administering of an independent variable as well as after the removal of the independent variable.

APA   American Psychological Association

APS   Association for Psychological Science

Analysis of variance (ANOVA)   Used when you have an independent variable with three or more levels or when you have multiple independent variables.

Applied research   Research is conducted to solve a practical problem within a field of study.

Archival research   A nonexperimental method where the researcher uses existing records and selects portions of the records to examine.

Attitudinal measure   A measure assessing a person's attitudes to the topic.

Attrition   Participants systematically drop out of an experiment, changing the experimental results.

Attrition   Participants dropping out of a study or not returning to complete additional parts to a study.

Authority   The appearance of expertise in a field of study.

B

Basic research   Research is conducted to further the collective knowledge about a topic within a field of study.

Behavioral measure   A measure to investigate a person's behaviors.

Between subjects design   Participants will be exposed to only one level of the independent variable.

Between subjects factorial research design   A research design in which all independent variables are between subjects.

Biased sample   A sample in which not everyone in the population has an equal or known chance of being selected.

Bonferroni correction   Can be used when conducting multiple statistical tests. The correction is used to limit the possibility of making a Type I Error.

C

Carryover effects   These occur when the effects of prior treatment conditions influence subsequent treatment conditions.

Case study   A research methodology that is an in-depth observation of an individual, animal, event, or treatment method.

Ceiling effect   When scores fall primarily at the upper range of a response option.

Closed-ended questions   Questions in which the answers must be selected from a predetermined list of responses.

Cluster sampling   Involves identifying naturally occurring clusters of individuals from the population to select from to be included in the sample.

Cognitive measure   A measure of one's mental ability or knowledge of a topic.

Confederate   A participant in a study but is also part of the research team. The participation of confederates is meant to influence the other participants.

Construct validity   The likelihood that the device or scale used to measure a variable actually is related to the topic or theory of interest.

Content analysis   A research methodology where a researcher counts the number of times a particular piece of content occurs.

Control   Direct manipulation of a desired variable or the management or removal of unwanted factors that can influence observations or experiments.

Control group   The group that is not exposed to the independent variable.

Convenience sampling   A procedure which involves using those participants who are readily available or will volunteer to participate.

Convergent validity   States that your measure should converge or be similar to other measures of the same variable.

Correlational research methods   Research methodologies that evaluate the relationship between variables.

Counterbalancing   Involves making sure that all combinations of the order of presentation occur in a study.

D

Degree of response   A measure of intensity of a response.

Demand characteristics   The change in the dependent variable is due to the researcher somehow communicating to participants how they should act or behave.

Dependent t-test   Used to determine if the mean difference between pairs is significantly different from zero.

Dependent variable   The variable in a study that is observed or measured.

Describe   The first goal of psychological research is to *describe* behavior or mental processes.

Descriptive statistics   Used by researchers to describe data sets.

Diffusion of treatment   Change in the dependent variable is due to participants in different groups communicating with each other.

Directional research hypothesis   A hypothesis that predicts a specific direction that the results will occur.

Divergent validity or discriminant validity   Argues that your measure should be dissimilar to measures of different variables.

Double blind study   An experiment in which neither the participant nor the researcher knows which group the participant have been placed into.

E

Effect size   The amount of overlap between populations.

Empirical   Acquisition of knowledge via objective and systematic collection of data.

Ethnography   Used to describe a culture in detail by recoding and transcribing events that are witnessed.

Everyday experiences   Using experience from life to obtain a research idea.

Experimental group   The group that is exposed to the independent variable in a study.

Experimental research   A class of research methodologies that involve manipulation of a variable.

Explain   The second goal of psychological research is to *explain* behavior or mental processes.

External validity   The extent to which the obtained results in a study can be generalized to other settings.

Extraneous variable   Variable that is not controlled for in the experiment that may have an effect on the dependent variable.

F

Factorial research design   A research design that uses more than one independent variable.

Failing to reject the null hypothesis   Indicates that there is not a statistically significant difference between the means of the groups in the study and that the means are equal.

Fatigue   Occurs when participants become tired during an experiment.

Floor effect   When scores fall primarily at the lower range of a response option.

Frequency of responding   A sum of the number of times a person/group responds to a question.

Functional problems   Using real-world problems as a source for a research idea.

H

History   An event beyond the researcher's control that can explain the change in the dependent variable.

Hypothesis   A statement about the relationship between variables.

I

Independent t-test   Evaluates whether or not two means are significantly different from one another.

Independent variable   The variable in a study that is being manipulated.

Inferential statistics   Used so that inferences can be drawn about a population from the sample used.

Influence   The fourth goal of psychological research is to *influence* behavior or mental processes.

Instrumentation   Change in the dependent variable is due to how the dependent variable was measured.

Interaction   Occurs when the effect of one independent variable depends on another independent variable.

Internal consistency A reliability assessment similar to a split-half method. However, the splitting occurs more than once and an average of the correlations is taken.

Internal validity Confidence in saying the observed change in the dependent variable is due to the independent variable and not due to any outside influences.

Internet A worldwide, publicly accessible network containing vast amounts of information.

Interrater or interobserver reliability A reliability assessment used when a research design calls for observations of an event. Two or more observers compare results from their observations. The higher the observer consensus, the higher the reliability.

Interval scale Classification of data on a scale that assumes equal distance between numbers.

Intuition Understanding through the use of common sense based on observation.

L

Large number of records Occurs when a researcher uses terms in a search engine that are too broad.

Level of significance The probability of obtaining data assuming the null hypothesis is true. This is indicated by the alpha level (α).

Levels of the independent variable The number of conditions for a specific independent variable.

M

Main effect Determining if an independent variable has had an effect on the dependent variables while ignoring or collapsing across the other independent variables in the factorial research design.

Matched subjects design A methodology where participants are matched on a particular characteristic before being assigned to the different levels of the independent variable.

Maturation The change in the dependent variable is due to internal changes within the participants over time.

Mean The average of the scores in the data set.

Measures of central tendency Numbers that represent the scores in the data set.

Median The number in the middle of a data set.

Mixed subjects factorial research design A research design in which not all of the independent variables are one type (i.e., one independent variable is between and the other within subjects).

Mode The most frequently occurring number in a data set.

Multiple baseline designs A methodology where researchers have a small number of participants receive the independent variable at varying times.

Multiple dependent variables Most studies have more than one dependent variable. Having multiple dependent variables increases the amount of information collected.

N

Naturalistic observation A research methodology where a researcher observes people or animals in their natural setting.

Negative correlation Two or more variables vary in opposite directions.

Nominal scale Classification of data into one of two or more categories.

Nondirectional research hypothesis A hypothesis that does not make a prediction about the direction that the results will occur in.

Nonexperimental research A class of research methodologies that involve the study of how variables are related.

Nonprobability sampling procedures A procedure where not all individuals within the population of interest have an equal likelihood or known probability of being selected.

Normal distribution of scores Occurs when most scores cluster around the middle, and few, but equal, numbers cluster on the extremes.

Nuisance variable A variable that is not controlled for in the experiment that influences all participants in the same manner.

Null hypothesis Hypothesis that states there is *no* difference between scores on the dependent variables.

O

One-sample t-test Used to determine when a mean is significantly different from a constant.

Open-ended questions Questions in which a response is elicited and there is not a predetermined list of responses.

Operational definition Defines how a concept or idea will be measured.

Order effects Effects of a study are due to the participants experiencing the same order of presentation of the levels of the independent variable.

Ordinal scale Classification of data into an order or rank of magnitude.

P

Parallel-forms method A reliability assessment in which a measure is divided in half and given to two groups of people. The reliability is high if each measure given is highly correlated.

Percent correct Average of correct responses to overall responses represented as a percentage.

Physiological measure Measures that are biological in nature (i.e., heart rate, pulse, blood pressure, etc.).

Placebo An inert substance that has no effect.

Placebo control group Exposed to an inert substance or object that is similar to the independent variable but has no effect.

Placebo effect Change in the dependent variable is due to the participant believing a change will occur.

Population The entire group of individuals in which you are interested in studying.

Positive correlation Two or more variables vary in the same direction.

Power The probability of rejecting the null hypothesis when it is indeed false.

Practice effects Participants improve performance due to subsequent experiences on the same task.

Predict The third goal of psychological research is to *predict* behavior or mental processes.

Prior research Using what others have done as a starting point to obtain a research idea.

Probability sampling procedures A procedure where individuals from the population have a known probability (or chance) of being selected for a study.

Pseudoscience Any theory, method, or belief that appears to be based in science but is not.

PsycARTICLES® A full-text electronic psychological database by APA.

PsycINFO® Largest electronic psychological abstract database by APA.

Q

Qualitative Research methodologies where researchers seek subjectivity through in-depth collection of information and emerging hypotheses.

Quantitative Research methodologies that seek objectivity through testable hypotheses and carefully designed studies.

Quota sampling In quota sampling, a convenience sample is selected that is comprised of subgroups similar in number to the population.

R

Random assignment A procedure in which a selected participant has an equal probability of being placed into each group of a study.

Ratio scale Classification of data on a scale that assumes equal distance and a true zero value.

Regression to the mean The change in the dependent variable is due to extreme scores moving toward the mean on later measures.

Rejecting the null hypothesis Indicates that there is a statistically significant difference between the means of the groups in the study.

Reliability The consistency of your measure to produce similar results on different occasions.

Replication A research experiment or study that is reproduced using the exact methodology and procedure.

Research hypothesis Hypothesis that there *is* a difference between scores on the dependent variables.

Research matrix A visual representation of a research design.

Research question States a research idea in a clearly defined manner that is testable.

Research topic A broad concept or idea.

S

Sample Smaller group of individuals that is representative of the larger population.

Sample size The number of individuals needed or that are selected for a study.

Sampling with replacement Individuals are selected one at a time with each individual being replaced before the next is sampled. Here, each selection has exactly the same probability of being selected.

Sampling without replacement Individuals are selected and are not replaced before the next is sampled. Here, the probability of being selected changes with each removal.

Science The accumulation of knowledge via systematic observation or experimentation using the scientific method.

Selection Change in the dependent variable is due to how participants were selected for the experiment or how they were assigned to groups.

Self-correcting A system of challenges by which scientific claims can be verified.

Simple probability sampling All individuals in a population have a equal probability of being selected.

Single blind study A study in which the participant has no knowledge of which experimental group he or she may be participating within—only the researcher knows.

Single case design A design that focuses on a single participant, single group of participants, or a small group of participants.

Skewed distribution A skewed distribution is one in which the most frequently occurring scores are not in the middle.

Small number of (or no) records Occurs when a researcher uses terms in a search engine that are too specific.

Snowballing sampling A procedure where a sample is acquired by a referral process among similar individuals.

Split-half method A reliability assessment in which a measure is split in half and the two halves are compared. If the correlation is high, the measure is said to have high reliability.

Statistical variance The degree of spread among data when surrounding the mean.

Stratified probability sampling A probability sampling technique where a researcher begins by identifying subgroups (or strata) and then randomly samples from each subgroup.

Subject variable A characteristic or attribute of a participant that can impact a study.

Survey research A research methodology where one designs a questionnaire to obtain information regarding behaviors, attitudes, or opinions.

Systematic probability sampling Random sampling in which a systematic approach is used.

T

Tenacity The persistence to maintain over time.

Testing Change in the dependent variable is due to the participants becoming more familiar with the test or testing procedures.

Test–retest Reliability A reliability assessment where your measure is tested on two different occasions for consistency.

Theory An overarching principle that explains separate research findings in an area.

Treatment conditions Refers to levels or number of groups in the independent variable.

Type I Error Occurs when a researcher rejects the null when the null is in fact true.

Type II Error Occurs when a researcher fails to reject the null even though the null hypothesis is false.

U

Using synonyms When conducting searches, you may need to think of a synonym for your research topic.

V

Validity The accuracy of a measure to evaluate what it is supposed to measure.

Variable An event or characteristic that has at least two possible values.

W

Within subjects designs Design in which participants are exposed to all levels of the independent variable.

Within subjects factorial research design A research design in which all independent variables are within subjects.

INDEX

A

ABA designs, 235–236, 311

AB designs. *See* Pretest–posttest designs

Abstract (APA style), 265

Action figures and negative body image, link between, 185–186, 188

Acupuncture treatments, research on, 173–176

Alpha level. *See* Level of significance

American Idol, 161–162

American Psychological Association, 311

ethics code, 47–48, 54–55

debriefing, 44, 50

deception in research, 43–44, 50

duplicate publication of data, 46–47, 51

humane care, 44, 50

informed consent, 38–39, 42

institutional approval, 38, 48–49

offering inducements, 43, 49

plagiarism, 46, 51

publication credit, 46, 51

reporting research results, 46, 51

research data sharing and verification, 47, 52

research participants, 42

reviewers, 47, 52

use of animals in research, 44–45, 50–51

learning goals linkage. *See* APA learning goals linkage

membership in, 4–5

psychology courses, 4–5

Analysis of variance, 255, 311

Animal research, 50–51

APA ethics code for, 44–45

ANOVA. *See* Analysis of variance

Antidepressants, research studies of, 87–88

APA. *See* American Psychological Association

APA learning goals linkage, 78–79

communication, 79, 143, 160, 227, 262, 284

ethical and social responsibility, 32, 56, 78, 97, 120, 142–143, 159–160, 178, 242, 283

knowledge base in psychology

APA's Code of Ethics, 55

classic research, 193

contemporary research, 193

factorial designs, 226

goals of psychology, 15, 31–32

psychological research, 158

research question, 119

single case designs, 241

subjects designs, 209

variables, 97

professional development, 16, 284

scientific inquiry and critical thinking, 261–262

APA's Code of Ethics, 56

correlational methods, 78

factorial designs, 226–227

hypotheses, 120

introduction and discussion, 283

levels of independent variables, 142

nonexperimental methods, 78

reliability and validity, 97

research methods, 15–16, 32, 177–178, 193–194

research question, 120

sampling, 159

single case designs, 241–242

subjects designs, 210

APA style, 269–270

abstract, 265

discussion section, 268

introduction section, 266–267

method section, 267–268

mistakes, 263–264

practice exercise on, 279–281

reference, 270–271

reference list, 274–275

results section, 268

tables and figures, 269

title page, 265

typical sources, 275–278

within-text citations, 271–274

Applied research, 20, 311

vs. basic research, 22–24

APS. *See* Association for Psychological Science

Archival research, 60, 311

Association for Psychological Science

membership in, 4–5

psychology courses, 4–5

Astrology, 9

Attitudinal measures, 129, 311

Attrition, 168–169, 188, 311

Authority, 10, 311

Autism in children and TV viewing, link between, 162–163

B

Balanced reporting, 8

Basic research, 311

vs. applied research, 22–24

description of event, 19

explanation of behavior/
process, 19
prediction of behavior/process,
19–20
Beautiful Mind, A (movie), 106
Behavioral measures, 129, 311
Belief, commonly held
blind obedience to authority, 10
sexual activity and marital status,
link between, 6, 10
Belmont Report, principle in, 35
beneficence, 36
justice, 36
respect, 35–36
Between subjects design,
182–183, 311
advantages of, 189
classic research and, 184–185
contemporary research and,
185–187
disadvantages of, 189
ways to minimize, 191
factors to consider, 187–189
practice exercise on, 190
Between subjects factorial
research design
definition of, 213
practice exercise on, 214–216
research matrix, 213–214
variable of hurry, 213
Biased sample, 311
biased sample probability
sampling, 148
Bonding behaviors and oxytocin
levels, link between, 258–259
Bonferroni correction, 255, 311
Books (type of sources), 276–277
Box Office Mojo, 123

C

Caffeine and alertness levels, link
between, 87, 182
between subjects design, 183
within subjects design, 197
Carryover effects, 188, 311

Ceiling effect, 131, 311
Cheerleader effect, 246–247
Child development, research
experiments on, 231
Childhood parentification.
See Parentification
Classic research, 184–185
between subjects design, 184–185
within subjects design, 198–199
Class rankings, 135
Closed-ended questions, 71, 311
Cluster sampling, 149, 311
Coca Cola Co., 195
Cocurricular activities, faculty
mentorship, and ethnicity,
relationship between, 45–46
Cognitive impairment,
research on, 191
Cognitive measures, 129, 311
Cold condition and movie genre
preference, relationship between,
123–124, 183
College classroom performance, 134
Confederate, 311
Consent form to participate in
research, 38–42
Construct validity, 92–93, 311
Contemporary research
action figures and negative body
image, link between, 185–186
between subjects design, 185–187
within subjects design, 199–201
Content analysis, 311
Control group, 86, 311
Convenience sampling, 311
Convergent validity, 93, 311
Correlation
analysis, 292–295
positive and negative, 61–62
Correlational findings, 7
Correlational research methods,
61, 312
advantages and disadvantages
of, 64
practice exercise on, 62–63
Counterbalancing, 312
Cultivation theory, 29
Customer satisfaction, 59

D

Dannon, FTC press release
against, 12
Debriefing, 50
APA ethics code for, 44
Deception in research, 43–44, 50
Degree of response, 131, 312
Demand characteristics, 171, 312
Dependent samples t-test, 254, 312
Dependent variable, 82, 132,
141, 312
assessment method, 131
measures of, 129–130
Descriptive statistics, 312
conclusions from, 252–254
purpose of, 251
Diffusion of treatment conditions,
170, 312
Directional research hypothesis, 312
Discriminant validity, 93, 312
Discussion section (APA style), 268
Divergent validity. *See* Discriminant
validity
Divorce likelihood and marital
satisfaction, correlation
between, 62
Double blind study, 172, 312
Duplicate publication of data,
46–47, 51
APA ethics code for, 46–47

E

Ebbinghaus forgetting curve, 234
Educated consumer, importance of
being, 5–6
Elite athlete performance and mental
imagery, 238
Emotional instability, 53
Emotional parentification, 287, 298.
See also Parentification
negative adult outcomes of,
296–297
and perceptions of unfairness,
287, 290, 299
"Emotional Parentification" score,
291, 293–295

Entertainment media, popularization of myths in psychology, 6
EPS. *See* "Emotional Parentification" score
Ethics, research
    IRB and, 35–36
    Wichita Jury Study and, 33–34
Ethnicity, faculty mentorship, and cocurricular activities, relationship between, 45–46
Ethnography, 312
Everyday experiences, 105, 312
Exam grades, distribution of, 256–257
Experimental group, 86, 312
Experimental research, 61, 312
External validity, 92, 312
Extraneous variable, 162–163, 312

F

Facebook
    advertisement, 83, 85
    messages to deceased individuals, 19–20, 30
Facial expressions, 52–53
Factorial research design, 312
    definition of, 212–213
    mixed subjects. *See* Mixed subjects factorial research design
    people's response to mail survey, 211–212
    research matrix, 212
    results of
        interactions, 223
        main effects, 221–222
        practice exercise on, 224–225
    between subjects. *See* Between subjects factorial research design
    within subjects. *See* Within subjects factorial research design
Faculty mentorship, ethnicity, and cocurricular activities, relationship between, 45–46

Father of the Bride Part II (1995), 6
Federal Trade Commission, 12
Field studies. *See* Naturalistic observation
Floor effect, 131, 312
Frequency of responding, 131, 312
Friend networking sites, 164–165
Functional problems, 105

G

Generalization, 8
"Getting Married and (Not) Getting Sex," 6
Ghost Busters (1984), 6
Gift giving and new acquaintance situations, 245–246
Graduate Record Examination, 91
GRE. *See* Graduate Record Examination

H

History, 165–166
Homework and children's scores, 207
Horoscopes, 8–9
Human aggression, theories on, 29
Humane care, 50
    APA ethics code for, 44
Human memory research, 233–234
Hurry
    and helping behavior, research on, 190
    variable of, 213
Hypotheses, generating, 116, 290
    practice exercise on, 113–115
    relationship between caffeine and alertness, 110–111
        directional research hypothesis, 112
        nondirectional research hypothesis, 111–112
        null hypothesis, 111
        research hypothesis, 111

relationship between textbook and writing quality
        nondirectional research hypothesis, 112–113
        null hypothesis, 112
        research hypothesis, 112
Hypothesis, 28–29, 312
    testing, 116, 246
        null hypothesis. *See* Null hypothesis
        and replication, 250–251
Hypothetical exam grades, 256–257

I

IIT. *See* Information Integration Theory
Impression, 181
Independent samples t-test, 254, 312
Independent variable, 140
    definition of, 82
    selecting levels of, 124–127, 140, 313
        practice exercise on, 127–128
    treatment conditions
        control group, 86
        experimental group, 86
        Mozart effects, 86
        placebo control group, 87
        teaching statistics and new method group, 86–87
Inducements for research participation, APA ethics code for, 43
Inferential statistics, 312
    conclusions from, 254–255
    purpose of, 251
Information gathering
    authoritative figure, 10
    intuition, 9–10
    restaurants, 59
    tenacity, 10
Information Integration Theory, 106
Information source, 4–5, 7

Informed consent, 38–39, 42
  APA ethics code for, 38–39
  for psychological research, 38–39
  for recording voices and images, 42
Institutional approval, 38, 48–49
  APA ethics code for, 38
  for psychological research, 38
Institutional Review Boards, 37, 54
  Belmont Report. *See* Belmont Report, principle in
  functions of, 35
  reasons for formation of, 35
Instrumental parentification, 287, 298. *See also* Parentification
  feelings of self-efficacy and, 297
  negative adult outcomes linked to, 296
  positive adult outcomes linked to, 288–289
"Instrumental Parentification" score, 291, 293, 295
Instrumentation, 170
Interactions, 223, 312
Internal consistency, 90, 313
Internal validity, 91–92, 313
Internal validity, threats to
  attrition, 168–169
  control for, 172
    double blind study, 172
    placebo as, 172
  demand characteristics, 171
  diffusion of treatment conditions, 170
  history, 165–166
  instrumentation, 170
  maturation, 166–167
  placebo effect, 171
  regression to mean, 167–168
  selection of participants, 168
  testing, 169
Internet, 107–108, 313
Interrater reliability, 90–91, 313
Interval scales, 136
Introduction section (APA style), 266–267
Intuition, 9–10, 313

IPS. *See* "Instrumental Parentification" score
IRBs. *See* Institutional Review Boards

J

"Jerusalem to Jericho" study, 213–214
Journal article, 275–276

L

Level of significance, 247–248, 313

M

Mail survey, factors influencing people's response to, 211–212
Main effects, 221–222, 313
Marital satisfaction and likelihood of divorce, correlation between, 62
Matched subjects design, 313
  definition of, 206
  examples of, 207
  practice exercise on, 207–208
Maturation, 166–167, 313
Mean, 252, 313
Measures of central tendency, 252, 313
Media
  influence on users, 186
  and psychological research, disconnect between, 7
  sources, 6
Median, 252, 313
Media outlets, 5
Media research and cultivation theory, 29
Media violence and aggression, link between, 6
Memory distortion and eyewitness recall, studies on, 104

Memory research, 233–234
Me, Myself, and Irene (2000), 6
Mental imagery and elite athlete performance, 238
Method section (APA style), 267–268
Microworld simulation and monitor size, 196–197
Milgram, Stanley, 145
Misinterpretation of numbers, 8
Mixed subjects factorial research design, 313
  definition of, 213
  examples of, 218–220
Mode, 252, 313
Monitor size and microworld simulation, 196–197
Mother's oxytocin levels and bonding behaviors, link between, 258–259
Movie genre preference and temperature, relationship between, 123–124, 183
Mozart effect, 83–84, 86, 153
Multiple baseline design, 237, 313
Multiple dependent variables, 131, 313

N

Nash, John, 106
National Association for Stock Car Auto Racing (NASCAR) race, 135
National Basketball League, 240
National Research Act of 1974, 35, 54
National Sleep Foundation, 70
Naturalistic observation, 76, 313
NBA. *See* National Basketball League
Negative body image and action figures, link between, 185–186, 188
Negative correlation, 61–62
Nominal scales, 135, 313
Nonexperimental designs, 75
Nonexperimental research, 61, 313
  hypothesis, 313

Nonexperimental research methods, 60
  archival research, 60
    advantages of, 69
    definition of, 68
    examples of, 68–69
  case study
    advantages, 68
    Clive's memories and behaviors, 68
    definition of, 67
    feral children, 67
    human sexuality, 68
    language deprivation, 67–68
    personality and brain parts, link between, 67
  content analysis, 70
  ethnography, 65
  naturalistic observation
    advantages of, 66
    chimp behavior, 65
    definition of, 65
    disadvantages of, 66–67
    examples of, 65–66
    interactions with parents, 66
    men's selection of urinal and urinating behaviors, 65–66
  survey research, 60
    advantages and disadvantages of, 74
    definition of, 70
    participants' behavior and sleep patterns, 70
    questionnaire formats, 70
    survey construction, suggestions for. *See* Survey construction, suggestions for
Nonprobability sampling procedure, 147, 313
  convenience, 151–152
  definition of, 151
  practice exercise on, 152–153, 157
  quota, 152
  snowballing, 152
Nonverbal cues of women, 186–187
Normal distribution, 252–253, 313
NSF. *See* National Sleep Foundation

Nuisance variable, 162, 164, 313
Null hypothesis, 313
  failing to reject, 247–249, 312
  level of significance, 247–248
  rejecting, 247–249, 314
  and type I error, 249–250
  and type II error, 250

O

Obedience, Milgram's research on, 145, 156
Observational learning, 103
Offering inducements, 43, 49
Olympic Games, 138
One-sample t-test, 254, 313
Open-ended questions, 71, 313
Operational definition, 133–134, 313
Order effects, 188, 313
Ordinal scales, 135, 313
Osteoarthritis, acupuncture treatments for, 173–176
Oxytocin levels and bonding behaviors, link between, 258–259

P

Paired samples t-test, 254
Parallel-forms, 90, 314
Parapsychology, 6
Parentification
  alcoholic parents and, 287, 289
  in context of attachment theory, 298
  emotional. *See* Emotional parentification
  factors leading to, 287–288
  and impostor phenomenon, relationship between, 288
  instrumental. *See* Instrumental parentification
  prevalence in society, 287
  shame-prone individuals and, 288
  workaholic parents and, 287–288

Parentification, positive and negative adult outcomes linked to, 288–289
  being less organized and practical, 296
  examination of
    correlation analysis, 292–295
    "Emotional Parentification" score, 291, 293–295
    hypotheses, generating, 290
    "Instrumental Parentification" score, 291, 293, 295
    materials and procedure for, 290–292
    Parentification Questionnaire, 290–291
    participants, 290
    "Perceptions of Fairness" score, 291, 294–295
    research questions, 291–292
    study limitations, 298–299
  lower college GPAs, 296
  negative self-perceptions, 297
Parentification Questionnaire, 290–291
Pedometers, 154
Penn & Teller: Bullshit! (television show), 3
"Pepsi Challenge, The," 195
Pepsi Cola Co., 195
Percent correct, 131, 314
"Perceptions of Fairness" score, 291, 294–295
Perceptions of unfairness and emotional parentification, 287, 290, 299
Physiological measures, 129
Placebo, 172, 314
Placebo control group, 87, 314
Placebo effect, 171, 314
Plagiarism, 46, 51
  APA ethics code on, 46
POF. *See* "Perceptions of Fairness" score
Population *vs.* sample, 147
Positive correlation, 61–62, 314
Power, 155, 314
  of suggestion, 3–4
Power table, 156

Practical significance *vs.* statistical significance, 257

Practice effects, 188, 189, 314

Pretest–posttest designs, 235, 311

Price and customer satisfaction, relationship between, 60

    restaurants, 59

Princeton Theological Seminary students, 184–185

Prior research, 105–106, 314

Probability sampling procedure, 314

    biased sample, 148

    cluster sampling, 149

    definition of, 147

    examples of, 150–151

    practice exercise on, 150, 156–157

    sample, 147–148

        with replacement, 148–149

    stratified, 149

    systematic, 149

    unbiased, 149

Pseudoscience, 3–4, 314

    astrology, 9

    authority, 10

    definition of, 9

    intuition, 9–10

    vs. science, 11

    tenacity, 10

PsycARTICLES, 107, 314

Psychological organizations, membership in, 4–5

Psychological research, 5

    APA ethics code, 47–48

        debriefing, 44, 50

        deception in research, 43–44, 50

        duplicate publication of data, 46–47, 51

        humane care, 44, 50

        informed consent, 38–39, 42

        institutional approval, 38, 48–49

        offering inducements, 43, 49

        plagiarism, 46, 51

        publication credit, 46, 51

        reporting research results, 46, 51

        research data sharing and verification, 47, 52

        research participants, 42

        reviewers, 47, 52

        use of animals in research, 44–45, 50–51

    data sharing, APA ethics code for, 47, 52

    design. *See* Research design

    facial expressions, 52–53

    interpretation in media, guidelines for. *See* Research interpretation in media, guidelines for and media, disconnect between, 7

    population *vs.* sample, 147

    reporting results of, 46, 51

        APA ethics code for, 46

    sample size, 155

    sampling techniques. *See* Sampling techniques

    types of, 60–61

    uniforms and student behavior in school, 34–35

    verification, 47, 52

Psychological research, goals of, 18

    applied research, 20

    basic research

        description of event, 19

        explanation of behavior/process, 19

        prediction of behavior/process, 19–20

    influencing behavior/process, 20

    practice exercise on, 20–24

    scientific method and. *See* Scientific method

Psychological topics, information sources on. *See* Information source

Psychology, myths in

    book examining, 5–6

    media sources, 6

PsycINFO, 107, 108–109, 314

Publication credit, 46, 51

    APA ethics code for, 46

Q

Qualitative research, 60, 314

Quantitative research, 60–61, 314

Quota sampling, 314

R

Random assignment, 153–154, 314

Ratio scale, 136, 314

Reference (APA style), 270–271

Reference list (APA style), 274–275

Regression to mean, 167–168, 314

Reliability, 93–94, 96, 314

    assessment methods

        internal consistency, 90

        interrater reliability, 90–91

        parallel-forms, 90

        split-half method, 90

        test–retest reliability, 89–90

    definition of, 89

Replication, 250–251, 314

Research design

    matched subjects design. *See* Matched subjects design

    nonexperimental designs, 75

    subjects design. *See* Subjects design

    between subjects design. *See* Between subjects design

    within subjects design. *See* Within subjects design

Research hypothesis, 314

Research ideas, 102–103

Research interpretation in media, guidelines for

    balanced reporting, 8

    correlational findings, 7

    generalizations, 8

    locating original source, 7

    misinterpretation of numbers, 8

Research matrix, 183, 314

    action figures and negative body image, link between, 186

    factorial research design, 212

    for between subjects design, 197

    for within subjects design, 197

Research methods, 77
    converging, 75
    sources of information, 4–5
    Wichita Jury Study, 33–34
Research participants, 42
    APA ethics code for, 42
    consent form to participate
      in research
        format of, 40–42
        specific topics of, 38–39
    rights of, 35
        Belmont Report. *See* Belmont
          Report, principle in
Research process, 28–29
Research question, 314
    Bandura's experiment, 104
    definition of, 103
    memory distortion and
      eyewitness recall, 104
Research question, formulating, 102
    conducting searches
        Internet, 107–108
        PsycARTICLES, 107
        PsycINFO, 107
    research idea, getting, 104–107
        everyday experiences, 105
        functional problems, 105
        prior research, 105–106
        using previous theory, 106
    search, starting, 108–109
Research topic, 314
    Bandura's experiment, 103–104
    definition of, 102
    memory distortion and
      eyewitness recall, 104
Results section (APA style), 268
Reversal designs. *See* ABA designs
Reviewers, 47, 52
    APA ethics code for, 47

S

Sample, 314
    vs. population, 147
Sample size, 155, 314

Sampling techniques
    biased sample, 148
    nonprobability. *See*
      Nonprobability sampling
      procedure
    probability. *See* Probability
      sampling procedure
    with replacement, 148–149, 314
    without replacement, 314
Scales, 141
    examples of, 134
    practice exercise on, 136–140
    types of, 135–136
Scholarly resources, 4–5
Science, 314
    definition of, 10
    empirical, 11
    measures of control, 11
    vs. pseudoscience, 11
    self-correcting, 11
Scientific method, 18
    definition of, 10
    hypothesis, 28–29
    practice exercise on, 27–28
    steps of, 28
        data analysis, 26
        data collection, 26
        hypothesis formation, 25
        problem identification, 25
        reporting of findings, 26
    theory, 29
Search engine, 108–109
Selection of participants, 168, 314
Self-correcting, 11, 315
Sexual activity and marital status,
  link between, 6, 10
Sexual selection theory, 29
Simple probability sampling
  procedure, 147–148, 315
    with replacement, 148–149
Single blind study, 172, 315
Single case designs, 229, 315
    conducting
        ABA or reversal designs,
          235–236
        AB or pretest–posttest
          designs, 235

multiple baseline design, 237
    practice exercise on, 238
definition of, 230
limitations of, 239
reasons to use, 232–233
use in field of psychology,
  230–232
Skewed distribution, 253, 315
Sleep, television viewing, and weight
  in children, link between, 70
Snack foods, subliminal advertising
  of, 17–18
Snowballing, 152, 315
Social characteristics in social
  interaction, impact of, 181
Social interactions, 181
Sources, types of (APA style),
  275–278
Spatial reasoning skills and Mozart
  effect, 83–84
Split-half method, 90, 315
Standard deviation, 254
Statistical significance *vs.* practical
  significance, 257
Statistical variance, 188, 315
Stratified probability sampling
  procedure, 149, 315
Student's college experience and
  racially diverse campuses, 76
Subjects design, 182
    between. *See* Between
      subjects design
    within. *See* Within subjects
      design
Subject variable, 84–85, 95, 315
Subliminal advertising, 17–18
Subliminal messages, 17–18
Survey construction, suggestions
  for, 71–73
Survey research, 60, 76, 315
Systematic probability sampling,
  149, 315

T

Tables and figures (APA style), 269
Television advertisement, 83, 85

Television viewing, sleep, and weight in children, link between, 70

Temperature and movie genre preference, relationship between, 123–124, 183

Tenacity, 10, 315

Testing, 169, 315

Test–retest reliability, 89–90, 315

Texting while walking, 81, 94–95

Theory, 29, 315

Threats to internal validity, 165–166
  attrition, 168–169
  control for, 172
    double blind study, 172
    placebo as, 172
  demand characteristics, 171
  diffusion of treatment conditions, 170
  history, 165–166
  instrumentation, 170
  maturation, 166–167
  placebo effect, 171
  regression to mean, 167–168
  selection of participants, 168
  testing, 169

Title page (APA style), 265

Tooth decay and weight of children, relationship between, 61, 62

Treatment conditions, 96, 315
  control group, 86
  experimental group, 86
  Mozart effects, 86
  placebo control group, 87
  random assignment, 153–154
  teaching statistics and new method group, 86–87

t-tests, 254–255

TV viewing and autism in children, link between, 162–163

Type I error, 249–250, 315

Type II error, 250, 315

U

Unbiased probability sampling procedure, 149

Uniforms and student behavior in school, 34–35

V

Validity, 94, 96, 315
  definition of, 91
  types of, 91–93

Variability, measures of, 254

Variable, 95–96, 315
  definition of, 82
  dependent, 82
  examples of, 82–83
  extraneous, 162–163
  independent, 82
    treatment conditions
      control group, 86
      experimental group, 86
      Mozart effects, 86
      placebo control group, 87
      teaching statistics and new method group, 86–87
  nuisance, 162, 164
  practice exercise on, 85–86
  and reliability. *See* Reliability
  subject, 84–85

Variance, 254

Video games, influence of amount of blood in, 186, 189

W

Walking, texting while, 81, 94–95

Warm condition and movie genre preference, relationship between, 123–124, 183

Weight of children
  television viewing, and sleep, link between, 70
  and tooth decay, relationship between, 61

Wichita Jury Study, 33–34, 36–37

Within subjects design, 196, 315
  advantages of, 201–202
  classic research experiments, 198–199
  contemporary research experiments, 199–201
  definition of, 196
  disadvantages of, 202–203
    ways to minimize, 203–204
  factors to consider, 201–205
  practice exercise on, 197–198
  research matrix for, 197

Within subjects factorial research design, 315
  definition of, 213
  job applicant evaluation, 216–218
  music preference while playing computer games, 216
  practice exercise on, 217
  research matrix for, 216

Within-text citations (APA style), 271–274

Writing abilities, discussion about, 101

Y

Yelp, 59